No Holds Barred

The Complete History of Mixed Martial Arts in America

Clyde Gentry III

TRIUMPH
B O O K S

Library of Congress Cataloging-in-Publication Data
Gentry, Clyde.
  No holds barred : the complete history of mixed martial arts in America / Clyde Gentry, III.
    p. cm.
  ISBN 978-1-60078-545-0
  1. Mixed martial arts—United States—History. I. Title.
  GV1102.7.M59G46 2011
  796.800973—dc22

                                                              2010053748

This book is available in quantity at special discounts for your group or organization. For further information, contact:

Triumph Books
542 South Dearborn Street
Suite 750
Chicago, Illinois 60605
(312) 939-3330
Fax (312) 663-3557
www.triumphbooks.com

Printed in U.S.A.
ISBN: 978-1-60078-545-0
Design by Sue Knopf

CONTENTS

Preface v

Acknowledgments ix

MMA Glossary xi

1 Genesis of the Warrior 1

2 The Origin of Groundfighting 13

3 The Gracie Challenge 29

4 Recruiting an Ultimate Fighter 43

5 Showtime 57

6 Battle of the Styles 67

7 "The Sport of the Nineties" 81

8 Changing of the Guard 93

9 Clash of the Titans 109

10 The Age of the Wrestler 123

11 Extreme Competition 139

12 Quest for the Big Apple 153

13 The IFC Story 169

14 Revenge and Redemption. 181

15 Tournament of Champions 193

16 A Striker's Vengeance 205

17 From One Extreme to Another 217

18 Growing Pains 231

19 Ultimate Betrayal 247

20 Dark Ages 257

21 2001: A Zuffa Odyssey 271

22 Fighting the 800-Pound Gorilla 289

23 Real Fighting versus Martial Arts 311

24 Life as a Fighter 325

25 Fighting for a Mainstream Sport. 345

26 Japanese MMA: History and Beyond. 361

27 MMA Around the World 373

Appendix I: The Best of Tank Abbott. 391

Appendix II: Bas Rutten: The Flying Dutchman 395

Appendix III: Mixed Martial Arts:
An Illustrated Look at Basic Positions and Submissions. . 401

References and Interviews 411

Index 417

PREFACE

On January 8, 1999, I remember walking through the sparsely packed Pontchartrain Center in Louisiana for Ultimate Fighting Championship XVIII. Tito Ortiz sat on the cement between sections, gazing upon the Octagon. But no one gave him a second look. Backstage, Mark Coleman seemed ready for his fight, with a scruffy-looking Ken Shamrock, dressed in camouflage, standing by his side. And Dutchman Bas Rutten was nowhere to be found, most likely holing up in one of the back rooms, preparing himself for his UFC debut. The crowd didn't really seem to care; most were still caught up in the mystique of "no rules" fighting, and the flow of beer probably didn't help. As for me, I had found my own personal nirvana, seeing all of these fighters under one roof, each very approachable and charismatic in his own way. Thus began my journey of telling the incredible story you are about to read.

It has taken 10 years for this book to mature as the definitive history of American mixed martial arts. When I started writing it, the UFC was on its last legs, and I thought I might be chronicling the demise of a would-be sport. It was always a sport to me and to everyone else involved. But outside that vacuum, the media no longer cared, the cable industry wanted no part of it, and I wanted to show people this world from the inside out. I remember Joe Silva, who was something of a consultant for the UFC at the time, telling me the only way to make sense out of this story was to interview as many people as I could and get my hands on as much material as possible. I took that advice to heart.

Over a lengthy research period, I conducted interviews with fighters, promoters, cutmen, and everyone in between; spent hours in the library and on the Internet; and attended every mixed martial arts (MMA) show I could make. I wanted a challenging project that would require every ounce of tenacity I had. But the more interviews I conducted, the more questions I felt needed to be answered. As I dug deeper and deeper, it became quite apparent that one book would not do the sport justice, just as 30 or even 50 interviews would not. The title of the book used a misnomer for the sport's name, but at that time, what collectively became known as mixed martial arts went by many different names. The first *No Holds Barred* was published in July 2001, and then it was picked up by UK publisher Milo Books and was reissued as a hardback (May 2002) and a subsequent paperback (April 2005) that ended up being sold here in America.

When Triumph Books gave me the green light for a fourth edition, I jumped at the chance. I painstakingly perused the entire book, along with all of my notes and boxes of information, and transcribed more tapes of interviews I had conducted 10 years earlier. The original *No Holds Barred* was supposed to be the first in a series of books, so the timeline ended in 1997. Thus, many interviews didn't make it into the book because the series never happened. I interviewed Chuck Liddell in 2000; he was such a minor player at the time that I didn't use even a word from his interview. Times have certainly changed. Nearly every chapter has been not only updated but clarified with new information and new pieces of the puzzle.

Dozens of interviews with subjects old and new were conducted to ensure *No Holds Barred* stands the test of time as the definitive American MMA history book. Instead of ending in 1997, two brand-new chapters have been added to update the story, along with a few other surprises. Owners of the original book will also note the addition of chapters on the international scene. I removed all the fight results since Sherdog.com keeps up with all the results of every pro MMA event it can verify; it's an incredible resource.

You won't find any bombshells about Chuck Liddell, Anderson Silva, Georges St. Pierre, or Fedor Emelianenko. Mixed martial arts has arguably become a mainstream machine, and you can find shelves of autobiographies of top fighters, along with countless technique-centric books. This final version of *No Holds Barred*, while it has its share of crazy stories, is a history book, plain and simple.

The sport has reached an apex where it doesn't have that many hills left to climb, and the only thing added to history is the evolution of the athletes themselves. All of the hard-fought legal battles for sanctioning have now given MMA a home in virtually every state, New York being the biggest holdout. You can buy action figures, Octagon playsets, video games, collector's cards, paintings, and the list goes on and on. You can readily see fights on a half-dozen channels with at least one pay-per-view each month, not including the specials and feature films that showcase MMA stars. But the history contained in *No Holds Barred* gave life to the sport we see today and will continue to see in the future.

Since November 12, 1993, MMA has struggled to evolve from spectacle to sport. The grassroots movement propelled it past the "fad" stage that nearly killed it in the late 1990s. And while MMA continues to grow as a mainstream sport, you'll find the road to where we are now was a battle well worth fighting. I hope that anyone who reads this book will walk away with a better understanding of the relentless passion I found in virtually every person involved in shaping the greatest sport on earth.

Clyde Gentry III
October, 2010

ACKNOWLEDGMENTS

Special acknowledgment must go to Joe Silva for his guidance and the overwhelming degree of wisdom about mixed martial arts that always kept this book on track. I must also thank Dave Meltzer for his insight into the pro wrestling scene, as well as his business acumen about MMA pay-per-view.

Art Davie has the most amazing memory with the documents to prove it. I am so thankful he took the time to review a lot of the incredible backstory of how the UFC came to be. I would like to thank Clint Santiago Dahl, who has promoted fights with me in the past and also became a great resource for reaching out to people I couldn't get a hold of. I also really appreciate the transcription work from Daniel Thomason, who meticulously rifled through hours of tape. I must also thank Paul Viele of World Martial Arts, Peter Walsh of Milo Books, and Paul Smith of the IFC for giving this book a chance when no one else would. Finally, I must give special thanks to Robert Pittman of MMA Worldwide and Triumph Books for giving a 10-year-old book its final overhaul.

Thanks to all the people who took time out of their day to be interviewed for a project that has been more than a decade in the making.

And to my parents, sister Sherry Gentry, friend Zeus Smith, and business partner Bill Coe for all their patience and support for allowing me to step back in time one last go around to get it right!

MMA Glossary

Here is a basic but not comprehensive list of terms used throughout the book. There were multitudes of other styles that practitioners used, but some of them (Joe Son's Joe Son Do) were highly self-serving.

BRANCAILLE: French term describing an agreement between two participants to allow strikes in what is otherwise a wrestling match.

BRAZILIAN JIU-JITSU: Brazilian Carlos Gracie adapted Japanese judoka Conde Koma's teachings to create an effective ground-based system of fighting that utilizes submission and grappling techniques. His younger brother Helio later improved those techniques, which became known as Brazilian jiu-jitsu.

CAPOEIRA: Native Brazilian martial art that is most widely accepted as a dance, combining acrobatics and wide-ranging movements.

DIM MAK: Ancient martial art meaning "death touch." Consists of striking certain points on the body to cause illness or death. Most of what is preached is hyperbole.

FREESTYLE WRESTLING: One of two wrestling styles whereby practitioners are allowed to attack their opponents below the waist.

FULL-CONTACT KARATE: Sport karate that served as a precursor for American kickboxing. Only allows for kicks above the waist, and practitioners must wear 8-to-10-ounce gloves and footwear.

GRECO-ROMAN WRESTLING: One of two wrestling styles whereby practitioners are not allowed to attack the legs, so they must clinch and attempt to throw their opponents.

HIMANTES: Ancient Grecian boxers or pugilists wrapped their hands with these soft ox-hide straps to strengthen their wrists and steady their fingers.

JEET KUNE DO: Meaning "way of the intercepting fist," it was never actually a style; Bruce Lee's fighting concepts instead stressed what worked in a real situation.

JOB: Where one fighter agrees to throw a fight, allowing his opponent to win. Sometimes "jobs" are company decisions where only one fighter knows what is supposed to happen while the other fights for real. This term is normally associated with professional wrestling.

JUDO: Jigoro Kano took elements of informal jujutsu styles and created a way to use an opponent's strength against him. Judo means "gentle way," and throws, grappling, and strikes were part of the style. As it gradually became a spectator sport, the real art suffered in favor of crowd-pleasing throwing techniques.

JUDOKA: One who practices judo.

JUJUTSU: By the seventeenth century, there were over 750 forms of jujutsu in Japan. This diversity meant that the term embraced everything from weapons and strikes to grappling. Jigaro Kano's judo eventually replaced Japanese jujutsu.

KARATE: Meaning "empty hand," this Japanese martial arts style was based on older striking-based styles from Okinawa. There are several systems in karate including shotokan, kenpo, and shorin-ryu.

KATA: Formal training exercise where students execute precise sets of movements that emulate real fighting situations.

KENPO: As the first Americanized martial art, the style emphasizes attacking vital areas on the body with a variety of strikes. Ed Parker, known as the Father of American Kenpo, took the style to new heights and brought formality to its processes. Zane Frazier and Keith Hackney used kenpo in the UFC.

KICKBOXING: Generally accepted term for the sport that includes punches, kicks (above and below the waist), and sometimes knees.

KLIMAX: When a victor could not be declared in pankration (see p. xiv), both fighters drew lots, with the winner positioning his opponent any way he chose. With the loser remaining still, the other fighter was allowed to strike in any fashion without his opponent dodging the blow. Then, if that fighter still remained, he would do the same thing to his opponent. Seldom did it last more than a few turns.

KUNG FU: Although the name has been associated with martial arts, it actually means "skill" or "ability." Several styles of kung fu exist (wing chun, five animal, etc.), but typically they are broken down into northern (long-range fighting and kicking) and southern (hand movements for shorter-range fighting) schools.

KYOKUSHINKAI KARATE: Known as both a style and a sport. Fighters strike without gloves or protection of any kind but cannot punch to the head. Kicks to the head are legal.

LUTA LIVRE: A freestyle form of Brazilian jiu-jitsu without the gi. Luta livre became an early rivalry amongst the practitioners in Brazil.

MIXED MARTIAL ARTS: General term used to describe the convergence of striking, grappling, and submission techniques into one forum, whereby fighters can win by knockout, technical knockout, tap out (verbally or physically), referee stoppage, corner stoppage, or judge's decision. Other terms include *vale tudo, freestyle, no holds barred, cage fighting, extreme fighting, reality fighting,* and *ultimate fighting.*

MOO YEA DO: Created by Grandmaster Tiger Yang, it is a mixture of tae kwon do, aikido, and kung fu. Mark Hall used this style in the UFC.

MUAY THAI: Adapted from Thai military arts. Practitioners can punch, kick, knee, and elbow. Also known as Thai boxing. Most fighters don't last more than a few years due to injury. The term "Muay Thai kick" often describes a devastating maneuver where the shin collides with the opponent's thigh. Anderson Silva and Wanderlei Silva are both known as strong Muay Thai exponents.

NINJUTSU: Feudal Japanese discipline that combined martial arts with commando tactics and alleged magical powers, among other things. Skeptics believe the ninja never existed but were just a hoax to scare up the art's large merchandising ploy with costumes and ornate weapons. Scott Morris and Steve Jennum both fought under some semblance of this style.

NO HOLDS BARRED: Misnomer for mixed martial arts used during the sport's infancy. It was originally used to separate matches with closed-fist strikes (NHB) and open-hand strikes (Pancrase style).

OCTAGON: Engineered fence used by the UFC. Once thought to be a gimmick, the octagonal shape gives structural support. The Octagon is 30' in diameter and stands 5'6" (six inches were added after Tank Abbott tried to throw Cal Worsham over the fence at Ultimate Ultimate '96).

PANCRASE: Karl Gotch supposedly coined the term (a variation of *pankration*) for Masakatsu Funaki's new organization, which became Pancrase Hybrid Wrestling. During the event's infancy, only open-hand strikes were allowed to the face. Because several states in the United States did not allow closed-fist strikes to the face for nonboxing events, pancrase became a relative term for this style of fighting.

PANKRATION: The third combative sport added to the ancient Olympics in 648 BC, meaning "all strength" or "all power." There were two types of pankration: ano (which only allowed for fighters to stand and was used during training) and kato (used in the games where fights could go to the ground).

PENCAK SILAT: Indonesian martial arts form where proponents fight very low to the ground with gliding movements that often attack the legs. Alberto Cerro Leon used this style in the UFC.

PIT FIGHTING: Another term for street fighting created by Art Davie for use by Tank Abbott and Scott Ferrozzo.

POINT KARATE: Nonrealistic matches between karate practitioners were decided by points, and fighters were not allowed to follow through with their strikes.

PUGILISM: Derived from the Latin word "pugil," meaning to fight with fists, this term was used during the ancient Greek Olympics and ultimately became known as "boxing."

QUEENSBERRY RULES: After the decline of bare-knuckle pugilism, the English Marquis of Queensberry established modern rules for boxing in 1867, including the introduction of padded gloves, to make it more organized and humane.

SAMBO: Russian martial art that uses a combination of grappling and submission techniques and literally means "self-defense without weapons." Much of the art resembles judo, but it includes arm and leg submissions. Oleg Taktarov used his sambo training in the UFC.

SAVATE: French form of kickboxing without knee strikes. Gerard Gordeau used this style in the UFC.

SHOOT: Term generally used to describe a completely legitimate match between athletes. It is also a wrestling term for moving toward a takedown.

SHOOTFIGHTING (also known as SHOOTWRESTLING): Bart Vale copyrighted the term "shootfighting," which describes the converged style in mixed martial arts using strikes, grappling, and submission techniques.

STAND-UP MARTIAL ARTS: Collective term used to describe martial arts styles that do not involve any ground techniques or grappling, including boxing, karate, kung fu, and tae kwon do.

STIFF-WORK (*see also* WORK): While the match still has a predetermined ending, both fighters land harder strikes, often grappling and moving to a submission for real. The Japanese UWF matches and the Kingdom organization often employed stiff-worked bouts.

SUBMISSION: The act of a fighter physically or verbally relenting to punching or submission damage (*see also* **TAP OUT**).

SUMO: Adapted from sumai (meaning "struggle"), this Japanese sport relies on men of gargantuan portions to push and flip their equally large opponents outside of a circular mat. While the style and its ancient traditions are respected in the martial arts world, both Teila Tuli and Emmanuel Yarbrough could not use size to win their fights in the UFC.

TAE KWON DO: Meaning "art of kicking and punching," this Korean fighting style has become the most popular in North America and Great Britain. Unfortunately, the commercialism of the art has watered down much of its original effectiveness.

TAP OUT: The act of a fighter physically or verbally submitting during a match. Often times the fighter taps the mat or the opponent to relent, whereby the opponent stops activity.

TOMATO CAN: Promoters often bring in tomato-can fighters, also known as ham-n-eggers and palookas, to build up records and/or protect budding stars. These fighters have a puncher's chance, but usually lack the skills and conditioning to beat opponents that promoters are trying to protect.

TUF NOOB: Term used to describe new fans of *The Ultimate Fighter* reality show who may not know of the history of MMA outside the show and the UFC in general.

UNIFIED RULES: The general term used to describe the rules for modern-day mixed martial arts. While some variances do exist, most states assimilated these rules that were originally codified for the New Jersey State Athletic Commission in 2000. Through the valiant efforts of several individuals, the genesis of these rules stemmed from California, but the commission did not have the budget to support the sport until 2006.

VALE TUDO: Portuguese term coined by a Brazilian newspaper journalist that means "anything goes" and was used to describe the early matches between Brazilian jiu-jitsu and other martial arts styles.

WORK: Both fighters agree on a predetermined ending for the match without undue harm; in other words, a fix. American pro wrestling matches are called "works."

1

GENESIS OF THE WARRIOR

As smoke pours through a cascading flash of neon lights, the restless crowd grows louder. Two warriors emerge from the darkness. Their hands and feet are physical weapons outmatched only by minds teeming with knowledge of strategy and submission. This is the ultimate test for a fighter unbound by one-dimensional game play. Each man must be a tremendous athlete, versed in many fighting disciplines, who understands that one mistake can lead to surrender. All the months of preparation can lead to an outcome that may only take seconds or minutes. The crowd roars as both combatants launch themselves forward to punch, kick, grapple, and grind toward a finish.

Many believe this sport was what the late Bruce Lee truly envisioned with his notes on martial arts, fighting, cross-training, and physical fitness. In the 1960s, even before he had attained movie superstardom and sparked a worldwide craze, Lee made it his life's work to find the integral link between traditional martial arts and the unpredictability of genuine hand-to-hand combat. Lee's influential book *Tao of Jeet Kune Do* showcased his views on changing the way we look at fighting by scientifically and realistically examining its natural processes. He refused to be constrained by any single style or method of combat, preferring instead to keep an open mind, to adopt or adapt what worked and to reject what didn't. "Bruce was way ahead of his time," said Dan Inosanto, Bruce Lee's best-known student and authority on Jeet Kune Do (meaning "way of the intercepting fist"). "Bruce said, 'If there's one thing we should guard ourselves against, let it be a partiality. It robs us from our understanding of the whole picture.'"

Since the dawn of time, man has been drawn to physical challenges that dwell in a primal state. The Greeks made wrestling the first combative sport of their Olympic games; indeed many believe that Alexander the Great's conquests brought martial arts to India, which led to the creation of kung fu in China. Almost two millennia later, bare-fisted brawls for cash in the Old West were outlawed to eventually create boxing. Today television viewers may experience the same visceral thrill when watching a fiery crash in a stockcar race, or a high-sticking fracas enraging two ice hockey players to duke it out. While the art of war (martial arts) has many faces, there can be no denying the power of Bruce Lee's central theme: the converging of combative styles into one forum. In fact, jeet kune do, which is not a style but a philosophy about martial arts, is often referred to as "style without style."

The 1990s saw the emergence of a new sport that, for the first time, put this to the test. It seemed to come from nowhere and, in America at least, created impressions of the kind of bloodsport or fight to the death often featured in low-budget action films. It became known as *no holds barred* (NHB) when in fact there are plenty of holds that are barred, and several rules for fighter safety. Today the sport is almost unanimously referred to as *mixed martial arts* (MMA), a more appropriate term, even though "martial arts" has denoted several interpretations. Tainted by fraudulent practices, mail order black belts, chop-socky movies, and Tae Bo infomercials, the collective martial arts could be anything and everything. Kickboxing and even professional wrestling have been called mixed martial arts. In Brazil, it is known as *vale tudo*, meaning "anything goes" in Portuguese. Since *The Ultimate Fighter* reality show debuted in January 2005, the sport has shed most of its negative image in favor of

2

the mainstream term of mixed martial arts. So for the purpose of this book, mixed martial arts will be used to describe any competitive contest whereby participants can punch with a closed or open hand, kick, wrestle, and perform submission techniques under strict guidelines in a professionally supervised setting. Fighting sports of this type have been around a lot longer than people think; their origins can arguably be traced back as the blueprint for martial arts.

North America bore witness to the first major commercial MMA event when the Ultimate Fighting Championship (UFC) debuted on November 12, 1993. Other promotions soon followed, though most of them died off after continued political pressure destroyed the sport's most lucrative cash stream, the U.S. pay-per-view television market. Since that time, the rules have been reworked, the UFC regularly beats out pro boxing and pro wrestling pay-per-views, and the sport continues to flourish at many different levels worldwide. Today, one can find as many as a dozen different events occurring somewhere around the world each week. The sport has drawn martial arts back to its original form and given bored boxing fans something new to cheer about. Thanks to the age of the Internet and new forms of mass media, MMA has become the hot ticket for a new kind of sports fan. Thousands of competitors and hundreds of submission fighting schools around the world endeavor to produce the ultimate warrior. And as history proves, it has always been a sport born from a need to find the perfect athlete.

◆ ◆ ◆

IN EVERY CULTURE, in every place, in every time in history, men have fought on instinct alone, with or without proper training. There is a clear difference between fighting for cause and fighting for sport, and only the latter is the subject of this book. Sport fighting can be traced back to the Trojan War in 2000 BC, but for practical purposes, most will agree that pankration, the third combative sport of the ancient Olympics in Greece, was the first mixed martial arts contest. From 776 BC to 720 BC, the Olympics was built on running sports until wrestling was introduced in 708 BC. Combatants stripped naked, doused themselves with olive oil, and covered their oily skin with sand to gain a better grip. Nudity was a way to make everyone equal, regardless of social class standing. In 688 BC, pugilism, or boxing, became widespread. Though men did not have gloves per se, they wore straps of leather called himantes to protect their hands. Boxing was a popular sport in the Olympics, and it created controversy as to who was a better fighter: the boxer or the wrestler.

The year 648 BC brought forth pankration, which means "all strength" or "all power," to the 33rd Olympics. No one really knows how pankration originated. Greek mythology often cited Hercules and Theseus as being the men responsible for bringing pankration to the Olympics, but that was mere fairy tale. Some historians pointed to soldiers having to use all their skills in hand-to-hand combat. Others cited civilizations dating back to 2600 BC, particularly Egypt, as being likely candidates that spawned the sport. Egypt has often been named as a source for cultural advances made by Greece, and arguably laid the foundation for Greek mythology.

The Greek author Philostratos claimed the best pankrationist would be a strong man who could be called the best wrestler amongst boxers and the best boxer amongst wrestlers. Men could strike by punching, kicking, or using other body parts, and they could wrestle and continue fighting on the ground. Eye gouging and biting were the only two illegal maneuvers in pankration, and fighters would be flogged for violation by umpires stationed close by. Combatants fought in the nude but, unlike in boxing, didn't wear gloves or himantes. The object of pankration was to submit your opponent by any means necessary. Fights continued until submission, death, or sunset; in the latter case, a *klimax* was executed to decide the victor. In klimax, each fighter drew lots, with the winner positioning his opponent any way he chose. With the loser remaining still, the other fighter was allowed to strike in any fashion without his opponent dodging the blow. Then, if that fighter still remained, he would do the same thing to his opponent. Seldom did klimax last more than a few turns.

A pankrationist could raise a hand to call an end to the fight. Joint dislocations, broken bones, and primitive strangulation made pankration a violent sport, of which champion boxers and wrestlers wanted no part. Greeks elevated the pankrationist above boxers and wrestlers because he proved his prominence by doing both. Boxing, wrestling, and pankration all had one thing in common: participants were only matched by age, not weight. Heavier men usually chose pankration as their sport. While several fights ended by knockout, the majority ended up on the ground, where fighters rolled around in the sand and mud viciously striking or strangling their opponents.

There were two types of pankration: *ano*, which was used for practice and only allowed for stand-up fighting, and *kato*, which included ground-fighting and was generally used for the games. The Olympic sportsmen were not amateurs; they were professional fighters. A pankration champion was well paid, didn't have to pay taxes, and was fed for life by the city. Pankration not only became an Olympic game, it became a way of training. Schools were set up and different pankration styles evolved, all of which were held secret from other schools.

In Rome, pankration led to even more vicious spectacles, where men could not only use their hands and feet, but brutal weapons to savagely destroy their opponents. As Roman society became chaotic, gladiators moved into more dangerous forms of combat. It is believed that popular Greek pankrationists didn't compete in these types of events, for it ruined their image in the Olympics. In 393 AD, the Roman Emperor Theodosius decreed the Olympic games should stop, citing that his Christian beliefs would not tolerate them. Ruler Honorius discontinued gladiatorial combat in 404 AD.

Though pankration officially ended with the ancient games, it continued in occidental forms around the world. In Europe, pankration most likely mixed with other forms of combat among several tribes, including the Celts and the Batavians. In Provence, France, a traditional wrestling match often crossed over to *brancaille*, when both men agreed that punching would be allowed. These types of matches were said to have continued through the 1940s in the south of France, only to move underground after World War II.

There is evidence to support claims that MMA matches took place in Asia in the second half of the twentieth century. Famed martial artist and creator of Chinese Goju, Ron Van Clief, took part in one such event in 1969, held in Taiwan. "It involved grappling, and over 90 percent of the matches ended on the ground," he remembered. "It was a more interesting way of looking at the martial arts from a combative aspect." Van Clief competed in another event in 1982 called the World Freefighting Championships, held in Hong Kong. Though all martial arts styles could compete and grappling was legal, matches frequently stopped every time both men went to the ground or strayed from the fighting circle. Karate, kung fu, tae kwon do, and other Asian stand-up martial arts were tested against one another, but the fights kept going to the ground. That event was important because it proved that two standing fighters in a free-form setting would eventually grapple and go to the ground, even if they didn't know what they were doing down there. Clearly, some form of pankration continued to exist in parts of the world since the days of Ancient Greece.

◆ ◆ ◆

FOR YEARS, various forms of fighting developed outside of boxing in the United States. The first documented modern-day boxing match was held in 1681, but a phenomena known as "rough-and-tumble" fighting began to take shape nearly 100 years earlier in the Southern backwoods of Virginia and the Carolinas. Whether for personal gripe or money, when two men squared off they agreed to fight under Broughton's Rules or rough-and-tumble. Jack Broughton was an early heavyweight pugilist who on August 16, 1743—over 100 years before the creation of today's Queensbury Rules—created the first documented rules on boxing. These rules stated that hitting a downed fighter was strictly prohibited. In rough-and-tumble fighting, that's usually when things started up as fighters could do everything sans weapons; these were true no-holds-barred contests. Punching, kicking, and grappling were just as fair as scratching, biting, and eye gouging.

Paul Smith, commissioner for International Fighting Championships, fondly remembered competing in no-holds-barred matches during the mid-1980s. There was a Texas event called the Iron Gladiator Championships that was held in Houston, Fort Worth, and San Antonio. "This was a completely illegal event in the vein of Clint Eastwood's *Every Which Way But Loose*, as most of the fighters were just bare-knuckle, barroom brawlers," said Smith. "The fights did go to the ground, though, and I won the tournaments because I had submission training." Wealthy businessmen set up these events in bars and warehouses to whet their appetites for brutal action. Fighters found out about the matches from neighboring martial arts schools just days before the events were to be held. Though most of these events had referees and some rules (such as no biting, no eye gouging, or no groin shots), this was hardly a uniform sport.

Before the Ultimate Fighting Championship came along, arguably only two MMA matches had gained any sort of renown. On December 2, 1963, judoka Gene LeBell fought professional boxer Milo Savage. The match lasted four rounds before two-time national judo champ LeBell finally choked Savage out. The match took place in part because writer Jim Beck's article in *Rogue* magazine in August 1963 claimed judo was fraudulent and any practitioner wouldn't last against a boxer. Beck even chose Savage, a respectable middleweight, and the match took place in Salt Lake City, Utah, where Beck and Savage resided. Savage wore brass knuckles covered with leather, but he also wore a karate gi top (according to the rules set between them), making it easy for LeBell to grab him by the lapels. Years later, LeBell served as referee for one of the best-known MMA matches of all time: Antonio Inoki vs. Muhammad Ali.

Held June 26, 1976, while Ali was in his second reign as world heavyweight champion, this "fight" would go down as one of the oddest—and most boring—of the century. Inoki, a Japanese professional wrestler, needed a way for his organization, New Japan Wrestling, to increase ticket sales over rival All Japan Wrestling, which had substantial ties to America's top pro wrestling stars. "New Japan had to create new stars, so one of the things they came up with was the idea of making Inoki the world's martial arts champion," said Dave Meltzer, the premier authority on professional wrestling. "What they would do was take guys from other sports and put them in 'worked' matches with Inoki. The most famous was Willem Ruska, a multi-gold medalist in Olympic judo." But to really put Inoki over with the crowd, he needed to beat the best, and during the mid-1970s, no one qualified more than boxing superhero Muhammad Ali.

Originally, the two had worked out a predetermined ending. "Ali would beat up Inoki, then he'd want to stop the fight because Inoki was taking such a horrible pounding," said Meltzer. "Ali would talk to the referee about stopping the fight, and Inoki would come up from behind and give him a kick to the back of the head. Ali would fall down and be pinned." Ali would be paid $6 million for his troubles. Two days before the fight, Ali called it off, unwilling to lose, and they tried unsuccessfully to devise another finish. The rules were eventually altered to make a real, or shoot, match nearly impossible for Inoki to win. Inoki was told he could not throw or submit to Ali in any way.

Before a capacity crowd at the Budokan Arena in Tokyo, Ali threw a total of six punches and landed only two in 15 rounds. At the start of each round, Inoki ran to the center of the ring and fell on his back, from which position he would rotate back and forth, kicking Ali's legs. Ali was utterly confused and could hardly sting like a bee. The match was ruled a draw, and Ali walked away with only $1.8 million. He unsuccessfully sued for the rest. Actually, Ali didn't do much walking, as he was taken to the hospital due to blood clots caused by Inoki's kicks. This was an inglorious moment in boxing history; even worse, it nearly destroyed pro wrestling in Japan. To rebuild his reputation, Inoki continued to fight in mixed matches—none of which were legit—but the plan worked and Inoki became one of the greatest legends in Japanese pro wrestling.

The masses popularized martial arts through sports competition, but in most cases, the sport siphoned the martial from the art. Since the late 1960s, the United States had staged thousands of martial arts competitions ranging from *kata* and weapons to point karate, full contact, and kickboxing tournaments. Point karate tournaments were the mainstay of stand-up martial arts competition until one of their champions, Joe Lewis, voiced his concern over the unrealistic nature of these events. Lewis began his martial arts training at age 20 while stationed in Okinawa in the U.S. Marines during the early 1960s and earned a black belt within one year through his dedication. Training in the Orient was tough, and he often donned hard-surfaced *kendo* gear to engage in full-contact sparring. Returning to the USA, he entered point karate competitions and won without even knowing the rules. But he didn't like the start-and-stop motion, especially having to pull his punches when he had been trained to strike with power. In 1969, he convinced a local promoter to host the first full-contact karate match on January 17, 1970. The announcer mistakenly called it "American kickboxing" when he saw Lewis wearing boxing gloves and knew he would be kicking.

The martial arts community was outraged by this portrayal of karate, protesting that it would affect enrollment and give the Japanese art a bad name. The term "kickboxing" was associated with Muay Thai in Thailand. Muay Thai is the roughest full-contact, stand-up martial arts contest, where the average fighter's career lasts only a few years. Elbows, knees, clinching, and all kicking and punching techniques are legal. It is often referred to as Muay Thai "boxing" or "kickboxing," but in actuality, the Japanese abridged the Muay Thai rules to create "kickboxing." In Thailand, either name is an insult, and it is only referred to as Muay Thai. In America, even Japanese kickboxing didn't sit well with the martial arts community. "Some of my friends who owned their own karate schools came up to me and said, 'Joe, you're ruining the karate business for all of us. Tell people that kickboxing is bad for martial arts and that people shouldn't do it,'" remembered Lewis. "And these were the guys that eventually became some of the head referees for these full-contact events."

While purists fought to remove "karate" from the sport's name and call it "kickboxing," the media felt just the opposite. Karate was starting to become very popular, and kickboxing was still associated with Muay Thai, though the American rules did not allow elbows, knees, or kicks below the waist. "The reason for that was that CBS did an audience response survey where they put an applause meter on it and found out that the largest response was when someone got kicked in the head, the second was when someone attempted a kick to the head, and the third-largest was when someone got punched to the head," said former kickboxing promoter Howard Petschler.

Lewis recalled a conversation between him and John Martin, president of ABC's *Wide World of Sports* back in 1970. "He told me, 'Mr. Lewis, we have no interest whatsoever in karate. However, we will go anywhere in the world to film your kickboxing matches.'" Lewis remembered the last time martial arts was on television. "The only time it had been on national TV was 1965 for the national championships on ABC. It was a bloodbath between Mike Stone and Pat Worley at Jhoon Rhee's National Championships. At the end of that match, ABC, NBC, and CBS blacklisted it. I was the one who got martial arts back on television."

The media and the sanctioning bodies for boxing had no idea what to make of it. "I was trying to figure out ways to generate press," said Petschler. "What helped was when the [boxing] commission came out and…one commissioner said, 'We don't sanction the sport and don't have anything to do with it, but we are watching it very closely because it is dangerous when you kick someone in the head—you can kill them!' And of course I sold the event out after that. Back then [in the 1970s], there was a big mystique about a black belt, the death touch, and all that stuff. While the general public thought we could do supernatural things, we were just really trying to find out what worked and what didn't, and kickboxing, like MMA, made us reevaluate much of the traditional technique—a mini revolution in martial arts spearheaded by Lewis."

Unlike point karate tournaments, full-contact karate contestants needed to be in tip-top shape, as there would be constant movement.

"Many of the early fighters lacked technique. They were not used to applying their skills in all-out, to-the-knockout fashion," said authors Al Weiss and David Weiss in their book *The Official History of Karate in America*. "Many fighters lacked the conditioning that kickboxing required and the resulting contests were lackluster and brawlish."

Kickboxing sputtered along until 1974, when Lewis and promoter Mike Anderson drummed up spectator interest for their new "international" full-contact karate circuit. An elimination tournament was held in Europe with top competitors, and an agreement was made with husband-and-wife team Don and Judy Quine to bring the event to Universal Television. The event was broadcast on ABC's popular *Wide World of Entertainment*, and point karate legends like Bill "Superfoot" Wallace, Howard Jackson, and Lewis all made the transition into full-contact karate. One month before, the Quines' and Anderson created a sanctioning body called the PKA (Professional Karate Association). Howard Petschler became one of the original PKA commissioners.

Participants wore karate pants and gloves and, to separate it from boxing, each man had to throw at least eight kicks per round. Jhoon Rhee, the father of American tae kwon do, added a very important element to full-contact karate when he created the "Safe-T-Chop"—foam gear to be worn on both hands and feet. It was introduced in the 1970s and "a high percentage of the kickboxing matches in the first decade used that gear," said Petschler. "Eventually boxing gloves for the hands and foam pads on the feet become the standard. Everybody wanted to know what worked, and of course many traditional instructors refused to acknowledge the sport."

The PKA's success led to other organizations, each one claiming different stars who could be called "world champions." The sport was so well received that a full-contact match preceded the famed 1975 Ali-Frazier "Thrilla in Manila" boxing title bout in the Philippines. By the late 1970s and early 1980s, full-contact karate had become widely known as kickboxing. Other events were still touted as full-contact karate but were not held in a ring and bore little resemblance to full contact. Kickboxing was created to distance itself from events like *kyokushinkai karate*, which was bare-knuckle but did not allow punches to the face. Since the original fighters in full contact wore gloves and could kick, the term "kickboxing" was no longer seen as a threat, and the media accepted it as such. Around 1980, knees and sometimes clinching was allowed to bring the sport closer to its Japanese cousin.

The heyday of these matches drew to a close after the PKA dissolved in 1987, and real martial arts competitions lost what little appeal they sustained on U.S. cable television by the early 1990s. For the first time, well-decorated martial artists had been given the chance to show what they could do in a fight and the audience was unimpressed. Many fighters looked downright clumsy, failing to display the graceful moves people saw in the movies and wanted to see replicated in tournaments. Countless fly-by-night kickboxing organizations came onto the scene, creating a political rivalry between promoters to keep the best matches from taking place. Most of the sport's heroes faded into the world of low-budget film or continued their martial arts careers only inside the pages of magazines. Realistic combat sports were going nowhere, save for Japan with the emergence of K-1.

2

THE ORIGIN OF GROUNDFIGHTING

Before the Olympic Games were outlawed, Alexander the Great and his conquering Macedonian army may have inadvertently spread pankration to the rest of the world. In 326 BC, his armies followed a successful campaign in Egypt with the conquest of India. India is said to be the birthplace of kung fu, and, though no one knows for sure, some believe Alexander and his men indirectly taught the Indian monks. Alexander led his troops on long, arduous journeys, and many pankration-trained soldiers remained in the countries they had conquered. These men may well have mixed their martial skills with the fighting forms of other cultures, laying the framework for what we know today as the martial arts. In 500 BC, the Indian monk Da Mo (Boddidharma), who trained in the Indian martial arts, journeyed across the Himalayas until he came in contact with the Shaolin temple in China. This meeting sparked the birth of kung fu, and Da Mo founded Zen Buddhism. Evidence does exist of a primitive form of Chinese wrestling called jǐao dǐ that took place around the same time; it is unknown whether the two were related. Though pankration is clearly not responsible for the philosophies of Eastern and Asian martial arts, it almost certainly aided the perfection of the fighting systems.

During the Choon Chu era (772–481 BC) in China, empty-hand (unarmed) fighting techniques were prevalent and filtered throughout neighboring countries such as Japan. A wrestling sport known as chikura kurabe led in 230 BC to the birth of jujutsu (meaning "the gentle art"), founded on various principles ranging from empty hand and submission to weapons and wrestling. As civil unrest plagued Japan, it was necessary for soldiers to become better equipped on the battlefield. Between the eighth and sixteenth centuries, Japan's martial arts blossomed into many different styles, each with its own set of beliefs. Most of them were tested in combat. In 1532, Tenenuchi Hisamori created what is believed to be the first formal jujutsu school.

By the seventeenth century, wartime had come to a close in Japan, creating the Edo era (1603–1868). More than 750 systems of jujutsu existed during this time, and refinement was needed to expel forms and techniques based on weapons. When the power of the Shogun was given to the Japanese emperor after the Edo period, an imperial law made practicing martial arts in the name of the samurai (the warrior class) illegal. Unarmed fighting techniques useful in everyday life became a fixed part of jujutsu, rather than the deadly aspects used in war. Jujutsu practice had to exclude weapons, but, with varying philosophies employed, the term *jujutsu* included one school that believed only in punching and kicking, as well as another that focused on groundfighting.

In 1878, a sickly, lean pacifist named Jigoro Kano began jujutsu practice as a way to better his physical condition. He studied under numerous jujutsu masters but found that many of the techniques were not applicable in real life. He also concluded that the systems held little "spiritual balance" to govern their usage. At the age of 22, Kano learned enough to make a startling revelation. "Knowing that every one of the jujutsu schools had its merits and demerits," said Kano in an 1898 lecture, "I came to believe that it would be necessary to reconstruct jujutsu even as an exercise for martial purposes. So by taking together all the good points I had learned of the various schools and adding thereto my own devices and inventions, I founded a new system for physical culture and mental training as well as for winning contests. I called this Kudokan judo." Kano did not like the harmful taint and violent use of jujutsu on the street. He created Kodokan judo (meaning "a place to study the gentle way") to bring an overall philosophy to the martial arts founded on three sets of techniques: throwing, groundwork, and striking. There was also a code of conduct that had to be followed, and exhibitions for money or fights in the streets were strictly prohibited.

Kano's judo soon became so popular that a rift between jujutsu schools culminated into a challenge in 1886. In the ensuing competition, Kano's students dominated the jujutsu practitioners, winning most of the matches. On July 24, 1905, 18 jujutsu masters joined Kano's ranks to follow his art. Jujutsu was dead, and judo (meaning "the gentle way") replaced it with uniformity, honor, and sport. Part of Kano's plan was to spread the teachings of judo to the rest of the world, and from 1889 to his death at age 77 on May 4, 1938, he made 10 trips, including America and Europe. Japan became enamored of judo, and from 1905 to 1910, the physical focus of the art moved away from striking and dangerous techniques toward a safe yet competitive sport. In 1909, the Kudokan became an official Japanese foundation, and sport judo became an international pastime. Punching, kicking, and dangerous submissions were only taught to higher-ranking *judoka*, or judo players, who could not use these techniques in competition. As a sport, judo consisted of throws and some groundfighting with submission only; highly injurious techniques such as ankle locks were often eliminated. In Europe, many judo factions still honored jujutsu and often claimed that a black belt in one system would automatically be a black belt in the other.

In 1903, Yoshiaki Yamashita, one of Kano's top judoka had success in the United States and sent for more Kudokan players to join him. Arriving on December 8, 1904, Mitsuyo Maeda and another senior judoka, Tsunejiro Tomita, found themselves in great demand for judo demonstrations. Over the next couple of years, Maeda and Tomita performed demonstrations at colleges, military academies, and for anyone who would have them. Maeda would eventually start entering challenge matches and performing in pro wrestling bouts, something that Kano would not have approved of. Though only 5'5" tall and weighing 154 pounds, Maeda competed in over 2,000 matches and never lost a jujutsu/judo competition. He traveled all throughout the U.S., Europe, Cuba, Mexico City, and Central America performing in matches and demonstrations. While on tour in Spain in 1908, Maeda became known as "Conde Koma" (Count of Combat) in the ring, and eventually made this part of his legal name.

Maeda eventually traveled to Brazil, landing in Porto Alegre on November 14, 1914, but ended up settling in Manaus, near the Brazilian Amazon, in December 1915. After establishing himself, he moved east to Belem, where he married in 1917. Maeda's challenge/fighting career was coming to a close, but it wasn't quite over. João Alberto Barreto recounted a story his father-in-law told him about a capoeira fighter's challenge to writer Marcelo Alonso for *Full Contact Fighter* in January 2002. Upon meeting, the Japanese bowed as a show of respect, but Pé de Bola, the capoeira, didn't know what to make of it and extended his hand instead. "I think, hypothetically, that the Japanese thought that it was the beginning of the fight," said Barreto. "When he held Pé de Bola's hand, he squeezed it so hard, that made the capoeira fighter get down on his knees and give up, just with the hand squeezing. That would be the first recorded vale tudo, here in Brazil."

Barreto's father-in-law, Samuel Pinto, was a prominent doctor in Belem and had many connections, including a Brazilian scholar and politician of Scottish descent named Gastão Gracie. Pinto formed a friendship with Gastão's oldest son Carlos and decided to take him over to Maeda's judo academy, Clube Remo, which he had opened in 1921. Though there are varying accounts as to what happened next, the most known story stemmed from Maeda teaching Carlos judo in exchange for Gastão helping Maeda secure a consulate post. With Gracie's help, Maeda became a major force in Japanese immigration to Brazil in 1925 and adopted Brazilian citizenship in the 1930s. Maeda would continue to teach in his remaining years, passing away at age 63 on November 28, 1941, just one day after receiving his seventh dan in judo.

◆ ◆ ◆

BORN TO A WEALTHY FAMILY, Carlos Gracie was the oldest of five brothers. He took judo/jujutsu instruction from Maeda at age 14 for four years.

Carlos continued to study under Maeda's Brazilian assistants until he moved his family to Southern Brazil from Belem. He formed his own jujutsu academy in Rio de Janeiro in 1925 and took it upon himself to teach jujutsu to three of his brothers and to friends. He had a fourth brother named Helio (the "H" is silent), a frail child who was 11 years younger. "At 14 years old, my daddy was so weak and skinny that he could not even run or he would pass out," said Relson, Helio's second-eldest son (all Helio's children's names begin with the letter R, which is pronounced as an "H" in Portuguese, so Relson is "Helson," and so on). "Carlos focused on making him better by perfecting the Gracie Diet. Carlos was a doctor and went to the university for more than six years. He studied plants and the combination of fruits. [Helio] started the diet in six months and then he was playing soccer again." The Gracie Diet, something the entire family holds sacred to this day, involved eating lots of fruit and combinations of certain foods at certain times, while avoiding pork and foods high in sugar.

Helio was told not to partake in his brother's jujutsu activity until a moment of circumstance. "My dad was about 16 years old. After spending a couple of years watching my uncle Carlos teach classes, one day a student showed up to class and my uncle Carlos is nowhere to be found," said Helio's eldest son, Rorion. Helio apologized for his brother's absence and told the student that if he wanted, he could take lessons from him for the day. The student agreed. When class was over, Carlos finally showed up. To his dismay, the student told Carlos that from that moment forward, he wished to take instruction from Helio. A new teacher was born, and Helio, who had once been too weak for any sport, had found something to make him only stronger. As he became more proficient in jujutsu, Helio realized that many of the things he had been taught required more energy than was needed. "Helio started changing those techniques, as a form of trial and error, gradually so that he could use them, and that is what gave birth to Brazilian jiu-jitsu," said Rorion. Instead of judo throws, Brazilian jiu-jitsu (BJJ) emphasized groundwork and submission techniques like chokes and arm bars. Judo replaced jujutsu in Japan, while in the rest of the world it would more often assume the new spelling of *jiu-jitsu* and would be used more to describe groundwork than throws or striking. The term "Japanese jiu-jitsu" was relegated to yet another traditional stand-up art to be taught throughout American dojos.

As the Gracie name became more widely known in Brazil, and associated with jiu-jitsu, challengers came out of the woodwork to discredit Helio and the family. Jiu-jitsu was virtually unknown compared to boxing and the native art of *capoeira* that ruled Brazilian martial arts. Just as Maeda had to prove himself and his art, Helio now became the defender of the Gracie name. Of all the brothers, Helio fought in the most challenge matches for the family, starting with his 1932 victory over pro boxer Antonio Portugal in 30 seconds. "Carlos dedicated everything to help Helio become a champion," said Relson. Soon *O Globo*, Brazil's biggest newspaper, was carrying accounts of his fights, which employed punching and kicking as well as grappling. One reporter dubbed these matches *vale tudo*, which means "anything goes" in Portuguese. "When the Gracie family first started fighting, we were looked at as traitors in Brazil," said Relson. "We were representing jiu-jitsu, which was Japanese martial arts, and we were fighting against capoeira, which was the national martial art. Every time we went to compete, people were throwing bottles and chanting, 'Traitors go away!'" Helio continued winning, and eventually the Gracie name and jiu-jitsu spread throughout Brazil as the real deal, far more so than the colorful but less effective capoeira. João Alberto Barreto remembered securing a gymnasium his father had built for Helio to fight a capoeira stylist at the age of 15. He would go on to live with Helio for 12 years and became one of Helio's first instructors under the Gracie Academy banner in Brazil.

Indeed, the Gracies were to become perhaps the most remarkable family in the history of martial arts—some say in the whole history of sports. While Carlos dedicated himself to his dietary research and Helio did most of the fighting, both spawned large families, and many of their children would become dedicated jiu-jitsu students, outstanding competitors, and later instructors. They stressed technique above all else and preached a mantra that most genuine fights end up on the ground, so that is where they are likely to be won or lost. Develop the skills to finish an opponent on the floor and a smaller man (or woman) can defeat a much larger foe. As the Gracie offspring grew older, their children in turn would mature to extol the family combat art as the best and most effective of all.

As headlines made big news of Helio's success in the ring, a local Japanese group that had continued Maeda's teachings sought a judoka who could knock him off his pedestal. Back in Japan, Masahiko Kimura had accomplished everything he had set out to do. Born in 1917, he had reached seventh dan in judo at the age of 29. For 13 straight years, he never suffered a single defeat. In 1950, he made the decision to leave judo to earn money in pro wrestling and judo challenge matches, just as Maeda had done before him. In July 1951, Kimura and two other judo players were asked to compete in Brazil, where Helio made an open challenge to Kimura. Believing Helio was unworthy, Kimura told him to battle one of his juniors first, so a fifth-degree black belt named Kato accepted.

One week before their match, Helio suffered a broken rib in training but still managed to fight to a draw. Helio was ready for Kato the second time, just 30 days later. The Japanese fighter threw Helio around with ease initially, and at one point Kato began to apply a choke. Reversing the position, Gracie beat him to it and choked Kato unconscious in six minutes. Gracie's popularity surged, and, having passed the test, he now wanted Kimura himself. Kimura's second and much larger judoka, Yamaguchi, declined for fear of injury, so Helio got his wish.

It would be Helio's greatest challenge. The Brazilian was 39 years old and 140 pounds; Kimura was six years younger and outweighed him by nearly 50 pounds. As in the match with Kato, Helio implemented rules dictating that the fight could only be won by submission; throws did not matter. Also, if Kimura could not beat him within the first three minutes, then Helio should be considered the winner. According to Kimura's biography, Gracie followers situated a coffin next to the ring for the Japanese fighter. On October 23, 1951, Brazilian newspapers reported that 20,000 spectators gathered inside the massive Maracana Stadium in Brazil to bear witness to "The World Championship of Jiu-jitsu."

During the first of 10 rounds, Kimura treated Gracie like a rag doll, throwing him around the ring. Kimura tried several submissions, but Gracie held strong and evaded his opponent's attack. Three minutes into the second round, Kimura had Gracie in an arm lock. The Brazilian would not give up until his brother Carlos threw in the towel minutes later. The match lasted 13 minutes. There seems to be some confusion as to whether Helio's elbow was actually dislocated. Rorion Gracie said it was not, but Kimura's own biography along with other accounts said otherwise. There is no doubt that Gracie suffered his first defeat, and the arm lock that was formally known as the "reverse ude garami" became known as the *Kimura* or *Kimura lock*, a term still used today.

Gracie's final match took place on May 24, 1957, under vale tudo rules, against former student Waldemar Santana. Santana had been a family friend for over a decade until he and Helio had a falling out that escalated into a heated tabloid-slinging exchange. The Brazilian headquarters of the YMCA in Rio hosted the fight. "At that time, more people came in and joined the Gracie Academy [jiu-jitsu school] than any other period in the Academy's history," said Rorion. A 50-year-old man fought his much-younger pupil (Santana was 23), who outweighed him by 50 pounds, for nearly four hours. João Alberto Barreto saw the fight and said that Waldemar had great respect for Helio and that it was a friend of his, a psychiatrist, who had issue with the family. He said that Helio was in no condition to fight and was ill, but fought anyway. "Despite Waldemar being very strong and knowing how to fight, because we taught him, Helio resisted for 3:45 and in the end, he didn't have the strength to do anything," said Barreto. So Santana picked up Gracie, threw him to the ground and kicked him in the face. This was the longest recorded, uninterrupted match in MMA history. Even though Helio finally was knocked out, how could anyone not see the advantages of jiu-jitsu in such a fight? Of course the family had to be vindicated, so brother Carlos asked Waldemar to pick between Helio again, Barreto, or his own son Carlson for the rematch. With Helio's retirement, Waldemar picked the 17-year-old Carlson Gracie, who fought Santana five times, winning two and drawing three. Ironically, during his last pro wrestling/ judo tour in 1959, Santana challenged Kimura to a submission match. Kimura submitted Santana with the move that pegged his moniker; they had a vale tudo rematch that ended by 40-minute months later. Kimura passed away at age 75 on April 18, 1993, from lung cancer.

Carlson continued fighting through the 1960s and, because of his success against Santana, which had been a huge hit on television, freestyle fighting became a true spectator sport in Brazil. As Rorion remembered, "It was called *Vale Tudo on TV*, and of course it reached very high ratings; eventually other television networks were getting very political against that." These fights aired sporadically on Brazilian television throughout the 1950s and 1960s, creating heroes for the audience at home. Relson recalled another show his father Helio produced, called *Herois do Ringue* or *Heroes of the Ring*. "That was in 1959 at TV Continental," said Barreto. "When I was in law school, I would get out of school and go straight to fight." As more and more people learned about Brazilian jiu-jitsu, other incarnations developed, such as *luta livre*, or freestyle grappling without a gi. "The name 'luta livre' comes from my daddy's event," said Relson. "My daddy promoted an event called Luta Livre Americana back in 1958 because America is wild. In Brazil, Americans were looked at as fighting very mean, like a streetfight, stemming from John Wayne movies. In Brazil, we had this image of the Americans fighting bare-fisted."

Vale tudo made heroes out of fighters other than the Gracies, such as Ivan Gomes. According to Brazilian MMA journalist Marcelo Alonso, who wrote an article about Gomes in the American magazine *Fightsport*, "[Gomes is] known in the Brazilian northeast as the best vale tudo fighter ever. [He] fought in more than 200 consecutive vale tudo matches...not one ended in defeat." At a time when Carlson Gracie was at his best, he fought Gomes to a draw in 1963 and proclaimed it was the toughest fight of his career. Gracie befriended Gomes, who later ran one of his gyms in Brazil before competing in Japan thanks to Antonio Inoki. In August 1976, Gomes defeated three opponents and retired with a record of 199–0–6.

• • •

THE GRACIE FAMILY BECAME LEGENDARY for their exploits. During the mid-1980s, crime was at an all-time high in Brazil, and even the beaches were not a safe haven. One afternoon, Rickson and Royler Gracie (Helio's middle sons) went surfing, a common pastime for Brazilian youth. Royler was very even-tempered but got into a disagreement with another surfer. "Six guys tried to beat up Royler, but Rickson was able to get him away," said brother Relson. "Some guys were kicking Royler on the ground, so finally Rickson went to the car and grabbed a bat. Rickson laid into the guys with the bat to get Royler to safety, and, as they spun away in the car, the guys were throwing rocks and broke the back windshield." The following week, a German journalist had his camera stolen and was subsequently stabbed to death. Something had to be done.

"The equivalent to the SWAT team came to my dad's [jiu-jitsu] school, and the whole team was there," said Relson. "They got 15 of us to walk with them through the beach. When the cops walk through the beach, the bad guys would hide drugs and weapons in the sand. When we walk through the beach, we were like normal people with shorts; this was to surprise the guys." Relson walked in front, Royler 30' behind, and they had plenty of reinforcements. "I approached a group of four of the troublemakers and talked to them about coming along quietly to talk with the police," said Relson. "They didn't want to go. One guy stood up and pushed me and then punched me so I choked him out. The other guy tried to kick me so I took him down and choked him too. The third one ran into the water, and then I jumped on his back and choked him out too in the water. The fourth one also got into the water and started to swim away. I swam behind him and choked him out." Relson had to bring the fourth one back to the beach with the others, and soon, his family and students surrounded them. "They resisted and some of the other bad guys showed up to make more trouble from the corner of the beach, but they were in for a surprise. The cops showed up and found weapons and drugs and arrested them."

♦ ♦ ♦

ON NOVEMBER 30, 1984, a pivotal event called Vale Tudo No Maracanãzinho pitted Gracie students against other styles. The historic importance of this event not only shaped combat sports outside of submission wrestling but established a new hero amongst the Brazilians: Marco Ruas. A teenage Ruas had begun his martial arts training under the tutelage of Uncle Zinicius, a judo black belt and well-respected teacher in Brazil. He eventually took up tae kwon do, capoeira, and Thai boxing before boxing coach Santa Rosa took him under his wing. During his twenties, Ruas trained and taught steadily under the guidance of tae kwon do and Thai boxing teacher Flavio Molina. Although Ruas experimented with luta livre, he concentrated on stand-up martial arts until an incident with the Gracie family forced him to look at the bigger picture.

Sometime in early 1984, Molina's brother-in-law, a tae kwon do practitioner, got into a street fight with Charley Gracie and Gracie lost. "My cousin Renzo was in a nightclub and got into a fight with some guys from luta livre," said Relson. "Those same guys got into the street fight with Robson's son, Charley Gracie, and mobbed him up." According to Ruas, Charley went to his uncle Rolls Gracie and told him about the encounter, saying, "This tae kwon do guy was saying that jiu-jitsu was bad!" The Gracie family wielded an almost mythic power with jiu-jitsu at this point, one that few dared to challenge. While Relson was known as the streetfighter of the family, Rolls was noted as the most technically skilled—but not on this occasion. Armed with several students, Rolls stormed Molina's school with a vengeance. "He [Molina] taught kids, but some of his students were black belts, and the jiu-jitsu guys came and put the guys to sleep," said Ruas.

"Because of these fights, it gave them [luta livre] the ego to think they can beat us," said Relson. "It created a stir in Brazil to start up the challenge matches again. For years, nobody challenged us; I only fought in the streets." Maracanãzinho was a nickname given to a smaller convention center in Brazil compared to Maracana. Originally, the Gracie family was going to face Molina's crew, but the decision was made to let Gracie students compete instead. Molina, Ruas, and others competed as "kickboxers" and fought as a team in the event, which was promoted by Robson Gracie. Just two months prior, Roberto Leito Sr. contacted Ruas and offered his services to teach him ground defense. Known as the father of luta livre, Leito Sr. learned jiu-jitsu from the Gracies but built new techniques and strategies upon the art. The only chance Ruas had to defeat Carlson Gracie student Fernando Pinduka (Ruas was originally going to fight Relson Gracie) would stem from learning Brazilian jiu-jitsu. "Leito taught me some techniques, and the guy could not submit me," said Ruas. "I landed a lot of punches and knocked his tooth out. Everybody around the ring was for the Gracies, and the referee was a black belt in jiu-jitsu." Though Molina was choked out by Relson Gracie brown belt Marcelo Bhering, 23-year-old Ruas fought to a draw. Pinduka controlled the pace on the ground and had the crowd behind him, but Ruas stayed out of his traps and stunned him several times standing up. This experience changed Ruas forever, and it put him on the road to enlightenment about knowing both sides of the coin. (Jiu-jitsu and luta livre practitioners constantly tested themselves and their machismo attitudes against one another, not realizing that knowledge should be shared and adapted.)

Ruas developed his own following, but he only fought in three other vale tudo-style matches in Brazil. "The Gracies only liked to fight guys from one style like capoeira or kung fu, guys who knew nothing about jiu-jitsu," said Ruas. "The Gracies considered me an enemy, and it was hard for me to get sponsors or to get fights again. It wasn't personal; it was just about jiu-jitsu." Rorion Gracie has quite a different take on the matter. "Every single one either learned directly or indirectly from the Gracies, and there was no such problem in allowing them to fight against us." At times, vale tudo became synonymous with jiu-jitsu, but the latter was more accessible and safer for public consumption. Eventually, its brutal cousin all but disappeared, relegated to underground events. As time went on, challenges made to the Gracie family became fewer and fewer; their art had proven its effectiveness and there was no point in disputing it any longer. But Helio's eldest son, Rorion, didn't want to stop there.

• • •

RORION GRACIE BEGAN LEARNING JIU-JITSU at such an early age that he said he had a diaper on under his gi. He had grown up with a family name that meant something on the rough-and-tumble streets of Brazil. By young adulthood, he felt it was time to spread that fame. Against his relatives' advice, the 17-year-old Rorion journeyed to the United States in 1969 in search of a dream. He found himself sleeping on newspapers and panhandling for food instead. Returning to Brazil periodically, he graduated with a law degree from his native land and learned English. He also refused to give up. Rorion settled permanently in the U.S. in 1978, with one thought in mind: to teach jiu-jitsu to anyone who wanted to learn the most potent system of fighting. The drive behind Gracie Jiu-Jitsu, according to Rorion, was "if these people never have access to learning jiu-jitsu, they will be forever oppressed by the big, tough guys in their neighborhood."

But without any advertising, Rorion's dream of teaching the smaller guy how to defeat the bigger guy would have to wait. While cleaning houses to make extra money, he met a woman with a TV/film producer husband who thought he would be great in front of the camera. Gracie stumbled on an unlikely career as an actor. Over the course of the next 15 years, the tall, dark, and handsome Rorion appeared in major television series like *Hill Street Blues*, *Fantasy Island*, *Hart to Hart*, and *The Love Boat*. Gracie enjoyed his new job, but that didn't prevent him from bringing people from the set to his garage to show them the family art. "I had a small house on Muscle Beach, and after every shoot, I would drag whoever I could and give them an introductory class," said Gracie. Erik Paulson had devoted his life to the martial arts and was training with Dan Inosanto in Jeet Kune Do when he heard about Rorion training people out of his garage. "I went down, and I took my first private and thought I was going to get my ass kicked," he said. "I trained with Rorion, and it was an eye opener and one of the nicest experiences I ever had. First of all, he shook my hand; he was very nice, complimentary, and he really explained the elements of Gracie Jiu-jitsu and the leverage factor."

Although his first dojo was basic, Rorion knew he was on to something. He believed in jiu-jitsu so much that he registered the name Gracie Jiu-jitsu. "The term Gracie Jiu-jitsu was carved by me [in the USA], and it identifies my source of instruction," said Rorion. "When the Gracie name became very famous, a lot of relatives of mine started to capitalize on the work I had done. Unfortunately, they don't have the sense of professionalism and ethics that I wished they did, and because I owned the Gracie Jiu-jitsu name, I would refuse to let those guys sell and prostitute the name."

The Machado family, cousins to the Gracies, also called America home. When Rorion started conducting seminars, he brought over Carlos Machado to work with karateka and film star Chuck Norris in Las Vegas. Machado eventually moved to America, and, through Norris, Carlos and his brothers dabbled in films while teaching with Rorion in his garage. According to Rorion, the Machados began teaching students behind his back, as well as undercutting his prices and changing the way the art was taught. They were eventually ousted from Rorion's group and even sued over use of the Gracie name. Rorion ended up sending several cease-and-desist letters to family members over use of the name.

Carley Gracie, Rorion's nephew and son of Carlos Gracie, was a different story. He settled in America several years before Rorion in late 1972 but failed to find a niche for jiu-jitsu. When the UFC exploded onto the scene, he restarted his school and contested Rorion's registered trademark. Carley filed a lawsuit in December 1994, calling for the registration's cancellation on a number of grounds, including Carley's prior use of "Gracie Jiu-jitsu" in Florida and an alleged "secondary meaning" because the public associated the term with the entire Gracie family as a martial arts style. A San Francisco jury tried the case in November 1997. The verdict found that Gracie Jiu-jitsu was indeed more than a teaching style; it was a style of martial arts. The District Court ordered the USPTO to cancel Rorion's service mark registration. That said, the case was not over, and Rorion would reign victorious in July 2000 for Carley violating the triangle logo trademark; Rorion would be awarded $108,000 in damages, along with $620,000 in attorney's fees. As for Gracie Jiu-jitsu and Brazlian jiu-jitsu, the "style" improved by Helio Gracie now belonged to the world.

Issues over the name withstanding, Rorion's attempt to popularize the art in the States had not worked out as he had hoped. After all, there was no reason to venture into someone's garage to learn martial arts when one could pick and choose from countless dojos promoting every flash-in-the-pan style from Asia. While word of mouth attracted a small though loyal following, it would take a new spin on the old family tradition to reach the masses.

3

THE GRACIE CHALLENGE

In 1982, one of Rorion Gracie's pupils ventured into a traditional karate school and bragged of jiu-jitsu's superiority—to put it simply, how his teacher could defeat their teacher. The karate instructor responded by issuing a challenge to Gracie, with $1,000 going to the winner. Gracie was more than happy to oblige, but the instructor backed out at the last minute. However, legendary kickboxing champion Benny "The Jet" Urquidez was a close friend of the instructor and agreed to take on Gracie instead.

Born into a fighting family (his father a boxer, his mother a pro wrestler), Urquidez shot up through the kickboxing ranks in the mid-1970s, capturing title after title. He also paved the way for Americans to test their skills in the Orient by becoming the first Westerner to beat the Japanese at their own game. Japanese audiences were so taken by his showy performances in the ring that Urquidez became a superstar. Though doubts surround his unblemished 58–0 record, there is no doubt The Jet is one of kickboxing's greatest legends. Rorion Gracie had no idea who he was.

Gracie and Urquidez met at the local YMCA in West Valley, California, where the kickboxer frequently taught.

"Do you want to do this on mats or the hardwood floor?" asked Urquidez.

"That depends," said Gracie, "Do you want to land on the mats or do you want to land on the hardwood floor?"

They both laughed; Urquidez pulled out some mats. It was not a real fight by any means, just a sparring session between masters of two arts. With no wager in place, Gracie took Urquidez down at will; he also made him tap several times. The kickboxer was amazed with what Gracie could do, but that wasn't the point of the exercise—it was to show how good jiu-jitsu was, not the person using it. To demonstrate further, Gracie matched his student against one of his opponent's top pupils, who was 40 pounds heavier. It didn't matter. Just as Gracie had instructed him, the smaller man rushed Urquidez's muscular purple belt and quickly took him to the mat where, after a struggle, he made him tap with an ankle lock. The kickboxing legend was impressed and agreed to help spread the word about Brazilian—make that Gracie—Jiu-jitsu. Rorion wondered if this would finally be the answer to his problems.

A week passed, but there was still no word from Urquidez. After repeated calls, Gracie gave up. It seemed that every time he called, The Jet was too busy with something else. A few months later a documentary filmmaker contacted Gracie at his home and asked if he would contribute to a martial arts piece he was doing. The filmmaker was intrigued by the "challenge" angle and wanted to set up a fight between Gracie and a well-known kickboxer. As fate would have it, the kickboxer turned out to be Benny Urquidez. The kickboxer, realizing what was at stake, drove a hard bargain. According to the filmmaker, Urquidez would fight under the following conditions: five rounds of five minutes each, but if it went to the ground, they would have to be stood back up after 60 seconds. No matter the outcome, Gracie would have to pay Urquidez $100,000. If Urquidez lost, he would give Gracie his world champion-ship kickboxing belt. "So I'm hiring him to fight me for $100,000," said Gracie. "What would I do with a world championship belt? I'm not a kickboxer." To level the playing field, Gracie made a counterchallenge: same number of rounds and time limits, but if the fight went to the ground, it stayed there. Urquidez would put up $75,000; Gracie would put up $100,000. If the fight went to a draw, Urquidez could keep the

$100,000. The filmmaker was puzzled that Gracie would concede such an apparently unfair advantage to his opponent but told him arrangements would be made. Gracie never heard back.

News of what transpired didn't necessarily bring flocks of students to his garage dojo, but it created more hype around the Gracie Challenge. In one such match, well-known tang soo do practitioner Ralph Alegria (winner of multiple championships in tournament play) fought Rorion Gracie in a ring. Alegria tapped in less than two minutes. A watching film producer was so impressed with Gracie's abilities, he asked for his help in choreographing the fight finale between Mel Gibson and Gary Busey in the 1987 blockbuster *Lethal Weapon*. Gracie worked with both actors for two months in preparation for the sequence, which included submissions. Gracie also worked with Rene Russo in *Lethal Weapon 3* and had a small part in the film.

• • •

TWO MORE YEARS PASSED before Rorion Gracie got the break he was looking for. Respected freelance writer Pat Jordan was working on a story about an arm wrestler when his subject recommended Gracie, having worked out with him in his garage dojo. Jordan spent three days with the jiu-jitsu master. In September 1989, his lengthy article on an "unknown sports hero" appeared not in *Black Belt* or some other karate rag, but in the mass-market *Playboy* magazine. Headlined "BAD," it called Rorion "the toughest man in the United States" and was a compelling account of his attempt to achieve the American dream through his father's legacy. It also declared that he would fight any man in the USA for $100,000, winner takes all.

The "Gracie Challenge" took on a life of its own. No longer was it a singular wager made with Urquidez; it was now something the Gracie family staked its entire reputation on. A slew of letters about the article poured into the *Playboy* office, and the martial arts community soon recognized the Gracie Challenge with a follow-up in *Karate Kung Fu*

Illustrated. Rorion and his brothers suddenly had their hands full with new students and new challenges.

On the other side of Los Angeles, adman Arthur Davie kept the *Playboy* article for another reason. He worked for top advertising firm J & P Marketing and was faced with the dilemma of finding an outlet to create brand awareness for Wisdom Imports' Tecate beer. Noting the beer's Mexican/Asian appeal, an extreme sport seemed logical, but the category manager didn't think highly of Davie's idea of using kickboxing or boxing events. With money and research invested in the project, a thick folder was all that was left, waiting for someone with initiative to act on it. Davie was no stranger to taking things into his own hands, as he had already built a reputation for creating spectacles out of his ad campaigns. He had made the May 1980 issue of *TV Guide* by playing a giant motorized zucchini for Honda and had even jumped off a 10-story building for a television commercial promoting his San Diego auto dealership at the time.

Born in Brooklyn, Davie had dabbled in amateur boxing in his youth and kept it up when he was drafted into the Marines during the Vietnam War. In 1969, a fellow soldier returned from a lengthy R-and-R session in Bangkok full of stories about mixed martial arts bouts he'd seen in nightclubs over there. It became a never-ending source of locker-room fodder, wondering if Sugar Ray Robinson could have beaten Bruce Lee. More than two decades later, that thought still lingered in Davie's mind. Rorion Gracie's newly acquired profile was about to bring that concept to fruition—in the United States.

Davie dropped by Gracie's new school in Torrance in the spring of 1990, only to find contractors milling about with younger brother Royce and father Helio working on the juice bar. He left his card. Two weeks later, Davie was called and asked to come down. Though the school was unfinished, Davie was invited to a challenge match held that Saturday night. He didn't know what to expect, waiting attentively in a crowded room with everyone dressed in white gis. Suddenly the door opened and a horde of karate guys based in the gang-ridden L.A. suburb of

Compton poured in. In typical good-guy-versus-bad-guy fashion, they wore black gis. Their karate instructor wanted to prove himself against one of Rorion's younger brothers, Royler, who weighed a nimble 155 pounds. Davie watched in astonishment as Royler choked out his man two or three times. It was clear the karate practitioners didn't have a clue what was going on. Looking around the room, Davie spotted a vaguely familiar face, Hollywood director John Milius, one of Rorion's Tinseltown protégés. Davie was a big film buff, and he and Milius hit it off immediately. Before long, Davie was taking private classes from Gracie on Tuesday nights, right after Milius. On several occasions the three would sit around Gracie's office chatting about jiu-jitsu vs. karate and every type of combination in between.

After leaving the advertising company in late 1991, Davie needed a new creative outlet and agreed to help his newfound friend promote a videotape series called *Gracies in Action*. Each tape showed several fights, from black-and-white footage of Helio to recent challenge matches held in the Gracie dojo. Hapkido experts, wrestlers, and so-called masters of every conceivable martial arts style barely had time to strike a pose before being taken to the ground and tapped out. It was uncanny. Davie devised a hot direct-mail scheme that soon had the orders piling up. "When I saw the reaction to the tape from fans, I said, 'Let me see if I can come up with something to create a show around this,'" said Davie. Rorion had been approached about such an event before, but nothing had ever transpired. The thought of recreating what the Gracie family had done back in Brazil was more than appealing to Rorion; it was something always in the back of his mind.

Rorion remembered the time when he was 10 years old in Brazil, watching vale tudo matches at home with his family on television. There was one long, exhaustive match where one fighter sat in the corner on the ground while his opponent loomed over him. "The guy in the middle of the ring reaches his hand down, appearing as if to let the other guy up," said Rorion Gracie. "The guy sitting down reaches up to the friendly hand that has been extended. With his hand extended, the guy standing up grabs the other guy's hand and kicks him in the face on national television. Everybody at home went crazy from the excitement. This is the type of thing that I envisioned for what would become the UFC."

On November 25, 1992, Davie and Gracie formed WOW Promotions and set up shop in Torrance, California. Davie then developed a proposal for a limited-rules tournament called War of the Worlds, and he and Gracie were pitching it to John Milius in under a week. Milius, who scripted *Apocalypse Now* and directed Arnold Schwarzenegger's breakout picture *Conan the Barbarian*, was excited about the idea. In a letter addressed to Gracie on January 3, 1993, he said, "I feel [War of the Worlds] connects the present to the past by recreating the classical Greek and Roman contest of pankration." At that time, Davie and Gracie envisioned that an open tournament of this type could never take place in the United States. Originally the show was to be held in Rio de Janeiro on October 30, 1993.

Before setting things in stone for Brazil, Davie conducted his own research to clarify the viability of hosting the show stateside. He knew that most states would be problematic but, by chance, had found a flyer for what appeared to be a mixed martial arts show that would be taking place right down the street in Irvine, California. On February 21, 1993, he attended Cage of Rage at the Bren Center, which promised a spectacle of martial arts madness. The show took place in a 10' high octagonal cage with spikes on the top, but with colorful costumes, over-the-top martial arts moves, and whacky theatrics, the show was nothing more than a glorified pro wrestling event. Promoter Greg "Kazja" Patschull was only allowed to run the show in California if all the matches were predetermined. War of the Worlds would be the real deal, but what state would allow it to happen unhampered?

After an exhaustive amount of research, Colorado became a logical choice. As it turned out, a July 1, 1977, law had repealed all state statutes governing boxing and wrestling matches, save for one: participants must be 18 years old to compete. Davie could live with that. "Colorado was the only choice given there was so little indicating that we couldn't do this," said Davie. To make matters even easier, it was learned that Colorado, at the time, was one of the few states where a limited liability company could be formed. On May 12, 1993, WOW Promotions was set up as an LLC that would ultimately be out looking for investors. But first they needed a vehicle to broadcast these fights, and pay-per-view was the answer.

Months earlier—beginning in January 1993—Davie had contacted two major pay-per-view companies, TVKO and SET. Television exposure would be essential. But no one wanted to listen; no one understood what Davie was trying to sell. At that time, pay-per-view was not making the big money everyone had hoped. Shows were expensive to produce, since cable companies were taking 50 percent, with 10 percent going to the distributor and 40 percent to the producer. This was also a difficult time for sports shows that had dominated pay-per-view, like boxing and pro wrestling. The heyday of boxing pay-per-view, the Mike Tyson era, was gone, with Tyson languishing in jail for a rape conviction. People weren't interested anymore in shelling out a lot of money for one headliner and two or three no-name fights. Pro wrestling came under a lot of scrutiny when steroid abuse allegations led to World Wrestling Federation owner Vince McMahon being put on trial.

Davie found himself with one last alternative—the small but unconventional Semaphore Entertainment Group (SEG). Based on the East Coast, SEG was a joint venture between the giant Bertelsmann Music Group (BMG) and Robert Meyrowitz, who had made his name as the foremost producer of innovative radio programming. Once described as "a riverboat gambler who sinks formidable sums into promoting concerts and other entertainment programming," the avuncular Meyrowitz had worked with Hollywood icons and had created the *King Biscuit Flower Hour*, which became America's longest-running nationally syndicated radio series and a veritable "Who's Who" of rock music. He was also behind novelty sports events such as the "Battle of the Champions," an exhibition tennis match between Jimmy Connors and Martina Navratilova. Davie thought SEG was just the kind of progressive, freewheeling company that might go for the unusual. As he'd done with TVKO and SET, Davie gathered copies of the *Playboy* article and the *Gracies in Action* tapes and sent them to SEG's main office in New York.

Luckily, maverick programmer and one-time stand-up comedian Campbell McLaren intercepted them. McLaren, a former film student, wasn't interested in boxing, didn't like wrestling, and didn't know much about music. But he saw pay-per-view as an appealing avenue for genres previously unexplored by commercial television. At the time, he had been toying with ideas ranging from the world's biggest demolition derby to Mexican pro wrestling because of its "superhero" charm. When the *Playboy* article crossed his desk, McLaren dismissed his other ideas. He had found what he was looking for.

David Isaacs, SEG's youthful vice president of marketing and planning, was also trying to find the right business for the firm, since all of its pay-per-view events had barely turned a profit, if they made money at all. He was shown the tapes. "I remember seeing Rickson on the beach [a match with Hugo Duarte from *Gracies in Action 2*], and the office just filled up with people watching it," said Isaacs. "And you were like, 'Oh my gosh, I've never seen anything like this!'" On April 27, 1993, Davie received a fax from McLaren inviting him to New York to talk about his proposal for War of the Worlds. When he got there he found an enthusiastic McLaren trying to win over bossman Robert Meyrowitz. "He didn't know tae kwon do from moo goo gai pan," remembered Davie. "He wasn't sure what the hell we were talking about." But one thing was sure: Meyrowitz's track record with pay-per-view wasn't cutting the mustard. Fast approaching age 50, he needed something as fresh as the *King Biscuit Flower Hour*, which had put SEG on the map in radio. He trusted McLaren enough to make the right choice and move forward with the project.

◆ ◆ ◆

ON JUNE 3, 1993, SEG sent an agreement to solidify the deal between the company, Art Davie, and Rorion Gracie. As it stood, WOW and SEG would each own half of the show, but WOW would be responsible for producing and paying for the live show, including the fighter purses and overhead. Through the LLC, Davie and Gracie each held 45 percent, so they developed a private placement memorandum and began pitching it five days later with John Milius confirmed as creative director. The show would now be called *The World's Best Fighter*. A meeting was called, and 65 students of Gracie's academy were invited to hear more about the project. After everything was said and done, 10 percent ownership was given to 28 investors with just under $250,000 raised. Davie and Gracie only lent their expertise—nothing out of their wallets. Campbell McLaren was in attendance; at the conclusion of the meeting, Davie turned to him and said, "By the way, this isn't just a pipedream or hypothetical." McLaren eased the WOW investors by telling them that SEG was investing $400,000 into the first show, making it a done deal.

The first event was slated for October 2, 1993, with SEG Sports Corp., a wholly owned subsidiary, and WOW working in tandem to plan the logistics. SEG had just scored big with a New Kids On The Block concert that became the highest-grossing pay-per-view entertainment event ever. But while that looked great on paper, it didn't mean SEG was the one making the money, said Isaacs. "We had been doing lots of music shows where there were a lot of difficult and legal aspects to doing those deals: working with artists, recording labels, and licensing content from third parties. From a business side, [The World's Best Fighter] was very appealing. Instead of being a content licensor, we would be a content creator."

But what exactly were a veteran ad man, a jiu-jitsu black belt, an action film director, and a fledgling pay-per-view company supposed to create? Initially, it was to be a 16-man single-elimination tournament worth $122,000 in cash and prizes, including Grecian crowns and the title, "The World's Hand-to-Hand Combat Champion." SEG eventually agreed on an eight-man tournament with varying fees given to fighters for just showing up.

The fights would be held in a circular pit some 20–25' in diameter, to be designed by John Milius. He originally devised a pit with Greek structures surrounding it. That idea was thrown out, but a conventional boxing ring was out of the question too. Rorion Gracie pointed out that a ring could not contain the fighters in this type of combat. More often than not, they ended up falling through the ropes and onto the floor; the injuries sustained outside the ring might even be worse than those in it. Campbell McLaren suggested a completely open ring with a copper panel that would be electrified for effect, or a plexiglass enclosure with barbed wire running along the top. "Then we had a doctor tell us that if anyone landed on it and was sweaty, it could cause ventricular imputation and someone could have a heart attack," remembered Davie. Trying to add a bit of gimmickry himself, Davie envisioned a crocodile-infested moat surrounding a pit. That idea was discarded for the sake of visibility.

Eventually, SEG contracted film set designer Jason Cusson, who brought reality back into the picture by establishing parameters agreeable to all parties. After several designs were submitted, an octagonal cage was approved. Cusson would be credited as the show's art director. The chain-link fencing stood 5'6" tall and was 30' in diameter. Despite popular belief, the octagonal shape was not for the sake of theatrics but a design strong enough to support the action contained inside. Little did anyone realize the cage concept would become a fixture in other MMA events produced around the world.

While "War of the Worlds" and "The World's Best Fighter" were bandied about as names for the show, it was SEG's Vice President of Affiliate Relations, Michael Abramson, who coined The Ultimate Fighting Championship. Abramson was a long-time promotion manager with companies such as Island Records and Chrysalis, a solid salesman whose job was to market SEG products to affiliates. "Ultimate tested very well because it implied that there was nothing beyond that," said Davie. The logo was actually inspired by a television commercial icon, Mr. Clean, and represented a character of great power but no specific ethnicity.

Though SEG was hot on the project, it was still important to get Bertelsmann interested, since they would be fronting the money. Meyrowitz and McLaren met with their German partners at a ritzy Italian eatery in Manhattan. After three vodka martinis, Meyrowitz prodded his partner to go in for the kill.

"Oh yeah, it's like the martial arts," said McLaren. "It's kind of like you had Bruce Lee fight Muhammad Ali."

"But isn't Lee dead?" asked the Germans.

It took some time for both parties to get on the same playing field, but the Germans finally committed to the event despite not understanding what it was about. What they really wanted was for SEG to get rockers ZZ Top...but that would have to wait.

With everything else in place, it was time to pitch the show to cable companies. October 2 became October 30 due to logistical problems, and then it became early November when the Viewer's Choice distribution network needed a show rundown. But how do you present a show rundown for a live event like this? "We couldn't for the life of us project what the quarter-hour breakdowns were going to be like because we didn't really have a clue," said McLaren. That prompted the question, "How long are these fights going to last?" Rorion Gracie claimed that fights could go on for eight hours because it sometimes took jiu-jitsu a while to "cook" a guy. Davie, on the other hand, told McLaren that guys could get their heads ripped off. "What were they talking about? Eight hours, cooking...I couldn't follow," exclaimed McLaren. Since Viewer's Choice didn't quite know what it had, the final airdate was pushed back to November 12, 1993.

Though the Denver Coliseum had previously been booked for October 2, it now became the neighboring McNichols Sports Arena that would play host to the inaugural UFC. The event would be sanctioned by the International Fighting Council, which had been organized on June 7,

1993, with Art Davie as commissioner. *Enter the Dragon* star Jim Kelly, Jeet Kune Do exponent Paul Vunak, and karate gold medalist Ben Perry were on the IFC's advisory committee but didn't really do much of anything. The IFC was to review and certify fighters, select referees and judges, oversee medical examinations, but above all, "regulate and oversee the development of the new full-contact mixed martial arts," according to a one-pager. The IFC was strictly set up as a way to self-sanction the event, so if Davie and company wanted to do something, they had de facto IFC approval.

In terms of promoting the event, the "sport" aspect was never emphasized. Full contact karate and kickboxing weren't marketable, so the idea of selling a new martial arts show would need a lot more pizzazz in order for it to whet the appetite for the PPV consumer. The show was built on a simple premise: how various martial arts disciplines would fare against one another in a realistic contest with no weight classes and virtually no regulations. But was it sport or spectacle? "I remember sitting in John Milius' office with Rorion, Campbell McLaren, and Bob Meyrowitz, and we sat around debating that issue," said Davie. "I reminded everybody that I had sold it to Bob on the basis that it was a spectacle. It was designed very much as a spectacle. We did not feel it was a sport. Everyone felt that it had a lifespan of maybe about two years." McLaren also liked the gimmick of a man in a gi using his skills to battle an opponent from an entirely different background. After all, martial arts competitions had traditionally been intramural: karate only fought karate, and so on. "I like to think I took this circus, this pseudo-gladiatorial atmosphere, and placed it on top of the Gracie Challenge," summed up McLaren.

SEG's three-shot deal of "different programming" was about to unfold. The first was controversial comic Andrew Dice Clay's "No Apologies" concert, the second was a horror/magic show featuring British heavy metal band Iron Maiden, and the third was The Ultimate Fighting Championship. Clay's show did extremely well, but Iron Maiden didn't catch on big with the American public: in a test screening, one of the senior members of BMG passed out upon seeing all the blood and gore in their stage act, supplied by the same team that had handled the *Hellraiser* movies. The show did find an audience overseas, but the real question would be if the UFC would find an audience at all.

With the particulars taken care of, it was time to scout for fighters. Over the course of several months, ads were placed in martial arts magazines calling for the best fighters in the world to test their skills against each other. All of the problems with point karate tournaments, all of the martial arts styles that weren't "sport-oriented" and, quite simply, all of the frauds that turned a tidy profit from peddling their watered-down arts were in for a big surprise...the *ultimate* surprise.

4

RECRUITING AN ULTIMATE FIGHTER

A rt Davie and Rorion Gracie began their search for seven fighters to participate in The Ultimate Fighting Championship in June 1993, but they already had one recruit. After all, someone had to represent the art of Brazilian jiu-jitsu and, according to the *Playboy* article, the choice was obvious. Rickson Gracie was younger than his brother Rorion by eight years, and his more muscular frame marked him out from the rest of the family. He was also acknowledged as the "champion" of the Gracies, having built his reputation competing in vale tudo and jiu-jitsu matches in Brazil.

However, some months earlier Rickson had been forced to leave the Gracie Academy in Torrance after a disagreement with Rorion. Rorion learned of Rickson teaching students on the side, just as the Machados had done before. Rorion felt he needed to protect the name Gracie Jiu-jitsu, which represented not only an art but a way of teaching that art. This rift in the family created an unlikely warrior. With little time to prepare for the first UFC, Rorion turned to 27-year-old Royce Gracie, a sibling who had remained loyal to both his professional and personal aspirations.

Royce had come to the U.S. in 1985 at the age of 17, on an invitation from Rorion to babysit his children. Like his brothers, he had been taught jiu-jitsu since birth and now found himself part of a famous fighting family. "It was so natural to watch them [train jiu-jitsu]; it would be stranger to see someone speaking Japanese than watching a fight," remembered

43

Royce. Upon joining his brother in America, Royce also became an important partner in the family business. But he had to learn how to speak English first; the only words he could speak were "Stop!" and "Like this," a result of assisting Rorion in teaching jiu-jitsu classes. He watched a lot of *Sesame Street* and went to English class for six months. As Art Davie recalled, "He was just a nice kid from the gym who would go to his brother Rorion on Saturday afternoons to get spending money for his favorite hangouts at the beach." Royce was 6'1", weighed under 180 pounds, and, with his handsome, unmarked face, looked little like the conventional image of a vicious bruiser. He participated in dojo challenges but had no professional fighting experience. Royce never saw his participation in the UFC as being anything more than doing what his older brother asked of him.

Rickson was less than happy. "It's my fight. I've been waiting for this all my life," he told Rorion when he heard of the event. But the decision had been made. Rickson ventured off to Japan to drum up interest for himself to compete but came back one week later after finding that no one knew who he was. Swallowing his pride for the family, Rickson began training his brother. Royce stopped teaching and put all of his energy into a combination of running, swimming, weightlifting, and, of course, lots of jiu-jitsu.

Though Rorion owned half of WOW, he left the day-to-day operations to Art Davie, whose task was simply to find martial artists willing to fight. Davie sent letters to anyone listed in a legitimate martial arts organization or directory he could muster. He found most potential prospects fell into one of two groups. The first group felt the very idea of a mixed tournament broke the martial arts code of using a style's skill for sport. After all, many martial arts schools never engaged the fighting aspect but merely taught when and how these skills could be used. They proffered self-discipline, honor, respect, pacifism, and varying Eastern philosophies as valid reasons for not competing in this type of forum. The other group simply believed their style was too deadly for fighting. "They had a lot of sparring, but not that much fighting experience," said

Davie. "But their system and their guru told them they were the best, that they were deadly, and people would die doing this." Neither group was willing to put years in the dojo on the line, but that didn't stop Davie from eventually rounding up his magnificent seven.

Making use of his old contacts in the defunct kickboxing/advertising tie-in, Davie was able to reach kickboxer Patrick Smith through Karyn Turner. Turner, the top female martial artist of 1974, had subsequently moved into promoting martial arts events. Her kickboxing promotions in Colorado with Coors as a sponsor were well-known in the U.S. Smith had recently won the heavyweight championship of the Sabaki Challenge, a kyokushinkai karate (no punching to the face) event. As a youngster, his only martial arts experience had been mimicking the moves of his idol Bruce Lee. In successfully using these techniques against schoolyard bullies, 13-year-old Smith caught the attention of a school security guard who was a master of an African martial art called Robotae. This was the beginning of Smith's formal training. He later earned a third-degree black belt in Robotae, a first-degree black belt in tae kwon do, and competed in various events. At 6'2" and 217 pounds, he had an overall win-loss record of 17–2 and was ranked seventh by the World Kickboxing Commission. He had also been working with Bobby Lewis, a boxing trainer who had turned ex-con Ron Lyle into a heavyweight contender who lost to Ali for the world title and gave George Foreman all he could handle in a memorable brawl. Smith's mean-spirited reputation for roughing up his opponents and even referees made him a shoo-in for the event, especially after Davie saw him fight live in Denver. But Smith's girlfriend had reservations. "I told him right then and there I wanted to do it, but she said, 'Give us until Wednesday,'" remarked Smith, who ended up signing three days later. "I was the first one entered in it, besides Royce."

To highlight the contrasts within martial arts, it was imperative to get a sumo wrestler, a man of enormous size and strength. Davie initially garnered the interest of Matsui Fata, a reigning champion from the Juryo Division of the Japanese Sumo Federation, but money became an issue, and he was soon discarded. Davie eventually found Teila Tuli (also known as Taylor Wiley, his Anglo name) via John Jacques of the American Sumo Association. Tuli, who hailed from Honolulu, made a better match for the UFC, partly because he had been thrown out of several dojos for behavioral problems. He was the first non-Japanese to win the all-Japan collegiate sumo championships and earned a slot in the Makushita Class of the Japanese Pro Sumo Association. Tuli had been retired from sumo competition for four years, but the 6'2" Hawaiian still tipped the scales at a monstrous 410 pounds. He jumped at the chance to compete in a "no rules" tournament in America and was paid a $6,000 premium for his participation.

While sumo, karate, and professional wrestling were all popular in Japan, it was hard to classify the Universal Wrestling Federation. It was not the preordained comic-book theatrics of an American pro wrestling promotion (known in the business as a "work"); much of the action looked real (termed a "shoot"). Maverick wrestler Akira Maeda had made the UWF a success in 1988 after a failed attempt years earlier, but in 1991 part of the organization broke off into Yoshiaki Fujiwara's Professional Wrestling Fujiwara Gumi (*gumi* means group), or PWFG. Fujiwara had trained extensively under the tutelage of Karl Gotch, one of the original foreign talents to become a star in Japanese pro wrestling. Gotch was known as a hooker, describing his real—as opposed to faked—submission techniques. He taught this shoot style of wrestling to several of Japan's top pro wrestlers, becoming known more for his training than his wrestling exploits. The UWF style evolved from more realistic pro wrestling to very stiff-worked matches, meaning they would have predetermined endings but would "shoot" for position. Wrestlers sold their punishment to the audience and took frequent bruises, but the UWF was still a "worked" event. Frequently, "real" fighters competed for added hype, and Maeda wanted non-Japanese to be part of the crew. Masami "Sammy" Soranaka, the husband of Gotch's daughter, was the perfect man for the job since he lived in Tampa, Florida, and could recruit fighters from there.

In 1990, a professional wrestler of a different kind crossed paths with Soranaka. Kenneth Wayne Shamrock was a muscular All-American athlete who had been fashioned by his adoptive father Bob into a money-making enterprise. Shamrock competed in toughman contests and every other type of ruffian sport as an outlet for his aggressive nature. By the age of 21, he was bored with construction jobs so his father suggested that he try pro wrestling. He joined the small-time circuit of the South Atlantic Professional Wrestling Association, among others, and rubbed shoulders with numerous wrestlers vying for a chance at the big time. Assuming the stage name Vince Torelli, Shamrock enjoyed only minor success, making as little as $50 a match when it cost more to drive to the venues, but the up-and-comer did have his share of great tag team partners, including Dean Malenko, a second-generation wrestler whose famous father was the "Great Malenko."

Shamrock's pro wrestling career was threatened when he had a run-in with another tag team, aptly named the Nasty Boys (Brian Knobbs and Jerry Sags). They were moving to a larger organization and had little regard for the small-time players they were leaving behind. After a brief skirmish in a bar with Shamrock, the two Nasty Boys jumped him from behind in a neighboring hotel room later that night. Shamrock was beaten unconscious and suffered serious facial injuries, busted ribs, and a broken sternum. The experience was a wake-up call: as he lay in a hospital bed the next morning, he knew he was lucky to be alive. Malenko might be his ticket to the East. "Soranaka was working out of Malenko's school, so obviously they were getting pro wrestlers and getting guys who were tough, teaching that style and bringing them to Japan," said Shamrock. "Malenko knew that I had a reputation for being tough...so he showed me some tapes and thought I would be good at that." Shamrock was intrigued by the idea of learning something new and caught a plane to Tampa. He made his Japanese pro wrestling debut during the final months of the UWF in 1990, before joining up with Fujiwara and PWFG.

Shamrock fought several times for PWFG before that company split, and pro wrestlers Masakatsu Funaki and stablemate Minori Suzuki formed Pancrase Hybrid Wrestling in early 1993. Wayne Shamrock, as he was now known, followed them. Funaki was tired of having to "put over" [deliberately lose] to old-timers and yearned for the chance to put his skills to use in authentic matches. Karl Gotch came up with the name Pancrase, since the organization promoted itself as doing shoots, hence pankration. "You saw the change [in Pancrase] as opposed to earlier matches [in UWF] because they all ended rather quickly," said Shamrock. Instead of systematically changing position for excitement, Shamrock defeated Funaki by choke at 6:15 in the first Pancrase event held on September 21, 1993. Shamrock fought again for Pancrase before another fighter, Scott Bessac, told him about the UFC.

At first, he believed the show was an American aberration of the UWF and had his doubts: "I thought they were definitely going to tell us we couldn't do [certain moves] or ask me to put some guy over, and I definitely would have told them that I would walk. So I was waiting for that to happen and fully expecting for the fight not to go on." But after making a call to Art Davie, the 6', 220-pound Shamrock agreed, filled out an application, and sent it in. With his chiseled build and potential "hero" status, it didn't take long for Shamrock to be made one of Davie's elite eight. Still unsure if the event was going to take place, Shamrock fought in one more Pancrase match just four days before the UFC.

◆ ◆ ◆

THANKS TO A PRESS RELEASE that Rorion Gracie had sent out, Dutch gym owner Johan Vocsh learned of the event and had several karate players and kickboxers to pick from for a slot in the first UFC. None was interested in fighting outside his sport, however, except for Gerard Gordeau. Tall and balding, Gordeau was nearing the end of his career, having participated in competitions for over two decades. In 1988, he had even fought in a supposedly legit MMA bout in Japan against Akira Maeda for the UWF. At the time, Gordeau had competed only in karate tournaments, so he didn't have much experience fighting with gloves on. When he arrived in Japan, he was told to wear boxing gloves, while

Maeda fought bare-fisted. Gordeau knocked Maeda out, but an extended count and numerous stops by the ref allowed Maeda to recover and eventually gain the upper hand, and he submitted Gordeau by leg lock. The Dutchman had learned his first groundfighting lesson.

At 6'5" and 215 pounds, Gordeau had a sleek build and solid martial arts credentials. He was Dutch Karate Champion from 1978 to 1985 and earned sixth place in the World Championship Karate competition held in Osaka, Japan, in 1991. Gordeau's primary style was savate, or French kickboxing (without knee strikes). In savate competition, he had swept top European honors from 1988 to 1991 and had taken the World Championship in 1992. With a 27–4 fight record, he was one tough customer. Gordeau was often hired as a bodyguard and bouncer for illegal raves held around Europe and also worked security for the underground porn business. He cited his lack of schooling (he had only five years total in grade school) and his knack for throwing a punch as reasons why he made fighting a chosen profession. Whether in the ring or on the street, Gordeau enjoyed fighting and didn't care where he did it.

An advertisement in a run-of-the-mill martial arts magazine attracted the attention of kickboxer Kevin Rosier. Rosier was a super-heavyweight in every sense and had won several titles in kickboxing, though many were one-shot deals. "These guys would make you fight for nothing in one of their bullshit shows, promising you would get paid more for the next one," said Rosier. "Then the show would fold, and I'd just throw the belt in the trash." From the age of six, he had accumulated numerous black belts in varying karate systems and Chinese forms and had fought in over 200 competitions. He retired in 1990 and found work as a bouncer and bodyguard for pop acts such as Debbie Harry and Billy Idol. Over the course of three years of working for some of the toughest clubs from New Orleans to New York, the 6'4" Rosier ballooned to a staggering 345 pounds. Still, he phoned Davie and Rorion Gracie and barraged them with questions about the event. "What is this bullshit show you have going on here?" he asked. They knew who he was and didn't seem to care that he was a "little" overweight.

The only fighter Rorion recommended for the event (aside from his own brother) was Zane Frazier, a meaty, 6'5" kenpo (an Oriental martial art) stylist. Frazier had been studying martial arts since 1980 and had been fighting for just as long. He held a fourth-degree black belt in kenpo and had even had the chance to study with the late Ed Parker, the father of American kenpo karate. Rorion had seen Frazier take an opponent to the ground in a scuffle that ensued during a Long Beach karate tournament. Impressed that a "karate guy" knew groundfighting, Rorion sent Royce and Art to check him out at a local martial arts expo in July 1993. Frazier was not there to muck it up with fellow martial artists; he went to seek out an old nemesis—Frank Dux, the man who "inspired" the movie *Bloodsport*.

As the kickboxing craze died out in the early 1990s, Frazier had needed to make some money, so a friend—Mr. Tae Bo himself, Billy Blanks—introduced him to Dux, who was coming off the success of the movie *Bloodsport*, based on the allegedly true story of Dux's participation in a secret fighting tournament, the Kumite, held in the Bahamas in 1975. While the movie became a guilty pleasure for much of the martial arts community, its source material was mere hyperbole. However, it enabled Dux to build a promising school that needed an instructor with more time on his hands than its owner. A deal was worked out between the two, but it fell apart when Dux reneged. Frazier opened up a neighboring school and took his students with him, only to face alleged death threats over the phone.

So when Frazier confronted Dux at the expo, the bad blood came to a head. Dux tried to push him away, but a quick exchange of punches and kicks gave Frazier the upper hand. According to Frazier, Royce Gracie was there to see it, while Art Davie bore witness to the aftermath. "Wow! You are definitely in the UFC. Hell, I don't need to see any more," Frazier remembered Davie telling him. "You beat the *Bloodsport* guy!" When asked to substantiate the story, Davie said Frazier's account was "pure poppycock! I never went to a martial arts expo at the Century Plaza Hotel, with or without Royce. Rorion was friends with Frank Trejo, and

Frank recommended Zane to him, and Rorion relayed that to me." Trejo is an icon in the kenpo karate world, having trained extensively under Ed Parker; he trained Frazier and worked his corner for the fight.

Though there were differing stories as to the magnitude of the Frazier/ Dux "fight," something definitely went down. Dux subsequently sued Frazier and the Century Plaza Hotel (where the expo was held) for failing to prevent the attack. The case dragged on for three years and ultimately exposed the fraudulence of Dux's claims. In fairness, he did have a martial arts background, but his vivid imagination and unbelievable fighting claims caught up with him. Frazier claimed to have found school records proving that Dux could not have been in the U.S., in the military, and learning to be a ninja while fighting in over 365 matches all at once. After Dux faked a seizure and postponed a deposition for not admitting to "being a fraud," according to Frazier, a court order finally made him come forward. "Frank Dux goes into the deposition and said, 'I talked to my master's second in command, and if I reveal any information, my family will be killed, I will be killed, and everyone in this room will be killed if I reveal anything about *Bloodsport*, the Kumite, and my secret training as a ninja,'" remembered Frazier. Despite these ridiculous and melodramatic goings-on, Dux walked away with $500,000 from the Century Plaza, while Frazier was absolved without further duress. Dux later authored a book entitled *The Secret Man* about his alleged career in the CIA. *Soldier of Fortune* magazine penned an article using overwhelming evidence to prove that Dux lived in a fantasy world.

◆ ◆ ◆

IF THERE WAS TO BE A TOURNAMENT to decide the best fighter, no style qualified more than boxing. The "sweet science" was the largest mainstream fighting sport *per se*, and many felt a boxer could knock out a martial artist with ease. The difficulty was in finding a boxer ranked in the top 10 who would be willing to fight under something other than Queensberry Rules. An exhaustive search turned up notables such as James "Bonecrusher" Smith and Leon Spinks—both former heavyweight champions—but money or age proved to be insurmountable hurdles. Enter Ernest Hart Jr., former middleweight karate champion of the 1970s, who wanted to be part of the UFC any way he could. Though too old to compete himself, Hart thought that, by getting a fighter into the event, he might have a shot at announcing. Hart contacted 6'1", 196-pound "King" Arthur Jimmerson, a fellow St. Louis native, who didn't really know what to make of the event. Jimmerson was no slouch, having been named in *Ring* magazine's "Fights of the Year" edition in 1988 with his knockout of Lenny LaPaglia at Madison Square Garden. That win also made him the World Boxing Council's 10th-ranked cruiserweight contender. Add to that a list of impressive sparring partners, an exhibition with kick-boxing Hall of Famer Don "The Dragon" Wilson, and a record of 29–5, and Jimmerson was in the show. Little did anyone know, however, that Jimmerson had recently hit pay dirt when a friend who came into a lot of money made him a salaried employee at $100,000 a year, and Jimmerson had stopped training. He did need a fight, though, as he was scheduled for a match with Thomas "Hit Man" Hearns just a month after the UFC.

The grand prize was $50,000. The fighters would get $1,000 to show, and purses would increase as winners advanced. The total prize money was $110,000, with extra funds logged in for "commercial purposes." When he realized the lack of rules, Jimmerson backed out of the event for fear of getting hurt and possibly ruining his boxing career. After some tricky negotiating, he was offered over $18,000 just to show up, win or lose. That was the same amount he would earn for the Hearns fight, so without another thought, Jimmerson was back. "I was out of shape and had not been in a gym in eight months," recalled Jimmerson. "They called me at my weakest moment. When I went in there, I had no idea what I was doing and didn't know what jiu-jitsu was or anything."

◆ ◆ ◆

ALL OF THE FIGHTERS WERE REQUIRED to arrive a week before show time to acclimate to Denver's mile-high altitude and to promote the event. As most viewers wouldn't know the fighters, Rorion Gracie wanted a name that people would recognize. He called Chuck Norris and asked him to commentate, but the action star doubted the event would come off and declined. Instead, SEG and WOW secured Bill "Superfoot" Wallace and Kathy Long, two heavyweights in the martial arts world, to fill the bill. American football legend Jim Brown was added for good measure.

Rorion Gracie received a fax from the Jiu-Jitsu Federation of Rio de Janeiro on July 16, 1993, recommending João Alberto Barreto and Helio Vigio Gomes (both were Carlos Gracie Sr. and Helio Gracie black belts) and Pedro Valente Sr., a Helio Gracie black belt who had studied under the grandmaster since the age of 12 after he and his father watched him fight Kimura, to officiate the event. All three men had numerous years of vale tudo refereeing experience, but Barreto (18 years of refereeing experience) and Gomes (16 years experience) got the nod; each was paid $500 for his troubles. Barreto started training in Brazilian jiu-jitsu at age 15 after his father introduced him to Carlos and Helio Gracie. He subsequently lived with Helio and trained for 12 straight years. Barreto made his vale tudo debut in 1958, where he and Gomes had both defeated their opponents.

Little is known about Gomes—who certainly had his time as a popular vale tudo fighter alongside Barreto—but Art Davie remembered a particularly interesting story while having lunch years after the UFC with Reylson Gracie, son of Carlos Gracie Sr. Reylson recalled being out on the streets late at night during his youth in Brazil. "[Gomes] pulled up in a van and said, 'Hey, it's late and kind of dangerous to be out here on the streets so let me give you a lift home.'" Reylson got into the van, sat between two bucket seats, and began to hear something rolling around in the back behind a curtain that separated them. When he asked Gomes what was making the sound, the driver simply told his passenger they were hams. Reylson was confused by the term, but after he had reached his destination, Gomes pulled over and showed him what was back there: two dead bodies. "What they do when they assassinate someone is that they gut them, and they fold them in half, and they wire the legs and the neck together and fold the body in half so with no intestines in it, it sinks, and the gas doesn't allow them to come up," Reylson relayed to Davie, who said that Gomes was apparently part of the Brazilian secret police. "And that's how they would dispose of the body. A lot of people were afraid of me at the time because I knew Helio Gomes, and they thought that I had some type of connection."

Fighters, trainers, fans, managers, and journalists showed up one by one at the Executive Tower Inn, not knowing what lay in store, much less who was supposed to fight. "I don't think it really had set in that this was going to be the real deal," said Shamrock. The day before the show, everyone convened at the Brahms conference room of the hotel to go over the rules. Most of them thought the event was "no rules," but that wasn't strictly true. Fighters would be allowed to wear clothing according to their style. In a strange rule-making anomaly, Rorion instructed that six-ounce boxing gloves were required *if* the fighter's usual art employed closed-fist strikes to the head; otherwise, bare knuckles were permitted. Everything else was allowed with the exception of eye gouging, biting, and groin strikes. There would be five rounds of five minutes each, divided by one-minute breaks. There would be no judges—no one thought the fights would go past the first round. Although the Brazilians were fairly calm, confusion over the rules filled the air with testosterone. "There was a lot of politics, going back and forth," remembered Tuli. "It started to really get ugly."

It was then announced that hand wraps could not be used. A wrap protects the wrist and the hand from injury, and so would favor the punchers, but Rorion allowed the wrap to be used just below the knuckles only. This launched a debate between Rorion and fighter Zane Frazier. "This is bullshit, because you are setting us up to fail by taking everything away the night before the fight," stormed Frazier. The kenpo fighter had every reason to be upset. "My coaches told me that they could stop fights on cuts, so we should wrap my hands in such a way that they could act as razor blades," he said. Rorion asked if someone said something bad about Frazier's mother, would he run home and wrap his hands before fighting that person in the street? The room erupted in laughter, but Frazier was not amused and contended to start the UFC one day early. The biggest man in the competition, Teila Tuli, had enough, signed the waiver, and headed for the door with his brother in tow. The room went silent after some confusion as to whether Tuli signed or not. "Hey, I don't know about you guys, but I came here to fight. If anyone came here to party, I'll see you tomorrow night at the arena."

Back upstairs, Rorion Gracie and Art Davie told Tuli that after he signed, all the bickering stopped and everyone else followed suit. It was a big relief on the part of WOW, but Tuli didn't look happy. "At that time, I was in mourning. They came in and saw a T-shirt. One of my older cousins had passed away that week. It was hanging up in my room with a lei and all that. I made a shrine to him. Rorion said, 'You have to put this past you. When you cry, you lose a lot of energy.' I was like, 'Man, it's too late. I've been crying all week.'"

The meeting in the conference room was the first time everyone saw each other. Kevin Rosier had recently had a tooth pulled; he was shot up with Novocain and sat there in a daze. Gordeau never uttered a word, having only arrived a day before via a 24-hour plane trip. Frazier played conspiracy theorist. Jimmerson had already decided Ken Shamrock would be the man to sweep the tournament when he caught him working out earlier that day. (Shamrock had merely been trying to loosen up after an exhaustive flight from Tokyo to Denver the night before.) Royce Gracie, the smallest fighter of the group, remained calm, pleasant—and seemed utterly unthreatening.

With all the hype and experience these men brought to the table, only the following night could answer the boundless questions on everyone's minds. Would a man with 30 years of martial arts experience be able to fight for real under such conditions? Would size and strength matter? Would someone die? One thing was clear: these 10 men (two alternates would fight for a shot in the next tournament) were about to change the way the world viewed martial arts forever.

5

SHOWTIME

On November 12, 1993, the stage was set for the first Ultimate Fighting Championship...well almost. Just hours before the event was to take place, the agreement between SEG and WOW had yet to be finalized. Though Bob Meyrowitz had flown out to meet with Art Davie and Rorion Gracie in Torrance, California, for a full day to work out the details, there were still snags in the original agreement. It almost became a point where SEG producer Michael Pillot wanted to tear down the Octagon and call it a day. "In a last-minute conference call—we had our attorney, Bob's brother, on the call, and Campbell was in his suite, while I was in my suite getting my tuxedo together to get ready," said Davie. "We finalized our deal, and what I got them to agree on, a concession at the last minute, was that they would pick up the fighter purses starting with UFC II." WOW and SEG would own the UFC 50/50, with WOW getting an escalating guaranteed fee per show.

While this was going on, Clay McBride accompanied the fighters in a huge van to take them to the McNichols Arena. McBride remembered Zane Frazier being cocky about his chances to win, Kevin Rosier serving up comedic fodder, and Ken Shamrock sitting quiet and composed. When they arrived, the fighters saw the Octagon for the first time. "We were all joking and looking at this thing, and they were saying, 'We're really going to get in this thing and fight in front of a bunch of people and hammer each other,'" recalled McBride. The fighters bounced around on the matted floor and banged against the cage meshing, testing out the fenced enclosure. Art Jimmerson ran his hand over the top of the Octagon and walked all the way around, perhaps as a way to absorb where he would soon be going to war.

No one knew what was going to happen. As exterior shots of Denver rolled across televisions in homes across America, commentator Bill Wallace introduced the public to the "Ultimate Fighting *Challenge*." Wallace not only got the name of the event wrong, he did everything from belching into the mic to saying, "You could say it's an octagonal octagon." He also mispronounced and erred on several names, including announcer Rich "The G Man" Goins, whom he renamed "Ron" four times. There had been some controversy as to who would do the play-by-play, but the original UFC press materials listed Wallace, Kathy Long, and Jim Brown as color commentators. The veteran full-contact karate exponent ended up doing the job (something typically reserved for seasoned public speakers, yet this was Wallace's first time). If Wallace seemed unprepared, so was everyone else.

The first match of the evening pitted Teila Tuli against Gerard Gordeau, the most extreme clash of styles the event had to offer. Tuli made his way to the Octagon dressed in a flowery Samoan garb. Gordeau then entered and made an astonishing gesture: he turned to all four corners of the ring and, with the television cameras on him, gave what appeared to be a series of Nazi salutes. It was an uncomfortable moment, especially given the partnership between Germany's BMG and SEG's Jewish president, Robert Meyrowitz, who did not attend the first event. Gordeau, smothered in tattoos and sporting a bald, pale head, looked like an Aryan Nation poster boy. Yet he was actually giving the salutation for his art of savate. "I'm Jewish too... all my family were killed in World War II by the Germans," he later said. As the two men were set to square off, Tuli stared into the eyes of his opponent. "The way he was looking at me while we warmed up," said Tuli, "it took so long to introduce us that it gave him a long time to size me up. I just got so nervous. I knew he was going to chop me down."

Tuli barreled toward his lofty matador and absorbed several punches to the head. "I like sumo and I know what they do…I knew he was going to come at me like kamikaze," said Gordeau. Tuli thought that he had a good chance of connecting to Gordeau's chin, but as the Dutchman back-pedaled, "the next thing I knew, my face fell into the fence," remembered Tuli. "That stunned me." The sumo wrestler had partly tripped on the soft matting, and Gordeau took advantage by placing a well-executed round-house kick to his face, launching a tooth into the crowd. The Dutchman followed up with a looping right hand that connected hard, and the ref stopped the action even as the bloody, confused Tuli motioned for the match to continue. Tuli's brother threw in the towel, which angered the big man. "I couldn't see out of my one eye," said Tuli. "I wasn't going for the win anymore. It was life or death to me at that point. I'm happy it ended right after." Tuli left with blood and tears in his eyes, and the crowd had witnessed a Streetfighter 2 game gone awry. It was all over in just 26 seconds.

As the commentators tried to make light of the quick finish, Kevin Rosier and Zane Frazier prepared for war. When Rosier's hooded cloak was removed as he entered the Octagon, it revealed a physique that looked less than battle-ready. "He sent us this great press kit and then shows up 75 pounds overweight," remarked Campbell McLaren. "I saw Rosier in the gym with a pizza and a Heineken." Despite more than 50 years of martial arts experience between the two, their match looked more like a street fight between barflies than a technical exhibition between athletes. Rosier scurried clumsily at Frazier and clobbered him with a right hand, which sent them both to the ground. The fight went back and forth, until a game Rosier landed enough haymakers, drop-ping the kenpo stylist down for the count. But there was no count. "I stomped on his head, but I pulled back like professional wrestling and put [his foot] down so it looked more dramatic," exclaimed Rosier. "I could have driven my heel into the lower part of his spine and crippled the guy." Frazier's handlers knew when to quit and threw the towel in after the second stomp.

Sitting five rows back was boxer Art Jimmerson. He could not believe the brutality; it was unlike anything he had ever seen. Not only had he not trained for the event, he had hardly given it a thought. He had come with a large entourage, including his wife and cousin, but hadn't bothered to bring gloves. His doubts first surfaced when he entered the hotel and heard stories about what the Gracies were capable of: "Don't get Royce mad or he'll break a limb," said one of the refs. Art Davie's kid brother managed to scrounge up a pair of eight-ounce gloves for him as the event started, but as Jimmerson walked from his seat to the backstage area to prepare, boxing gloves were the least of his worries. As Jimmerson entered the changing area, Kevin Rosier was popping his jaw back into place. It was clearly broken. Zane Frazier was on a stretcher heading for a nearby hospital; unbeknownst to everyone, he had suffered a severe asthma attack during his fight and couldn't breathe unaided after returning to the dressing room. "It was the third time that it had happened that year; I later found out that I had exercise-induced asthma," said Frazier.

What Jimmerson saw next was truly hard to believe. Doctors were feverishly trying to remove two of Tuli's teeth that were embedded in Gerard Gordeau's foot. "They tried to get them out, but they were too far down into his foot," remembered Jimmerson. They finally decided to put Vaseline and tape on it, leaving the teeth in for the rest of the night for fear of exposing the wound anymore. On top of that, Gordeau's hand was broken in several places. Yet the savate champion, cigarette dangling from his mouth, showed no signs of quitting and had blocked the pain out of his mind.

Seeing all three men injured to various degrees was more than Jimmerson could handle. "Finally my managers came over to me and said, 'This is what we're going to do: go in there, and at the first sign of trouble, we're throwing in the towel,'" he later recalled. After all, Jimmerson's payday was locked in no matter what, so why should he risk injury?

Of the next two combatants, Royce Gracie was the first to the Octagon, led by the Gracie train of Rickson, Royler, Relson, father Helio, and others. "It's kind of ironic that Royce Gracie is going to wear his judo top," said Wallace, a further sign of his ignorance. The audience erupted at Gracie's introduction, while Jimmerson walked down the aisle sporting only one glove. Art Davie sat in a van outside, watching the monitor. "I almost went ballistic," he recalled. "What the fuck was he doing? What was this one glove shit?" Jimmerson's goal was to dance around for five minutes, make it to the second period, and give the audience a show. Wearing a token glove was his idea, a pointless one since he was going to lie down for Royce. "I asked for one boxing glove so I could throw him off," remembered Jimmerson. "My thought is that if I hit him in the face too hard I would break my hand, and that would mess up my fight with Tommy Hearns."

Until the night of the show, no one had known who they were fighting. The brackets were left up to Art Davie, who juggled the card several times. Gracie and Shamrock were the two main variables, since he felt they were the strongest competitors. "My first match was supposed to be with Royce Gracie," remembered Gordeau, "but when I got to Denver, all the Japanese press came to me and made pictures, and SEG asked, 'Who is that guy?' And [the Japanese] said this Gordeau was very dangerous and had a lot of fights in Japan." Gordeau believed his fight with Gracie was switched because of this, but according to all the fighters and Davie, the matchups were changed several times.

In contrast to the previous fighters, Jimmerson and Gracie took a minute to feel each other out. The crowd groaned. "I waited and waited, and he didn't come in to take the initiative, so I stepped on it," said Gracie. Without one punch thrown, the Brazilian took Jimmerson down and worked his magic. Moving into position, he head butted the boxer to show he meant business. Jimmerson tapped, indicating surrender. Unseen by the referee, his corner had also thrown in the towel as soon as Jimmerson went to the ground, but it caught on the Octagon fence. The ref was so surprised by the boxer's sudden action that he asked him if he wanted to continue. He didn't; the charade was over. Jimmerson walked away as rich as if he had lost in the finals. The boxer never faced Thomas Hearns; instead, he lost by technical knockout to Orlin Norris, which was the third time he had ever been stopped in a fight. Jimmerson believed his time in the UFC cost him his career because the easy paycheck had stripped him of his motivation. From 1994 to 1999, Jimmerson's boxing record was 4–9. He retired and went to work for Pepsi Cola. Jimmerson briefly came out of retirement in August 2001 and lost four straight matches before finally hanging it up. He had a 29–5 record going into the UFC, with 15 straight back-to-back wins.

Kickboxer Patrick Smith against shootfighter Ken Shamrock looked like the best match of the night. To make things even more exciting, their respective records had been beefed up. Smith now sported an unbeliev-able 250–0 record, and though Shamrock had only three "real fights" in anything but toughman contests, he was credited with two dozen wins. Since Pancrase was so new and he had beaten founder Funaki, Shamrock was named the No. 1 shootfighting champion of Japan. The crowd didn't know any better and seemed happy to buy into these loaded résumés, especially that of hometown Colorado boy Smith.

What was not embellished was their dislike for one another. As Shamrock, his father, and accompanying crew walked toward the entrance, Smith and an army of followers were waiting for them, dressed in black and red. They taunted Shamrock with, "You're going down! He's going to fucking kill you!" The kickboxer stared down his opponent, who didn't want to start trouble for fear of his father getting hurt in a melee. But as they moved past each other, Shamrock turned to Smith and said, "I'll see you in the ring."

With the fight underway, Smith got off one kick before Shamrock took him to the ground. Smith clung to Shamrock's underside and landed several kidney shots with the balls of his feet before the grappler set him up and went for a heel hook. After a brief moment of desperation, Smith screamed out in agony, violently tapping the mat with both hands. Like a lion with its kill, Shamrock had to be pulled away. "It wasn't satisfying enough that he tapped out because he was still talking, so I didn't want to end it there," said Shamrock. "I wanted to keep going. The satisfying thing would have been to nail him in the mouth and beat on him." Smith had said earlier that his strength was his toughness, but all of the talk outside the ring couldn't save him from a kind of fight he knew little about. The crowd voiced its disapproval with profanity-laden chants. They thought their hometown favorite had been part of a fix. The absence of a large-screen monitor also prevented more than half of the 4,800 in attendance from seeing what was going on at all. Since much of the action took place on the ground, the audience's blocked view became a problem.

◆ ◆ ◆

THE FIRST SEMIFINAL pitted Gordeau against Rosier; both men deserved nods for coming out with injuries. Rosier tried his patented caveman technique, but it was no match for Gordeau, who produced a classic one-two combination followed by a powerful leg kick. Gordeau did this twice more, then engaged Rosier with a flurry of punches and elbows. The attack was so profuse that at one point Rosier sat down with both hands over his head. Unlike in boxing, with its eight-count, the referee let it go, and just as Rosier had done to Frazier, Gordeau began stomping. Rosier instantly tapped out, and the ref stopped any further punishment. Rosier had said earlier that his strategy was to let his opponent hit him; it worked a little too well.

It was now time for the two best grapplers to mix it up. Both Gracie and Shamrock had scored very easy wins over their opponents. Shamrock thought Gracie was just another guy in a gi who practiced katas: "I understood that they did some stuff on the ground, but it looked pretty slow and boring to me, and it didn't look like it was effective." Though Shamrock came into the tournament not really knowing what to expect, he felt his submission training and natural athletic ability enabled him to best any man that night. And to anyone watching, it looked like a mismatch. Gracie was giving up size and strength to an opponent who knew about submission.

However, Gracie wasted no time in rushing Shamrock to get him to the ground. Shamrock positioned Gracie just as he had Smith, but the jiu-jitsu fighter followed his lead. The wrestler went for the leg. Unfazed, Gracie moved with him, and when Shamrock tried for the ankle again, it was too late. The Brazilian trapped Shamrock's neck from behind and applied a rear choke. Shamrock tapped immediately, but, as Gracie let go, the referee came up to them and ordered, "Fight." Shamrock grabbed the ankle again. "I didn't know what was going on. I was just reacting," he said. Gracie moved back into position. "That's when I went to his ear," said Gracie later, "and told him, 'You tapped. You tapped, Ken.'" There was no doubt that Shamrock had tapped or admitted to tapping…the match was over. Gracie's jiu-jitsu was foreign to Shamrock's experience of grappling and, with this win, the crowd had a new hero—the small man who was able to beat the big man, plain and simple. Almost as if he had forgotten what he'd said about his match with Smith being too easy, Shamrock told the postfight interviewer, "I'm just not used to this kind of stuff."

People have since wondered why Ken Shamrock, a man of submissions, would give his back to Royce Gracie and allow him to apply a choke with ease. Shamrock and the Japanese fighters had learned from wrestler Karl Gotch, and, since the UWF was a worked organization, Shamrock points out that "they didn't emphasize chokes because it was entertainment and the action had to continue, so moving from arm bars to leg locks to rope escapes would be much more exciting than getting a guy's throat and choking him." When he moved into Pancrase, chokes became more prevalent, but Shamrock didn't spend much time on them and never expected to fall victim to one. He really didn't understand the gi either and said that was how Gracie choked him, not his arm. "You're looking at adding a foot to two feet on a choke, because the position he was in with me going for the leg lock had that gi wrapped around my neck. Now without that gi, I end up with the leg lock." The rules had clearly stated shoes were not allowed if the fighter wanted to kick because they would be weapons. Ken argued a gi was a weapon too.

◆ ◆ ◆

BEFORE THE FINALS, a qualifying match provided the audience with the type of action they had expected all along. Kung fu stylist Jason DeLucia squared off against kenpo exponent Trent Jenkins to decide a slot in the next tournament. Both gave flashy performances with well-executed high kicks. DeLucia ultimately took Jenkins to the ground and applied a rear naked choke that ended the fight. Rod Machado, a Gracie student working as commentator, called it a classic Gracie choke, as if the move was unique.

It certainly got the crowd going. As fights broke out in the audience, Jim Brown commented, "This is probably the most alive audience I've ever seen. In fact, I'm a little worried." The crowd didn't let up while a presentation was made by the Gracies to honor father Helio as the first Ultimate Fighter. Helio spoke a few words in Portuguese before it was time to see if the striker or the grappler would be crowned as the Ultimate Fighting Champion.

For the last match of the night, a visual for "Round One" rolled across the television screen, signaling for the first time that these fights actually had rounds. With a bandaged foot (the teeth still embedded) and broken hand, Gerard Gordeau could barely move, much less fight. He didn't get off a strike before Gracie took him to the ground. "The doctor went to the Gracie camp and told them that I broke my hand and foot, and because Gracie knew everything, he blocked the good side of my body...you only see him grab my left side," said Gordeau. After a few punches had softened him up, Gordeau rolled to his stomach and solemnly whispered a string of expletives. The Dutchman felt he had been had and was angry that the "Gracie Mafia" ran the event. Gracie applied the rear naked choke, forcing Gordeau to tap not only the mat, but Gracie's arm. Gracie wouldn't let go of the hold because Gordeau had played a bit of funny business. "He got a piece of my ear," said Gracie. "He didn't take a piece off, but he bit my ear, and I had to pull it out of his teeth. He was trying to bite it, but it just got scratched and bled a little bit." Gracie finally let up, and as Gordeau pulled away the blood on his ear was visible. For his part, Gordeau would need lengthy treatment in Holland for the injury he suffered kicking out Tuli's teeth: "I had to spend nine weeks in bed, and they had a drain stuck in my foot to clean it with water every hour to prevent infection for fear of blood poisoning."

Royce Gracie complained to the official about Gordeau for a few seconds, then began to celebrate, as his family clambered into the Octagon. Soon he had a medal around his neck (inscribed *Per Aspera Ad Astra*, meaning Through Adversity to the Stars) and a check for $50,000; a new type of martial arts superstar was born. The fighters would convene hours later for the postfight party, which has become a rite of passage for nearly every MMA event thereafter where winners, losers, and everyone who helped make the event a success get together for drinks after the pressure is off. Clay McBride remembered that Rorion Gracie was so concerned that Teila Tuli did not attend the event that he personally sent someone for him to be part of the festivities. "He said, 'You must come down to the party and you have nothing to be ashamed of. You fought a terrific fight for the first time in a very unique event. It's a process of learning and discovering for everyone involved.'"

Tuli eventually came down and joined the pioneers of what would become the single greatest impact on the martial arts since Bruce Lee. "I watched Ken Shamrock and all the fighters having a good time with each other," said Tuli. "They were so professional. They looked at me, and they knew everything I was feeling. They came up and gave me a hug. They said, 'Don't worry about it. It happens to the best of them.'" Despite all of the problems, the show was also a tremendous success. Perhaps the concept was not entirely new, but it was new to the American public, and the style-vs.-style aspect was a great gimmick to attract fans. This would be the first chapter of a legacy that even the creators behind the UFC never envisioned.

6

BATTLE OF THE STYLES

S EG held the reins to what one pay-per-view analyst called "the first breakout franchise hit." Yet no one knew why it was successful. It had no promotion on mainstream television, no regular advertising, and no on-screen build-up to its events. "The UFC succeeded without television," said Dave Meltzer, who runs *The Wrestling Observer*, one of the best industry publications on pro wrestling and MMA. "When I look back at that period, there is no reason that the UFC should have ever made it." Certainly in answering the compelling question of who was the greatest martial artist, the UFC held an advantage over kickboxing, pro wrestling, and toughman contests, all of which had no chance without some sort of cross-coverage on television. And at $14.95 a pop, the pay-per-view income stream (UFC I did 86,592 buy rates) promised to be substantial. To keep the momentum going, it was time to develop the sequel.

Art Davie had struggled to find martial artists to compete in the first show but received 246 applications for the follow-up. This time he had the luxury of turning people down. "I remember this recluse from Alaska by the name of Cunningham. He sent me these pictures with him posing as if he were a monk by a river, claiming he had a death touch. I had a lot of guys who seemed more incredible than real." Many felt the first UFC's combatants had been over-the-hill veterans who didn't best represent their styles. The April 1994 issue of *Black Belt* magazine came out just before the airing of UFC II with an article entitled "Shotokan, Taekwondo and Kung Fu Challenge Jujutsu," describing how masters of these arts would dismantle Royce Gracie's techniques with their own traditional moves. The martial arts community felt Gracie deserved respect but pointed out that many arts had not been represented at all. Davie got the message and put together a motley list of pure styles to battle it out.

With so many worthy competitors, Davie and Campbell McLaren discussed doing a 16-man tournament. "And then [Campbell] promptly forgot about it; he did not tell David Isaacs or Bob Meyrowitz and got caught with his pants down," said Davie. "I had faxes going back and forth that discussed it. When they came to Denver, they were unprepared. Bob put Campbell on the carpet and told him he had lost control and that Art Davie made that decision unilaterally." It would throw out all of the timings for the scheduled television slot: the preliminary round started two hours before the pay-per-view broadcast at 5:00 PM in Denver on March 11, 1994. "We went through with it because that was the kind of organization we were," said David Isaacs. "A lot of other organizations would have just told the other guys to get back on a plane and go home." There were a total of 18 competitors, ranging from an 18-year-old tae kwon do practitioner (Sean Daugherty) to a 39-year-old karate stylist (Johnny Rhodes). Patrick Smith and Jason DeLucia returned from the first show, as did Royce Gracie, to prove BJJ was no fluke. Over 10 different styles—including ninjutsu, pencak silat, and sambo—were represented to quiet the naysayers.

To improve on the first show, changes were made. Davie sent a fax to McLaren 12 days after the first show. Rounds were out, since no fight had made it past five minutes. Matches were to be decided by lots to prevent bias. Interestingly, celebrities were often picked to draw the lots. At the weigh-ins for UFC VII, basketball bad boy Dennis Rodman literally drew names out of a bowl as UFC President Bob Meyrowitz filled in the slots on a dry erase board. "After listening to all the debate after the [first] show, with all the letters to the editor at *Black Belt*...saying that strikers were handicapped by rules like no groin shots, I pushed Rorion [who didn't like the idea] and SEG to allow them in," said Davie. "I felt that they [groin shots] answered the karate segment, which trained to use them. I thought that wearing a steel cup would minimize the real damage. Campbell loved the dramatic barbarism of allowing them, as he was still in the grip of no-rules fever."

Bill Wallace did not return as commentator. Almost immediately after his UFC experience, Wallace slammed the show and said in a *Black Belt* column that it was bad for martial arts. "His column came out so quickly that he must have written it the day after the event and got it rushed in," said former UFC scribe Clay McBride. "I thought that was very disingenuous. Wallace had to knock this thing down immediately because it was not what he was teaching on the circuit. He knew this would impact him in his pocketbook." A public war of words began between Wallace and the UFC. Art Davie hit back through letters in *Black Belt*, while McBride even suggested a charity match between himself and Wallace to *Black Belt* editor Jim Coleman. McBride, who wrote a column called "Reality Check" for *Inside Kung Fu*, was willing to put his limited jiu-jitsu experience under Rorion Gracie to the test. Neither Wallace nor *Black Belt* responded.

Fighter Kevin Rosier, for one, was scathing of the critics: "Eighty-five percent of the people that buy *Black Belt* magazine are punks that don't even go to karate dojos. They do it at home; they listen to these bullshit articles. The people that own *Black Belt* magazine don't know anything about martial arts. The people that write these articles don't know anything about martial arts. When [film star] Steven Seagal came [onto the scene], you had 20 or 30 people in the Yellow Pages teaching aikido. It is very hard to become an aikido instructor. When Brazilian jiu-jitsu comes out, the next year in the Yellow Pages you have people saying we teach jiu-jitsu, circular jiu-jitsu, linear jiu-jitsu...17 years of experience. Half of these instructors didn't even know what a guard or a mount was and now they're in the Yellow Pages selling it. They all want the mystique. People are going to train for realistic stuff, and then all these karate schools with the magazines and marketing are going to lose money. That's why they badmouth the UFC. They realize that, 'Oh shit, if our students find out that the shit we're teaching really doesn't work...that's going to be bad for karate.'"

Just as Joe Lewis's full-contact karate had created a rift in the martial arts community decades before, the UFC started a revolution of its own. "A number of people who own martial arts schools have up to 80 percent of their enrollment as kids," said Lewis. "And when parents see an event like the UFC coming out and saying, 'These are the best of the martial arts, this is what martial arts is really all about,' and then they see people kicking teeth out of heads and blood splattering everywhere and people getting dumped upside down and breaking bones, well, that terrifies parents. And now they don't want to believe it's safe because of what they saw on TV. The complaint about mixed martial arts mainly came from the people who owned commercial schools, not necessarily spectators." The gap between fighting and traditional martial arts was being revealed before everyone's eyes—and it didn't look pretty.

There had been other misjudgments. Between matches during the first UFC, two small children had been sent into the Octagon to clean the mats. "I let my son Ryron and Rickson's son Rockson—both 11 years old at the time—wipe the blood off the Octagon floor," said Rorion. "A lot of women wrote in and complained, 'How can you put kids in there cleaning up the blood from the mats?' It was a very crazy concept. I thought it was a brilliant idea at the time." Others were disgusted.

◆ ◆ ◆

THE REFEREES FOR THE FIRST EVENT, despite all their experience, didn't really work out either, so one of Davie's recommendations was "No referees in Octagon—replace with [two] IFC 'Observers' on Octagon's apron in corners, who scrutinize fighters and advise the corner if fighter is in serious trouble; only the fighter or his corner can stop the fight." The Brazilian referees were not invited back; it had seemed that in one fight they stopped the action too soon, while in another they acted as if the man on the losing end was learning a lesson. The UFC II rulebook stated that outside interference would be kept to an absolute minimum and that only the fighter or his corner could end the match. Fortunately, McLaren and Rorion Gracie knew that someone had to be in the Octagon to officiate, even if they didn't have any power. "There was naïve thinking going on, because if you look at what [Davie] was saying, you'd think that fighters would be reasonable, and if they get the shit kicked out of them, they'd tap or their corner would throw in the towel," said John McCarthy, who became the Octagon's key ref.

McCarthy was a second-generation police officer with the Los Angeles Police Department; his father Ron had served for over 25 years. After working a gang unit for five years and putting in his time as a patrolman, McCarthy asked to become a tactical instructor for the Los Angeles Police Academy, since teaching was also part of the family tradition (Ron had become an instructor too). When a group of policemen were cleared of the brutal beating of Rodney King—despite compelling video evidence against them—Los Angeles erupted into rioting. McCarthy was subsequently asked to serve on the Civilian Martial Arts Review Board, which banded together martial artists from around the country to decide on proper "use of force" tactics for the police. Martial arts legends Benny Urquidez and Gene LeBell attended, as did Rorion Gracie. Gracie and McCarthy became friends and swapped training tips: Gracie went through police training for a rookie; McCarthy learned jiu-jitsu. After training at the Gracie Academy, Gracie entrusted McCarthy with holding the first UFC medal that would be given to Royce after his win. After getting his wife Elaine's travel agency a profitable gig with the UFC, McCarthy was asked to take over as referee from the Brazilians.

McCarthy had no experience refereeing, but Gracie felt his ability to make split-second decisions, learned as a police officer, was prerequisite enough. It didn't hurt that McCarthy was 6'4" and weighed over 250 pounds. Art Davie later added the nickname "Big" to John McCarthy, and, though McCarthy didn't expect it, he would become as much a staple of the UFC as the Octagon. He refereed in the beginning as a favor and was unhappy at being told he was not allowed to stop fights on his own.

Just as "Are you Ready to Rumble?" had become boxing announcer Michael Buffer's calling card, John McCarthy would come to be known as the man who said, "Are you ready? Are you ready? Let's get it on!"

He would start every match this way, and the crowd screamed in a frenzy just waiting to hear those familiar words to start the action. "I was thinking of something from judo, but Davie insisted that it had to be something American," said McCarthy. "I knew that [boxing referee] Mills Lane had used 'Let's get it on!' Not in the fights, but in his fighter presentation in the beginning. He would say, 'Are there any questions from the challenger? From the champion? Let's get it on!' I didn't think I was infringing upon anything; I just thought that was the way to start these fights."

With no footage to market the original UFC, Campbell McLaren devised "There Are No Rules!" as its unofficial service mark. This wasn't strictly true, but it was seen as a handy promotional motto to distinguish the tournament from the plethora of kickboxing and karate events that advertised in the same media. Art Davie, a veteran ad man, was apprehensive about stressing the sport's harder edge, "but they [Campbell McLaren and SEG producer Michael Pillot] felt the best way to reach the larger audience was to sell the blood, guts, and fear aspects of it."

McLaren also drafted the official press release for UFC II. It was a document that would come back to haunt him and the UFC time and again. According to this press release, "The competition has no rules—only two suggestions—no eye gouging or biting." Though the official rules said these techniques *were* forbidden, the next line nullified this: "Use of these attacks *does not* disqualify a fighter, but will earn him a $1,000 fine." Thus, someone could actually win by playing dirty and only lose a measly grand next to the big winnings of the championship. Luckily, no one took advantage of the loophole.

It was the scary remark that McLaren then added that would cause all the trouble: "Each match will run until there is a designated winner—by means of knock-out, surrender, doctor's intervention, or *death*." The press only remembered the last word, arming critics who lambasted the UFC over the next few years. "That was pure circus," admitted McLaren. "He [Meyrowitz] could have and probably should have fired me for that, but he didn't and went with it. I was vilified in the pay-per-view industry."

When the UFC became the subject of a spot on *Good Morning America*, McLaren was accompanied by Jim Brown, who tried to gloss over the "or death" comment by comparing the UFC to football.

Gold's Gym had sponsored the first UFC and could have taken the event in a more lucrative direction had it not been for sumo wrestler Teila Tuli's tooth. According to UFC fighter Kevin Rosier, Tim Blind, president of human resources and public relations for Gold's Gym, sat ringside during the first show. The company had quite a bit of money tied up in advertising because they wanted to bring the concept of cross-training (martial arts and weightlifting) to the attention of the exercise community. "When Gerard Gordeau blew out Teila Tuli's tooth, it flew right by the people at Gold's Gym whom I had dinner with later that night," said Rosier. "Right when that happened, they looked at each other and said, 'Shit! This will never fly at corporate.' So that's how you had a major sponsor like Gold's Gym all of the sudden just drop sponsorship for the next show."

If that wasn't enough, McLaren created another untruth—that the UFC was banned in 49 states. This was patently false, as the UFC took place in several states during its infancy. No one seemed to notice. Both Davie and Isaacs felt that those initial story plants by McLaren certainly went too far, but the matter was blown out of proportion. Isaacs described it as "viral marketing," wherein the press began quoting the press to play the bloodsport angle like a broken record. Although *TV Guide* called the UFC, "disgusting, dumb, and depraved," the second show garnered 125,732 pay-per-view buys—a 45 percent increase.

◆ ◆ ◆

THE SHOW WAS ORIGINALLY SLATED for an 8,000-seat auditorium but had to be moved to the 3,000-seat Mammoth Arena after the local Denver mayor used a clause in the deed to object. Despite the name, Mammoth Arena was much smaller than the show's first venue, the 18,000-seat McNichols Arena. This presented numerous problems for the production team, as they had to put up fighters in two different hotels, turning one across from the arena into a quasi-dressing room.

Jason DeLucia remembers that site well. "It was a potentially volatile situation. There were 16 fighters, and maybe four or six of them got special treatment. The rest were stuck in a giant room, a bullpen type of thing that also housed the caterer." DeLucia claimed the disturbance caused by the caterer may have been intentional, to make the fighters lose their concentration. That wasn't the only problem. Things got so out of control that Davie asked alternate Fred Ettish if he would serve as gopher, since he wouldn't be fighting. Ettish went back and forth readying fighters to enter the Octagon. What he found was a prostitute-infested motel that "didn't smell so good. Things were broken, doors didn't always lock or close, and people were making sidewalk pharmaceutical deals in the rooms."

The first round of the 16-man tournament provided some interesting matches. The third fight of the night pitted Johnny Rhodes against David Levicki, a 6'5" wing chun practitioner. Rhodes attempted a spinning back kick as Levicki crept up to him with showy hand movements. Neither move worked, and after a brief scramble on their feet, the remainder of the match was spent on the ground. Although he didn't know what he was doing, Rhodes settled into Levicki's guard position (the bottom fighter has the top fighter positioned between his legs), and his size created enough space to take Rhodes out of striking range. The position also gave the audience a bird's-eye view of Rhodes's backside, as his gi pants kept coming down due to Levicki's wrapped legs. "My pants could have just came on all the way down; it wouldn't have mattered...I was not going to let go of that hold no matter what," said Rhodes. Referee McCarthy humorously had to pull them up several times during the match, but that didn't stop Rhodes, who eventually found his opening and started slugging the bigger man in the kidneys and face.

A bad cut over Levicki's left eye prompted him to call it quits. "You're the better man. I'm going to give it to you," he told Rhodes. But McCarthy didn't hear anything, and a pause gave Levicki his chance for revenge. Rhodes resumed punching as well until McCarthy finally stopped the fight, with blood streaming down Levicki's face. Levicki needed five stitches beneath and six stitches above his left eye. "I could have broken his neck using a hold I learned in the Special Forces," he said later in an article for *Penthouse*. "But I couldn't do it. I didn't come here to kill anyone." Rhodes also thought his spinning back kick would have done the trick. Even when reality set in, some fighters still held onto misconceptions and death touches.

The match had lasted more than 12 minutes, almost as long as all of the bouts from the first UFC combined. Rhodes was exhausted after the match, but remembered Levicki's mom coming over to him. "She said, 'You hurt my baby!' I told her, 'Well, you have a very big baby that was trying to hurt me!' (laughing). We exchanged phone numbers. He wanted to learn how to punch and stuff like that. He gave me a call and I never heard from him again."

◆ ◆ ◆

THE NOW-RETIRED GERARD GORDEAU brought in Dutch sambo player Freek Hamaker as a last-minute favor to Art Davie; the original fighter he was going to bring got stabbed. Hamaker was a porn theatre owner but also the Belgian Heavyweight Sambo Champion. Thaddeus Luster, a seventh-degree black belt in kung fu san soo, was his opponent. Luster firmly believed his art was "the most potent fighting system on the planet," but that didn't stop Hamaker's immediate takedown and eventual submission by arm lock. Luster couldn't even get off a punch. Hamaker, who fought on three days' notice, just wanted to see what it was like to fight in one of these events; at that point he had no intention of continuing. He was fine but told officials his hand was broken.

Fellow Dutch import Remco Pardoel had a somber face and pudgy physique but held jiu-jitsu championship titles from four countries. Pardoel took judo lessons at four years old from his father, a martial arts instructor. When he turned seven, he took up tae kwon do and at age 11 trained in jiu-jitsu. He heard about Brazilian jiu-jitsu and invited well-known jiu-jitsu stylists Jacare and Fernando Yamasaki to conduct a seminar in November 1993, the month of the first UFC. Pardoel sent in his application to compete in that event, but Davie put him in the second show since the first card was full. He faced Spaniard Alberto Cerro Leon, master of pencak silat, an Indonesian martial art form that keeps the practitioner low to the ground, making him less vulnerable. "Alberto was the reason to enter the UFC for me," said Pardoel. "In Europe, the guys from pencak silat and wing chun were badmouthing all other styles by saying and writing that they were invincible, which [they] weren't. So the best way to prove that they were wrong was to challenge them."

Often going by the name "El Toro," Leon had won several championships throughout Europe and Asia and claimed he once broke both legs of an opponent in a match. The Spaniard's moves were unconventional and intense, but his style was no match for Pardoel's takedown. However, the Dutchman had difficulty submitting Leon, his jiu-jitsu obviously not on par with Royce Gracie's BJJ. "For me, this was the first fight in my life which wasn't a sports fight," commented Pardoel. "The UFC is sports too, but on a different level." After trying a choke and an arm lock, the big man finally submitted El Toro with a cross-arm choke. "Normally when you crank someone's arm, they will tap," said Pardoel. "He didn't and I respect him for that, but at the party afterwards, he couldn't use his arms anymore, so I think the locks were decent in a way."

Minoki Ichihara was the smallest man in the tournament, standing only 5'7" and weighing a nimble 178 pounds. He arrived with over 200 reporters from his native Japan to represent traditional karate. He came with Royce Gracie in mind, but once again the shortcomings of stand-up arts versus ground arts became apparent. Ichihara tried to create as much distance as possible, but Gracie took him down and mounted the karate player with ease. "As soon as I took him down, he just locked himself out and hung on and hung on for dear life," recalled Gracie. "But since there was no time limit, I just waited and waited and worked on him until he got tired." Gracie finally wrapped himself around Ichihara like an anaconda, performing both a choke and an arm bar simultaneously. Out of breath, the second-degree karate black belt tapped before the arm was fully extended.

In the most one-sided match of the night, ninjutsu stylist Scott Morris rushed kickboxer Pat Smith in the first semifinal, only to find himself mounted and bludgeoned to a dizzying state with 14 punches and 10 elbow strikes to the face. Morris staggered to his feet, blood tattooing his left eye from a gash that required 28 stitches. Morris's teacher and cornerman was Robert Bussey of Robert Bussey's Warriors International, who had been given an honorary award for his dedication to the martial arts at UFC II. During the match, McCarthy screamed for Bussey to throw in the towel, but when their eyes locked, Bussey turned and threw the towel into the crowd, even though his fighter was taking so much abuse. "Pat thank God got off of him," said McCarthy. Bussey believed his art was combat-tested and tough as nails and would rather have let his fighter get hurt than protect him from unnecessary punishment. That said, the action was over so quickly that a corner stoppage would still have been too late; the referee should have been allowed to stop it. Thankfully, Smith stopped the match himself, and yelled, "What's up?" as a way of showing the crowd that he was a different fighter from the first event.

Frenchman Orlando Weit came into the UFC as a favorite and showed off his Muay Thai skills in a feverish massacre of New Yorker Robert Lucarelli. At one point, Weit turned away and raised his arms in victory, but his fallen opponent had not tapped out, so the match continued. Again McCarthy yelled at Lucarelli's corner to throw in the towel and end the punishment. Weit slammed five hard elbows to the back of his neck before they finally got the picture. His injuries resulted in 10 stitches to the head.

Weit's quarterfinal match against Remco Pardoel provided a surprise, as everyone, including Pardoel, thought Weit would win. "I watched his first fight from the locker room and was shocked," exclaimed Pardoel. "I was sure that I would lose in a standing situation, and I was nervous before the fight, as in any fight." He wasted little time in closing the distance early and hip-tossed the man nicknamed "The Gladiator" to the mat. Holding him in position, Pardoel launched seven elbows to

Weit's head, the third knocking him unconscious. The commentators had pegged Weit to win by sizing both men up on looks alone. They couldn't have been more mistaken. Pardoel, who had said Weit might clinch the grand prize, was even more stunned. Weit won the 1994 Muay Thai Kickboxing Championships just 11 days after UFC II.

• • •

EVERYONE WANTED TO PROVE HIMSELF against Royce Gracie, but no one more so than martial arts journeyman Jason DeLucia. Though he had no formal fighting competition ranking, DeLucia was a book of knowledge on the martial arts. He had made it his life's calling to seek out styles from East to West, adding anything to better himself, and had regularly competed in backroom prizefights in Boston's Chinatown. DeLucia eventually moved to California with one thought in mind: to fight film star and aikido exponent Steven Seagal. "At that time, Steven Seagal had stated in a magazine that he would take on anybody, anytime, anywhere," said DeLucia. With very little money to his name, DeLucia made the trek to California, crashed on a friend's sofa, and went to Seagal's dojo morning, noon, and night for three months. Seagal was never there. DeLucia learned a lot about aikido and ultimately found his calling when he instead took the Gracie Challenge, fighting Royce (the match is shown in the *Gracies in Action* video).

DeLucia quickly learned that five-animal kung fu and his myriad honorary black belts didn't truly prepare him. "I thought that I could at least last through the fight long enough," said DeLucia, believing his stand-up base could keep the Brazilian at bay. After being submitted in less than two minutes, DeLucia contacted Rorion to fight Royce in the UFC, but all the tournament slots had been filled. By winning a qualifier against Trent Jenkins in the first UFC, he earned his chance at redemption against Royce.

DeLucia attempted a side kick during the first few seconds of the match but broke the fibula bone in his foot when it collided with Gracie's shin. Going to the ground, DeLucia pulled Gracie off him, narrowly escaping a choke, only to leave his arm exposed for the jiu-jitsu man to finish him. DeLucia stood up, but the arm bar was locked, forcing him to fall to the ground, frantically tapping the mat. DeLucia would not be seen again in the Octagon for over five years, choosing to fight in the Pancrase organization thanks to Ken Shamrock. "The experience was the best single thing to happen to organized martial arts," DeLucia said. "And for that, everyone should thank Rorion Gracie because he did it. If not, we would all be working in the mill."

Patrick Smith could have worn himself out in a long stand-up battle with fellow semifinalist Johnny Rhodes, who had punished last-minute entry Fred Ettish to a bloody pulp. Instead, Smith opted to finish Rhodes with a guillotine choke just minutes into their bout. "I wasn't in a lot of pain; I just was out of gas and knew there was nothing else that I could do so I tapped," said Rhodes, who submitted with his foot. Afterward, Smith seemed as cocky as ever, muttering, "No one can really take me down!" As for Rhodes, he was set to compete in the next show but ended up rolling his truck three times in a terrible accident that ended his short-lived fighting career. He continued to teach martial arts in Las Vegas, incorporating ground fighting.

In jiu-jitsu vs. jiu-jitsu, Royce Gracie gave up over 100 pounds to Remco Pardoel to decide who would be the second finalist. Pardoel should have been able to detain Gracie and beat him at his own game. Instead, he froze and Gracie took him down early. "He followed every move and took his time," said Pardoel. "He was going for back mount, and he had a good trick of wearing his belt really loose around his waist. When I tried to throw him, I couldn't pull him because of his belt. Gracie choked Pardoel into submission by using his own gi against him (known as a lapel choke). It was becoming very clear that Brazilian jiu-jitsu had something over other submission arts. In the UFC, labels, titles, records, and rankings didn't mean much. "Royce is the best in the world on the ground," said Pardoel. "On that day, I was his child and he was my dad and could play with me any way he chose. After the UFC, I got enthusiastic. I devoted my life to build Brazilian jiu-jitsu in Europe, with the help of my Brazilian friends, of course."

After 13 matches, only Pat Smith and Royce Gracie remained. Both men would be fighting for the fourth time in just under three hours, though each had disposed of their respective opponents with relative ease. Smith had greatly improved since his first time in the Octagon; with "Redemption '94" stitched across his jacket, he seemed ready to take the championship from Gracie. But as the match started, Smith got off just one kick before being taken down to the ground and mounted. Smith tapped the mat at 1:16 after Gracie threw some short punches in order to create space. The kickboxer capitulated because he felt there was nothing else he could do. "I thought he was going to put up more of a fight," said Gracie. "I was hoping that he was going to turn around so that I could get him in a choke."

In a tournament that tested so many styles, Royce Gracie affirmed his grappling art had superiority over traditional standing styles that dominated the martial arts. While the cynics retreated to magazines to snipe, there was no doubt that the quest to beat Gracie was made for a new kind of warrior. But when would this warrior emerge? After winning the $60,000 prize, Gracie smiled from ear to ear. The answer to that question would have to wait till the next event.

7

"The Sport of the Nineties"

Though Royce Gracie swept the competition at UFC II, WOW promoters knew that opponents would only get tougher. The decision was made to replace Royce with his brother Rickson Gracie, who had won an MMA tournament called Japan Vale Tudo '94 on July 29, 1994. Although Rorion Gracie stated that he intended merely to alternate members of the Gracie family, Art Davie emphatically believed the intention was to replace Royce with an even stronger fighter. Rickson was a legend in Brazil, where he had won numerous jiu-jitsu and vale tudo matches during the 1980s. Moodily charismatic, physically powerful, and a technical master, he was considered the true fighter of the family, and WOW saw him as the next superstar in the Octagon. "I always wanted Rickson for the event; he was a Brazilian Marlon Brando and I was always putting the pressure on Rorion because I was nervous about Royce," said Davie.

A month before UFC III, Rickson met with brothers Rorion and Royce, father Helio, and Art Davie at the WOW office one Saturday morning. Art contended that both he and Rorion had approached Rickson before, so this meeting laid everything out on the table. Royce sat on a couch away from where the others discussed Rickson's participation. He watched a piranha swim around in a tank that Davie had somehow inherited at the WOW office, and paid little attention to the conversation. "Rickson at some point turned to Royce and asked him in Portuguese, 'Is this what you want to do?'" according to Davie. "Royce nodded and said, 'Yes.' Rorion explained that this was in the best interest of the family."

Rickson, on the other hand, mused that it was in the best interest of Rorion and that he had other plans—his success in Japan was indication of that. Rorion and Rickson batted the matter back and forth until Helio rose to speak. He was a man of few words, but everyone listened as he pointedly told Rickson, "When I fought and when your uncle Carlos fought, money was not our primary consideration." The room went quiet. Rickson protested that Rorion would make over $1 million from the UFC, and so he should make the same for competing. It was clear Rickson wanted to go his own way. He would no longer even work Royce's corner in the Octagon. Many Brazilians felt Rickson's spine was in Royce's body during the first two events. Could Royce succeed without him?

Though another brother, Relson, had worked out with Royce for the first two shows, he stepped up his commitment level for the third. "We had a meeting with Royce after Rickson and Royler left," said Relson. "It was my dad, Rorion, Royce, and all my brothers. We agreed to keep it going. I pulled Royce aside and I said, 'You have to forget about Rickson and Royler.' They had trained him for over two months before the first fight." Now he had to do it without them. He sparred 10-minute sessions with each brother and "we would save the best for last, which was me," said Relson with a laugh. Relson was something of the tough guy in the family and had more of a name for fighting in the streets than anywhere else. "When I was training with him, everything was allowed, and I head butted him to prepare him for that," remembered Relson. Royce would be ready to face a whole new group of combatants.

Style against style was the original concept for the UFC, but it wasn't the reason most people watched the event. In a focus group conducted by SEG, "only 27 percent of the audience were martial artists," said Art Davie. "The vast majority of the audience were guys who enjoyed NFL football, monster truck pulls, and pro wrestling. They wanted action." They didn't care about the nuances of martial arts, let alone what styles labeled the combatants. So a change in marketing strategy was devised, turning the third event into a reality-fighting contest with a pro wrestling spin.

Since pro wrestling was something people could identify with, SEG exploited the ready-made angle of Royce Gracie facing off against Ken Shamrock for UFC III. Shamrock had all the makings of a star, despite his earlier loss to Gracie, and Campbell McLaren wanted to focus on that. He sent Shamrock a letter after the first show stating his intention to build him up for the media. When Shamrock couldn't make the sequel due to a broken hand, he was given some interview time and spoke of a rematch. Marketing material pushed the Gracie/Shamrock confrontation: two-time champion vs. No. 1 contender.

Davie, now inundated with fighter applications, packed the show with competitors who looked and acted larger than life. Sitting in his office just a few weeks before UFC III, his attention had been drawn to the roaring of a Porsche convertible pulling up out front. Out stepped a short, stocky Asian man sans shirt, while a menacing figure with tattoos adorning his muscular body fell in behind him. Joe Son announced himself to Davie as a minister who was there to bring the gospel of the Lord to the Octagon by way of his student, Kimo Leopoldo. The tattooed Kimo never spoke a word, but his undeniably fierce demeanor was his first-class ticket into the show.

Born in Munich, Germany, but raised in Honolulu, Hawaii, Kimo was an ex-gangbanger whose life had been spinning out of control in a haze of drug use and bad behavior. He moved to Newport Beach, California, to escape his demons and restart a college football career. When that failed, Kimo sought refuge in religion and befriended Joe Son, who was part of an extremist Christian group. There was no mistaking his dedication; the word "Jesus" was tattooed to his stomach while a cross tattoo donned his entire back. Though just a streetfighter, Kimo was elevated to a third-degree black belt in tae kwon do for the show. Aside from seeing the *Gracies in Action* tapes, Kimo was as green as they come. "To be honest with you, we really didn't even train; we read Bible scriptures," said Kimo. "I think we physically trained once before the Ultimate and did takedowns. It was just a bond." Son and Kimo felt the UFC was a fad that could lead to bigger things.

Emmanuel Yarbrough was a different story. Davie had watched him in an open sumo tournament earlier that year and, for six months, had tried to get him interested in the UFC. At 6'8" and a truly enormous 616 pounds, "Manny" was the proverbial gentle giant. Davie said Yarbrough didn't really want to fight but, after enough coaxing, agreed to enter the competition. Harold Clarence Howard was another character, a Canadian wildman with long golden hair, a beard, and piercing eyes that said as much as his colorful speech. With multiple black belts and a nifty parlor trick of breaking a cement-filled bag with his bare hand (used in his promotional segment), Howard cranked up the show's bigger-than-life appeal even further.

Other so-called martial artists wanted to talk the talk without walking the walk. Wing chun stylist Emin Boztepe attacked the Gracies in martial arts magazines, pointing out how his skills could defeat jiu-jitsu. "Royce and Rorion openly challenged him to come to the show," said Campbell McLaren. "We never heard from that guy. With all the guys that we openly challenged, there was always some excuse: 'You don't do this...you don't do that.'"

◆ ◆ ◆

SCHEDULED FOR CHARLOTTE, NORTH CAROLINA at the Grady Cole Center, on September 9, 1994, UFC III appeared much slicker and better-produced than its predecessors. The Octagon canvas was changed to blue from white, since it was more photogenic. It was also made less springy, with the 2" thick pad under the canvas being replaced by one of ¾", aiding fighter mobility. Music channel MTV introduced the UFC as "the sport of the nineties" and different fighters hammed it up for the intro to the pay-per-view broadcast. The so-called "Laws of the Octagon" were announced as no rounds, no time limit, and no way out—phrases that played on the raw perceptions that had created so much heat from McLaren's UFC II press release.

Not everyone was enamored. In an article that appeared two weeks before the show in *Newsday*, sports columnist Woody Paige of the *Denver Post* referred to the previous event as "the most disgusting, horrifying thing I've ever seen. It's basically taking cockfighting and putting it in human form." The phrase "human cockfighting" would echo over the next few years as the UFC came to wider notice and more and more objectors appeared.

Though North Carolina was on the original radar for hosting shows, that was no longer the case. The local police, no doubt spurred by an ever-increasing political disdain for the UFC, were considering bringing in video cameras and recording the actions in the Octagon as possibly an "organized brawl, assault and battery inside the cage," said Davie. "At that point, alternate fighter Steve Jennum said he wouldn't be able to fight because he was a sworn police officer and couldn't participate in something like this because he would lose his badge. We had civil attorneys working for us but had to hire criminal attorneys for fear of being arrested." The North Carolina Attorney General tried to get the event banned but was unsuccessful because the state did not have any relevant statute to shut them down. Thankfully the show was allowed to happen without incident.

There was at least one very positive difference between this show and its predecessors. John McCarthy told Rorion Gracie he would never serve as a referee again if he couldn't stop a fight, because "I knew that a fighter was going to get hurt, and I wasn't going to be able to do anything about it. I cannot be in there and allow some guy [who is] knocked out to be hit if I can't stop it because there's no tap or towel." Gracie gave the go-ahead for McCarthy to use his own judgment in stopping a fight. After the brutal beating of Scott Morris, the relentless damage inflicted by Orlando Weit on Robert Lucarelli, and the "enough is enough" torture committed on Fred Ettish at UFC II, Big John was now allowed to intervene for the sake of fighter safety. This was an important step in establishing the UFC as a credible sport, but it still had a long way to go.

The first match of the evening brought out sumo giant Manny Yarbrough against Keith Hackney, a kenpo stylist who had taken the place of fighter Roger Theriault on just three days' notice. "Davie asked me if I wanted to fight, and I thought about for about 10 seconds, and I knew that if I said no, they would never call me again," said Hackney. "I said, "You know what Art, I haven't been training the way I want to train, but you know what, I'm ready to fight and don't care who it is.'" To prove himself capable of competing in the UFC, Hackney was asked to battle Thomas Ramirez in a makeshift sparring match held in a nearby North Carolina gym. If Hackney looked impressive, he would compete on the card; if not, SEG would pay for his expenses, and he would watch from the front row. The 350-pound Ramirez had lashed out at Davie in *Black Belt* magazine but wasn't much for backing up his smack talk. "I put him in the ring with Keith, and he smacked him around, and I thought, 'Oh this Keith is better than whatever I could dream,'" said Davie. Hackney got the nod to face Yarbrough, whom he had seen curl 315 pounds on a straight bar with relative ease. With little time to prepare, he worked on low kicks before the match to keep the sumo wrestler off him.

The crowd was bloodthirsty in the hot, dry venue as the 5'11" Hackney stared up at his massive foe. McCarthy started the match, and it didn't take long before Hackney nailed Yarbrough with a ridge hand (Hackney called it a tiger strike), much like a bat hitting a home run. The big man fell back with a resounding thud, and Hackney pounced on him to finish the job. Yarbrough mounted a brief comeback, swatting Hackney's head with his huge paws. As the two staggered back up, Yarbrough's strength sent Hackney crashing through the Octagon fence and into the audience. A quick restart saw the smaller man put Yarbrough down on all fours after sweeping his leg, forcing the giant to trip and fall. Without hesitation, Hackney took control and pounded his opponent's head 41 times with his fist and forearm, breaking two metacarpal bones in the process. "Realistically, I would have beat him all day just to keep him down," said Hackney. The war could have ended a lot sooner with less injury to Hackney if he had known submission or thought to use an elbow to finish it. Afterward, Yarbrough said it "was part of the strategy to take some abuse, but you can only go so far."

Next up was Ken Shamrock vs. Christophe Leininger. Leininger was two years older than Shamrock and was once ranked No. 2 in the U.S.A. for judo. His father had been one of the originators of sport judo in Europe prior to the 1964 Olympics and had taken the art to Arizona when he moved there with his family in 1959. Leininger learned judo from his father and understood the need to study jiu-jitsu tactics as well. While leading the U.S. judo team in the 1986 Olympics, he met Brazilian jiu-jitsu instructor Megaton Diaz, who gave him a better understanding of mat work as opposed to throws. The two ran a school in Phoenix for several years. After his judo career waned, Leininger thought it would be interesting to enter the UFC. He had the best credentials of any judo player who submitted a résumé.

"My whole strategy was that this guy was going to try and bum-rush and overpower me, and at that point, I would set up a guillotine," said Leininger. "But Shamrock didn't budge and did exactly what I didn't want him to do, which was just stand there." After the crowd moaned over a slow start, Leininger made the first move, believing he would earn points for aggression, as in judo competition. He went for the takedown, but Shamrock was ready. He cross-faced Leininger so hard that the judo man later admitted to being knocked out for a second. Down on the mat, Shamrock was in Leininger's guard. After a failed attempt at a triangle choke (where the attacker uses his leg with the opponent's own arm for the choke), Shamrock slipped out and took Leininger's bac k. The judoka turned to the side to prevent a choke but was now pressed up against the fence. Lying in Leininger's guard, Shamrock stayed clear of his opponent's attempt at an arm bar and landed some hard shots. "I got tired and had the back of my head against one of the posts and he jacked me up. With a couple of hits, I was done," said Leininger, who tapped. He suffered a minor concussion and wouldn't return to the Octagon until UFC XIII.

Harold Howard's match against hometown boy Roland Payne provided much-needed fireworks but not before he had one of the craziest intros for the pay-per-view audience. With dark shades, he announced, "We have a saying back home that if you're comin' on, come on!" before ripping the shades off and staring into the screen. Though Payne had a Muay Thai background, karate practitioner Howard came out blazing with more effective strikes and knocked out Payne with a devastating elbow to the back of the head. He followed that up, but McCarthy stopped him—something he wasn't allowed to do in the previous show.

This was the perfect warm-up for Royce Gracie's return. Gracie made his usual entrance led by a line of his brethren, heads bowed and hands on each other's shoulders, but nothing could best the appearance of his opponent. As dried ice poured out of the backstage area, Joe Son emerged with a hooded Kimo carrying a wooden cross on his back. "I was carrying that cross for God so the fight didn't really matter," exclaimed Kimo. "I was calm, and whatever happened in that Octagon, just happened." It was something of a surprise to the promoters. "People were buying reality, and we didn't want the taint of sports entertainment," said David Isaacs. "We wouldn't have let something like that go because we didn't want people to think we were professional wrestling." To prevent the promoters from nixing his clandestine religious message, Joe Son had told Art Davie the large box shipped to the arena was "special training equipment." On his walk to the cage, Kimo dropped to his knees and prayed. Onlookers wondered if this man was for real. Just seconds before the fight, Kimo realized "it was a straight streetfight, but I wasn't mad. We just got into the Word, and it kept me calm."

After ref McCarthy initiated the battle, Kimo rushed Gracie with ferocious intensity, barely missing with wild punches. "This match was difficult for me," said Gracie later. "I tried to match power against power instead of all my other matches, where I used technique. I just wanted to see how strong he was." Gracie and Kimo clinched, with the latter holding his own until another break in the fence forced them momentarily outside the cage. Kimo thought they would break, as in the Yarbrough fight, and restart from their corners, but McCarthy signaled for them to continue once they were back inside. According to Kimo, this gave Gracie the chance to strengthen his grip, with Kimo losing a contact lens in the process as a result of a headbutt. The two finally went to the ground, but unexpectedly, Kimo took Gracie's back and tried to sink in a rear naked choke. If he had been more astute on the ground, he might have choked Gracie out.

Unable to sink in his hooks (wrap the legs around the bottom man to tighten the grip), Gracie eventually turned to his back with Kimo hovering over him. The Brazilian landed several shots to Kimo's face, which was now bleeding, and used the bigger man's ponytail to keep him in place. "I couldn't breathe too well because of the way I was angled, and I couldn't pull my head back," remembered Kimo. The clash became so intense that Gracie pulled Kimo's ponytail apart, leaving hair strewn about the canvas. As they moved to the side of the fencing, Gracie sunk in an arm bar. Kimo tapped as his arm barely locked out. The battle had been the toughest of Royce Gracie's UFC career. Victorious but exhausted, would Gracie be able to continue?

As Ken Shamrock watched the action before him, he knew he had to win one more fight before he could bury the memory of his loss to Gracie, the plague that had taken over his life. Shamrock wanted a shot at Gracie more than anything but first had to dispatch kickboxer Felix Lee Mitchell, who replaced Keith Hackney when the latter dropped out due to his broken hand. Mitchell came in wearing boxing gloves but was forced to take them off because he didn't show them to McCarthy during the prefight instructions. Shamrock, who had time to change his tights between matches, fought cautiously and took more than four minutes to get the kickboxer to the ground. He was then able to win within seconds after taking Mitchell's back and sinking a rear naked choke. But at what price? Shamrock hobbled away with an injured ankle as his father Bob comforted him.

Harold Howard was confident about taking on Gracie. He believed he had found a way to integrate karate and jiu-jitsu to defeat the Brazilian champ—and his opponent was in bad shape. As the Gracie train made its way to the Octagon, Royce felt devoid of energy. "We stopped for the cue to walk in front of the camera and I laid down. I don't remember laying down," he said. Royce called out to older brother Relson for some watermelon juice. It was feverishly hot inside the venue, and he was dehydrated. To this day, Royce doesn't remember any of this, a sign of his disorientated state. When he got inside the Octagon, McCarthy asked if Gracie was okay. "I said yes, but suddenly my vision went off—it shut down—and I couldn't see anything. That's when I turned around and said [to his family], 'Guys, I'm doing my job. Now help me out here and do your job. I can't see anything.'" McCarthy knew something was wrong and asked again if he was all right to continue. Still unable to see anything, Gracie responded just to the voice. He couldn't even see Howard, who was jumping around in his corner. Gracie pleaded with his family to do something, but after McCarthy came over a third time, the towel was thrown in and Gracie was helped backstage. It turned out he was suffering from hypoglycemia, an abnormally low level of sugar in the blood, though Dr. Joseph Estwanik who examined him after the fight chalked it up to dehydration.

Howard jumped for joy, though he had won only by default. As he and his manager celebrated and returned to the back, Joe Son and Kimo burst into the cage and made a mockery of the situation, jumping up and down like something out of pro wrestling. Kimo said he didn't mean any disrespect to the Gracies; he just wanted to show he was okay and could still fight. The incident outraged Relson, who felt Son in particular needed a lesson. "I approached Joe Son later on and said, 'Hey motherfucker! Let me tell you something, you want to walk with me outside now because you walk like a punk,'" said Relson. "'You want to go outside with me alone. You call me names so let's go outside and see for real.' He turned to me and said, 'No! No! Royce is great. I respect you guys a lot.' I told him he didn't respect my family, my daddy, or me so let's go outside with no TV or anything and let's settle it. He grabbed both of my hands and bowed to me and apologized and said it was just for show." Kimo later wrote an apology letter to Royce for the incident. But there was something strange in the air that night. Everyone was fighting...in the stands, even out in the parking lot, where Art Davie and Joe Son almost got into it. "That show had everybody pissed off at everybody," said Davie. "Michael Pillot, Rorion, and I were knocking heads because we couldn't decide on how to go forward with the show."

• • •

THE FINAL WAS TO BE HOWARD AND SHAMROCK, but Shamrock had no more will to fight now that Gracie was out. "When something is taken from you, you lose everything," he said. "Everything I had trained for, everything I had wanted...you get so hyped up for it and now it's gone." Shamrock was not coming out. His father tried to explain how much money he would make from winning the championship, but it didn't matter: Shamrock was so stubborn that Howard could have forfeited the match, giving him a win by default, and it wouldn't have made any difference. The Lockeford, California, native would have to suffer a little longer for his revenge. He was the only one who understood that obsession. "When I woke up in the morning, I saw Gracie's face," said Shamrock. "I had a hard time living with my wife and my children because that's the only thing that I ever wanted was to face him in the ring because as an athlete, I had been doing this a long time."

With Gracie and Shamrock out of the picture, an alternate would have to compete in the final. Ninjutsu exponent and Nebraska police officer Steve Jennum stepped up to the plate to face Howard. (Jennum was originally going to replace Gracie to fight Howard in the semis, but with time running out on the pay-per-view, they let Howard have a bye.) Interestingly enough, they couldn't find Jennum, and the pressure set in. "I found Jennum walking to his car in the parking lot and told him we needed him for the final," said WOW coordinator Kathy Kidd. "He thought the whole show was over with and was headed home; it's remarkable we were able to find him in time because we only had about 20 minutes left for the pay-per-view."

As the match got underway, Howard did a forward flip, either to show off or to disdain Jennum's abilities. As Jennum moved in, Howard locked him in a guillotine choke, and they both fell to the ground, but Howard didn't have the choke sunk in right and had no knowledge of how to correct it. Jennum pulled out and the two went toe to toe, each landing punches. Moving to the clinch, the policeman tripped Howard and mounted him. Howard tried to protect himself, but Jennum rained down strikes until the Canadian lost the war of attrition. Two towels were thrown in, and a man who had fought in only one match claimed a $60,000 check and could legitimately be called the Ultimate Fighting Champion.

The first two shows had put the effectiveness of martial arts on trial in a realistic situation. Now the competition was tougher and, for the first time, there was a problem with the tournament format. In eight matches, there had been two alternate replacements and one bye. Could this still be called The Ultimate Fighting Championship? The show left many unanswered questions, though that wasn't necessarily a bad thing. "It was like a great pro wrestling tournament. Ken didn't really lose, Kimo hurt Royce but lost, and he was so big and colorful...he was a big star. Then you had this alternate win the tournament," said Dave Meltzer. "The marketing of pro wrestling is the only way to make this work. Many people think that's a dirty word, but it's not. It's the same with boxing. You have to create curiosity."

Spectator sports are built on curiosity and personalities, which drive the audience to watch athletes perform. Would boxing be anything without the likes of Muhammad Ali, George Foreman, and Mike Tyson? These three men were great boxers, but, more importantly, they were performers who enticed crowds by clever marketing of their colorful appeal. Though the UFC sold itself as being real, it also needed those same types of performers to take it to the next level. UFC III (which again rose in pay-per-view buy rates at 126,840) worked off a pro wrestling model with real fights. Its success took the show to new heights but was also leaving a trail of controversy in its midst. After watching a video of the event, the Charlotte City Council voted on May 24, 1995, to permanently ban the UFC from ever returning to Charlotte. Charlotte's mayor pro tem called the UFC "another form of pornography."

8

CHANGING OF THE GUARD

While the pro wrestling slant made the UFC more marketable, SEG wanted to focus on establishing credibility. "It took a few events until we got certain things better controlled, like what we needed from the fighters and entourages," said David Isaacs. "We wanted to run it like a sport, and we wanted to treat these guys like athletes."

There would also be a major shift in the production team. Producer Michael Pillot brought in Bruce Beck, a veteran Madison Square Garden staffer who had served up energetic play-by-play commentary for boxing, kickboxing, and 20 other sports in his 12-year tenure at the famous New York venue. Beck didn't know what to make of the UFC at first but found it compelling and, more importantly, *real*. He told SEG he would approach it like any other sport, calling the action like he saw it, and recommended Jeff Blatnick as color commentator. Blatnick, the 1984 Olympic gold medalist in freestyle wrestling, had been doing commentary since 1987 for national collegiate wrestling championships. He saw the UFC as a natural extension of amateur wrestling, far removed from the bigger-than-life entertainment of the undeniably more popular pro wrestling. Ironically, Blatnick had done color for Shootwrestling, a series of U.S. pay-per-views that had been passed off as real when they were nothing more than old stiff-worked Japanese events left over from the UWF era.

UFC IV would be the first time a "real" wrestler tested his skills against other martial artists. "Some people wouldn't recognize wrestling as a martial art," said Blatnick. "Wrestling is a common denominator of combative sports by learning how to put someone on his back." Though the sport doesn't have karate chops, punches, or fancy kicks, it is arguably the forerunner of every grappling art known to man. Yet with three UFCs in the books, no wrestler with exemplary credentials had ever entered the Octagon. Ken Shamrock had done well with a wrestling background but nothing like that of collegiate or Olympic-caliber grapplers. Campbell McLaren pushed to have them in the event, although "a lot of wrestlers thought it was interesting but didn't seem to want to get involved." He talked to Olympian Dave Schultz and even his brother Mark, who both declined.

Until 1988, wrestlers and other athletes had to scrape by and couldn't compete for money if they wanted to go for amateur gold. When professionalism was finally allowed and jeopardizing amateur eligibility was no longer a threat, men like Daniel Severn could finally make a better living. The Michigan native, who held over 70 amateur wrestling records, was polishing his career on the independent circuit in a pro wrestling camp in Ohio when a friend showed him a tape of the UFC. Severn found a martial arts magazine and filled out an application inside to try out for the event. He was surprised when there was not a listing for "Wrestler" among the various styles and had to check off "Other." After sending in mug shots but not hearing anything back, Severn forgot about the event and secured a pro wrestling gig in Los Angeles instead. Phyllis Lee, a grandmotherly type who served as manager for numerous pro wrestlers, took up the slack and made calls on Severn's behalf to Art Davie, whose office was nearby. Davie eventually went to see Severn in action and set up a meeting later that night.

Just days after UFC III, Davie watched Severn and pro wrestler Al Snow engage in a shoot-style pro wrestling match for GAME (Great American Mat Endeavors) in the upstairs area of a Chinese restaurant. Afterward, Davie sat down with Severn. "You realize this is real, don't you?" he asked. Severn admitted he had no professional fighting record to speak of, but he was a competitor. For over 20 years, he had wrestled in the amateur leagues all over the world, from Cuba to Japan. He told Davie of an experience while in Turkey at the age of 17, where instead of wrestling another teen, he took on an ex-serviceman twice his age. His opponent grabbed the back of Severn's head and headbutted him right above the eye. "As I backpedaled, I had my hand up beside my face, blood trickling down. I thought the match would be over with my opponent being disqualified for unsportsmanlike conduct. The referee stepped between us and cautioned me for passivity. He told me I was stalling!" This was in the first 15 seconds of the match, one that Severn ended up winning. Though it was not "anything goes," it was Severn's introduction into a foreign environment with questionable rules—and showed he had guts. Davie was not convinced, and it took over a month before Severn heard anything back.

Eventually Severn filled out the application that read, "In case of your accidental death, we are not liable." *What could possibly be accidental,* Severn thought, *if the only things I can't do are poke you in the eye and bite you?* He had only five days to prepare and returned to Ohio to work out with Al Snow and two other pro wrestlers. None of them knew anything about fighting, but they had a pair of old boxing gloves and devised a game called "Hit Dan." In amateur wrestling, some moves can become illegal with just a turn of the wrist; Severn now practiced those moves, taking down his friends and making them "scream in pain." But punching, kicking, and headbutting were not in his repertoire; Severn entered his first UFC as a pure wrestler, albeit a veteran one. The odds were stacked against him.

But with the tagline "Revenge of the Warriors" accompanying UFC IV, SEG wanted Kimo back. "I knew I was going to get another shot," said Kimo. "I felt that [Joe Son] and I were on a mission from God, so if it was him doing it, fine by me. We strong-armed SEG, saying if Joe Son didn't get his shot in the UFC, they would never see Kimo again." SEG made Royce Gracie vs. Steve Jennum their marquee matchup. (To avoid the confusion of alternates winning tournaments without paying their dues, all alternates were now required to fight *before* they stepped into the tourney.) The show also featured a veteran of another kind: Ron "Black Dragon" Van Clief. As a birthday present to himself, Van Clief wanted to enter the Octagon at the ripe old age of 52, still sporting the sculpted physique of his earlier days. Van Clief took martial arts in the 1950s, bounced around from style to style in the 1960s, and became the "Black Dragon" when he turned actor for the Shaw Brothers film company in the 1970s. He signed a four-picture deal for the Hong Kong company known for its over-the-top kung fu films and ended up doing 15 chop-socky flicks over a 10-year period. Van Clief also did voiceovers for Shaw films being exported to the States, usually dubbing for villains. Having competed in Hong Kong's World Freefighting Championships in 1982 and winning several point karate and full-contact karate matches, Van Clief saw the UFC as the epitome of what martial arts was about. Tai Mak, a student of Van Clief's and star of the film *The Last Dragon*, pushed his master to compete in the event.

But getting into the UFC was no easy task. After SEG president Bob Meyrowitz turned him down because of his age, Van Clief finagled his way into Campbell McLaren's office one afternoon. He didn't arrive alone. "Ron came in unannounced with four acolytes, these muscular, six-foot-something white guys who towered over him," said McLaren. The Black Dragon sat before him as the four men circled McLaren, making him feel uneasy. In his soft voice, Van Clief murmured, "Let me remove my shirt." As he took it off, Van Clief's men exploded in outrage and berated McLaren.

"You have humiliated our sensei!"

"You have embarrassed us!"

"How dare you make him take off his shirt!"

McLaren was perplexed, since Van Clief had acted without prompting. Then he asked McLaren to punch him in the stomach. "No, what if I just touched you," said the SEG vice president of programming. Once again, the henchmen were indignant.

"He touched our sensei!"

"We cannot allow this!"

McLaren, who was getting spooked, protested, "Guys, he asked me to do this." Finally, the veteran martial artist asked permission to perform a test of strength. "I thought he was going to karate chop my desk. It seemed like something right out of a movie. If that was planned, those guys were geniuses." Parlor tricks aside, Van Clief also said he had entered the New York City Marathon. McLaren agreed that if he completed the race, he was fit enough for the UFC. Van Clief did finish the race, and the Black Dragon was in.

• • •

BUDDY ALBIN PROVIDED THE ON-SITE PROMOTION for UFC IV and brought in two kickboxers: Anthony "Mad Dog" Macias and Dallas native Guy "The Sandman" Mezger. WBF Intercontinental Boxing Champion Melton Bowen was the second boxer to make his way to the UFC after the Art Jimmerson debacle. As for Royce Gracie, this would be the greatest test of his abilities in the tournament format.

After some initial problems with Oklahoma trying to ban the event before it began, UFC IV was held in Tulsa at the Expo Square Pavilion on December 16, 1994. Lots were drawn to decide the card. Van Clief smiled when he saw Gracie was his opponent in the first match of the evening. SEG, however, was far from enthusiastic about having its two-time champion mix it up with someone nearly twice his age. Though Van Clief had been involved in numerous martial arts competitions over his lifetime, he was taken down and submitted at 3:51. He was still all grins after being handed his defeat and hugged Gracie for the experience. "I've received a lot of flack from different people for going in there and doing it," remarked Van Clief. "Hundreds of people gave me flack about going in because, as a grandmaster, I shouldn't be doing that. How many guys, just two weeks from turning 52 years old, would step into the UFC, especially as a grandmaster? One!"

• • •

"LOOK AT HIM! He's scared! You're going to kill him!"

As Keith Hackney (dubbed the "Giant Killer") readied himself for Joe Son, the religious man's followers sought to intimidate the kenpo artist. Hackney watched Son as he struggled to carry the long, balsa wood cross on his back. The act wasn't as original the second time. Son bull-rushed Hackney at the start of the match and then caught him in a guillotine choke on the ground. Despite his hand being unhealed, Hackney used groin shots to full advantage—for the first time in the UFC—punching Son six times. Though he wore a cup, Son's eyes squinted in pain. Hackney broke free, stretched out Son's 5'4" body, and grabbed his throat. "I was waiting for him to arm bar me, but I had a tight grip on his Adam's apple and probably would have ripped it out had he tried to push my arm out of the way," said Hackney. Son didn't go for it and subsequently tapped out.

Returning UFC champion Steve Jennum went toe-to-toe with boxer Bowen. After taking some hard shots, Jennum got the mount and pounded on Bowen, then arm-barred him for the tap out. Unfortunately, Jennum's hands swelled up so much that he could no longer make a fist due to the punishment he dished out; as a result, he couldn't continue in the tournament. For the last quarterfinal, amiable training partner Al Snow led Dan Severn to the cage, but who was leading who? "Everyone thought that Al was me until the day of the press conference, when I was sitting up there with the rest of the fighters," said Severn. Snow always dressed in tank tops and shorts, while Severn looked like the handler in a sports jacket. Even Severn's wife and four children back home didn't know what he was doing that night; save for papers she had to sign a day before the event, his wife might never have known.

Severn vs. Anthony Macias turned out to be the match of the night. Macias was an Oklahoma native and, though he had a solid wrestling background, claimed Muay Thai as his style. The 260-pound Severn shot in on him "but he had so much baby oil on him that you'd swear someone had dipped him in by the ankles," recalled Severn. Macias connected with knee strikes and hard elbows, but the bigger man used his Greco-Roman background and dumped the kickboxer with two devastating back *souplesses* (pro wrestling bastardized this term, calling it a "suplex"). Severn later admitted to trying a belly-to-belly throw, but Macias was too slippery. After eating plenty of good shots, Severn had his man down and choked him out without throwing a single punch. He had proven that amateur wrestling deserved to be in the UFC.

Hackney made it to the semis, though his ankle had to be injected with cortisone for the pain. He put up a tremendous fight against Royce Gracie and kept him from the takedown by throwing bombs. At one point, he even grabbed Gracie's gi and slugged away, but the Brazilian tied him up and fell to his back holding Hackney's arm. Hackney desperately tried to fight out of it and broke away momentarily, but the jiu-jitsu fighter kept his cool. By clenching Hackney's right arm, Gracie could move his hips out and wrap his leg around his opponent. It was only a matter of time before Hackney fell to the mat and tapped out to an obviously painful arm bar. "When I saw the first two UFCs, I thought [the Gracies] were very arrogant," said Hackney. "I thought this shit didn't work, and I'm going to go in there and show them. After talking with the family and meeting them though, they were the nicest guys in the world. And I give them a lot of credit for bringing a lot of stuff to the martial arts." The other semi was less dramatic: Dan Severn choked Jennum's replacement, Marcus Bossett, to submission in less than a minute without throwing a punch.

In a challenge match to decide a spot in UFC V, long-haired fighters Jason Fairn and Guy Mezger made their own rule amendment. "We both need hair appointments, so we can either have a girl fight and pull each other's hair or we can have a gentleman fight?" asked Mezger. With elbows and headbutts also off the table, it was a good scrap, but Mezger ground and pounded his way to victory—hair intact. After 20 minutes of dead time for SEG to push merchandise, it came down to grappler vs. grappler. The much larger Severn easily took Gracie down and outpositioned him. He caught Gracie with a couple of slaps to close the distance but wasn't able to finish him, and both men remained up against the fence for over 15 minutes. Severn looked down at Gracie. He had him in place and knew what had to be done. But he was also having to come to grips with something his first two matches hadn't exposed: after more than 15 minutes of fighting, Severn was physically spent. Gracie locked in a triangle choke on the oblivious Severn as color commentator Jeff Blatnick noted the wrestler was in trouble. At 15:49, Severn tapped. "Did I tap because Royce Gracie beat me, or did I tap because I was unwilling to hurt another individual that night?" That was the question Severn had to answer if he wanted to continue fighting.

When the match was over, Severn shook his head in frustration. He felt it was his mind that had lost the fight; his body could have finished it.

Gracie hoisted the $64,000 check over his head. He was back on top and had claimed his third title. But for SEG and WOW, disaster had struck. The show was only scheduled for a two-hour TV block, since cable companies did not treat the UFC as a legitimate sports event, which would have garnered three or more hours. With all the time wasted in the show, the finale ran over by almost four minutes. Many people watching at home were suddenly cut off during the final crucial moments of the Gracie–Severn match. They went nuts. Complaints poured in and money was refunded, costing SEG millions of dollars. What should have been the UFC's biggest-profit show was relegated to the financial status of a local event whose primary cash stream was ticket sales from a small venue in Oklahoma. Still, the pay-per-view buy rate improved to 160,805 at $21.95. Oklahoma subsequently banned the UFC from ever returning, and state officials in Mississippi put a stop to it before the show had a chance to take place there. In March 1995, the attorney general in Kansas said that criminal charges would be filed against anyone attempting to hold a UFC there as well.

• • •

SEG TRIED SEVERAL DIFFERENT VENTURES on pay-per-view, but nothing worked as well as the UFC. On June 17, 1994, they took a chance on actor David Hasselhoff's singing career by making a pay-per-view special called *David Hasselhoff and His Baywatch Friends*. Any success that it might have enjoyed was cut short when O.J. Simpson took his infamous ride in the white Bronco that same evening. Despite the Hasselhoff disaster, SEG President Bob Meyrowitz became good friends with Hasselhoff's manager, Jan McCormick, a starmaker in Hollywood who had also managed the late Brandon Lee, son of Bruce.

Meyrowitz approached McCormick about the Gracie family and set up a meeting with Royce. McCormick immediately took to Gracie's charm and boyish sensibility and couldn't believe he was the one beating all these muscle-bound warriors in a cage. Anticipating something big, Meyrowitz asked Art Davie, "Can you get Rorion, Royce, and yourself into a corporation for the purpose of carrying Royce forward as an entertainment property? I want 10 percent, Jan wants 10 percent, and William Morris, as a theatrical agency, gets 10 percent." Meyrowitz knew he could work with Davie but not with Rorion, who liked to call the shots. A meeting was set at William Morris early in 1995 involving all the principals, including Jeff Sheinberg, the CEO of William Morris, and Mike Simpson, president of the giant agency's TV division.

A $15-million-dollar movie was discussed for Royce. Davie recalled the favored plotline. "The yakuza are furious that Helio Gracie brought jiu-jitsu to Brazil, and now with Royce becoming the Ultimate Fighting Champion, they're hijacking Japanese jiu-jitsu from Brazil, and what right does Helio have to do that? So the yakuza go and kidnap the old man from Brazil and take him to Tokyo. The Gracies, who never really got along, must band together like the Magnificent Seven and, led by Royce, go over to Japan, kick butt, and get the old man back." Things seemed promising until Rorion spoke up, asking if his student John Milius could direct. Sheinberg shot that down, since Milius had not had a hit in years. "[Rorion's] with his brother in the movie, but he's not supposed to talk," said Davie later. "Things ended on that note, and a lot of steam came out of that meeting. Bob came out and said, 'What the fuck was that? I thought you were going to control this guy.'"

Davie went to Rorion and tried to salvage the relationship. He told him Meyrowitz wanted a three-year management deal, but Gracie wouldn't take it. "Rorion, do you realize the magnitude of the meeting you were watching in that room?" asked Davie. "Most martial artists would give one or both of their testicles to be in that room, having someone build a $15-million-dollar film for them and outline a potential career. Do you understand that?" But Gracie didn't feel comfortable with Meyrowitz, who reputedly wanted a lot more than 10 percent of a film deal. "In essence, he wanted to own everything that Royce and I did," said Rorion. "I said absolutely no way. Bob said that after the agreement is made, everything that the Gracie Academy makes, he gets a percentage of that. He knew that a deal like that would affect T-shirts, classes, and videos. I said absolutely no deal. Every coin has two sides. I'm Brazilian, but I'm not stupid. Jiu-jitsu did not get this far because I'm a nice guy."

Davie went back to Meyrowitz with the bad news. "He embarrassed me in front of those people, and now he's telling me he doesn't want to pay me? Fuck him," said Meyrowitz, according to Davie. A film that spun real life into art could have done a lot of big things for the UFC and the Gracie family, but it never transpired. A few months later, the UFC appeared in the Russell Crowe film *Virtuosity* and came off looking like a blood sport. It even portrayed more than two fighters in the Octagon doing battle at the same time. "It took the worst elements of what the UFC was known for, which was people brawling in the ring," said Davie. At the time of the original authoring of this book in 2000, Rorion Gracie claimed to have finished a tome on the life of his family and hoped to turn that into a movie one day—on his terms.

◆ ◆ ◆

MEANWHILE, ROYCE GRACIE WAS BACK ON TOP. After winning three tournaments, the decision was made to retire him from the tournament format to compete in single "superfights." But whom would he fight? It was unfair to bring UFC II semifinalist Pat Smith back into the loop. Marketing reports said Ken Shamrock was the most popular fighter in the UFC, but he had never finished a tournament. Besides, both Shamrock and Gracie were popular, and using the pro wrestling model, two "baby faces" couldn't fight one another. Davie hatched a plan to bring in a star from the traditional martial arts realm to battle Gracie. At first, the obvious opponent was Emin Boztepe, a kung fu stylist who had earlier blasted Gracie and the UFC in martial arts rags. Rorion Gracie was able to get Boztepe's attorney on the phone, but that was as far as it went. Next they tried getting Bart Vale, who had made a name for himself from his stiff-worked matches in Japan. No dice.

Davie's best choice was kickboxer Dennis Alexio, because he wanted someone that martial arts purists could identify with, and Alexio's star-like quality on the mic was perfect for the UFC. "I got his home phone number and offered him $50,000 and really couldn't get him excited," said Davie. "He said he would get back to me but never responded. We were still experimenting with the format. We wanted a major name from the kickboxing world to face Royce." In the end, Davie kept coming back to Ken Shamrock. He knew the fighter wanted Gracie more than anything, even though Shamrock's adoptive father Bob no longer supported him in the event because he had pulled out of a winnable tournament at UFC III. The idea of a superfight came about to ensure that both Gracie and Shamrock would fight each other. "That's the only thing that I trained for and wanted," said Shamrock. "I could have fallen apart, and my life would have been over. I mean, my wife could have left me and my kids would have been destroyed because I couldn't deal with that. I was very difficult to live with. I begged Bob Meyrowitz and Art Davie not to let this go."

UFC V returned to Charlotte, North Carolina, the same setting as their proposed second meeting at UFC III. Only this time, fate had nothing to do with it; Shamrock would get his shot.

Dan Severn also felt he still had something to prove, something to conquer. He wrestled with the rules in his head and came to the conclusion that there was nothing wrong with striking an opponent. "I looked at the UFC as the ultimate challenge. It wasn't for the money or the fame," said Severn. "It was the ultimate test of spiritual, mental, and physical fortitude when you step out there. There is no room for mistakes." Severn made good on those words by dismantling judo stylist "Ghetto Man" Joe Charles in just over a minute, opening up a cut over his left eye, taking his back, and sinking in a choke.

Russian immigrant Oleg Taktarov came into the show with a busted knee that popped in and out of place as a result of a training injury. Though he looked impressive in the quarterfinals, Taktarov entered the Octagon against Severn believing that, since he was another grappler, there would be no striking. He could not have been more wrong. After taking him down, Severn launched several knees to the Russian's face, opening up a gash that drenched the canvas with crimson. "Gokor, he's cut!" yelled referee John McCarthy to Taktarov's trainer, even as the bloodied fighter tried to work an arm lock. The fight was stopped at 4:21 when Gokor Chivichyan threw in the towel.

Another first-round match produced one of the few examples of serious foul play in the UFC. The 6'7", 295-pound John Hess outweighed Texan Andy "The Hammer" Anderson by 60 pounds and was a foot taller. The week of the fight, Hess had been in bully mode, pushing people and berating them with tough talk. His manager even challenged commentator Jeff Blatnick to a fight. "A lot of people came in with the bravado, but as the old saying goes, 'Their only claim to fame is to have no shame,'" said Blatnick. Hess's manager believed in his client's fighting style, which he dubbed Scientific Aggressive Fighting Technology of America. Anderson was a self-made millionaire who owned several businesses, including the Totally Nude Steakhouse in Longview, Texas; the place became so popular, yet offensive, that the city actually paid Anderson to shut it down. He was also a sixth-degree black belt in tae kwon do and agreed to donate his UFC fight purse to one of three charities: School for the Blind, Feed the Children, or a cerebral palsy foundation.

As the match got underway, Hess lumbered toward Anderson throwing sloppy slaps with little technique. "Instead of hitting, he scratched my eyes while we were standing," said Anderson. "Then he continued to scratch and hit me. I finally got him on the ground and got on top of him, and he shoved one thumb into my eye so that I could barely see. Then he bit a chunk out of my hand, grabbed the back of my head, and shoved a thumb in my eye, popping it out of socket. I lost 20 percent of the peripheral vision in my right eye." McCarthy stepped in to stop the bout at 1:23; Anderson was visibly disgusted when Hess's hand was raised. Hess was fined thousands of dollars for his dirty deeds, which was paid to Anderson and given to the School for the Blind. Backstage, Anderson found Hess balling his eyes out. He was exhausted, and since his hand was broken, could not continue.

A year and a half later, Hess chastised the UFC as a publicity stunt, opinions which were due to appear in *Inside Kung Fu* magazine. To prove his point, he picked an "easy" fight with an 18-year-old jiu-jitsu stylist. The match lasted 15 seconds. The jiu-jitsu man was Vitor Belfort, who demolished Hess with super-fast punches. Hess was never heard from again. Anderson continued working in the sport behind the scenes.

Though he came in as a replacement for the injured Hess, Canadian wrestler David Beneteau had solid credentials. He won the Junior Championships from 1984 to 1987 and captured the U.S. Junior Open in 1987 as well. He had lost to Dan Severn in amateur wrestling 10 years earlier. Beneteau had not competed in three years since getting his degree in sports medicine, but he managed to knock out his first two opponents with relative ease. As the finals got underway, Severn shut down Beneteau's striking game by tying up with him. Severn eventually swept Beneteau's leg, took him to the ground, and gained side mount. Beneteau was trapped next to the fence, and Severn immediately performed an arm lock that tapped him out at 3:03.

As Severn raised his hands in celebration, the fierce look in his eyes prompted commentator Bruce Beck to dub him "The Beast." He was no longer the quiet, reserved gentleman who people had known outside the Octagon. And his heavyweight championship belt for the professional wrestling organization, National Wrestling Alliance, would no longer be needed to build up his status in the real fighting realm. The Beast had been born. Daniel (Dan) Severn had conquered all to win the ultimate challenge—for now.

◆ ◆ ◆

THE PRESSURE FOR THE GRACIE–SHAMROCK SUPERFIGHT had been building for months, with each side predicting a consummate win come fight time. It was a match that needed to take place, but the crowd would grow bitterly disappointed. Ken Shamrock had waited a year and a half to conquer his demons, but, nestled in the guard of Gracie for nearly 30 minutes, he was unable to get that image of being submitted out of his mind. He didn't want to chance it, didn't want to risk a mistake. He felt uncomfortable in the guard, but "all I knew was that if those legs got up around my arm or head, I was getting choked," said Shamrock later. "And he was not going to get there." The crowd booed with displeasure as all expectations for an exciting fight began to disappear. For Shamrock, it bothered him that hours before the match, he was told there was going to be a 30-minute time limit. "I think Ken respected Royce's abilities too much," said Bob Shamrock, and Ken freely admitted to being overly cautious. For his part, Gracie found a 27-pound weight disparity a problem for the first time, even though he had fought and beaten heavier men. Neither man took the initiative, and it went down as one of the most boring matches in UFC history.

After 30 minutes, Bruce Beck commented on the overtime: could five more minutes decide a victor? With his hands grasping the fence, Bob Shamrock was beside himself with frustration. "I don't usually cuss, but I was cussing Ken out left and right," said the elder Shamrock, who dramatically yelled out the countdown to Ken. As the five-minute overtime was instituted, Art Davie noticed the crowd getting restless, since the two seemed content with a stalemate. "I was screaming at McCarthy," he said, "and finally he looked over and saw my thumb saying *stand them up.*" McCarthy obliged; Shamrock finally landed a solid punch that made Gracie's eye swell up like a balloon. The two went back to the ground, and, after 36 exhausting minutes, the match was ruled a draw, since there were no judges and no other decision could be made.

The recriminations began almost immediately. "He should be embarrassed for not beating Royce," said Rorion. "If I was as damaged from the punch as he [Ken Shamrock] said, why didn't he finish me?" returned Royce. There was controversy from all sides, and both men claimed they would have finished off the other had the match continued. It was an anticlimactic end to the sport's first great rivalry. The match catapulted the event into unimaginable pay-per-view buys: 286,256 at $24.95 a pop. Rorion Gracie felt the match fell short of his vision of what The Ultimate Fighting Championship should represent: a truly realistic forum. "It [no time limit] forces the fighter to chase victory, knowing that he has to finish him off now or he might get caught later. It makes it real, like a street fight." But the UFC was not a street fight; it was a spectator sport that had to play out within a suitable, sustainable time frame for a pay-per-view audience.

After the fourth show ran over, time limits became a necessity. "Rorion always saw it [the UFC] as simply a means for his family's style to get over [with the mainstream]," said Davie. Davie also felt the mounting pressure of American states unwilling to hold the event. And there was growing friction between WOW and SEG. "We were always going over the expenses because we split the profits 50/50, and I didn't want some Jim Rockford type of deal," said Davie (a reference to the *Rockford Files* television character, played by James Garner, who always got shafted at the end of an episode). "I felt that Bob was going to be a real problematic partner, along with the fact that we were under such political pressure." Davie and Gracie weren't getting along either. The Brazilian held Davie personally responsible for Royce Gracie getting punched, since he had told McCarthy to stand them up. "Rorion was so furious over that because it was not realistic and not a real fight," said Clay McBride. "You're breaking them and standing them up." The UFC was bigger than any one style; it was and grew to become a profitable spectator sport that demanded more.

If the show was to move forward, something had to change. According to Rorion, "Art had gotten in cahoots with Bob and wanted me out of the decision-making process. They thought, *Let's find a way to get Rorion out of this.* So Art came to me and said, 'Let's sell WOW.' He told me he was tired of it and it wasn't going to work." Rorion didn't want to sell, knowing that more money was to be made. But he relented, if only because a new show was in the works, as he and Davie had discussed. "Bob liked being in business with me, and I liked being in business with Rorion, but the three of us didn't work," said Davie. "Bob and I were two guys from Brooklyn and we could talk, but when you got the three of us in the room, it was very strained." On April 19, just 12 days after UFC V, Rorion Gracie and Art Davie sold their share of the UFC to Bob Meyrowitz. "We had an international event that spawned one of the best franchises on pay-per-view," said Meyrowitz. "We needed to step up the production and rules had to be changed." Gracie, for his part, believed that judges would never perceive that a fighter on the bottom of a ground match might possibly win.

Gracie signed a two-year noncompete clause but knew there was a way around it. "As soon as we sold WOW, Art and I went to meet with some guys in Chicago about another show. They decided not to do the deal, and Art gets hired the next day to work for SEG [as matchmaker]. It got to show me what type of person Art was, and I wasn't happy about that. I felt betrayed." Davie claimed Meyrowitz called him up out of the blue. Either way, it was apparent that Gracie was no longer needed. He wanted to put real fights on television, while SEG wanted a television show with fighting.

Gracie and Davie were paid hefty sums for their share of the UFC, even though they never put in one dime. Through a loophole, the original 28 investors, who had put in $250,000, were left with nothing. "I really thought this was horrendous, not just because I was losing money, but because I thought it was very bad press for him in the martial arts community," remarked McBride. "Rorion and Art walked away with money and left all the investors high and dry." Since they were students of Gracie's, Rorion agreed to pay the principal plus 10 percent back to each investor. Davie bought a boat, settled in Las Vegas, and was paid $25,000 per show as matchmaker. "To this day, Rorion and I are the only ones to have ever profited from the UFC," said Davie. That is, till 2005.

Naturally Royce would not continue fighting in the UFC and stepped down. He then voiced complaints about the show in numerous magazine articles and eventually made his comeback nearly five years later for Japan's Pride organization. A party was held for Royce Gracie's triumphant reign in the Octagon, at which he received a jeweled samurai sword adorned with UFC logos. The event would never be the same without Gracie, the smaller man who defeated the bigger man to collect three championship titles and only a handful of bumps and bruises. In the process, a sport had been born—and it was bigger than jiu-jitsu. The Gracies had shocked the martial art system into growing again. Now it was time to mature.

9

CLASH
OF THE TITANS

Oleg Taktarov stared calmly across the Octagon into the cold, blue eyes of a monster named Tank. It was the finals of UFC VI, dubbed "Clash of the Titans." Since the stoppage that had kept him from the finals of the previous show, Taktarov's leg had healed, he'd had more time to train, and his mind was focused on the fight rather than where his next meal was coming from. Before him stood a rampaging foe who had just crushed two men in less than two minutes combined. Taktarov was unfazed. He had endured far worse.

The story of Oleg Taktarov's involvement with the UFC was something right out of a movie. He was born in Sarov, just east of the Ural Mountains in Russia, one of the 10 "secret cities" of the so-called Soviet nuclear archipelago and home to one of the country's largest H-bomb research centers. Taktarov grew up inside the confines of a secret nuclear testing site, autonomous from the rest of city and surrounded by an electrical fence; like much of the populace, his family worked in the complex. At the age of 10, his father took him to a sambo/judo school nearby. Sambo is the premier Russian martial art, a mixture of wrestling and judo. For seven years, Taktarov learned sambo and spent his summer months in a special training camp. At the age of 17, he took part in a sambo match that would decide his fate. If he won, he could fulfill his mandatory two-year military service in Gorky, competing for the army in the sport division. If he lost, he would be sent to the regular army and stationed as far away as Afghanistan. During the contest, his opponent snapped Taktarov's ankle, as leg locks were an integral part of sambo. Taktarov writhed in pain but would not yield, and the bout continued until the referee stood them up. With only one chance to end the match, Taktarov grabbed his opponent by the gi lapels and slammed his head to the ground, knocking him out. He could continue his sambo training for the Russian military.

The army was supposed to give Taktarov the best training of his life. Instead, it was mundane, leaving the sport maniac yearning for more action. Though it was risky, he would go AWOL at 5:30 AM to train at his old sambo school for two hours, returning to the army camp in time for daily training. This worked out for a short while until a general caught him coming back late. Drenched in sweat, Taktarov told the officer he just wanted to make the army happy by training under his own conditions. The general didn't buy his story. Within a few days, Taktarov was shipped off to a remote forest camp for a six-month assignment as punishment for his "good intentions."

Becoming a tactical officer and learning how to read radars was not exactly what Taktarov had planned. Before long he was back training in the forest. He lifted logs, ran, and wrestled around with his comrades to build up his strength. During one session, an intense pain in his side prompted him to seek medical aid. He was told dismissively it was probably overtraining. Taktarov went AWOL again, but this time it was life or death. Trekking over five miles through the Russian countryside, he finally made his way to a doctor. It turned out he had a ruptured spleen. "If you had been 20 minutes late, it would probably have come open inside of you and you might have died," said the doctor. This time, Taktarov was not disciplined for leaving his post. He eventually resumed training and became so strong that the army felt he should represent them in weightlifting, so he was sent back to Gorky.

In a chance meeting with the general who had sent him away, Taktarov pleaded his case: "I'm different now and know what I did was wrong. I will still work hard and achieve my goals. Please let me come back and practice sambo again so I can fight in the world competitions." Taktarov was granted that opportunity and won the nationals a couple of months later against the best in Russia. He finished his two years with the army and continued training for another two years in the top sambo school. But with nothing more to achieve, Taktarov became bored and no longer wanted to train. For a short while he took a job teaching sambo for the government to special forces, KGB, and other members of the Russian elite police. It was called counterterrorist training. Taktarov was surprised by his students' inexperience in hand-to-hand combat.

This gave him the chance to make some money. Before long, he had opened up a lucrative training business that supported his regained interest in sport competition. Moving away from sambo, Taktarov competed in full-contact jiu-jitsu events, where strikes were legal. He won four times. When news of the UFC surfaced, he went to the Baltic cities in Latvia and competed in similar MMA events. After finding success there, he set his sights on fighting in America and eventually settled in a Russian community in Los Angeles. The Russian-speaking neighborhood provided Taktarov with a safe haven, since he couldn't speak English, but his money dried up. Soon he was sleeping in a car he had rented with his last remaining dollars. He was bored of training and fighting, and his childhood dream of becoming an actor seemed hopeless. That was when a dazed and confused Oleg Taktarov found himself walking into the Gracie Academy in Torrance. Returning to fighting was the only thing he could do if he was to survive in a world he did not understand.

Taktarov grappled at the academy (against Pedro Sauer) that day and later claimed he had no problem holding his own, as he was much stronger and was accustomed to wearing a gi. Rorion complimented his skills, and some other students in the school told him about the WOW office across the street. After changing into street clothes, Taktarov walked into the office to find Rorion sitting across from Art Davie. Taktarov's limited English was a problem, and after Gracie left, Davie had to get his Russian-speaking brother-in-law on the phone to translate. "I gave him some money because he was starving," said Davie. "He came back later and gave me a videotape. After looking at it, I thought, *This guy can really fight.* While having dinner with Davie over a year after his participation in the UFC, Taktarov learned the truth: "Davie told me that Gracie said, 'That guy is nothing. Do not use him. He sucks.'" Though Rorion Gracie denies this, Davie corroborated the conversation and recalled a similar story about getting Alexander Karelin into the UFC. Karelin was a Russian wrestler of superhuman strength with a long list of record-setting titles to his credit and was known as "The Experiment" for his seemingly superhuman prowess—but after wrestler Mark Schultz lasted 30 minutes with Rickson Gracie in a sparring session (Gracie finally tapped him), Rorion didn't want either one to enter the UFC. Because Rorion had taken such a stand against Taktarov, Davie decided he had to be in the show.

It wasn't difficult to locate Taktarov, who had taken refuge in his car literally parked daily in front of the WOW offices. Davie arranged for the eager UFC participant to train under the auspices of UFC on-site promoter and manager Buddy Albin in Texas. Though Albin accepted him, the experience left the Russian with a bad taste in his mouth. Living in a rundown apartment complex in Dallas, Texas, Taktarov found he could speak more English than the rest of the tenants. "I stay in a room with a boiler behind the wall so that I could hear the water bubble all night long," he remembered. The Russian's weight dipped down below 200 pounds, and his knee was in bad shape for his appearance at UFC V. If he was going to continue, Albin and his present location would not do him any favors. "Listen Buddy, I can't train in Texas because there is no one for me to train with, no food, and I'm so depressed here," Taktarov admitted to the on-site promoter. "Ken Shamrock came over for a seminar so we grappled, and he wanted to learn submissions from me, and I wanted to train with him because he was much stronger than anyone else around." Taktarov ended up moving out to Northern California, and the stability with the blooming Lion's Den gave him the training he needed to fight at a world-class level. He lived in Bob Shamrock's house and worked with Ken for two months in preparation for the next event, though he was still managed by Albin. Taktarov was a different man when he competed at UFC VI on July 14, 1995, in Casper, Wyoming.

◆ ◆ ◆

THERE WAS ANOTHER MAN who had turned up at UFC V but hadn't gotten the chance to show what he could do. David Lee Abbott hailed from Huntington Beach, California, and was introduced to Art Davie by his friend Dave Thomas.

"He's kind of like that guy from the Clint Eastwood movie and the fights," he told Davie.

"You mean *Every Which Way But Loose* and Tank Murdock [a character from that film]?" said Davie.

"Yeah, except he's Tank Abbott, and the guy can bench over 600 pounds!"

How would a street fighter with no martial arts experience perform in the event? Abbott was invited to attend UFC V, but Campbell McLaren and Bob Meyrowitz weren't sure they wanted him on the card because of the political pressure they were facing. It was bad enough that some traditional martial artists couldn't cut the mustard, but what about some bar brawler who tried to go in there and really hurt people? Abbott showed up and proceeded to down vodkas like water; SEG didn't know what to do with him. "When Abbott came in, he looked like the prototypical bad guy, the biker at the bar who looks like he really does want to rip your head off," remembered David Isaacs. Abbott got so inebriated at UFC V that he lost his tickets and had to be seated up in the rafters. He later used his key to get into the wrong room, the one belonging to SEG president Meyrowitz.

Sporting a potbelly and a shaven head with a contrasting bushy goatee, Abbott was a walking time bomb of testosterone, a vicious animal who was about to take the UFC to a whole new level. He called himself the "anti-martial artist," and the only true no-holds-barred fighter to ever enter the Octagon. Abbott was born to a middle-class family and started wrestling at the age of nine. He wanted to try out for the gridiron, but his football coach father wouldn't let him, only his older brother. Abbott claimed to have been a fighter from a very early age, though he can't pinpoint where his aggression originated. At college, he dreamed of being a champion wrestler and earning a degree in history. Only one of the two came to pass. At the age of 19, after a night of too much partying, "my buddy that was driving passed out, and, while going 50 miles per hour, he hit a light pole. I woke up with my teeth knocked out and my leg almost cut off. That fucked up my wrestling career."

After graduating in 1993 from the University of California at Long Beach, Abbott planned to become a teacher, "but it was a smokescreen. I knew in the back of my head that I could never be a teacher because of all my convictions for beating people up." Abbott took up boxing and found he had what are called "heavy hands," meaning his fists were like hammers. He quickly built a reputation around Huntington Beach for stirring up trouble. "A good time before I was famous was to go out, party, and then the tough guy in the bar gets his ass kicked! I'd come up to him—here I am, a kind of fat-looking guy, and didn't have a goatee then—I had hair. I'd be boogeying, going 'Woo, Woo!' and he'd go, 'Hey man, shut up.'" Baiting a guy in a bar and beating him up outside became one of Abbott's leisure pursuits.

Tank may have had a reputation as a streetfighter, but SEG needed to spruce up his "legitimate" background. Davie reinvented him as a "pit fighter," and suddenly he had a record of 7–0, which remains unsubstantiated save for drunken myths from the goon crew that accompanied him to many a show. When asked about the worst beating he'd ever given someone, a tight-lipped Tank only revealed the injuries. Apparently, someone had broken a pool cue over Abbott's head. The assailant ended up having "his leg broken in three places. All of his teeth were kicked out of his face—uh, did I say kicked? Well, they were missing. And he had 75 stitches in his face, with two and a half weeks in the hospital." Abbott had also served a seven-month jail sentence before fighting in the UFC. At the time of the tourney he ran a garage door business with his brother and worked several odd jobs.

Another storm was brewing in Casper, Wyoming, as Ken Shamrock and Dan Severn faced the prefight press conference before their super-fight at UFC VI. After most of the attention was given to Shamrock, Severn got up and headed for the door without explanation.

Shamrock, taking Severn's gesture as a sign of disrespect, said, "We'll finish this in the ring."

"In your dreams," retorted Severn's manager, Phyllis Lee.

This made Shamrock furious. Later on in the afternoon, visitors couldn't walk through the Hyatt Hotel without stepping on copies of a nondescript newsletter explaining how Severn was going to destroy Shamrock. The flyer further enraged Shamrock, though the gentlemanly Severn insisted it was "not in my M.O." Fueled by anger, Shamrock couldn't wait to face the Beast.

It became clear on the night of the show that each fighter would also be battling the altitude in a venue 5,140' above sea level. It was the first show that SEG had sole control of, and from its beginning, with Michael Buffer's famous "Let's get r-r-r-eady to r-r-r-r-r-umble," it was a show to remember. Buffer, the undisputed king of boxing announcers, had been brought in by his brother Bruce, a lifelong martial artist with a black belt in tae kwon do whose kickboxing career was cut short by an adverse MRI scan. The two brothers created the Buffer Partnership; Bruce masterminded turning Michael's famous catchphrase into a mul-timillion dollar enterprise, with video games, movies, songs, and even a television show. After becoming a fan of the UFC, Bruce called up SEG and pitched the idea of Michael introducing the show. A three show deal was cut from UFC VI to VIII, but the announcer's alignment with World Championship Wrestling eventually sidelined him after just two shows. "Michael would say, 'If it's not in the Octagon, it's not real,' and that really upset the people at WCW and Turner Broadcasting, which was owned by Ted Turner at the time," said Bruce. Turner, one of the most powerful media moguls in the world, usually got what he wanted.

The first few tournaments had been largely beneath the radar of national politicians and the media, being staged in states without boxing commissions and airing to a tiny, though growing, audience on pay-per-view. That all changed when someone had sent a video of an event to John McCain, the Republican senator for Arizona and future presidential hopeful. McCain, a former Naval Academy boxer and Vietnam prisoner of war, was disgusted. On June 6, 1995, he fired off a scathing two-page letter to Wyoming governor Jim Geringer, urging him to stop the UFC from taking place in his state the following month. "The 'Ultimate Fighting Championship' is a disturbing and bloody competition which places the contestants at great risk for serious injury or even death, and it should not be allowed to take place anywhere in the United States," McCain wrote. "Governor, I have been an avid fan of professional boxing for over 30 years, but there is absolutely no sport in the UFC, only ugliness and rule-less brutality. The viciousness of the UFC is truly appalling." Luckily the state could not find cause to shut down the UFC, so it was full steam ahead. McCain, though, was just getting started.

As the lots were drawn, no one wanted Tank Abbott more than the 350-pound John Matua, who was fighting to raise money for his brother in a hospital. Matua was a student of *kuialua*, the brutal Hawaiian art of bone breaking. Greg Patschull, the Cage of Rage and subsequent promoter of Kage Kombat, brought Matua to Davie. Since no scales were used in those early UFCs, his weight was listed as over 400 pounds. Abbott came in at a comparatively svelte 265 pounds and wore modified kenpo gloves, the first time gloves of this type were worn in the UFC. SEG had always dithered over whether or not to allow these four-to-six-ounce fingerless mitts that protect the hand but were small enough to grapple with. Abbott's usage prompted them to encourage gloves from that point on. "I have been in so many streetfights that I know that when I punch you, my hands are going to blow up," said Tank.

On McCarthy's order, Abbott wasted little time, making a beeline for Matua and mauling him with blows that sent the Hawaiian down to the mat—headfirst—with all four limbs outstretched like Frankenstein. Matua had suffered a major concussion, but Tank still came down one more time with a devastating elbow to his face that bounced his head off the canvas. McCarthy pulled Tank off; it was all over in 18 explosive seconds. "John Matua was rated G; I have hit rated X," said Tank. Looking down at his handiwork, he also mimicked his prey's rigid body in a most unsportsmanlike fashion. "That bothered me, and I actually felt the swell of anger," said color commentator Jeff Blatnick. "If there had not been a ref there, I would have kicked him in the face 10 times after I did what I did to him," exclaimed Abbott. "That means nothing to me."

That was the first of four quarterfinal matches that each took less than a minute. The 6'8" Paul "The Polar Bear" Varelans laid waste to Cal Worsham, the International Taekwondo Council's No. 1 point fighter. It was a good little scrap, with the 5'10" Worsham getting in some blows before his larger opponent downed him hard with an elbow to the back of the head. Then UFC veteran Patrick Smith performed a beautiful front thrust kick to the chest of Rudyard Moncayo that took the breath out of him and set up a rear naked choke with success. The big match of the night was supposed to be the return of Canadian wrestler Dave Beneteau against Oleg Taktarov. Beneteau took the sambo player down to the ground with ease and was in Taktarov's guard until the wrestler pushed him up to the fence. A brief stand-up melee didn't work to Taktarov's advantage, but the Russian survived Beneteau's onslaught. Going back to the ground, Taktarov quickly finished him with a front choke just three seconds shy of a minute.

The semis produced one of the strangest occurrences in the UFC. First up was Tank Abbott vs. Paul Varelans. Abbott took Varelans to the fence and pounded the giant Polar Bear's face with strikes. Grabbing the fence mesh, Abbott then pressed his knee into Varelans's face and looked up to the cameras with a big smile. He was enjoying the brawl and working the crowd at the same time. McCarthy finally stepped in and stopped the bout in Abbott's favor, though Varelans was still willing to continue.

A few minutes later, Pat Smith made his way to fight Taktarov but collapsed to his knees on the way and clutched his stomach in pain. Andy Anderson, who was escorting Smith, thought it was a response to pure fear. He told Smith to suck it up and go out anyway. "Pat claimed that he had stomach problems," said Davie. "And of course at the cocktail party he was eating ham sandwiches. I'm still to this day pissed at Pat about that." Smith may have not been fit to fight, but he was fit to call. SEG was so upset with Smith over making countless phone calls on their tab that they posted a sign up for everyone to see addressing him directly to stop. At first, Davie approached one of Paul Varelans' seconds, Brian Johnston, about taking the slot against Taktarov because there was a bit of a conundrum with the alternates. In two alternate matches before the tournament, competitors Anthony Macias and Guy Mezger both won, and Macias was picked to take Smith's place. There was one problem: Buddy Albin managed both Macias and Taktarov, as well as Mezger.

In a locker room meeting minutes before the match, Macias made a decision that would blight his career for good: he was ordered to throw the fight. "I was in on the conversation with Anthony Macias, Oleg, and Buddy [Albin]," said Andy Anderson. "Everyone knew that Oleg was going to need every ounce of strength he had to beat Tank. Buddy Albin told Macias that if you don't lose this fight, you will never fight again in another no-rules fight...ever." At that time, Albin was a major force in MMA, managing several fighters. He was also the on-site promoter and took as much as 40 percent of the gate receipts for the UFC. Unbeknownst to SEG, Macias agreed to throw the fight. In the cage a few minutes later, Taktarov submitted him by choke in 12 seconds. Commentators Jim Brown, Jeff Blatnick, and Bruce Beck were suspicious and openly called attention to the fishy ending. Though Tank had blown through both of his opponents, Taktarov was now fresh to face him in the finals.

◆ ◆ ◆

DAN SEVERN AND KEN SHAMROCK both looked to be at the top of their games for their superfight. Severn was six years older and outweighed Shamrock by 50 pounds, but from the start Shamrock attempted a shoot. Severn's takedown defense kept him at bay. They clinched and worked for position to dictate the pace of the fight, but neither man was willing to chance a mistake. Moving toward the fence, Severn shot for a single-leg takedown but with his head on the outside. Shamrock locked in a guillotine choke. The first one missed, but the second one cinched in tight, and when Shamrock gained leverage, Severn tapped immediately. "I proved my ability and I can wrestle," said an ecstatic Shamrock after the fight. "I wanted to see if he could throw me. I wanted to see what he had." According to Severn, he was running a high temperature and felt sluggish, but there were no signs of it in the fight. Shamrock also said that he had noticed Severn's head on the outside when going for a takedown, perfectly natural for amateur wrestling. For MMA however, it left the head susceptible to the guillotine. The two would fight again; their rematch would be entirely different.

It was now time for the tournament final between Taktarov and Abbott. The much stronger Tank took the Russian down early in the fight and landed several punches—Taktarov said later that he saw them coming and was unaffected—but within a few minutes, he began to tire. The altitude became a major factor, and by the 10-minute mark, both men were gasping for air. It looked like it would come down to who wanted it more. "When you keep in mind that you still don't have a Green Card, you gotta win, and that was my motivation," said Taktarov. After 15 minutes on the ground with both men attempting chokes, John McCarthy stood them up. They worked toward the fence. Tank's head was limp. He was out of gas and in position for a guillotine choke. "He had no neck," remembered Taktarov, so eventually he moved to Tank's back and sank a rear naked choke that ended the fight at 17:47. Both men had fought their hearts out. No one had thought that the out-of-shape Tank could make it past the first few minutes. Afterward, he shook his head and walked out of the cage like nothing happened. "All I know is that I fought two real fights and Oleg fought in one real fight," exclaimed Abbott. "They [SEG] did not want a real fighter; they wanted a real martial artist—some guy from Russia—to win it all."

Taktarov, on the other hand, had a gash on his head, a bloody nose, and remained still on the ground. Ken Shamrock jumped in to hold him down so he wouldn't expend energy. Taktarov claimed it was his toughest battle ever, not because of Tank, but because he felt like he was going to die after the match. "Then Buddy Albin found a gas mask, and in front of millions of people, he wanted to show that he knew what he was doing," said the Russian. "But they forgot to turn it on, and oxygen was not coming into the mask. So imagine that you cannot breathe and someone puts tape over your mouth! Another guy came in named Gokor [Chivichyan], who was trying to show off too, and they were both fighting over the mask." Taktarov eventually received competent attention and was rushed to the hospital, where he was told that he had lost a half-gallon of fluid. He laughed about it later, saying, "The oxygen couldn't go to my brain because my blood was dry!"

Taktarov won the grand prize, Anthony Macias never fought in the UFC again, and there was one more fight to be had—it just wasn't on the card. Pat Smith may have bowed out on purpose without injury, but he would still get to fight, even if it was unplanned. According to Tank Abbott, Smith went into a frenzy right after the Huntington Beach bad boy returned from his match against John Matua. "I'm pretty sure Art Davie had his finger in this by saying, 'Hey, we need to disrupt the flow of what is going on.' He [Smith] came running out...and threw a few kicks at my dad," said Abbott. Though Abbott doesn't know why he did it and Davie doesn't recall the episode, Smith certainly made an enemy by the attack. Paul Herrera, a collegiate wrestler and Tank's lackey, stood between them and got punched in the face for his troubles. Herrera wanted to get even with Smith, and, later on in the show, Tank himself tried to go after the kickboxer. Campbell McLaren watched Ron Van Clief, who had taken over as IFC commissioner from Davie, hold Tank back by grabbing his throat and telling him to stop. The streetfighter backed off for the moment, but things didn't stay cool for long. After a night of partying, Tank retired to his hotel room and crashed. Herrera and fellow wrestler Eddie Ruiz kept drinking. At one point, Herrera tried to pick up a beautiful girl who turned out to be Pat Smith's sister. She left for reinforcements in the form of Smith's crew. Herrera and Ruiz managed to get out of there and tried to wake Abbott. He was out cold.

The next morning in the hotel, Ruiz berated Herrera for not doing anything to Smith. With an evil look in his eye, Herrera put on his singlet and wrestling shoes as the whole crew got ready to go upstairs for breakfast. As the elevator door opened to the dining room, Pat Smith was standing in the entrance. He was in the wrong place at the wrong time. Herrera threw one punch that sent Smith down. "I put a boot in Patrick's ear twice, and Paul beat the living hell out of him," remembered Tank. Kickboxer Maurice Smith (no relation), who had been working with Ken Shamrock on stand-up, finally moved in and broke things up. "I saw Paul pounding on Pat because Pat was already on the ground and had been knocked down," said Maurice Smith. "I ran over there and tackled Paul to get him off, and Tank was already walking away."

Bludgeoned and bloodied, Pat Smith was carried to Andy Anderson's room. Art Davie was meeting with pseudo-star John Wayne Bobbitt, the man whose penis was severed by his enraged wife while he slept, who was interested in competing in the show. They heard the scuffle from outside. As Davie went to investigate, Abbott went one way and Herrera went the other. Davie accompanied Smith to the hospital. "He got beaten up worse than any of his UFC fights. He had stitches inside and outside his mouth." Smith never competed in the UFC again. Neither Herrera nor any of Tank's people were ever sued, but one thing was for sure: David "Tank" Abbott was a bona fide villain. He was also becoming a star for the rabid UFC fan base and a recurring story for the press.

So popular was Abbott that he would be put under contract with SEG and paid a monthly salary instead of a per-fight purse; he was one of the first fighters to get this arrangement, along with Randy Couture and Mark Kerr. SEG's Steven Loeb handled a lot of the fighter money and was once a bit tardy in sending out Abbott's check. To get the ball rolling, Abbott sent Loeb a bullet with Loeb's name inscribed on it. Needless to say, Tank got his money within the week.

As for the pay-per-view buys, they dipped to 194,463, which wasn't bad, but it signaled something that many knew all along: without a story, why would anyone pay? Sure the draw of style vs. style was still there and the controversial "no rules" stigma, but fandom is incited by names, faces, and a story they can swing either way. Nothing has happened, despite all the technology to which the world has been exposed, to change that.

• • •

UFC VII, HELD IN MEMORIAL AUDITORIUM in Buffalo, New York, on September 8, 1995, broke box office records with over 8,100 in attendance. The show mixed veterans and newcomers, culminating in a dramatic finish in the tournament final between Paul Varelans and Brazilian Marco Ruas, a veteran of old school vale tudo. Ruas was something of a mystery man, his age kept secret, but there was no denying his stand-up and submission abilities. "I had a very short time to prepare myself for that event," said Ruas. "I was very determined to win that tournament no matter what." Manager/promoter Frederico Lapenda gave him the moniker "King of the Streets" and a style: Ruas Vale Tudo. He wowed the crowd with his Muay Thai skills, but despite his formidable weapons, it took him over 13 minutes to finish Varelans, causing the show to run over its allotted time once again. (UFC VII dropped down to 155,965 buys.) A power blackout also caused problems; it seemed the UFC couldn't get a break. "We had a lot of momentum going into that show, but with the time running over, it probably cost us over $1 million," said chief operating officer David Isaacs.

No one expected the superfight between Oleg Taktarov and Ken Shamrock to go the distance either. Yet for 35 minutes, the two former training partners grappled and struck each other until a draw was declared. "I just wanted to show him that it was the wrong idea to fight, because a fight can never be exciting if two people know each other and train for many months together and you know every single move," said Taktarov. This didn't stop the Russian from bleeding (a frequent occurrence in his fights), and after the match, cut man Leon Tabbs went to work. "I go in there to stop the bleeding and he's halfway unconscious," remembered Tabbs. "He finally comes out of it and looks at me and says, 'Leon, why did you stop the fight?'" The Russian was made of stern stuff: to this day he has never tapped out from any match.

10

THE AGE OF THE WRESTLER

Two years after the UFC had begun, it was time to decide the champion, the man who could face and triumph over the best of the best: the Ultimate Ultimate warrior. The show returned to Colorado for the third time, though it now faced opposition even there. "The mayor said he didn't know if he could do anything legally, but morally, the UFC was an abomination," recalled Art Davie. "We were on the cover of *USA TODAY* in December 1995 with the mayor telling people, 'I don't know how this goddamn thing came into our town, but were not extending any courtesies to them and if the police can do anything, we support them to get them out.'" The state had its hands tied legally, however. As long as they didn't break any city ordinances or laws, the absence of a state athletic commission gave the UFC a free hand.

Ultimate Ultimate '95 featured four champions and four veterans who had made it to previous semifinals. Unfortunately, Ken Shamrock and Royce Gracie, the two most popular fighters and obvious choices, were nowhere to be found. Shamrock had never made it beyond the semis; Gracie was tempted with everything from a new truck to more money than any fighter had ever made, but it wasn't enough. "Meyrowitz wanted to sign Royce to a multifight contract, which we couldn't do," said Rorion Gracie. "If Royce won, he would be worth a lot more." As it stood, champions Steve Jennum (UFC III), Dan Severn (UFC V), Oleg Taktarov (UFC VI), and Marco Ruas (UFC VII) would face off against David "Tank" Abbott, Paul Varelans, David Beneteau, and Keith Hackney.

The show was held at the Mammoth Gardens, the notorious venue of UFC II. Paul Varelans was originally to be rematched with Mark Hall (Hall lost to Varelans in UFC VII) for a single fight on the card, but when Gerard Gordeau passed on his slot and Patrick Smith dropped out for no reason, Varelans moved into the main bracket. For the first time since the inaugural event, fighters would not be matched by lots but by Art Davie's decision.

It seemed a natural for Tank Abbott, who had spent his share of time behind bars, to face the ninja police officer, Steve Jennum. Abbott walked through Jennum, much to the delight of the screaming fans. All of the quarterfinal matches were over quickly as Hackney fell to Ruas via rear naked choke at 2:39 into the match, when most felt it would have lasted longer. "Physically I was in the best shape of my life, but mentally I wasn't there," said Hackney. "I wasn't sleeping right and wasn't eating right. I got wrapped up doing so many interviews that I just wasn't really in that fight at all." Hackney vs. Ruas provided the only trump card, as both men were adequate strikers. But the kenpo man had an off night, and grappling made the real difference in this match, since Hackney was still new to the ground game. This would be Hackney's last MMA fight.

Varelans quickly lost to Severn and, for the second time, Taktarov submitted Beneteau. Taktarov didn't waste any time, performing a crafty maneuver by rolling under the wrestler during a tie-up and going for an ankle lock. He won without suffering any damage and was fresh for his next match. Beneteau had really wanted the Russian and thought about quitting the sport after his second loss to him.

Both semis ended in decision, something that had not happened before—there had been no judges. Proper judging criteria had still not been established, creating plenty of controversy. Tank Abbott could hardly get off a punch as Dan Severn got the takedown and pinned him against the fence. Abbott wondered why McCarthy wouldn't stand them up; he and everyone else had been told that if there was no action on the ground for over two minutes, they would be stood up. For 17 minutes, Severn proceeded to knee, slap, punch, and elbow the street brawler over 250 times. "Dan Severn didn't do anything," claimed Abbott later, meaning Severn wouldn't stand up and trade punches with him. The wrestler's strategy was sensible, but Tank wouldn't give in or tap, and with the crowd growing restless, Severn let up, giving his opponent a last-ditch effort for three minutes. "The serious point of the match was pretty much over," said Severn later. "Nobody likes to see a grappling match, so I let him come to his feet so the crowd could get excited." The wrestler tried to perform a suplex, but time ran out. Severn was given the unanimous decision.

The first eight minutes of Taktarov vs. Ruas were exciting, with the Russian getting a guillotine choke on the Brazilian and the latter throwing some good kicks and punches. When a cut opened over Taktarov's eye, John McCarthy stopped the fight in favor of cutman Leon Tabbs' examination. The match continued. Then something strange happened: Ruas refused to engage. "Since he was already cut and it was getting hard for me to breathe, I just wanted to conserve my energy for Severn," he later said. For nine straight minutes, not a single punch was thrown, and at the 29-minute mark Taktarov was ruled the winner. Ruas's manager, Frederico Lapenda, was furious, charging the judges' table and voicing his anger. "How can you say you can put judges in a fight, but there are no rules written anywhere...like a punch is worth five points or whatever," he said later. "So I created a big fuss, but you couldn't back down from a fight, and sure enough, Ruas had the best contract in that show, and I know when I negotiated that I drove a hard bargain, but I took a gamble too. If Marco would have won, he would have won a lot more, but that wasn't good for the UFC." The lesson was that a fighter should never think he is ahead on points; he must chase victory as if victory is always within reach.

The finals rematched Severn with Taktarov. Although the Russian later claimed that doctors kept him from resting between his match with Ruas and the finals, it made little difference. Severn manhandled him, just as he had before. "This time his punches didn't land so bad and they missed a lot," said Taktarov. "He put two fingers in a scar on my face and tried to open it up." Taktarov was soon bleeding, and his opponent tried to force an early stoppage, but Tabbs twice let it go. The Russian put up a good fight, despite his mangled face, and even tried his rolling ankle lock trick again. The match lasted 33 minutes and went to a decision with a clear winner: "I delivered well over 300 head butts," remembered Severn. "Now they weren't big, whompaloozas—small ones here, small ones there—but that man's skull swelled up so much. Within 15 minutes of that match, they took him to the hospital. I think I took like two or three ibuprofen."

Severn won the largest purse since the first UFC: $150,000. "He was unbelievable that night," said Art Davie. "I meant it when I said to him, 'My God, you blew me away.'" Neither street brawler Tank Abbott nor sambo champion Oleg Taktarov could do anything to Severn, once again proving that wrestling was as much a martial art as anything else. The Beast had made a tremendous comeback. Soon he would face his nemesis, Ken Shamrock, one more time. Unfortunately the UFC was dealt another blow as the pay-per-view ran over its allotted time limit again and pay-per-view buys slipped to 154,167.

◆ ◆ ◆

SEG DECIDED TO TAKE UFC VIII to the Caribbean island of Puerto Rico— and unexpectedly ran into a political war. By the time of the Puerto Rico event, McCain was moving in for the kill. He and Colorado senator Ben Nighthorse Campbell led a determined crusade to destroy the sport, and urged Governor Pedro Rossello of Puerto Rico to stop the UFC from taking place in his territory. The national press was there in force for the first time too, sensing a story amid the palms and balmy beaches of the holiday isle. They reported that the government of Puerto Rico concurred with McCain that the event had "no place in a civilized society." "We had been approved and came into town and the Minister of Sport at the last minute decided that we might not be able to do it there and that this was something the Commonwealth of Puerto Rico would not want to do," said Art Davie. SEG's lawyers fought back, contending that the authorities could not stop the event because they had no regulations governing such fights. While arguing in court, Bob Meyrowitz got word that Cablevision had dropped the event just days before it was to take place. This enraged Meyrowitz. "He got pissed off and spent $10,000 on a spur-of-the-moment full-page ad in New York's *Newsday* lambasting Cablevision and its chairman, Jim Dolan," said Elaine McCarthy. "He put in [Dolan's] personal phone number. 'Tell Them You Want Your UFC' was what I think the headline was. Bob was pissed, and the guy had to have his phone number changed." The ad prompted people to call Dolan and demand the UFC be put back in the lineup.

The SEG legal team spent days trying to convince a district court judge, who finally gave approval one day before showtime. The show was on. Delivering his last hurrah, producer Campbell McLaren devised the theme: David and Goliath. He had always loved the Emmanuel Yarbrough–Keith Hackney fight from UFC III and felt that a tournament with big guys against small guys would be a surefire hit. Campbell would move on to other SEG projects after this show.

A new cast of characters entered the UFC for the first time. Tank Abbott brought in fellow troublemaker Paul Herrera, a high school coach with a solid wrestling background. Gary Goodridge had won the Yukon Jack World Arm Wrestling Championships and was interested in competing; Art Davie had seen him arm wrestle on television and didn't deliberate long about putting him in the show. Goodridge was a muscular, bald, mean-looking native of Barrie, Canada, who definitely fit the bill. Obviously, the 6'8" Paul Varelans was a shoo-in. And some believed that Joe Moreira, a Reylson Gracie student, would be the next big jiu-jitsu fighter to rock the event.

Though he faced Kimo Leopoldo in the superfight, Ken Shamrock brought in his first protégé to compete in the show. Just as the Gracies had their family, Ken had the Lion's Den, a submission fighting school that grew from the need to find suitable training partners for Shamrock. Enter Californian Jerry Bohlander, a former high school wrestler who was going through a tough time of working long shifts to feed his sisters and disabled mother. "I had a lot of pent-up aggression," said Bohlander, who got into numerous street fights as his form of release. When a friend turned him on to the UFC, Bohlander fell in love. He was especially fascinated with Shamrock, whom he sought out in California. Bohlander took self-defense classes from Shamrock for three months, before the UFC veteran asked him to try out for the Lion's Den. The tryouts were grueling, a crazy mixture of sparring, resistance running (carrying a guy your own weight on your back and running 160 yards), 200 squats, and, after everything else, pull-ups. Buckets were on hand for trialists to throw up in—and then carry on. Bohlander made it through the ordeal the first time out and was more than honored when his mentor asked him to fight. "I was a poor kid and didn't have anything. I almost cried, and I had a lump in my throat that I was the first one he asked to fight, to represent the Lion's Den." With only six months of training, the 21-year-old would be part of the sport he once watched with his friends.

Scott "The Pitbull" Ferrozzo was a 350-pound juggernaut who became a wealthy man selling collectible 1950s toy robots. When a collector spent over $60,000 and Ferrozzo found out he had pay-per-view ties, a few phone calls were made and he was in the show. Billed as a "pit fighter" (another Art Davie creation), Ferrozzo was a larger Tank Abbott: his tattoo-laden body featured a pit bull, stemming from a nickname he'd earned while playing college football. "In the Citrus Bowl, they have it on film where I'm ripping the quarterback's head from his neck," said Ferrozzo. "I've got his head twisted all the way around, and I'm screaming at him, 'Don't get up!'" Aside from football, he boasted a record of 117–7 in high school wrestling. Remembering his violent, steroid-induced days from school, Ferrozzo wanted to see if he still had what it took. "I saw it as the ultimate in one-on-one competition and was drawn to it right away."

Arizona native Don Frye was another newcomer: imagine a muscled-up Tom Selleck. Frye had wrestled for Oklahoma State and Arizona State University, where he trained under the tutelage of coach Dan Severn. He worked as a firefighter for six years and competed in pro boxing, but after compiling a 5–2–1 record, he decided to call it quits. After taking up judo,

Frye saw his old coach in the UFC and ventured to Wyoming to see him lose to Ken Shamrock. The two hooked up, and Frye became Severn's training partner for UU '95. Frye fought in several underground matches, one of which was held in an Atlanta dojo, to familiarize himself with mixed martial arts. (These shows became known as the Atlanta Underground; Ferrozzo coincidently fought in one of these shows to know what he was getting himself into.) Severn's new management team of lawyer Robert DePersia and trainer Richard Hamilton eventually took Frye on as their new "hot" property, and he earned a slot in the tournament. Around home, Frye was often called J.R., short for junior, but that wouldn't work for the UFC. While joking about "The Beast," Frye came up with "The Predator." It seemed like each fighter had to have a moniker that outdid the others. Though he didn't have as strong a wrestling background as Severn, Frye knew how to punch and was well aware of submissions from working with female judo teacher Becky Levi. That said, Frye was the next MMA fighter to adopt using the modified kenpo gloves as Tank Abbott had done before him.

In the UFC, no one wants the status of hometown favorite because they never seem to do well. Puerto Rican Thomas Ramirez, whom Keith Hackney had beaten to compete in UFC III, made his debut against Don Frye in the opening round. Ramirez looked out of shape but was marketed as having won over 200 challenge matches. He became a 10-second, one-punch casualty for Frye, who didn't even break a sweat. Joe Moreira's highly touted background didn't help either as he ran from Paul Varelans, who won a boring, one-sided match by decision. Scott Ferrozzo vs. Jerry Bohlander was another story. The massive Ferrozzo controlled the Lion's Den member for much of the bout. Both landed some hard shots, but stamina proved to be the key. With 52 seconds left, a gassed Ferrozzo held his head down around Bohlander's waist, allowing the smaller man to get him in a guillotine choke. "I panicked and didn't know what to do," said Ferrozzo, who tapped out.

The most spectacular fight of the night was the quarterfinal between Gary Goodridge and Paul Herrera. Goodridge had a boxing background but no formal martial arts experience. His only preparation had been sparring with heavyweight friends. When word of his UFC entry spread around Canada, Goodridge met up with a martial arts master skilled in *kuk sool won*, who made an interesting proposition: "We'll give you a fourth-degree black belt and buy you a gi if you represent our school." The arm wrestler accepted the offer and went to three classes but knew he was far from ready to compete. Two weeks prior to the fight, he started training with a collegiate wrestler. The only submission he learned was a maneuver called a goose neck (the legs trap one arm and the attacker's arms lock out the other, turning the victim into a human crucifix).

When Goodridge showed up in Puerto Rico, he heard rumors that Herrera was a racist (though Herrera dismissed the notion). "I got all worked up that no matter what, I was not going to lose to him," said Goodridge. He sent two of his training partners to watch the wrestler work out for a video segment used in the event's promotion. When they came back, they told Goodridge that Herrera shot in with a double leg the same way, every single time. So Goodridge remained still when their match started, and sure enough Herrera took the bait. Goodridge, in his black gi, trapped Herrera's arm and fell into the perfect position to submit him. Instead, he pounded Herrera's exposed head with eight power-bomb elbows to the face and temple, knocking him out in just 13 seconds.

Both Goodridge and Frye made it to the finals after taking out their semifinal opponents. The arm wrestler was just too powerful for Jerry Bohlander, who took a lot of punishment before referee John McCarthy stopped the fight. Frye had another easy round against the injured Varelans replacement, boxer Sam Adkins. Adkins looked intimidating but couldn't stop Frye's takedown and subsequent strikes, leading to a quick tap out.

Goodridge and Frye fought a short but memorable seesaw final. Goodridge threw Frye around with ease but took some dizzying punches in the process. In just under five minutes, the Predator finally gained an advantage on the ground, and, after a couple of shots, Goodridge was done. David had beaten Goliath. "At the elite level, it is still the skill level that really dictates what goes on inside the Octagon," said commentator

Jeff Blatnick. UFC VIII proved that a person's physical attributes weighed heavier than black belt status; the black belts (at least those who really had black belts) were growing thin.

Shamrock and Kimo both had similar builds. Each had failed to beat Royce Gracie, and each had something to prove for the superfight title. Shamrock had to show that the draws to Gracie and Taktarov could be balanced by strong wins like the one against Severn, while Kimo had trained with Matt Hume at AMC Pankration in Seattle to ready himself. As the match began, the Hawaiian ran across the cage in typical fashion toward Shamrock, who took him immediately to the mat and gained side control. Shamrock worked to a mount position, landed a punch, and forced Kimo to his stomach but didn't go for the obvious choke. The temperature inside the venue was a blistering 100 degrees, and he felt the move would be too risky, seeing how he could slip right off his sweaty opponent. Kimo eventually overpowered him and sat in Shamrock's guard. "I know that Kimo likes to pyramid up and open for a punch," said Shamrock later. "He caught me with one, but he also opened himself up for me to go for the leg." Shamrock swung under like a pendulum and, after missing the first time, was able to get the knee bar. Kimo tried to work out of it, but leg locks were Shamrock's specialty. Kimo tapped out at 4:24. The tattooed, religious zealot had suffered his second UFC defeat. "I was disappointed in AMC that they didn't train me in [leg locks]," recalled Kimo.

The night would not have been complete without another intrusion by Tank Abbott. Infuriated that his friend Paul Herrera had lost in such a devastating manner, Tank needed little prodding to be drawn into a fight. Moving out into the audience, the pitfighter noticed a vaguely familiar face in Brazilian Allan Goes. Before he had entered the UFC, the burly bad boy and his crew had visited Goes's dojo in California to study jiu-jitsu for a day. Goes, a Carlson Gracie disciple, had little trouble tapping out everyone and was rumored to be bragging about it at the show. Elaine McCarthy sat behind Tank, his girlfriend Andrea, and manager Dave Thomas. "Here, hold my teeth," Tank said to his girlfriend as he made his way toward Goes. According to Elaine, Andrea was egging Tank on to punish the Brazilian. That was the last thing SEG needed; they had fought tooth and nail to get permission to hold the show in Puerto Rico and didn't need any bad publicity.

Tank got off one hit as Goes buried his head into his attacker's chest. The two were eventually pulled apart. Goes later admitted he was partly to blame; he was frustrated and angry at seeing his friend Joe Moreira lose. "Why did you do that when you know we are already in trouble?" Elaine asked Andrea. When Tank walked back toward his girlfriend, Andrea pointed toward Elaine and indicated she had insulted her. Tank marched up to Elaine, got in her face, and said, "I will kill you, you fucking whore. You don't talk to me or anyone associated with me like that." A tearful Elaine went to Bob Meyrowitz and told him that if Tank wasn't fired, she and her husband John wouldn't be returning. "You like him and I know that, and you think he's important for your thing and that's fine, but I'm not doing anything else as long as he's around," said John McCarthy. The Lion's Den came to Elaine's aid and looked for Tank, but he was long gone, reportedly making more trouble at a Hard Rock Cafe nearby. Meyrowitz called Abbott and told him to take some paid time off. Art Davie devised a "suspension" smoke screen, using the skirmish with Goes as the reason, but SEG could not afford to lose their referee and one of their most valuable team players. Tank would not return until UFC XI. Though Puerto Rican officials never found out about the Tank matter, that didn't stop the private hospital that SEG booked to take care of fighter injuries from refusing service. "They decided they didn't want to deal with the fighters, so we had to move them to a public hospital at 2:00 AM early Sunday morning in San Juan," said McCarthy.

◆ ◆ ◆

IN A DEPARTURE FROM PREVIOUS EVENTS, SEG opted for a night of single matchups for UFC IX. That would not be the only difference. Meyrowitz, McCarthy, and a team of lawyers were battling with the Michigan district attorney, who was trying to prevent SEG from holding the event in Detroit. They were still in court at 4:30 PM on the day of the event, when the judge issued an ultimatum: the fights could go on as long as there were no headbutts and no closed-fist strikes to the head. Meyrowitz caved in. "We had become an easy target for these small-time politicians who were looking for free publicity," he said. McCarthy looked puzzled, as the two rules were implemented just hours before the fights started, but was reassured that, if breached, they would be only "minor" infractions. Any guilty fighter would receive a $50 fine, but, with a wink and a nod, everyone knew it was business as usual.

It was a small victory for the UFC, but they were losing the political war. Governor Rossello had vowed publicly that no UFC event would ever again take place in Puerto Rico. Ohio and South Carolina joined Kansas, Mississippi, and Oklahoma, reportedly banning the event, as did the Chicago City Council. "From the 'inside,' I can tell you, the pressure was enormous because we knew that the sport and our business's viability hinged on our getting each event off and on pay-per-view as planned."

The sport was even sent up in an issue of the satirical magazine *MAD*; its perceived high body count and bloody carnage filled the seven-page spread. UFC fighters Dan Severn, Royce Gracie, Kimo, and Ken Shamrock became Dan Septic, Royce Gravy, Chemo, and Ken Wayne Amtrak. Even Campbell McLaren (also known as Marky D. Sodd) was drawn into the piece—and subsequently bought the rights to the artwork.

A very powerful ally joined the opposition. In the run-up to Detroit, Lonnie Bristow, president of the American Medical Association, issued a ferocious statement decrying "these brutal and repugnant contests." He went on:

> Far from being legitimate sports events, ultimate fighting contests are little more than human cockfights where human gladiators battle bare-knuckled until one gives up, passes out, or the carnage is stopped by a doctor or referee. The rules are designed to increase the danger to fighters and to promote injury rather than prevent it.

The AMA is opposed to boxing in general as a sport in which the primary objective is to impose injury, and has worked to eliminate both amateur and professional boxing. Ultimate fighting contests are even more physically dangerous and morally abhorrent, and it is the opinion of the AMA that these blood-filled brawls should be banned immediately.

The AMA had already provided expert testimony in legal actions to stop the UFC, and Bristow said it would continue to "support state legislatures and city officials seeking to ban these brutal and barbaric contests which are being dispensed to the public as blood-soaked, crude public spectacles."

His widely reported outburst served only to enhance the curiosity value of the event and caused a run on tickets for the 11,000-seat Cobo Arena. The venue owners admitted it was "not exactly *Sesame Street Live*" but promised "a real exciting evening." They were not entirely correct. Dan Severn's second chance at beating Ken Shamrock highlighted an otherwise hit-and-miss card. Canadian Gary Goodridge was supposed to fight countryman David Beneteau, who had managed to slip through the medicals with ease with a broken hand. According to Beneteau, he was "ratted out" and disqualified before the fight. Davie and McLaren needed an immediate replacement and couldn't think of a better choice than 1994 Olympic gold medalist wrestler Mark Schultz, who accompanied Beneteau as his cornerman. Davie courted Schultz for four hours one night the week of the event, but the wrestler had reservations. He was in shape, but he hadn't trained for anything like this before. He didn't even have his wrestling singlet, just a toothbrush and shower shoes. But after taking the mandatory AIDS test, Schultz agreed to fight—for $50,000.

Just before the match with Goodridge began, McCarthy walked over to Schultz with a word of advice: "Try to hit him with open palms as much as you can." No one could ever doubt a wrestler's abilities again as Schultz, who was giving up 40 pounds to his opponent, took Goodridge down seconds into the match. Though he knew little about submission,

Schultz controlled Goodridge the entire time, and during the latter stages of the 12-minute bout he connected with several hard punches to the face. "Open hands! Open hands!" yelled McCarthy, but the wrestler paid no attention and beat Goodridge over and over. After several stoppages to check Goodridge's bloody mug, McCarthy finally put an end to his suffering at 12:00.

Reigning jiu-jitsu champion Amaury Bitetti replaced fellow Brazilian Marco Ruas to face Don Frye. "Because of my interview, the Ultimate Ultimate ended up running over," said Frederico Lapenda. "My relationship was really bad with the UFC, and then they invited Ruas to come back and fight Frye, but they gave a ridiculous offer. They were angry with me, because in a way, they lost money with me, so Ruas was done with the UFC." Weight was a major factor for Bitetti, as Frye was 15 pounds heavier. Though Bitetti came out aggressively, he was unable to take Frye down. While grabbing a standing fighter above the waist and forcing him to the mat is standard for a jiu-jitsu stylist, the tactic rarely worked against a seasoned wrestler. Wrestlers have great balance, and if one isn't trying to work an opponent's center of gravity (abdomen), it is very difficult to take him down. Frye chose to stay on his feet and dictated the fight against a man who could not outgrapple him. That was the least of Bitetti's problems. After tying up for the first minute, and a brief exchange, Frye battered Bitetti with punches and knees. The resilient Brazilian bounced back and even tried to take Frye down again, but the wrestler sprawled and outpositioned him on the mat. With barely two and half minutes left, Frye opened up more knees to Bitetti's head on the ground, and McCarthy finally stepped in to stop the punishment at 9:30. Bleeding and bruised, the jiu-jitsu champion had learned an important lesson.

Aside from a small circle "in the know," no one knew that closed-fist strikes were illegal for this event. "I was not going to fight," said Shamrock, who had Meyrowitz, David Isaacs, and his own father trying to convince him otherwise. "I was nowhere near confident that I could beat Dan. I didn't have the skills that night because my body and mind were messed up." In training for the fight, wrestler/bodybuilder Mike Radnov accidentally broke Shamrock's nose, and he had two bruised ribs and a dislocated knee to add to his problems. But the boys from his adoptive father's home for troubled teens would be watching, and *Sports Illustrated* was there to do a story on him. If he played his cards right, Shamrock was going to be on the cover of *Sports Illustrated* and be featured on *CNN Sports*. "Ken, you've broken Kazuo Takahashi's cheek [in Pancrase], and you've broken his jaw and nose with an open hand, so you don't need to close your fist," said Bob Shamrock. "So don't worry about any business decision that SEG makes; just don't do any headbutts, because you don't do that." It was not that simple. Shamrock had made up his mind but reluctantly gave in to the pressure to help out the show. The cancellation of his fight could have done substantial monetary damage to SEG.

Boos from Dan Severn's hometown Michigan crowd brought Shamrock's confidence down even further, but he made good on his word. Fighting was optional, however. When Shamrock's problem with the rules got back to Severn, he devised a plan to throw him off his game. Severn went out and bought a pair of boxing gloves, showing he intended to punch. And for 31 minutes, the fight that would be dubbed "The Great Dance" saw neither man make a move on the other. For the first 15 minutes, Severn walked around Shamrock without a punch thrown. "I took to the center of the ring understanding that I was going to be fighting for my life, and Dan never came at me," said Shamrock. While both men agree that it was one of the most boring fights in UFC history, Severn said in an interview in 2000: "the greatest psychological match ever." After the two finally tied up and went to the ground, Shamrock had one chance for a rear naked choke. "My leg was locking out," he said later, "and if you watch the fight closely, you'll see that I had one hook in, and I couldn't get in the other because my leg got locked out. That's when I lost the back mount." Shamrock lost the top position, then got hit a couple of times and started to bleed. The crowd went from hating

Shamrock to plain hating the fight. Rorion Gracie, watching from home, shook his head in disgust.

The result was a decision, one Severn knew in his heart he was going to lose; after all, Shamrock was their star. But the Beast's hand was raised. Severn had redeemed himself against Shamrock, but the match cost SEG millions. Their next event saw a 33 percent drop in viewership—the lowest since UFC III. "Ken lost his focus on the wrong thing," said Bob Shamrock, who was upset by his son's performance. "I didn't even stay for the party; I just went upstairs, grabbed my things, and got on a plane and went home." The two didn't talk for a week. Shamrock had missed his chance to shine. There would be no *Sports Illustrated* article or *CNN Sports* segment. To this day, Shamrock and Severn do not like one another. "As far as I am concerned, Ken Shamrock cannot hold my jock strap," said Severn. "And I'll bash that guy any time I get an opportunity just because I do not like what he represents." Shamrock's retort was more simplistic: "I don't like him either, and I really don't know why. There's just something about him."

Two months after the event, the governor of Illinois signed legislation prohibiting "ultimate fighting" exhibitions. Another state had gone. SEG had also lost faith in Shamrock, who was able to garner the highest buy rate of 189,532 since UFC VI. He would skip two shows before making his return. And the company dropped superfights for three consecutive shows. They couldn't afford any more debacles because the UFC was no longer the only show in town.

11

EXTREME
COMPETITION

O thers were bound to cash in on the success of the UFC eventually. Christopher Peters, the 26-year-old son of heavyweight producer Jon Peters, created the first similar event of any note. One month after UFC VII, his World Combat Championship (WCC) made its debut on pay-per-view on October 17, 1995. Peters was an avid martial arts fan and had approached both Rorion Gracie and Art Davie about doing a show in 1994. When that fell through, he pulled the finances together to produce the million-dollar WCC before a 6,000-plus crowd in Winston Salem, North Carolina. Martial artist Bob Wall helped Peters secure several fighters, including K-1 (Japan's premier kickboxing organization) stars Peter Aerts and Sam Greco. When K-1 realized what was going to take place, they pulled both from the show. That didn't seem to bother Peters, who desperately wanted to have a Gracie on the card. At one point, things looked promising for Rickson to make his debut, but money became an obstacle. Looking through *Black Belt* magazine, Peters found an ad for Renzo Gracie, cousin to Royce. Touting a $120,000 grand prize, it was easy to get him onboard.

UFC event coordinator Kathy Kidd joined Peters and the WCC after SEG had taken over for WOW. Though she had once dated Art Davie, she soon found herself dating then-*Black Belt* magazine executive editor Jim Coleman, who had been more than critical of the UFC and never gave it any respect. "Because I was dating him, I was always talking about [World Combat Championship] and was a fan of the sport, and I think

I was able to change his opinion and turn him around a little bit," said Kidd. In the October 1995 issue, the cover of *Black Belt* was American Bart Vale facing off against Renzo Gracie with an "all of the sudden" very positive preview for the show. Whatever the reason for Coleman's actions, Peters seemed sincere in his attempt to turn a spectacle into a sport. He used *Black Belt* as his sounding board, not realizing that Kidd and Coleman were more than just friends.

WCC boasted great production values and some exciting matches, but Peters didn't want to copy the UFC; he wanted to add his own twist. He set up the tournament so that strikers fought strikers and grapplers faced grapplers until the final match. "It was so unfair to the strikers," said Peters. "It was a stupid mistake, and I would be the first one to admit that." The tournament showcased decent talent like former IBF world cruiserweight boxing champion James Warring and three-time Olympic judo competitor Ben Spikjers. As for Bart Vale, he was a better marketer than fighter whose reputation was based on fighting worked and stiff-worked bouts in Japan. "I didn't know about any of that," said Peters. "As far as I knew, this was some legendary guy." After defeating Mike Bitonio in a gutsy battle, Vale had to withdraw due to injuries.

Erik Paulson was something of an unknown but had spent a lifetime in the martial arts. He had also been the first American to compete in the Japanese-based Shooto organization prior to the UFC in 1993. Paulson had trained with the Gracies in Rorion's garage and trained in Japan with real shooters, but Peters put the man who claimed Jeet Kune Do in with the strikers. "The strikers were the most beat up compared to the grapplers because all we could do was beat the shit out of each other," said Paulson. "I remember them standing me up saying I was going for a submission; the ref didn't know what he was watching." To add insult to injury, Paulson came out with his blonde hair in a ponytail when pulling hair certainly wasn't illegal. Paulson was also a part-time stuntman and was told not to cut his hair because he was getting a considerable payday to play a Viking heavy in a movie right after the fight. He tried to tie it up the best he could, but it only gave his opponents another weapon to use against him. "The first chance he got, Sean McCully grabbed my ponytail and used it as leverage to headbutt me," said Paulson, who would eventually TKO McCully. "Then James Warring got his fingers stuck into my hair. And I was just like, 'Come on man, you're 60 pounds heavier! Do you really have to grab my hair to beat me?' He took advantage of my stupidity." Paulson lost to Warring after 16 blistering minutes by TKO; when he returned home he found out the part that cost him his performance had now been given to someone else. Renzo Gracie easily swept the four-man tournament of grapplers—quickly submitting both—and tapped out Warring via choke in under three minutes. Gracie went a little far against first-round grappler Ben Spijkers—he stepped on his neck getting back to his feet. Spijkers had played a bunch of games before their fight said Peters and had talked trash about Gracie and his family, a move that didn't pay off.

According to Peters, the show made money and the sequel, "WCC 2: Meltdown in Mexico," was set to play out the following March. Strangely, the wife of the show's investor threatened divorce if he put in another dime, so the funding went out the door. With politics making things difficult, Peters folded up shop. He would later form Christopher Peters Entertainment and currently produces and distributes films. Kathy Kidd, along with former UFC scribe Clay McBride, had served as judges for the show. After breaking it off with Coleman, she would later marry Art Davie; it lasted only a year. Throughout 1996 and 1997 in a column called "Notes on a Tournament Format," Coleman would lambaste every UFC and MMA in general, sometimes leaving a paragraph to personally vent about Kidd. "He was an unhappy guy and that was his way to strike back, which was kind of silly," said Kidd. "At one point, I told him I would get an attorney to get him to stop." Coleman would be replaced with Robert Young in January 1998; Kidd is still on very good terms with Art Davie even today.

◆ ◆ ◆

PETERS MAY HAVE BEEN UNSUCCESSFUL in sustaining the WCC, but he wouldn't be the only one to try. Enter Donald Zuckerman—lawyer, boxing manager, musical talent manager (remember the group Scandal?), and former owner of the popular New York nightclub The Ritz. By 1993, several months before the inaugural UFC event, he was searching for a new avenue to flex his creative muscle. He dabbled in film production until a friend in the industry showed him a tape of some vale tudo fights, much as *Gracies in Action* had been shown to SEG. The idea was to make a film out of it, but Zuckerman felt it should be a fight show. Once described by the *Los Angeles Times* as "a raconteur...hot after bicoastal opportunities with a phone pressed to his ear," Zuckerman had connections inside the television sports networks ESPN2 and Fox International. He assembled all his money-making ducks in a row; all he needed was funds to produce the show itself. He went to Polygram and secured a deal with his friend John Sher, who headed up one of the corporation's production arms. Sher agreed to be a deficit financier to enable Polygram to pay for the show; Zuckerman would get his cut upfront and by selling video rights on the back end.

A deal was inked in April 1994 for the show to go into production just after Sher pulled off his brainchild, Woodstock II. However, when the budget of $19 million turned to $45 million for the outdoor concert—which also deteriorated into near-riot—Sher was fired, Polygram was out of the picture, and Zuckerman was left to start from scratch. The lawyer turned to a very unlikely alternative: Bob Guccione, the man who created the soft-porn *Penthouse* magazine and subsequently ran that company's parent entity, General Media Inc. The wealthy Guccione agreed to put up $750,000 and brought in his son Anthony to aid Zuckerman in running the new sister company, called Battlecade Inc. (The *Penthouse* connection was no surprise: in a 1979 issue of *Hustler* magazine, Benny "The Jet" Urquidez was featured in a lengthy article entitled "The Baddest Dude in the World"; 10 years later, Rorion Gracie received a similar treatment in *Playboy*. It's hard to believe, but true, that skin magazines brought more press to these two men than any martial arts rag, and that *Playboy* sparked the all-important union between Art Davie, Gracie, and SEG.)

Zuckerman didn't know much about martial arts, or at least not enough to produce a show comparable to the UFC. He had been trying to pull together facts and figures about this type of show, and word around town said Gene LeBell was the man in the know. LeBell was a two-time Amateur Athletic Union judo champion, but he was known more as a pro wrestler and Hollywood stuntman. His martial arts pedigree stressed groundfighting over stand-up techniques, and his knowledge of submission holds became legendary. After several discussions with LeBell, Zuckerman was introduced to one of his students, John Perretti, who he invited to be the matchmaker and on-air commentator for Extreme Fighting, the name of Battlecade's promotion. Perretti, a lifelong martial artist, accepted the offer. He had studied tae kwon do, tang soo do, and other Korean forms before moving on to wing chun kung fu, which he'd studied for 16 years. Perretti eventually moved into various competitions ranging from wushu (kung fu forms competition) to full-contact karate (he even fought Howard Jackson, who was ranked No. 10 in the world). After studying boxing, Perretti's thirst for martial arts wisdom took him to LeBell, "who unceremoniously convinced me that I knew nothing about fighting." He studied under LeBell and then moved on to other grapplers including the Machado family, cousins to the Gracies. Perretti held the veteran in such high regard that LeBell became the middle name of his first-born son.

With General Media's money, Zuckerman and Perretti were set to promote Battlecade's Extreme Fighting in New York on November 18, 1995, at the Park Slope Armory in Brooklyn. Pitching for the Big Apple was a bold move. Roy Goodman, member of the New York State Senate, held an eventual press conference to rally support for shutting the event down, but Zuckerman was quick to follow him, made the press laugh, and got some good press out of it. But he didn't stop there. "We were doing everything we could to drum up as much press as possible because we figured this was our debut, and just like the [UFC] was marketing that someone may die, we were trying to, in essence, do the same thing," said Zuckerman. "We even had pickets at our press conference; they didn't know they were working for us, but they were. We paid a bunch of kids to hold up signs saying that someone was going to die and to stop this now and that type of thing." The forced negative publicity may have worked a little too well.

Though Zuckerman's team ended up winning a court case that gave them permission to go ahead in the state of New York, it had become a risky endeavor. "Our lawyer said that no matter where we went in New York, the police were going to take it very seriously and close us down," said Zuckerman. Just two days before the show was due to take place, it seemed Zuckerman's own marketing ploys had pushed him into a corner. He had little choice but to change sites.

The plan was to move the show to North Carolina, which was becoming a prime site for the fledgling sport. Though a law had been passed to ban MMA in that state, it wouldn't come into effect for another month. The sellout crowd in Brooklyn was dumped and tickets were given away to fill up the North Carolina venue. With very little time to prepare, Zuckerman remembered an old client, film producer Dino De Laurentis, who had once built a sound stage there. The person who ran the sound stage just happened to be a martial artist and welcomed Extreme Fighting with open arms. "On Friday morning, we decided that we were going down there," remembered Zuckerman. "We sent everybody by plane, and the trucks started rolling since all of the equipment was still in New York. The morning of the show, everybody started to set everything up and we just made showtime." The entire production was moved from New York to North Carolina in just 36 hours. It would certainly not be the last chapter in the story of MMA in New York.

◆ ◆ ◆

A NEW GROUP OF WARRIORS was ready to battle in the larger, circular cage of Extreme Fighting. John Lewis was a former break dancer who grew up in Hawaii and quickly learned that "the culture was very much streetfighting oriented." He began studying martial arts because he wanted to test his skills against better opponents. Measuring 5'11" and weighing 159 pounds, Lewis had tattoos running from the neck down, accentuating his unbelievably sculpted physique. He eventually set up mats in his backyard and fought or trained anyone who was interested. "I would always get different guys in there from different arts to see how I would fare against them, and that's how I met John Perretti," said Lewis. After sparring with Perretti in his backyard in 1991, Lewis was introduced to Gene LeBell and became his first black belt. He eventually fought in his first official MMA match in a Hawaiian event called United Full Contact Fighting. With Perretti and LeBell in his corner, Lewis won by arm bar at 1:45. That took place just two months before the first Extreme Fighting show, and Perretti used four of its fighters in his events.

Having worked with the Machados, Perretti was well aware of the Gracies and hooked up with Frederico Lapenda, who managed several Carlson Gracie students who were ready to fight. Mario Sperry was a 1995 Brazilian jiu-jitsu champion, Carlson Gracie Jr. was a 10-time Brazilian jiu-jitsu champion, and Marcus "Conan" Silveira was a menacing, 6'3", 245-pound Brazilian specimen. Silveira started judo at the age of eight and, after five years, moved on to jiu-jitsu under Carlson in Brazil: "Carlson taught more than just the fundamentals of jiu-jitsu; he brought us the knowledge of being in a street fight with technique." Silveira moved to the United States in 1989 and, though he had never fought professionally, opened up a jiu-jitsu school in 1993. He was ready to test himself. Carlson gave him the nickname Conan, and he rarely went by anything else after his first professional appearance.

Perretti also found another Gracie in San Francisco: Ralph, brother of Renzo. And just as the UFC had Oleg Taktarov, Perretti had Igor Zinoviev, who had emigrated from St. Petersburg to Brooklyn in 1992 purely by accident: Zinoviev was supposed to meet a business contact in America, but when he didn't show up at the airport, Zinoviev ran into a fellow Russian, who showed him around town. He has lived in the U.S. ever since. His background in judo and sambo helped him win the heavyweight judo championship in the Empire State Games in 1995 and 1996. When a friend introduced him to Perretti, Zinoviev became his student in kickboxing and subsequently started to learn better groundfighting.

Perretti's talent as matchmaker stemmed from his varied martial arts experience and understanding of fighters as opposed to guys with black belts. "When I watched the UFC, I was laughing as I listened to these people talk about things they had no idea about," he said. He also didn't think much of Art Davie's matchmaking. Davie's criteria was, "How much do you weigh?" Extreme Fighting had decent talent, partly because it learned from the UFC's mistakes about putting in black belts who didn't know how to fight.

The action inside the circular cage, which had similar rules to the UFC, was more sport than spectacle, but with the tagline "Whatever it Takes to Win!" and pneumatic Penthouse Pets roaming the audience, there was more than a hint of the Roman Coliseum. Muscular television and film celebrity Mr. T fielded questions backstage, his ignorance of the sport and cartoonish persona seeming in direct contrast to what Perretti was trying to project. One difference from the UFC was major: instead of an eight-man tournament, there would be two four-man tourneys broken down by weight class.

The first show was a lively mix of striking, controversy, and competitive matches. Ralph Gracie started things off by quickly choking out Japanese karate player Makoto Murako, who was in midtap as he slipped into unconsciousness. Igor Zinoviev also looked impressive, knocking the wind out of Harold German with a hopping sidekick; after missing a knee bar, he punched German in the head more than a dozen times before tapping him out. Mario Sperry, who came in with an unverifiable fighting record of 272–0, finished Rudyard Moncayo with strikes, just as Silveira won his match over Zinoviev protégé Victor Tatarkin.

Silveira won the heavyweight tourney by beating wrestler Gary Myers by choke, despite a cut over his right eye that almost gave his opponent the win. The middleweight final was more competitive as Mario Sperry took on judo champ Igor Zinoviev. Within 40 seconds, the Brazilian took Zinoviev down and established side control—but not for long. The two volleyed for position, with Zinoviev even catching Sperry in a guillotine choke. Sperry broke free, but he couldn't break the Russian's iron grip.

The two eventually rose back to their feet against the fence, with Sperry behind Zinoviev. The Russian had entered the event with broken ribs, and his breathing became a factor.

With three and a half minutes left in overtime, Sperry leaped on Zinoviev's back to sink in a rear naked choke, but the Russian countered by ducking. Now Sperry was in front of him on the ground...a very bad position. Sperry caught a knee to the face but took Zinoviev down again. The fight stopped moments later when Sperry, with a huge gash over his forehead, tapped the mat once, though he was only wiping the blood away. Sperry didn't complain about referee Gokor Chivichyan's decision because of the rules. "Before the show, it was said that any cuts over the eyes would finish the fight," said Sperry. He felt the match could have continued, but when he got to his corner, he realized the cut was too severe (requiring 13 stitches).

Zinoviev became Extreme Fighting's first middleweight champion. Sperry's record was allegedly now 273–1, although Perretti said later the largely undefeated record was actually Carlson's idea. Records showed Sperry competing in one previous match, so his hundreds of wins were most likely in jiu-jitsu, if indeed they existed. Conan Silveira also had claimed a record of 17–0 when this was actually his first fighting experience. It's a gamble to pad résumés, and the show strained credibility by saying Rudyard Moncayo was 7–0 when he had just lost in UFC VI to Pat Smith.

As Carlson Gracie Jr., known as the "Prince of Jiu-jitsu," stepped up to face John Lewis in a superfight, he probably expected a quick match. Lewis trained with jiu-jitsu practitioner Andre Pederneiras and would be competing in his second MMA match but faced a more skilled opponent. Gracie mounted an aggressive attack but had difficulty controlling Lewis. At one point he got the takedown, but Lewis pulled guard and kicked him back with his tremendous grasshopper legs. Lewis returned with furious strikes while Gracie wanted the action to return to the mat. Working back to his feet, the Brazilian wasted his energy grappling Lewis, who had his arm wrapped over the top of the fence. Gracie finally got his man down, but Lewis stayed right on him and unloaded more punches. When the 15-minute time limit ran out, a 5-minute overtime offered much of the same, with a clinched stalemate against the fence. The fight was ruled a draw. "A lot of people thought that I won that fight," said Lewis. "I was in control the entire time and he just kept me in his guard." Sperry's loss to Zinoviev and the Lewis/Gracie draw also began to raise doubts about the strength of jiu-jitsu as a style, compared to the skill of the fighter using it.

◆ ◆ ◆

ALTHOUGH THE FIRST SHOW LOST MONEY due to all the free tickets, the scantily clad women, harder-edge promotion, and decent fights made it a success with fans. Zuckerman didn't want to take any chances with the follow-up show. He came up with a plan to hold Extreme Fighting 2 on an Indian reservation to steer clear of the American court system altogether. After contacting several reservations without any luck, he received a call from kickboxing promoter Mike Thomas, who had been running small shows in Kahnawake, a Mohawk reservation in Quebec, Canada. Thomas was a member of the Mohawk tribe and saw the fighters as possessing a warrior spirit, something the Indians could identify with. He became the on-site promoter and made several trips to Quebec to keep the authorities informed of what the Mohawks were doing. "There were a lot of tricks that the province [of Quebec] was trying to pull," said Thomas. "The Mohawk Council said that they were going to stand by us, which they did."

Unfortunately, the French press in Quebec played up the violence of the show and forced the Canadian government to take the moral high road. Its first measure was to prevent participants from entering the country. "Immigration sent back nine of my fighters and my cameraman, producer, director, ring announcer, and others," said Perretti. Zuckerman hired a Canadian crew, but faced with the threat of arrest, they soon quit. "We ended up doing the fight with a very light crew, less than a third of what's needed," said Zuckerman. At least 27 people with the show were turned away at the border, and Perretti claimed that it wasn't entirely because of the Canadians: "And then Bob [Meyrowitz] or the UFC paid my fighters not to fight. I discovered all these guys, and then they got a hold of them and paid them more money than I could not to fight. Unbelievable!" Mike Thomas also learned that SEG's David Isaacs tried to rent out the same venue for the same night, an obvious attempt to block their competitors. The Mohawks would not go around Thomas, so EF stood its ground. Campbell McLaren said later that luring fighters away to compete in the UFC, and trying to gain access to the same venues, was just part of doing business and being competitive.

It was only the beginning. After spending all afternoon in court, the promoters were dealt a devastating blow when the Quebec government issued an injunction to stop Bell Canada from carrying the signal to the pay-per-view audience. Luckily for Zuckerman, they didn't enjoin anyone else. "I got an uplink truck to drive 200 miles at breakneck speed and arrive 30 minutes before the show, and we went right up to the AT&T satellite and did it ourselves," he said.

Zuckerman and Perretti stationed all the fighters in a hotel outside of Quebec to keep them out of the limelight and decrease the possibility of deportation. At the hotel, Zuckerman told the fighters not to leave any word as to where they were going—answering machine or otherwise. "If one person leaks this, we're fucked," said Perretti, those words captured from a never-released German documentary of the event. Fighter Steve Nelson said he didn't believe anything was wrong until the promoters made them switch hotels at one point. He was told that they would be fine on tribal land. The police couldn't do anything on the Indian reservation, but they could try to stop people from getting there. UFC II veteran Orlando Weit was scheduled to fight Igor Zinoviev, but the pressure nixed his participation on the card. In an interview conducted for the aforementioned documentary, Weit said, "It's not fair from the promoters' side because they didn't tell the fighters exactly what was going on." Shortly after, Weit and his wife left the hotel bound for Holland. Perretti, who had made exhaustive efforts to keep Weit at ease, fumed. "He totally chickened out, and he used us as an excuse for some political nonsense." He was the only fighter who refused to go on.

Unlike the first show, this one provided few surprises save for the opener between newcomers Nigel Scantelbury and Jason Canals. Both men fought their hearts out and performed a clinic of ground techniques before the bout was ruled a draw, and deservedly so. All of the veterans on the card faced relative fighting "newbies" with genuine martial arts credentials who didn't fare too well. Newly awarded jiu-jitsu black belt John Lewis quickly outpositioned AAU National Wrestling champ Jim Teachout, who tapped after several hard elbow strikes to the back of the head. Conan Silveira also continued his reign of terror by knocking the 5'8", 218-pound Carl Franks senseless at 1:17. Zinoviev was left without an opponent, but Perretti matched him against wing chun exponent Steve Faulkner, who was originally supposed to face wrestler Paul Jones. Zinoviev had hardly trained for Weit in the first place and now wanted an extra $25,000 to fight his new opponent, not knowing his strengths and weaknesses. The Russian slammed Faulkner to the mat and quickly gained a rear naked choke, forcing him to tap out. Zinoviev recalled that Faulkner told him he normally fought five on one, "so this should be easy." Before the show, a tape was shown of Faulkner sparring with multiple opponents. His moves were quick and complex. Against Zinoviev, he never got off a punch, kick, or block.

Steve Nelson had serious amateur wrestling accolades, including being a five-time national sambo champion from Amarillo, Texas. Both of his parents were notable wrestlers: Nelson's dad was Gordon "Mr. Wrestling" Nelson, and his mother was Marie LaVerne, a popular female pro wrestler in her time. After winning a fight at the WCC, Steve Nelson said before his EF match: "Tonight, I want to make sure that I walk out as the world champion so when I look back on this, I can say that I'm the best who ever was." After taking his back, Ralph Gracie finished him in just 43 seconds with 15 punches to the back of the head.

After their opponents were turned away at the airport, Canadians Carlos Newton and Jean Riviere fought each other in an incredible seven-minute-plus bout. Nineteen-year-old Newton wore a gi and weighed 180 pounds, but the promoters listed his weight as 205 pounds in an attempt to match them better on paper; Riviere weighed in at 286 pounds. Newton was nervous and became fatigued, but he gave Riviere all he could handle before tapping out from exhaustion.

With only six bouts, and just two of them lasting more than two minutes, the show did not make the required hour and 45 minutes needed to secure the pay-per-view two-hour block. Bob Guccione added vignettes with *Penthouse* models between matches, but it didn't make much difference. The skeleton crew and short fights made for a strained relationship between EF and the pay-per-view operators.

As the sellout crowd began to leave, there was an immense sigh of relief backstage that the show had managed to go on despite numerous obstacles. But the following night, the chief of the Mohawk Peacekeepers, in conjunction with the Quebec police, raided the hotel and made eight arrests. "They wanted to make it look like it was an Indian action," said Zuckerman. "The chief [of the Mohawks] betrayed us, although we don't know that for sure." The police had a list of whom they were going to arrest, though Mike Thomas and Zuckerman were spared. As Zuckerman recalled, Conan's brother Marcelo didn't take this very well. "His brother was three inches away from my face, telling me that if I didn't get him [Conan] out of jail tonight, I was a dead man. At one point I was going to have him arrested." The locked-up fighters would be more than okay though, as word had spread about these no-rules gladiators. The regulars behind bars were scared out of their minds, especially at the sight of Conan, who had two eyes tattooed on his back.

Other arrests were equally unpleasant. "The Texan [Steve Nelson] was in bed with his girlfriend, and they literally opened his door with a passkey and stood there and watched her dress," said Zuckerman. As Nelson was put in the squad car with Igor Zinoviev, Nelson's girlfriend said, "If these fighters had known that this was illegal, I know my boyfriend, for one, would have never fought." Nelson was miffed over believing he was okay to participate in the event in the first place. "We spent two days in jail, and *Penthouse* got us out with charges dropped and gave us each $1,000 for our troubles," remembered Nelson. "There were seven of us, and the rest of the fighters hid out until they got out of Canada. It's a funny story now, but at the time, it was a nightmare. I was a teacher/coach and had to explain why I wasn't back at work that next Monday and Tuesday." Nelson would later form his own fighting organization, the United Shoot Wrestling Federation, and become a major activist in legalizing the sport in Texas. He also fought a rematch with Ralph Gracie, and it took Gracie over 11 minutes to beat him. Gracie, incidentally, escaped arrest by hiding out in a friend's hotel room for three days.

When John Perretti returned to the USA and found out about the arrests, he took the next plane to Quebec and got himself arrested so that he could be with his fighters. Zuckerman worked out an agreement with the Quebec police, and all charges were dismissed after he signed an apology letter stating he had taken part in something that was illegal and not a sport. Zuckerman made sure the fighters didn't have to sign anything. Thomas was never arrested but was charged with the same violation. The prosecutors came up with a plea bargain to admit guilt that would cost him a mere $100. "I was more interested in making a statement that this was a sport, and I was prepared to spend whatever it cost to win that battle," said Thomas, who anted up $50,000 during a lengthy court case. All charges against him were dropped four years later.

The arrests confirmed the Canadian judiciary's stance on mixed martial arts, shutting down something they didn't understand. But the pioneers weren't ready to give in. They were just getting started.

12

QUEST FOR THE BIG APPLE

Bob Meyrowitz was unprepared. He had walked into the hornet's nest of *Larry King Live*, CNN's top-rated talk show, just 10 days before the first Ultimate Ultimate in December 1995 and all he had with him was a promotional poster. Meyrowitz watched as Arizona Republican Senator John McCain entered the studio with a four-inch-thick book entitled *UFC*; his three aides each had a copy. The nervous SEG president made a quick exit to the bathroom, where he cut up his poster to make it appear that he had notes and was fully prepared. It didn't do him much good. He sensed disaster after overhearing Larry King say to McCain, "Hey John, I didn't see you at the party Friday night. I was wondering what happened to you."

Meyrowitz and McCain were there to debate mixed martial arts before the nation. In early 1995, McCain had led a rally to ban "ultimate fighting." The sport's defenders sensed a conspiracy, pointing out that brewing giant Budweiser helped finance McCain's election campaign and was also boxing's biggest advertiser—and boxing was perhaps the one sport that felt most threatened by fans switching interest to MMA. McCain had been on a witch hunt voicing his opposition to MMA in newspapers, writing letters, and even chastising fellow Republican and New York Governor George Pataki for not stopping UFC VII in Buffalo. Pataki had succeeded in forcing EF promoter Donald Zuckerman to rethink his plan and change venues for his first show.

On *Larry King*, Meyrowitz was joined on a studio feed by UFC sensation Ken Shamrock, while McCain had Nevada State Athletic Commissioner Marc Ratner in his corner. The blunt-speaking McCain pushed his case, arguing that the UFC "appeals to the lowest common denominator in our society." King piped in, "The object is to maim, isn't that right, Ken?" Both sides brought up good points, but the show's host cut off Shamrock before he could talk about the many deaths that had occurred in boxing. McCain pointed out that at least boxing had a referee, ignoring the fact that the UFC and other like events did too. He tried to make his case by saying that New York State Athletic Commissioner, former boxing champ Floyd Patterson, didn't like Ultimate Fighting. Ironically, Patterson would later be relieved of duty as a result of short-term memory loss caused by brain damage suffered from boxing. McCain said he thought the event would end up overseas, since 36 states had already banned it. Neither Meyrowitz nor Shamrock could convince the panel of their case, but that didn't stop *Wild, Wild West* star Robert Conrad from calling in and chastising the senator for worrying himself over a sport instead of balancing the budget.

From a political standpoint, the UFC and MMA was a safe issue to come out against: who wouldn't be against something dubbed a bloodsport? It didn't matter that there hadn't been any serious injuries or deaths, unlike boxing; because it didn't have a true regulatory body, it was an easy target. Meyrowitz did say he was all in favor of regulation. Few people picked up on this at the time, but it would become the UFC's ticket to approval by the various state athletic commissions.

SEG hired prominent Albany lobbyist James D. Featherstonhaugh, affectionately nicknamed "Feathers" for his knack of flying under the radar to get laws passed that might otherwise have been shot down in the Senate. Meyrowitz knew that time was against him, as Pataki and New York State Senate member Roy Goodman were joining forces to seek outlawing the sport in New York. Zuckerman's Brooklyn show had alarmed them, and Meyrowitz's Buffalo event had come close to being shut down. In a December 5 letter to SEG, Featherstonhaugh laid out a plan to persuade key legislators to show support for the UFC by lobbying for its regulation in New York. First on his list was Senate Majority Leader Joseph Bruno, who also happened to be Featherstonhaugh's business partner. Meyrowitz met with Bruno, and, during the first two months of 1996, things were looking up for the UFC. Goodman's bill to ban the sport on January 30, 1996, did not get a hearing by the investigations committee until April of that year. By June, Goodman was looking at an entirely different picture. Some senators showed resistance toward banning these events. Goodman folded; he now sought regulation rather than banishment. By July, a law to properly regulate MMA events had passed both houses and was on its way to Governor Pataki.

In mid-October 1996, Governor George Pataki of New York signed SB 7780 into law, placing "combative sports" under the control of the New York State Athletic Commission. It meant mixed martial arts events were "legal" in the state. Bob Meyrowitz had done it; he had won the Big Apple. "After an exhaustive investigation, they have come to recognize that ultimate fighting is a legitimate sport," he declared. "We look forward to bringing UFC live events to our many fans in New York." SEG's home state was now ready, if not exactly willing, to host MMA tournaments, and SEG immediately announced plans in an October 30, 1996, press release to hold its first sanctioned show at the Niagara Falls Civic Center on February 7, 1997.

Of course this wasn't the first time the UFC, or Extreme Fighting, had tussled with promoting their events in New York. UFC VII took place in Buffalo, New York, roughly one year before the law was signed on September 8, 1995. Governor Pataki's spokesman Bob Bulman said they "wanted to stop the event from taking place, but 'did not have clear authority' to intervene," according to Michael Finnegan's article in the *Daily News* on September 16, 1995. John McCain piped in saying, "It was very disappointing that New York state officials could not prevent this appalling event from taking place."

When Extreme Fighting tried to hold its inaugural event at the Park Slope Armory in Brooklyn on November 18, once again the New

York State Athletic Commission didn't have jurisdiction, but they had other tricks up their sleeve to stop the event. The New York Division of the Military and Naval Affairs simply revoked Battlecade's license from the Park Slop Armory. Zuckerman brought the issue to the State Supreme Court in Brooklyn on the preceding Thursday and won. The judge enjoined the state authorities from canceling the lease, but an automatic appeal kept things in court. "They postponed their decision till the Tuesday after the fight," said Zuckerman, "and said that since the state had deep pockets, if the state was wrong, monetary damages would suffice, so they would not issue an injunction." But plenty of doubt remained in his mind. He couldn't risk the first show going under before having a chance to prove itself, so, after securing plans the day before (Wednesday), Zuckerman moved the show to North Carolina in 36 hours. "The fight in New York was only using that venue," exclaimed Zuckerman. "Now we were dead in the water without a venue."

So it seemed that with all the political pressure and combative politicians, how could a bill possibly make it through for New York to legitimize the sport of MMA in 1997? Reporter Dan Barry of the *New York Times* began poking around on the story and phoned both Meyrowitz and his EF rival, Donald Zuckerman, for quotes. "Now that it was legal in New York, [the press] called to ask about my plans," said Zuckerman, who told the reporter he was planning a show in Manhattan on March 28. "They also called Bob, who bragged to Dan Barry that he had secured Featherstonhaugh to get the law changed." On January 15, Barry's feature appeared on the *Times* front page under the headline, "Outcast Gladiators Find a Home: New York." The lengthy article made the politicians look foolish. Barry quoted them saying they wanted the sport banned and were doing everything they could to prevent it from taking place in New York. How could a senator, a mayor (Rudy Giuliani of New York City), and a governor be so opposed to something and then pass legislation to see that "human cockfighting," as Manhattan State Senator Roy Goodman proclaimed it, was allowed?

The following day Barry blew the lid off everything with a new article, "Giuliani to Try to Prevent 'Extreme Fighting' Match." It detailed how Giuliani was going to try to block the Manhattan event and the law that Pataki had signed. Through Barry's research of the State Commission on Lobbying, he found where Mr. Featherstonhaugh had drafted a letter to Meyrowitz and was paid $48,000, plus expenses, for his troubles. Republican Senate Majority Leader Joseph Bruno denied the efforts of lobbying. Barry's next article on February 7, 1997, headlined "Seasoned Lobbyist Gave No Quarter in Quest to Legitimize Bloody Sport," pointed to "Feathers" and Bruno being business partners. Bruno was key in pushing the legislation through.

Barry's articles dropped like a bomb. Follow-up stories in the New York media over the next few weeks stoked the controversy—and Meyrowitz and Zuckerman ate it up. Though Meyrowitz denied it, Zuckerman claimed he and the SEG president talked on a daily basis during the press frenzy and even had lunch together. Kelli O'Reilly, Zuckerman's secretary and an Extreme Fighting associate producer, frequently received calls from Meyrowitz over the course of that week in mid-January. The rivals seemed to be acting in concert.

Though he guessed the politicians would be steamed up over the *Times* articles, Meyrowitz was relatively unconcerned. After all, the new legislation was a done deal. "I was at a breakfast for [Mayor] Giuliani when his chief counsel came up to me and said, 'We've got a problem. You'll find out, and I'm just giving you a heads-up.'" The *New York Times* then called Meyrowitz, but this time it was not for a victory quote; they said the law had been repealed. They went on to say that a set of rules (all of 111 pages) for the UFC had been issued by the New York State Athletic Commission, rules that would have to be adhered to for the events to go ahead. "I said, 'Well, that's not true because the only one it would affect is me, and they haven't gotten me this rulebook.'"

The *Times* did have the rulebook; Meyrowitz had them send it over, promising them an exclusive. It was true: the commission had produced a set of rules and told Meyrowitz several hours after he received them, "We're still working on them." Meyrowitz read the fine print with mounting concern. The strict regulations were an obvious ploy to keep the "ultimate" out of the UFC. Fighters were required to wear headgear, were not allowed to kick above the shoulders, and the 30'-diameter Octagon would now have to be 40' to meet the Athletic Commission's rule requirements. The rules were intended to hinder the UFC until the law could be repealed.

Just a day before the Niagara event was to take place, Donald Zuckerman issued a statement saying he was canceling his proposed show for Manhattan. Meyrowitz wouldn't give up so easily; he had everything riding on the 7,000-seat Niagara Falls venue, which had sold out. He brought suit against the New York State Athletic Commission and took along UFC XII competitors Mark Coleman and Dan Severn for support. Meyrowitz insisted the rules were unfair and dangerous, as the mixture of headgear and grappling could create neck injuries that would otherwise be unlikely. It was too late. The judge declared that the commission was allowed to make whatever rules it chose to govern any sport under its control. "The only time in the history of New York State that a law has been repealed using emergency power without a 30-day waiting period was the UFC," said Meyrowitz. The event couldn't take place in upstate New York—or anywhere in the state for that matter.

As for UFC XII: Judgment Day, fighters and employees began checking into a hotel in Niagara Falls the day before the event, when word came down around 2:00 PM that the venue had been changed to Dothan, Alabama. SEG had secured Dothan as a backup venue only eight days before, believing there was no way they could lose since the commission and the law was on their side. New York might have won this battle, but Meyrowitz chartered three jets to take the UFC crew and the Octagon to Alabama. "Many fighters saw their relationship with SEG as antagonistic, but this was the one show where everybody knew just how far we had gone, how much money we had spent, and how much effort we put into this thing," said David Isaacs. "We moved a million-dollar show in under 24 hours. The pressure was enormous. The sport and our business's viability hinged on our getting each event off."

Fighters were allowed to bring one person with them; friends and entourages had to either return home or pay an astronomical fee to catch the next flight to Alabama. "We were supposed to land in Dothan, but because Dothan couldn't fit the planes, we ended up having to land in Montgomery, Alabama, in the middle of the night," said Elaine McCarthy. "I had to wrestle up a bunch of buses to meet us there in the middle of the night and drive us several hours into Dothan. By the time we all landed, we were just exhausted, and thank God those buses were there. We finally made it to the hotels at 6:00 AM the day of the show; we had to split everyone up and just put people in random rooms. We all went three days without sleep."

"A half hour before we were supposed to go on, we were still painting the Octagon canvas," recalled Meyrowitz. "I thought the paint was going to stick to the athletes' feet. It's remarkable that we pulled it off." Considering the fatigue factor, it was amazing that the fighters were still able to perform as expected. Yet UFC XII turned out to be one of the strongest shows in SEG's history.

To Bob Meyrowitz, Donald Zuckerman is the man who prevented SEG from cementing the success of the sport in New York, the media capital of the world. "Meyrowitz always blamed Zuckerman because he was riding on [Bob's] coattails with the Extreme event," said Art Davie. "He was trying to grandstand and pull a New York City coup. But Meyrowitz knew that you do one or two upstate in Niagara Falls, to show them they could do the event under the law. Then, once that credibility has been established, come back to Manhattan, which was Bob's market." While Zuckerman admitted he was partly to blame because "if I hadn't decided to do a show in Manhattan, none of this shit would have hit the fan in the first place," he insisted he wasn't the only one. Zuckerman claimed that Meyrowitz telling the *New York Times* about the lobbyist turned a 66-to-1 vote for the law to be passed into an Assembly vote of 134-to-1 to ban the sport. "It was just as much his fault, because we both wanted to be in New York," said Zuckerman. Nowhere in the *Times* article did it specify where Meyrowitz named "Feathers" or that he bragged about getting the law passed. In fact, he praised the Senate for looking past the misinformation to pass the law. Meyrowitz did, however, have a show booked at the Nassau Coliseum one month after Zuckerman's proposed Manhattan event.

Essentially, Extreme Fighting was beating UFC to the punch. Not all publicity is good publicity. "Zuckerman should get 99 percent of the blame for stirring up the trouble in New York," said David Isaacs. "All Bob did was take a call when contacted by a *New York Times* writer already doing a story based on Zuckerman's event 'from an undisclosed location.' I find it striking, to this day, that SEG, that had planned for over a year, had lobbied, and passed a law in New York State—I went to Albany to draft it personally—had spent the money necessary and planned an event in the far corner of the state, and had established a good working relationship with the New York State Athletic Commission takes any blame along with Zuckerman. His publicity stunt, without anything to back it up, cost the sport dearly." If neither promoter had spoken with Dan Barry of the *New York Times*, the lobbyist's name and subsequent dealings with Senate Majority Leader Joseph Bruno might never have emerged.

◆ ◆ ◆

IN PROFESSIONAL ICE HOCKEY, people cheer as two players throw down their gloves to fight, and the ref usually takes his time to stop it. In a stock car race, the possibility of death is always present, as any wreck can end fatally. In boxing, fans root for their favorite to knock the other guy out rather than have the fight go the distance. Many people drawn to watching full-contact sports do so because of that innate curiosity to see another person injured, or worse. Few will admit it, but why else do people yell and scream for their man to "kill" or "beat" the other person when watching *mano a mano* sports? (How about parents, who become unglued watching their children in little league?) Without television or any footage to use as promotion, SEG opted initially to make the Ultimate Fighting Championship appear larger than life. To sell the concept, they had to play off that "deadly" mystique of the martial arts and say it was a brutal display unlike anything anyone had ever seen before. Did boxing do anything different in its hyping of, for example, Mike Tyson? Did Tyson himself do the "sweet science" any favors with his behavior?

From a layman's perspective, MMA appeared much worse than boxing: bare-fisted punching in a cage, compared to fighting with gloves in a ring. Why? Because sports fans are comfortable with boxing; it has been around a long time as a spectator sport. What many don't understand is that boxing gloves protect the hand, not the target the gloves are intended to hit. If two people fight bare-fisted, the person throwing the punch must think of one thing: how soon before the small bones in his hand will break? Despite popular belief, the head is much harder than the small bones in the hand. In the first few UFCs, there were very few knockouts or hard punches thrown. If a fighter broke his hand, he couldn't fight—plain and simple. In boxing, the fighter wears 8- to 10-ounce gloves and is permitted to have each hand wrapped in up to 18' of bandages held in place by 10' of zinc oxide tape. This combination allows the boxer to pound on his opponent without the level of risk a bare-fisted fighter faces. It has been estimated that a boxer takes over 500 shots to the head in an average 12-round boxing match (because of so many deaths and brain-related injuries from boxing, title bouts were shortened to 12 rounds from 15). Then there are the countless thousands of punches boxers take off sparring partners while training.

"The truth is, if we say, 'Safer than boxing! Men close the gap and eliminate brain-damaging blows,' that's not going to sell anything, right?" admitted Campbell McLaren. The marketing effort to portray MMA as being deadly may have worked a little too well, but the fact remains that it's safer than boxing. From November 12, 1993, to October 4, 2010 (the date this book was wrapped), there have only been three casualties in MMA. American Douglas Dedge died on March 16, 1998, from injuries to the brain sustained in an unregulated Ukrainian event. He took six to seven shots before the match was stopped. Dedge collapsed and fell into a coma as the decision was being read. "We heard through guys who were with him that he was blacking out during training," said Clarence Thatch, who also competed in the event. Several reports from people who knew him said he had a preexisting condition that should have prevented him from fighting in the first place. On November 30, 2007, Sam Vasquez passed away, after collapsing from a knockout that took place in a Texas amateur event on October 20, 2007. And on June 28, 2010, Michael Kirkham was knocked out and never regained consciousness stemming from a professional sanctioned bout in South Carolina; he passed away two days later.

Politicians have campaigned to shut down so-called "no holds barred" contests even while they have substantial proof of death in other martial arts-related sports. Twenty-three-year-old Redone Bougara died from a blood clot on the brain as a result of a Draka (Russian kickboxing with wrestling and throws) match in Friant, California, in 1998. In January 1999, Michael Struve Anderson was kicked in the head during the U.S. Open Taekwondo Championship and would be pronounced dead hours later. New York Mayor Giuliani was quoted as saying, "I happen to be a boxing fan, but this [UFC] goes way beyond boxing. This is people brutalizing each other." With an average of four deaths per year in boxing related to the cumulative damage to the brain because of blows to the head, how does MMA top death? Joseph R. Svinth maintains an ongoing project called "Death Under the Spotlight: The Manual Velazquez Boxing Fatality Collection," which Velazquez started in the 1930s. Using an extensive table with complete records, 67 boxers died in the 1980s, 78 died in the 1990s, and the last update was in 2007 where 68 boxers had already died in that decade.

Every full-contact sport is dangerous to some degree, but men and women make that choice and accept the responsibility for putting their bodies at risk. In the December 13, 2000, issue of USA TODAY, an article entitled "Death on the Playing Field" discussed the dangers of high school American football. The reason? Thirteen young men had died that year from the sport, more than from boxing and certainly more than from any other full-contact fighting sport. On September 19, 1994, Joseph Estwanik, M.D., sent a letter to SEG after he had tended to the fighters' needs at UFC III. After listing the minor injuries he had come across, he had this to say:

> *I believe it is appropriate to state that the Ultimate Fighting Championship III produced fewer cumulative injuries than I have medically treated from some high school football and soccer games. Despite the apparent "brutal" image, no serious injuries were sustained and all injuries sustained were of a rather minor and non-lasting category. I found all competitors respectful, sincere, and appreciated athletes. The Ultimate Fighting Championship utilizes true athletes as compared with my impressions of the Tough Man contests in which a drunken, inexperienced, and poorly trained competitor will be inappropriately mismatched.*

Several anti-MMA politicians seem to be boxing fans. Yet boxing matches end much the same way as in MMA: knockout/technical knockout, referee stoppage, decision, towel, or fighter submission. With 8- to 10-ounce gloves and shorter rounds, fights are geared to last longer than in MMA, as knockdown rules allow the punishment to continue. Boxers who are knocked down because of a hard blow are sometimes given a standing eight count, which can occur up to three times in a round, before a match is stopped. A fighter can be dazed, knocked out on his feet, and then told to keep fighting even though the match should have been over at that moment. This is very dangerous, as it sets up what is generally referred to as "second impact syndrome." In an article entitled "Concussions in Sports," neurosurgeon Robert Cantu was quoted as saying, "The athlete appears stunned but does not lose consciousness and often completes the round. In the next period of seconds to a minute or two, the athlete rapidly deteriorates from a dazed state to one of deep coma."

In MMA, there are no standing eight counts; if the fighter is knocked down, the match is still in progress (in Japan, the Shooto organization has standing eight counts). He can verbally or physically relent (tap out) and end any further damage or the referee can stop it, but either way, the match is over. Admittedly, UFC II should have never taken place, since the referee was told he couldn't stop the fight. That was a bad call: it put fighters at risk, and it shouldn't have happened. Since that event, the sport has shed its circus trappings and created an evolving, systemized set of rules, with judges and a referee who can intelligently make decisions to stop a fight at any time where the fighter is not intelligently defending himself or herself.

In boxing, a fighter has two options: punch to the head or punch to the body. The brain takes a lot of damage as it is constantly rocked back and forth inside the skull with every hit. In MMA, fighters have an array of moves to end a fight. By adding the ground game, MMA fighters can't just stand and slug away, since a takedown from either side is imminent. Submission holds and positioning also lessen the commitment to strike aimlessly. In the Japanese promotion Rings, Brad Kohler knocked down Valentijn Overeem and commenced to pound on him wildly. Though it seemed like Kohler had the upper hand, Overeem readjusted his position and submitted his opponent via toe hold in under a minute. In Extreme Fighting 4, Brazilian jiu-jitsu specialist Allan Goes could have traded punches with Todd Bjornethun, but he caught him in a triangle choke that forced a tap without a strike being thrown. At UFC 118, Randy Couture met heavyweight boxing champ James Toney. The match was over just after three minutes when Couture got the takedown and submitted Toney via arm triangle choke after softening him up with punches. Toney never got off a punch.

What makes MMA so appealing is the fact that every fight is different; some matches have lots of strikes, other matches have two submission fighters, each trying to tap the other out. As for submissions, no one has ever been seriously injured from a choke or arm lock, but sometimes pride enters the picture. Scott Adams and Englishman Ian Freeman were "deadlocked" in trying to apply leg submissions on one another at UFC XXV. Neither man would tap until the pain became unbearable; Freeman ended up tapping after Adams broke his foot. At UFC 48, Frank Mir's arm bar was so tight on Tim Sylvia, the bone could be seen breaking as the ref stopped the fight less than a minute into the bout. There have been arm, knee, shoulder, wrist, and leg injuries as a result of submissions, but nothing that hasn't occurred before in high school football.

One of the most serious injuries in MMA history came at UFC IX, when Cal Worsham suffered a punctured lung from a cracked rib. In every full-contact sport, there is potential for damage by a one-time blow. Though Worsham won his fight with relative ease, Zane Frazier hit him at the right time in the right place. Worsham's adrenaline shielded any signs of the injury until he was back in the triage area; he was fine after a trip to the hospital.

Since boxing is 100 percent striking, boxers take much more cumulative damage than people think. No one knows more about this than UFC cut man Leon Tabbs, who has spent over 50 years in boxing. He started in amateur boxing in 1945, has managed and trained professional boxers all of his life, and has been a cut man for champions such as Marvin Johnson and Bonecrusher Smith. Says Tabbs, "UFC is not as brutal as boxing, and I say that because in preparing a fighter for a fight, if he's doing a 10-round fight, he's boxing maybe six to eight rounds a day. At best, the headgear is stopping you from getting cut, but the damage is still there. There is no question about it; the training for boxing is actually more brutal than the fight. There is just no comparison between boxing and the UFC. Boxing is so much worse as far as the amount of punishment a man takes. I cannot even think of a fight in the UFC that would come close to some of the matches I've witnessed in boxing."

One of the UFC's head physicians was Dr. Richard Istrico, who also happened to be a ringside physician serving the New York State Athletic Commission. In a letter dated October 24, 1995, he summed up the injuries he had seen in 53 MMA bouts. They included "soft tissue contusions, lacerations less than one centimeter in length, anterior nose bleeds, and dehydration. These injuries required treatments as simple as steri strips and ice compresses." Similar reports have come out over the years, and the level of injuries has remained the same, save for the fluke accident.

Art Davie and the Ultimate Fighting Alliance (which was created from the International Fighting Council at UFC V) gave way to some of the first rulebooks, but as a sport, it needed to be sanctioned and governed by a completely independent body with set rules and regulations that cannot be altered on the spot. Thankfully today, state sanctioning bodies are far more proactive and work to the best interest of the athletes. Monte Cox (Iowa), Matt Hume (Washington state), Sven Bean (Colorado), Paul Smith (California), Doug Muhle (North Carolina), and Steve Nelson (Texas) are just a handful of individuals who have educated their respective states that have led to sound sanctioning over the years. Even John McCain, who was once voted one of the "25 Most Influential People in America" by *Time* magazine, said in a post-Zuffa documentary that while he wasn't a fan of the sport, the rule changes to make it safer had drawn his attention elsewhere.

As of this writing in October 2010, MMA is sanctioned in 44 states. Of the remaining six, Connecticut, Wyoming, and Alaska do not have athletic commissions; Alaska for one has actually had a healthy MMA promotion called Alaska Fighting Championship that has produced 75 events so far since 2004. Vermont, West Virginia, and New York have commissions but have not sanctioned the sport. Ironically, politicians have even scorned John McCain for not continuing his quest to ban the sport in New York. Could it be the old wounds left by the Dan Barry articles? With the sport readily seen on television and on pay-per-view, it's difficult to surmise why the issue hasn't been solved. Certainly MMA no longer has to battle the confusion over dangerous Toughman contests, where unskilled, ordinary people fight with little or no medical supervision. "In 2009, there was a poll in New York over legalizing MMA, and 68 percent of those polled thought it should not be legalized," said Dave Meltzer. "I was stunned. I don't know one person who would not want to legalize it, but some people still think it should be banned because they don't have a lot of awareness of it." With overwhelming medical evidence and MMA's undeniable safety record, along with major states like New Jersey, Nevada, and California safely sanctioning events and garnering millions of dollars of revenue, the battle for New York is far from over, but the reasons for not doing it are growing thin. Most MMA pundits believe New York will finally sanction the sport by 2012.

On January 13, 2011, Zuffa-owned UFC held a press conference at Madison Square Garden touting the details of a study conducted by HR&A Advisors on the economic impact of sanctioning MMA in New York. The study found that sanctioning MMA would garner $23 million in annual revenue, create 212 jobs, and based on data from other commissions, the state could host 70 events annually. The study pointed out that just two UFC events in New York could bring in as much as $16 million in revenue. With so many states cash-strapped due to the economy, it's hard to dismiss MMA's economic benefit.

13

THE IFC STORY

International Fighting Championships has been one of the few franchise promotions to outlast the host of UFC clones that started in the mid-1990s. Though it would ultimately call California home, it began with a show in Kiev, Ukraine. The story of how the IFC got there, and what took place, reads as good as any James Bond thriller. For those involved, it would be an experience they'd never forget.

Even before his defeat at UFC V, Andy Anderson was working with promoter Buddy Albin to secure on-site promotions to keep live show audiences happy. Despite Albin forcing the first "work" (Taktarov vs. Macias) in UFC history, he was too useful to the company to ditch. That changed when UFC VIII came around. The two flew to Puerto Rico and began to lay the groundwork for the show a full month before it took place on February 16, 1996. Albin was a decent local promoter, having spent years in kickboxing as well as putting on underground, no-holds-barred events since the 1980s. But sometime during the mid-1990s—though no one knows the full story—Albin "lost his mind to alcohol and other problems," according to Anderson.

After they had both spent a full day negotiating with a Puerto Rican company to acquire equipment for the show, Albin called Anderson later that night and began to tell him what happened, forgetting he had been with him just hours before. When Bob Meyrowitz called Albin for updates, Anderson returned the calls because his partner was too far gone to know what was going on. Anderson and Meyrowitz became friends, while Albin was relieved of his duties and subsequently fired. A week before UFC VIII, producer Michael Pillot surveyed the site and wasn't satisfied with the equipment that had been secured. He sent for all of his own equipment by boat from New York to Puerto Rico, at a $200,000-plus price tag.

On November 7, 1995, a Ukrainian group called the International Professional Kickboxing League invited Albin (before his dismissal), Anderson, Ron Van Clief, and former Soviet Union wrestling coach Gennadiy Fabrikant to meet with them from the 18th to the 30th to produce a show in Kiev, Ukraine. All expenses paid (including bodyguards), they worked with the IPKL to launch a show called Ultimate Warriors, to be held March 30, 1996. Albin patterned the Ultimate Warriors logo on the UFC's and produced a poster that strikingly resembled the one used for Ultimate Ultimate '95, advertising fighters such as Marco Ruas, Ken Shamrock, Tank Abbott, and Oleg Taktarov. Needing more experienced help, Albin looked to his old kickboxing days. Atlantan Howard Petschler had left the PKA in 1994 and set his sights on promoting an MMA show without the bloodlust angle. He attended a few UFCs to garner the interest of investors, and when his plans to assist Martial Arts Reality Superfighting (see Chapter 17) fell through, he took a call from Albin, who he had first met at UFC III. Albin claimed he had purchased the "international" rights to the UFC and wanted Petschler to ready a production crew bound for Kiev.

Petschler had experience producing shows for Showtime and pay-per-view in Montreal and had worked with local promoter Victor Theriault (brother of kickboxing legend Jean Yves Theriault). He convinced Albin to bring both Theriault and Mike Thomas, the future on-site promoter for Extreme Fighting 2, to the Ukraine as well. Thomas, a Canadian native and kickboxing promoter in his own right, had spoken to Albin only over the phone. Little did anyone realize that Buddy Albin was not dealing with just another sports organization in the Ukraine. "All the sports teams over there are backed by different factions of the Mob," said Petschler. "Buddy had backed himself into a corner when he told them he was a branch of the Ultimate [UFC] and that this was going to be exactly like the UFC." In fact, this author obtained an original document from the IPKL where Ron Van Clief signed on behalf of the Ultimate Fighting Championship for Albin's group. The Russian mafia thought they would be making a sizeable fortune from the Americans hosting fights in their country.

Three weeks before the show, Petschler and Albin were there to work on the production. "The Ukraine didn't have a whole lot that we could use for a production like this, so I really had to look around," said Petschler. "I just remember having two bodyguards with me and taking a different route to one of Albin's contacts, Yuri, every single day." Everyone else arrived in the Ukraine two weeks before the show fearing the worst. Instead, Customs officials were pushed out of the way by mobsters, and the fighters were treated like celebrities, transported from the airplane to the hotel in custom vans and gleaming Mercedes and Volvos in what looked like a presidential convoy. "They were driving us through the snow on the autobahn going 95 miles per hour," said fighter John Lober. The city of Kiev was decked out with Ultimate Warriors propaganda, and the Russians didn't want to risk anything happening to their new American friends. "They kept us in an Olympic training center with an 11' concrete wall all the way around it with barbed wire on top of that," said Anderson. Machine-gun-toting guards in trench coats stood around the building, and no one was allowed to leave without an armed escort. "For many, this was their first experience with capitalism," said Petschler.

Staying in the now-abandoned Olympic training center was a surreal experience for everyone. The Ukraine was old, cultured, and run down, with holes in walls, bad septic tanks, and water that one would think twice about drinking. While the fighters did train, they were distracted by the world outside the door. Vodka could be bought for two bucks right down the street, and the place was swarming with Russian prostitutes and dancers. "I remember hearing screams outside the complex and seeing one of our fighters, 6'8" Gerry Harris, running buck naked through the snow chasing one of the Russian girls," said Petschler. "It was all in good fun of course, but then we were all invited to a Ukrainian orphanage, and it really brought home some of the conditions people were living in. The kids put on a show for us, shook the hands of the fighters, and made little gifts for us out of trash. It really put things into perspective."

Fun and culture aside, not all was well. Customs officials made trouble when they confiscated passports from several fighters, although they had, by then, been there for a week—with little money for food. Albin smoothed things over, borrowed $5,000 from Anderson, and was rarely seen again until the night of the show. Interestingly enough, according to Petschler, the Ukrainians had a unique way of keeping tabs on Albin and company. "The Ukrainians had kind of arranged for Buddy to be taken care of by Yuri's sister to spy on him and stay with him. They had a little different moral standard than we do. She wasn't unattractive and she was watching over the money; they were living in a little apartment together."

When Albin did show back up, he pulled all the fighters together and told them, "Bob [Meyrowitz] bought the word "Ultimate" off of me for $1 million, so you guys are going to have no problem getting paid," according to Lober. Most of them bought it. Albin told the opposite to Petschler and everyone else: that he had paid $1 million to use the name Ultimate for the show. His lies were beginning to unravel. "If I see that logo anywhere, I will sue you for everything you've got," Meyrowitz told Albin over the phone the night before the event; he called Van Clief as well at 2:00 AM. Petschler had to convince Yuri to go in and paint over the title, sealed on the Octagon floor in black. So what was the show to be called? Originally, Night of Diamonds (a reference to the diamond shapes of the Octagon wire fence) was going to be the new name for the event until Petschler came up with International Fighting Championships.

The National Sports Palace was nearly full, with a house of over 18,000 on hand. Albin had promised that comedian Eddie Murphy and Muhammad Ali were going to be in attendance; a very drunk and out-of-hand Leon Spinks appeared instead. Dutch sensation Bas Rutten, who made a name for himself in the Pancrase organization, served as commentator, along with Van Clief. Anderson would not be fighting but had the best view in the house as referee. Aside from being a millionaire, Anderson had refereed numerous tae kwon do tournaments and was well versed in MMA rules. With 11 fights on the card, he would have his work cut out.

The show comprised four single fights and an eight-man tournament. The only all-American match was John "The Machine" Lober against Eric Hebestreit. Lober was a former firefighter and had competed in sports his whole life. He became hooked on submission fighting and couldn't get enough of his new "drug," since his school ran classes only two or three times a week. In an effort to train as often as he wanted, Lober took a unique approach to finding training partners. "A friend of mine and I drove in our van down to a particular part of town. My friend would get out and hold up a sign that said, 'Fight my friend for $5 for five minutes,' and all of this was in Spanish. People were accepting the offers and we were getting these big, fat guys. I got three or four off the street, and [I'd] wrestle them in the garage and videotape it: me grabbing them, slapping them down, choking them, and taking their backs. Some turned into real fights because these guys would get pissed off because I wasn't hitting them."

When the UFC began, Lober was training in jiu-jitsu and varying fighting styles thanks to UFC alumni like Kimo and Todd Medina. He took the opportunity to fight in Kiev because he wanted to compete one time for experience and then call it quits. Lober's father, a former college wrestler, was his driving force but couldn't make the Kiev trip after a terrible car accident. After beating Hebestreit, Lober called his father to tell him the good news. His brother answered the phone; Lober's father had passed away just as his son was about to fight. The event changed his life and he made the sport his calling.

◆ ◆ ◆

THE EIGHT-MAN TOURNAMENT set up four Americans—none of which were the ones advertised—against four Eastern Europeans. Paul "The Polar Bear" Varelans, Gerry Harris, John Dixson, and Fred "The

Mangler" Floyd were physically the largest MMA fighters from the U.S. Outweighed by 100 pounds and eight inches shorter, Russian fighter Igor Guerus knocked out Harris with the only punch thrown in a 15-second match. Both Varelans and Dixson took out their respective opponents with strikes. Valery Nikulin, Varelans' opponent, suffered a broken collarbone and a dislocated elbow that didn't hinder his attack until the big man finally put him away.

The final match of the opening round, Floyd vs. Igor Vovchanchyn, confirmed the Ukrainian fighters' ability to dish out as much punishment as they could take. Hailing from Kharkiv, Ukraine, the 22-year-old Vovchanchyn was a champion kickboxer standing 5'9" and weighing 207 pounds. In the longest match of the evening, he systematically pounded the 340-pound Floyd until the Mangler verbally submitted at 13:40. Vovchanchyn then destroyed Varelans with dizzying shots to the face. "I was sitting in my dressing room," said John Dixson, "and when Fred came back, his face looked like a watermelon. Then Paul came back and his face looked like a watermelon."

Buddy Albin picked Dixson for the IFC because he had fought for him before in kickboxing shows and was a lifelong martial artist, from praying mantis kung fu to tae kwon do to boxing. Dixson faced Vovchanchyn in the finals. Believing he was a better stand-up fighter than both of his American comrades, Dixson battled the Ukrainian with flying fists. A few minutes into the match, he threw a right hand that broke Vovchanchyn's jaw. But the Ukrainian kept coming. Just after the six-minute mark, Vovchanchyn hit Dixson with a looping left hook that made his nose bleed like a faucet. Dixson tapped out and later learned his nose had been broken in five places.

Conditions for the native fighters were not all they should have been. In one of the single fights, Peter Khmelev defeated Ruslan Kriviy after kicking him in the groin. Kriviy collapsed in pain; he was not wearing a hard, protective jock strap. As the night progressed, it took longer and longer for the Russian and Ukrainian fighters to emerge from their dressing rooms. "We sent someone back there to finally see what was going

Top: Masahiko Kimura works side mount on Helio Gracie during their 1951 match. *(Courtesy of Rorion Gracie)*

Middle Left: A Brazilian newspaper clipping announces Helio Gracie's 1932 match against Fred Ebert. *(Courtesy of Rorion Gracie)*

Middle Right: Carlos Gracie (left) flips Helio Gracie during MMA's early days in Brazil. *(Courtesy of Rorion Gracie)*

Right: A newspaper article announces a fight between the Gracie clan (George, Carlos, Oswaldo, and Helio Gracie) and a capoeira team.

Royce Gracie (left) and father Helio Gracie. *(Courtesy of Rorion Gracie)*

Left: Early artwork for War of the Worlds, the promotion that would end up becoming the Ultimate Fighting Championship. *(Courtesy of Art Davie)*

Right: Royce Gracie (left) ready for war at UFC II. *(Courtesy of Clay McBride)*

Left: Art Davie presides over the fighter meeting at UFC II. *(Courtesy of Art Davie)*

Below: Pancrase founder Masakatsu Funaki with the Lion's Den, (from left) Ken Shamrock, Frank Shamrock, Bob Shamrock, Jason DeLucia and Ken's first wife, Tina. *(Courtesy of Clay McBride)*

Above: Fighters pose at the UFC II after-fight party. From left are Royce Gracie, Robert Lucarelli, Thaddeus Luster, Remco Pardoel, Orlando Weit, Freek Hamaker, Fred Ettish, and David Levicki. *(Courtesy of Clay McBride)*

Keaith Hackney has his hands full with Emmanuel Yarborough. *(Courtesy of Clay McBride)*

Left: SEG's ringmaster Campbell McLaren and the 600-pound Emmanuel Yarborough. *(Courtesy of Campbell McLaren)*

Right: Alternate Steve Jennum defeats Harold Howard to win UFC III. *(Courtesy of Clay McBride)*

Royce Gracie (with shiner) holds tight on Ken Shamrock at UFC V. *(Courtesy of Clay McBride)*

Dan Severn unleashes the Beast. *(Courtesy of Dan Severn)*

Tank Abbott was victorious in his UFC debut against John Matua. *(Courtesy of Robin Postell)*

Left: Ken Shamrock goes on the attack against Oleg Taktarov during their UFC VII superfight. *(Courtesy of Robin Postell)*

Right: Marco Ruas chops down the giant Paul Varelans at the finals of UFC VII. *(Courtesy of Robin Postell)*

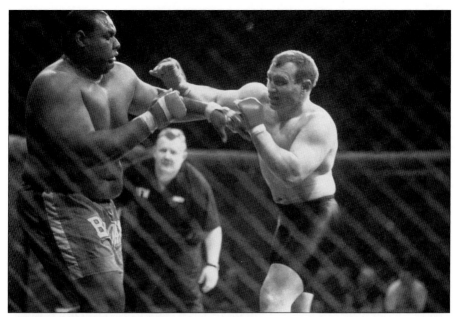

Fred Floyd (left) faces Igor Vovchanchyn at the inaugural IFC in the Ukraine. Referee Andy Anderson is in the middle. *(Courtesy of Robin Postell)*

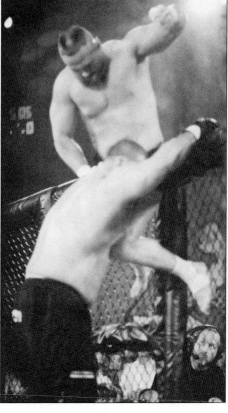

Above: Mark Coleman has Don Frye in trouble during their epic match. *(Courtesy of Robin Postell)*

Right: Tank Abbott tries to throw Cal Worsham over the Octagon fence. *(Courtesy of Robin Postell)*

Maurice Smith throws a kick at Marcus "Conan" Silveira at Extreme Fighting 3. *(Courtesy of Battlecade)*

Left: Pat Miletich tries to pick up Matt Hume at Extreme Fighting 4. *(Courtesy of Battlecade)*

Right: Vitor Belfort goes on the attack against Tank Abbott at the UFC XIII superfight. *(Courtesy of Robin Postell)*

on," remembered Howard Petschler, "only to find that all of the Ukrainian fighters had one jock between them." Apparently, Kriviy lost the coin toss to decide who would wear the jock. In the last fight, Vovchanchyn wore a jock that had been worn seven times by five other fighters that night.

The fights inside the Octagon were only the beginning of the war that took place outside. As Andy Anderson told it, "Buddy tried to screw Yuri, Yuri tried to screw Buddy, and Yuri said, 'Well, we didn't make any money.'" Judging by the size of the crowd, that was hard to believe. Buddy told Yuri he thought the show's tape recording didn't come out; although there was no pay-per-view, Petschler and his team filmed the event and planned to produce it for the U.S. market.

At a Russian bar after the fight, "I started drinking vodka—wrong choice for me," said Rutten laughing. "What exactly happened next, I don't know." According to John Dixson, Rutten and Paul Varelans got into a playful bit of roughhousing after having one too many drinks. Varelans apparently bit Rutten on the back, while Rutten threw him through a plate glass window. To the Dutchman, it was all in good fun; Varelans had to go to the hospital. That same evening, while at a topless bar, Rutten's antics were getting out of hand when a Ukrainian guard with automatic weapon in hand approached him. Rutten slapped him. In Holland, Rutten had a reputation for being a tough customer and had paid the price in jail on numerous occasions. The Ukrainian returned with reinforcements only to find Rutten onstage with the dancers. Anderson grabbed Rutten and carried him out only to smash Rutten's head into a mirror stationed on a nearby wall according to Petschler. Rutten then puked out the side of a van back to the hotel room. "All I remember is waking up in a different hotel room, only to hear a snoring Andy Anderson sleeping on the floor," said Rutten. "I asked Andy what I was doing in his room, and he told me that I had thrown up in my room. Okay, but it is a big bed, you don't need to sleep on the floor. Then Andy told me that I pissed the bed." Spot-checking the room, Rutten then noticed a television set lying on the floor. "The TV set tried to attack you and you were defending yourself," Anderson told Rutten. "Then he started to tell me what I did that night and I put my fingers in my ears and started humming; I didn't want to hear it anymore."

The following morning, Anderson was woken by a knock at the door. It was a representative from another Russian mafia group. Anderson was told that his good job as referee the preceding night would be rewarded if he and some of the fighters stayed for an additional six to seven weeks and staged another event. Anderson declined. "I don't think you understand," said the mafioso, "you are not allowed to leave." A guard took Anderson and three others back to the hotel, but the millionaire bribed the guard into putting everyone on the next flight out. "I ended up knocking the guard out because he wanted everybody to think that we kidnapped him, otherwise he would have gotten in a lot of trouble," said Anderson. Event coordinator Mike Thomas remembered another mafia group trying to get people to stay in the Ukraine. Anderson and company stopped off in Paris for a week before returning to the States.

As for Petschler, he stayed behind in the Ukraine with U.S. crew member Randy Kamay to create a rough master tape in NTSC format from the original PAL (standard European video format) shoot. The two worked on the transfer, only to be interrupted by two Ukrainians, who asked to take the tapes to Customs for inspection. Things seemed fishy, so Petschler declined and called Albin to sort out the problem. The Ukrainians muscled Kamay aside and took the tapes anyway, including one of two masters. Fortunately, they left one in the machine and Petschler had backups, save for the final match between Vovchanchyn and Dixson. Petschler retreated to his hotel and got on the phone to Albin, who told him to get out of the Ukraine any way possible. But leaving the country with the tapes proved impractical, as another mafia group convinced Customs that the "show" was actually an espionage attempt to film Chernobyl, the nuclear reactor site. To Albin's credit, he managed to get everyone on the next flight out, and Petschler dropped the tapes off at a Federal Express depot so they would not be confiscated. Sure enough, the IFC contingent was searched, and when the tapes didn't turn up, they were free to leave the country.

A week later, the tapes still hadn't arrived. Petschler called FedEx, who said that if he wanted them back, he would have to return to the Ukraine. Since Albin had not paid Petschler, going back to Kiev was the only way he could make any money. He had four men waiting for him at the airport and was whisked away in one car with another following for protection. "I was kept hidden and moved from apartment to apartment," said Petschler. He met with another sporting group run by yet another mafia crew, who agreed to help him safely get the tapes out of the Ukraine. They drove to FedEx, where the rear protector car (filled with gun-toting heavies) turned back; they did not want to face what danger lay ahead.

Collecting the tapes was actually no big chore, but the Russians sped away as if it had been a robbery and hid Petschler in another safe house. He then took an overnight train from Kiev to Odessa, stowing away in a sleeping compartment with a former Soviet wrestling coach of Ukrainian descent, who had arranged for the tape escape with a rival sporting club. "They were pretty slick because I didn't know we were short a tape until I got to Odessa," said Petschler. A local police captain met the intrepid IFC producer and threw him a party. Then he was sent home without the tapes again. A Moldavian general eventually took the tapes with him and shipped them back by U.S. mail. The missing tape contained the final match between Vovchanchyn and Dixson, so the U.S. commercial tape abruptly ends just after the last semifinal fight.

According to John Dixson, conditions in the Ukraine were so bad that Vovchanchyn went for days without food while preparing himself for the show. Those days are over. Vovchanchyn became one of the biggest MMA stars in the world, fighting in Japan, Brazil, and Russia. Georgy Kobylyansky, the Russian mob member who had backed the event, was not left out in the cold. A year later he hooked up with Frederico Lapenda, Marco Ruas's former manager, and produced a Russian MMA series called Absolute Fighting Championship. And though Ukrainian women are among the most beautiful on the planet, Howard Petschler swears he will never return there. Insiders speculate that he has been banned and would return home in a coffin if he did.

As a footnote, MMA journalist and editor Cal Cooper, who ran an Internet site called The New Full Contact, later befriended Yuri and received the tape of the final match. His intentions to sell the tape to fans were quickly thwarted by the IFC. To this day, they have never recovered the commercial copy of that match, but Lapenda sells the entire event. It's called Night of Diamonds.

• • •

AFTER SURVIVING SUCH A BUMPY RIDE, there was no turning back for the IFC team. Albin wanted to keep going and so did Petschler, but they needed money. Mike Thomas formed a corporation for the IFC in Montreal and, as a resident of Kahnawake—Mohawk Territory in the province of Quebec—he became the IFC president. It would be the first Indian native-owned company in international sports television industry. Thomas and Andy Anderson invested over $70,000 for a second show, to be held in Mississippi. When Thomas and Petschler showed up to see how Albin was doing at the event site, they found themselves sharing a room while Albin stayed in a two-bedroom suite entertaining guests. Anderson flew down to referee as a favor to Thomas, only to find that he would be staying in one of the hotel's smallest rooms.

IFC II didn't have the same star power. Anthony Macias made his comeback and won the eight-man tournament, but this show was important for another reason. Petschler had been updating his kickboxing rulebook for MMA and decided to test the waters with Mississippi. After meeting with the state's commission, IFC II became the first MMA event to be state sanctioned. Anderson returned to Texas to find a $26,800 American Express bill waiting for him. "Buddy told the hotel that my American Express card was a company card and to charge all the rooms to it," said Anderson. "He also charged money off the card as well." Taking a cue from Yuri, Buddy told everyone that the show hadn't made any money, when the event center had been packed to the hilt with screaming fans.

A third show in Mobile, Alabama, would be Buddy Albin's last. Thomas, Petschler, and Anderson read him the riot act at a meeting before the show. They still felt the IFC could continue with its original team, and when Thomas arrived at the show he gave Albin over $7,000, only to wake up the next morning to find that Albin had skipped town. Anderson and Jeff Weller had to lend money to Thomas, the investor, so that he could get back home to Montreal. To make matters worse, Albin had given Thomas the fighters' checks, but they were for only half the money agreed upon. Finally, because the second show had used up all the funds, there was no money left to shoot the IFC III video.

That was the final straw. Buddy Albin was officially ousted from the organization. "To make sure he got the axe, we actually threatened to have him arrested unless he signed away [his part of] the company," said Petschler. Petschler and Thomas agreed to let Albin have all the proceeds from the sale of the Kiev video, but first they had to buy back the rights from the first two shows; Albin had apparently sold the rights to a company in Atlanta for $5,000. They gave Albin $10,000 in exchange for his part of the IFC. Months later, Albin resurfaced with another show that had IFC written all over it. He was sent a cease-and-desist order. Save for some small shows in and around Texas, Albin was rarely heard from again.

The IFC led the way for others in Canada and has put together some great matches over the years. It also promoted the first-ever female match, on February 29, 1997, for IFC IV: Becky Levi defeated Betty Fagan in just under two minutes. After all the arrests from Extreme Fighting 2, Mike Thomas worked to secure a safe home for the IFC in Montreal, and he would find success by spearheading the first sanctioned event in the country on March 30, 1998. Andy Anderson continued to referee for the IFC as well as other events. Years later, Albin called Anderson and acted like nothing had happened, claiming it was Thomas who had used Anderson's credit card for the IFC II debacle. Anderson knew better, since Thomas had put his house up for collateral to keep the show going. By Anderson's estimate, Albin embezzled over $400,000 from Thomas and his Indian reservation in just two years.

For a promotion with so many ups and downs, the IFC continued to evolve by sanctioning other events and extending its brand name. In February 1997, martial artist Paul Smith, who had fought in several underground fights during the early 1980s, became part of the IFC team and ran shows inside Indian casinos. Mike Thomas eventually left his post as president of the IFC for other endeavors, while Smith and Petschler have worked together ever since. In March 1998, the IFC started the Warrior's Challenge, a successful show catering to up-and-coming talent that would be held on Indian reservations throughout California. This lucrative market (the casino pays an on-site fee upfront) became the blueprint for similar promotions like King of the Cage and World Extreme Cagefighting in neighboring casinos. Smith led the charge for MMA sanctioning in California, working to ultimately create what is known as the "unified rules." After churning out a series of smaller shows, the IFC stepped it up on September 6, 2003, for Global Domination held in Denver, Colorado. The event featured an eight-man tourney and international talent but failed to make much of an impact. The IFC continues to promote shows all over the USA, though its "international" scope may have narrowed.

14

REVENGE AND REDEMPTION

M ark Coleman was once again at a crossroads. The two-time NCAA wrestling champion at Ohio State had just lost in the semifinals of the 1996 Olympic trials and would be going home with his dream of glory shattered. He had faced this disappointment before. Coleman had made the 1992 Olympic team only to lose to a pair of foreign competitors he had beaten six months earlier. "I lost the eye of the tiger and started to head down the wrong path where I stopped training," said Coleman of the 1992 debacle. "I was drinking instead." It had taken everything in Coleman's heart to bring him back four years later, and his spirits could now have sunk even lower.

As fate would have it, trainer Richard Hamilton, who had worked with both Dan Severn and Don Frye, was at the Olympic trials recruiting new talent. He told Coleman that he was one of three wrestlers (Tom Erikson and Mark Kerr were the other two) being considered for UFC X just 30 days later. Coleman convinced Hamilton that he was the man for the job. With little more than a few street fights under his belt, Coleman had only his freestyle wrestling skills to employ in the Octagon—but they were considerable. From the age of six, he had been a career athlete, becoming an All-American in football, baseball, and wrestling. Wrestling was what the 6'1", 245-pound, Columbus, Ohio, native enjoyed most. Coleman knew that amateur wrestlers had few opportunities to make money on physical skills alone, and he felt the UFC would be the only chance he had to keep wrestling and provide for his future. "I watched all the UFC fights and felt that I wouldn't have any problems with anybody in the ring," said Coleman. "My confidence was believing that all those fights would be mismatches [if I had been in there]."

Coleman worked on his stand-up and trained at Hamilton's Arizona gym for submission, though he said Hamilton's idea of groundfighting was for Coleman to work out with beginners. Hamilton often told people he was a minister and had a strong alliance with the North Phoenix Baptist Church, which somehow assisted him in promoting karate tournaments. By aligning himself with the amateur wrestling team Sunkist Kids (a sponsored team that competed around the world), Hamilton was the ticket for any wrestler to get into the UFC. He trained Frye and Severn in minor capacities for their UFC appearances, though lawyer Robert DePersia was their manager. "He [Hamilton] envisioned himself as someone who could control all aspects of the athlete, not just the training," said DePersia. Hamilton became Coleman's manager, but that was okay with the wrestler, who saw this opportunity as an escape from his depression. Coleman felt that taking an opponent down wouldn't be a problem, and "grounding and pounding" would be all that was required to finish him off.

UFC X: The Tournament was held on July 12, 1996, at the Alabama State Fair Arena in Birmingham. The South should have been more open to holding these events, but political pressure was building even there, and misinformation created alarm. On the night of the fight, a policeman held up a video camera to film the event. "I told him he couldn't film because it was a copyrighted event and we don't allow any videography," said David Isaacs. "The officer told me he was going to arrest me if I didn't let them do it. Our local lawyer said they could arrest you and they will arrest you. I stepped aside. Every city was a battle." In terms of pay-per-view, UFC X would be another victim of UFC IX's Great Dance between Shamrock and Severn as the buys dipped to 142,039, the lowest since UFC III. "Every time we had a fight the public didn't like, the next show the buy rate would drop," said Art Davie.

There would be no superfight, since the Shamrock-Severn rematch had been so boring. SEG felt confident about their current champion,

Don Frye, and had enlisted a fresh crop of fighters to vie for the coveted UFC crown. Well-rounded athlete Brian Johnston, 6'4" and all muscle, had been wrestling since the age of 12 and had forged a brief career as a pro boxer and kickboxer. He wanted to make money fighting and, when kickboxing didn't pan out, the UFC was the only answer. Interestingly enough, he walked to the cage wearing a gi, a show of respect since he had emphasized judo throws in training. Another competitor, Moti Horenstein, had served three years in the Israeli army and was a three-time karate champion in his native country. With his brawny look, he hoped that "survival" (what he called his fighting style) would triumph.

While "Big Daddy" Gary Goodridge made his return after the loss to Schultz, traditional martial artist Mark Hall had high hopes for winning the tourney. He had destroyed Harold Howard at UFC VII, defeated Trent Jenkins at UU '95, and busted the nose of sumo wrestler Koji Kitao in the previous show. Hall was a good ole boy from Weatherford, Texas, who had grown up with a speech impediment. His classmates knew better than to tease him since it meant an automatic fight after school. The 189-pound Hall never backed down from anyone and trained heavily in martial arts inside his father's barn. He had taken moo yea do (a Korean style) to control his temper, and saw the UFC as a better way to earn a living than bouncing at clubs or teaching self-defense.

Unlike his previous appearances, Don "The Predator" Frye came to UFC X with a little more than just plain confidence. In prefight interviews, he poured on the heavy-handed bravado. "I didn't train that hard for the tournament, and I made the mistake of getting too cocky," remembered Frye. "I thought there was nobody out there who could handle me." As in his college wrestling days, Frye interpreted early success as a sign that he was doing everything right and didn't need to put in the extra time to better his skills.

Frye faced Hall in the quarterfinals and outweighed him by 25 pounds. He felt sorry for Hall and expected a quick victory over someone who lacked the strength or wrestling ability to put up a good fight. What Frye didn't count on was heart. With his traditional martial arts mentality,

Hall felt he could beat his opponent with his spinning back kick. He had practiced thousands of kicks in preparation for the one perfect shot, and at the beginning of the match, Hall got his chance—and one kick was all it took before he was taken down to the ground. Frye slammed Hall to the mat and stayed in his closed guard for the duration of the match—over 10 minutes. With his forearm pressed against Hall's throat, Frye battered Hall's ribs, bruising them to no end. As the match dragged on, the two argued about stopping the fight.

"You need to quit," said Frye.

"No! I can't quit," Hall fired back.

The punishment continued until John McCarthy put an end to it. Frye controlled his opponent but was exhausted. He would fight Hall twice more in the next five months.

Brian Johnston gave a shaky performance against fellow kickboxer Scotty Fiedler, who had him in trouble with a rear naked choke early in their quarterfinal bout. "I threw him and went right for the knee bar, but I didn't have experience with those techniques," said Johnston later. Fiedler didn't have the choke sunk in right; Johnston escaped and dropped bombs to the back of Fiedler's neck, which forced a ref stoppage. Gary Goodridge also had trouble from beefy biology teacher John Campetella, but he managed to short-circuit his opponent's wrestling ability and beat him down, forcing a tap out.

Coleman made his way to the Octagon sporting "Team Phoenix" on his shirt, an obvious advertisement for Hamilton's quasi-gym. But Coleman was there to represent freestyle wrestling in a way that had never been seen before. His opponent Moti Horenstein had been a martial artist since the age of five; it didn't make any difference. He threw one kick and Coleman went in for the takedown. The wrestler's ferocity, matched with his amateurish, albeit powerful, punching style, was too much for Horenstein, who was mounted and clobbered with a series of lefts and rights. The Israeli tried to defend, but Coleman landed enough bombs to make him cover up with both hands before tapping out. Coleman then lit up the crowd with a testosterone-injected celebration.

Frye and Coleman both had seesaw battles with their opponents in a lively semifinal round. Brian Johnston gave Frye a great fight by backing him up with his boxing skills, and it looked like an upset was in the making as the 25-year-old kickboxer trumped everything Frye could dish out. "He finally got a bear hug and...I couldn't get out of it," said Johnston. "I tried to go for a throw, but Don was a little too experienced for that." Frye took Johnston down and landed two sharp elbows to his forehead, which opened a small gash. With nowhere to run, the panic-stricken Johnston (who had never bled in a fight before) tapped out immediately.

Coleman battled a sharper Goodridge, and wrestling proved to be the bigger man's weakness. At one point, Coleman worked Goodridge over to his corner, but, with a wink to Hamilton, Goodridge grabbed the fence and laterally scaled to his own corner. Coleman held Goodridge from behind and landed several uppercuts, forcing him to turn around. Coleman began to fatigue, but after several takedowns, he finally moved into position for a rear naked choke. Coleman sunk in his hooks, but the Canadian knew he was done and tapped out.

The UFC X final was arguably the most personal in UFC history up to that point. Richard Hamilton and Don Frye had parted on bad terms, and Hamilton's foray into management was a smokescreen for his quest to find a terminator to destroy Frye. Coleman was his puppet. "He [Hamilton] made Don Frye out to be an evil person," remembered Coleman. "I have nothing against anybody, but the stuff he was telling me about Don made me want to go in there and kick his butt." Frye knew nothing of Hamilton's ruse and felt confident he could beat just another wrestler. Coleman outweighed Frye by 30 pounds, and he was far from just another wrestler.

In the 11½ minute war that ensued, Coleman set out to maul Frye. He landed countless headbutts, knees, elbows, and punches that closed both of his opponent's eyes. At one point, Coleman had Frye up against the fence in his own corner with Hamilton's face staring into Frye's. "Kill him! Make him suffer!" yelled Hamilton. "Hamilton was supposed to be some type of minister, but during the fight I heard a totally different person with the way he was talking to me," acknowledged Coleman. After pounding Frye for several minutes, Coleman eventually lost his blood lust and wondered why the match wasn't being stopped. "I felt that plenty of damage was done. I didn't like what was taking place."

Dan Severn, who had once coached and trained Frye in college, was sitting ringside as a special commentator. He looked to Frye's trainer, Becky Levi, a 6'1", 210-pound judo stylist and toughwoman competitor, and suggested she stop the fight, but it was trainer Steve Owen (Frye's longtime judo coach) who had to make that call. "Don told me that if he had a chance to win, do not throw in the towel," said Owen. Though Frye could do very little against Coleman, Owen felt he still had enough heart left. A cloud of concern fell over both camps. Frye's and Coleman's significant others, Molly and Tina respectively, circled the cage inches from one another. They were unable to hold back their anguish at what the men in their lives were putting them through.

Frye clung to the cage, but Coleman used all his strength to pick him up and slam him to the mat. McCarthy had stopped the bout earlier for doctors to check Frye's cuts, and now, after two hard elbows to the face, a second stoppage was all she wrote. Mark Coleman was declared the winner. In his postfight interview, he announced to the world that this was a win for wrestling. "It was important for me to promote [amateur wrestling], but now, I'm no longer a wrestler—I'm a fighter," said Coleman.

Frye had to be carried out of the Octagon. He was in bad shape. "I was devastated," said Becky Levi, who sat with Frye in the triage room. He could barely move as he inclined his head toward Levi when she spoke; he could not see her because his eyes were bruised shut. He dropped his head on her chest as she tried to stay calm. "When the doctor came in, I walked away to the shower area and cried my eyes out," she said. She rode with Frye in the ambulance to the hospital, where he spent the night with several fractured bones in his face and severe dehydration. (Mark Hall had already broken one of Frye's ocular sockets that looked like a mouse below his eye and Coleman's handiwork didn't make it any better.) His injuries were so extensive that he couldn't fly home for a week.

When Levi arrived back at the hotel, "the first thing I wanted to do was kill Richard Hamilton." Still covered in Frye's blood, she walked into a nearby bar and told Dan Severn of her intentions. As she left to find Hamilton, Severn grabbed Levi by the shorts and pulled her in close. "You aren't going anywhere, have a seat," he soothed. The Beast was able to calm her down, but the elusive Hamilton had taken his revenge.

Just four days after UFC X, Edison Media Research conducted a survey of 400 adults who had at least watched one pay-per-view; the sample was drawn from eight markets where the UFC was available and where cable operators had done an above-average job in promoting the event. Only 25 percent had seen UFC X. "We wanted to know who was watching," said Davie. SEG had assumed that there would be a high proportion of martial artists, but as it turned out, only 66.3 percent of those surveyed had heard of the UFC, and out of the UFC watchers, only 13.9 percent were martial artists. Though boxing was still king, there were some interesting demographics to be extrapolated. Out of the UFC viewers, only 56.5 percent were single, 79.6 were male, 79.2 percent were Caucasian, 51 percent had more than some college, 30.9 percent had income of $40,000 to $75,000, and the mean age was 29. UFC viewers were also big NFL fans, and one of the magazines that was frequently read the most was *Muscle & Fitness*. Though the audience for MMA would continue to evolve, just like the athletes, it was apparent that SEG now had a franchise, and they needed to ratch it up a notch if they wanted to keep their hold on the pay-per-view universe.

◆ ◆ ◆

DAVID "TANK" ABBOTT WAS FINALLY ALLOWED to return for UFC XI: The Proving Ground, after SEG pleaded with Elaine McCarthy (John's wife) to let them bring back their poster boy. For his unkind words in Puerto Rico, Abbott was supposed to write an apology letter to smooth things over with McCarthy. "I was totally and completely at fault," wrote

Abbott. "I was very distraught from the events that immediately preceded the crossing of our paths. As a result, I took a very defensive position at what I perceived as a threat." Actually SEG's David Isaacs penned the one-page apology and had Abbott sign it. Everything was kosher with Elaine, so it was time for the bad boy of the UFC to get back in training. He enlisted the help of Olympic heavyweight wrestler Tolly Thompson to roll with him. Unfortunately, Thompson dropped Abbott hard to the mat one day, reinjuring his knee hurt in his previous car accident. Abbott's mother suggested anti-inflammatories, and though the remedy worked for a short while, the effects eventually wore off. The streetfighter could barely move, and ballooned to over 300 pounds, but with his menacing visage emblazed across the event poster, Abbott *had* to show up.

Reigning champion Mark Coleman had been dubbed "The Hammer," and his focus and confidence were at an all-time high. From a commercial viewpoint, SEG desperately hoped he and Tank would square off. UFC XI was held at the Augusta-Richmond Civic Center in Georgia on September 20, 1996, playing to a rabid crowd hungry for the return of Tank. Much like at a pro wrestling event, Tank supporters held up banners. One read, "Tank is the UFC!" Along with Tank and Coleman, the show was a mix of veterans like Jerry Bohlander and Brian Johnston and relative unknowns such as Julian Sanchez, who had no sanctioned fighting experience and faced Coleman in the quarters. Coleman blew through the flabby Sanchez, taking him down and submitting him with a side choke at 0:44.

Iranian Reza Nazri advertised a set of instructional videotapes on Greco Roman wrestling in martial arts magazines, but he was pitting his skills against the formidable Brian Johnston. Seconds into the match, Johnston foiled Nazri's throw by crushing him to the mat. The impact knocked Nazri out, but Johnston was not finished. He mounted Nazri and landed a half-dozen headbutts and three solid rights before McCarthy rushed in and pulled him off, bloodying Johnston's nose in the process. The kickboxer was furious, believing McCarthy had broken his nose, but he was okay.

After Abbott quickly subdued boxer Sam Adkins with a forearm choke submission, the only competitive quarterfinal pitted Brazilian jiu-jitsu's Fabio Gurgel against Lion's Den fighter Jerry Bohlander. Gurgel's above-the-waist takedown couldn't match Bohlander's wrestling skill, but a solid right that opened a cut to Bohlander's face almost changed the course of the match. Gurgel took him down and mounted him, but Bohlander reversed and battered Gurgel inside his guard to win by unanimous decision.

Brian Johnston felt that he could take Coleman in their semi, but, as his parents watched from the stands, Coleman hardly hesitated in taking him down after the kickboxer had landed a couple of good leg kicks. "When he shot in, I elevated him and he hit the fence," said Johnston. "I didn't know that and thought he was Superman for recovering." Coleman stayed busy with headbutts and punches, which ultimately forced Johnston to tap out.

Backstage, Tank Abbott and Bohlander prepared for their semi. "You're not fighting," said Ken Shamrock to his disciple; Bohlander had hurt his hand against Gurgel, and Shamrock felt he was in over his head. According to Bohlander, he also had a headache and felt pressure behind one of his eyes; he thought he could have a concussion. "I told him he was too young, and there was no reason for him to go in there and get his ass beat up," said Shamrock. As SEG made the announcement with Bohlander stretcher-bound for the hospital, Abbott said in jest, "You're a pussy and your fighter is a pussy." Shamrock went ballistic. "I told him I was going to beat his fucking ass if I heard him say another word again. Jerry did not make that decision; I made that decision." The two exchanged a few more unpleasantries before going their separate ways. This marked the beginning of a longstanding feud that would never be resolved.

Abbott had trained specifically for Bohlander and had not expected to face a mirror image of himself. Scott "The Pitbull" Ferrozzo was more than ready to brawl with his fellow pitfighter. Ironically, Ferrozzo had lost to Bohlander in UFC VIII and had decided he needed better training if he wanted to continue fighting, flying Don Frye down to Minnesota to train him for four weeks. The two became good friends, and Frye became Ferrozzo's manager and training partner. Before making his way to the Octagon, a grinning Ferrozzo turned to Tank and said, "Now you're going to fight someone who isn't afraid of you." Tank's crew laughed it off, but Ferrozzo felt this was his day. A humble Frye accompanied him to the cage, with everyone in the entourage sporting shirts reading "Redemption."

Both men were 31 years old, but Ferrozzo outweighed Abbott by 50 pounds. Their bellies bulging, the two bludgeoned each other with heavy shots during the first minute, until Abbott stopped his opponent's takedown attempt and worked him against the fence. The fence opened a cut above Ferrozzo's right eye, but he was enjoying himself. As Abbott landed punches, Ferrozzo began taunting him. Abbott, whose knee was causing him too much pain to be boxing in the center of the Octagon, didn't respond. McCarthy separated the two several times, but on each occasion they gravitated back to the fence. The crowd only got glimpses of what might have been a great fight; instead they witnessed tedious fence-hugging. At times, Tank did nothing but hold on while his nemesis worked him over with belly punches, snarling at one point, "C'mon, you fucking puss," to get Abbott to move. It didn't work and the match went to overtime.

After 18 minutes, McCarthy raised Ferrozzo's hand as the winner by decision. "I got involved [in the UFC] for one reason, and that was to destroy Tank, and I did it," said an enthusiastic Ferrozzo. Abbott disagreed. "The guy [Ferrozzo] tries and does everything he can to beat me up, but that ain't nothing. I'm a man and can take a beating like a man, but I kicked his ass." Whatever, Ferrozzo glowed with elation instead of preparing for Coleman in the finals.

Coleman was ready to face anyone, but was anyone ready to face him? Ferrozzo had wasted all of his energy on Abbott and was on his way to the hospital to get checked out. He was on oxygen in the back, and the doctor told Art Davie he was dehydrated. "Dehydrated?" asked Davie. "The guy has enough body fat, how could that be?" But the doctor said he was gassed and couldn't go on. Brazilian Roberto Traven, who had won his alternate match, was to be his replacement, but he pulled out due to a broken wrist that Davie claimed was not broken. Davie and David Isaacs came up with a plan to have Tank Abbott come back out to face Coleman and give the fans their money's worth. "In that event, Bob literally dithered until we wound up not having a final," said Davie. "That was a huge fuck-up show. I'll lay that one at Meyrowitz's feet." Coleman was declared the winner by default and awarded $75,000. In an attempt to give the fans in attendance some kind of treat, Coleman and Kevin Randleman, his friend and protégé, staged a wrestling exhibition.

After UFC XI, Coleman fired Richard Hamilton as his manager. According to Frye's trainer Steve Owen, Hamilton had brought in 25 people and paid them to be Coleman supporters out of Coleman's purse, which explained why he had so many fans with ready-made signs for his first appearance in UFC X. "I found out that he was doing some stuff behind my back," said Coleman. "I also found out that his name wasn't really Richard Hamilton. Right before UFC XI, he had been involved in a crime in New York and was in the witness protection program, so why was he on TV with me? I really didn't like the situation at all." Hamilton hit back with a breach-of-contract lawsuit, but he had other problems. He would be indicted on one count of sexual abuse and six counts of sexual conduct with a minor just a year and a half later. In June 1998, a jury in Arizona sentenced Hamilton to 78 years for those crimes. Though Hamilton's spokesman proclaimed his innocence, he sits in jail at the time of this writing. He still settled out of court with Coleman on the breach-of-contract suit and received an undisclosed but substantial sum of money.

Coleman had been victorious in back-to-back events, but could he beat fellow two-time UFC champion and wrestler Dan Severn, who continually bounced back to refute his critics? Unlike any opponent he had fought in the past, Severn now faced one of his own at UFC XII's superfight. "I'm a realistic person," said Severn. "No matter who I fight, I simply write down pros and cons. I put down that he [Coleman] is younger, stronger, faster, better wrestler...I didn't come out looking too good on paper." Severn felt the only way he could beat Coleman was to take him beyond five minutes, when conditioning became a factor. Coleman had a different take on the matter. He felt invincible. There was nothing Severn could do to him.

After a brief standup, Severn shot for Coleman's leg, but Coleman sprawled, tied up Severn's head and pushed him back. Swinging wildly, Coleman landed a decent right, forcing the Beast to shoot for a second takedown. Coleman sprawled again and immediately took Severn's back. Now he had a difficult decision to make. "I knew Dan, and knew that he was a wrestler," said Coleman. "In the back of my mind, even though I was a grounder and pounder, I really didn't feel like going out there and punching him in the face a whole lot. We were somewhat friends, and we came from the same sport." Coleman softened him up with light body shots but refused to use elbows and headbutts.

Severn eventually rolled to his back, and Coleman took the mount. Severn tied up his opponent's head to keep him from punching. As he had done in previous bouts, Coleman transitioned to side mount and applied a headlock that became a very effective choke. Coleman trapped one of Severn's arms and squeezed his massive arms for over a minute. Severn tried to free himself with punches to Coleman's head, but at 2:59, he tapped from the pressure. The Hammer leaped to his feet with maniacal joy, scaled the fence, and pumped his fists. By beating two UFC champions from wrestling backgrounds, Mark Coleman was the undisputed king of the Octagon.

15

TOURNAMENT OF CHAMPIONS

The first Ultimate Ultimate had failed to live up to the hype, with three back-to-back decisions instead of clear-cut victories. The second couldn't have been more different. It was an exciting tournament, full of controversy and emotion, and not one match ended by decision. Ken Shamrock was out to prove to himself and to the world that he could face his demons and finish a tournament. Don "The Predator" Frye's war with Mark Coleman had made him even more popular, and it humbled him to the point of taking his training more seriously. And, after losing to Scott Ferrozzo, a leaner Tank Abbott was hungry for the fight of his life. Returning to the Alabama State Fair Arena, UU '96 was held December 7, 1996, a night no one present would forget.

Ken Shamrock had reached the end of his rope with Tank Abbott. Tank had pushed him too far with his off-color remarks toward Jerry Bohlander and himself. Since the show featured a tournament format, it was time for them to tangle. "I argued with them to put us in the first fight because Tank might not have made it to the finals, and that was a match that people wanted to see," said Shamrock. But SEG set up the brackets the same way they did for the first UU: four fighters they felt would win against four fighters who wouldn't. In other words, why put Tank vs. Shamrock in the quarterfinals, when the buildup would make it more exciting to see them later in the broadcast? One fly in the ointment could have been Mark Coleman, but he pulled out due to a virus three weeks before the show.

Ukrainian Igor Vovchanchyn and Brazilian Vitor Belfort were also supposed to fight, but for one reason or another each had to be replaced.

The first match pitted Shamrock against Brian Johnston, who had started to work out with wrestler Matt Furey and Don Frye, of all people. Johnston barely got off a leg kick before Shamrock took him down and pressed him up against the fence. In Johnston's open guard, the former King of Pancrase made good on his promise to be more aggressive. Perhaps it was his way of making up for the Severn dance, but Johnston paid the price. After being cautioned for holding the fence (a new rule to cut down on fighters using it to their advantage), Shamrock unloaded with hard rights to the face. Shamrock believed Johnston would tap from his punches and didn't try for a submission. "He was in a terrible position, but I just didn't know enough to do anything at that point," said Johnston later. Nearly six minutes passed until Johnston's hand raised up. After a moment of hesitation, he tapped out.

Unbeknownst to SEG, Don Frye, Mark Hall, Paul Varelans, and Kimo—all competing at UU '96—had just fought in another event dubbed U Japan less than a month earlier. It had been a way for sports agent/lawyer Robert DePersia to cash in on the fighters he represented, which was quite a few in 1996. "My presentation to [the fighters] was that because I had so many of them, it was like we were unionizing and could demand a higher wage, because they didn't want to pay anyone over a grand," said DePersia. "We were getting significant purses, and it was making Meyrowitz nuts, because if he wouldn't give me what I wanted for a fighter, I would just say, 'None of my guys are coming.' So I sort of controlled his events because I controlled all the talent." The U Japan show was set up just like the UFC, in an octagon, and featured nine UFC competitors in decent matches, save for a pro wrestling bout between Dan Severn and a hardcore Japanese wrestler.

Don Frye should have been in the best shape of his life for the December show. Becky Levi (who also fought and won her first MMA match in U Japan) and trainer Steve Owen had stepped up Frye's preparation. This was to be his chance at redemption. But just one day before the show, SEG fight consultant Joe Silva witnessed one of Don's training sessions: "When I went to see Don spar, he looked terrible. He was one of the favorites going in, but I could tell something was wrong seeing him work out. He told me that he had got himself in great shape but had caught a bad cold a couple of days before. I thought he was going to be in serious trouble."

Frye's first match would be against a new and improved "Big Daddy" Gary Goodridge. The Canadian was coming off a recent arm wrestling championship win, and trainer John Gnap slapped him across the face to psyche him up for the rematch. Goodridge and Frye tied up in the beginning, and while Frye was able to land several good knees and uppercuts, Goodridge was ready. He took the wrestler down and threw punches with reckless abandon, even thwarting an arm bar attempt. Working their way back to their feet, Frye clutched Goodridge's knee, and the Predator put the bigger man on his back. The crowd howled as the former UFC champion turned the tables, but Goodridge was exhausted and tapped out before any damage could be administered. At 11:20, it would be the longest match of the night.

"I was so tired, they had to drag me out of the ring," said Goodridge. "He's the only fighter who, after my fights with him, I ended up crying out of frustration and disappointment. I felt I had it, and then I lost it straight through my hands both times." It would be the Canadian's last appearance in the UFC for three years, but he found success in Brazil and Japan, exploiting his showmanship and distinct look. On December 31, 2003, Goodridge fought Don Frye a third time for Japan's Pride Shockwave. In 39 seconds, he delivered a devastating head kick (his first ever) and knocked out Frye. Goodridge said it was his retirement fight, but he continued competing for K-1 in kickboxing and MMA in several promotions worldwide.

Tank Abbott, who had recovered from his knee injury, faced ex-marine Cal Worsham. A doctor had shot his knee up with cortisone several times, and Tank had been able to run off some excess weight. Coming into the show, he was still a less-than-slim 273 pounds but far from the

298 he weighed against Ferrozzo. In his prefight interview, Worsham said, "Tank, don't even try to hang on to the fence. This is going out in the middle, and I'm taming the Tank." As the fight began, Abbott pushed Worsham up against the fence and proceeded to throw him out of the Octagon. Though Abbott denied the tactic later, he had Worsham high enough to slam him for several seconds, inviting him to counter with blows to Abbott's head. Abbott finally crushed him to the mat, moved from a side mount to the guard, and punished the tae kwon do champion with strikes to the abdomen.

Worsham held on to the fence, his eyes transfixed on Abbott as his cornermen shouted helpful advice such as, "You're going to lose Tank." Abbott moved in for the kill, but Worsham tapped. When McCarthy pulled them apart, Abbott got in one more shot. "I want him disqualified!" Worsham screamed at McCarthy, who pushed him back to the fence and got right in his face. Unlike any other referee in combat sports history, John McCarthy has become the judge and jury in the Octagon, and this was one of many times he manhandled a fighter to keep the peace. Though Abbott admitted to hitting Worsham after the break, he didn't see any problem with it: apparently Worsham had stuck a finger in Tank's eye, though he claimed it was an accident. McCarthy told Tank off, but the crowd erupted with pleasure upon seeing their bar-brawling bad boy make his comeback win. Because of Abbott's attempt to toss Worsham out of the cage, the height of the Octagon went from 5' to 5'6". Over time, the UFC would have cages of varying sizes, but the height would never dip below that.

Despite losing both of his previous UFC matches, Kimo Leopoldo had become a star. His fierce looks, mysterious demeanor, and brutish tattoos made him welcome on any card. Kimo had also been winning fights—just not in the UFC. In Japan, he'd defeated Patrick Smith, three Japanese fighters, and pro wrestler "Bam Bam" Bigelow. Now he faced Paul Varelans, who had replaced Mark Coleman. The Hawaiian weighed in 20 pounds lighter than before and spoke of being more of a "thinker" in the ring. As the match got underway, he wasted energy on an ankle lock and couldn't put the 340-pound Polar Bear on his back. Nestled against the fence, Kimo attempted to throw his massive opponent (who outweighed him by 100 pounds), but Varelans wound up on top. With blood trickling from his left eye, it looked as if Kimo would suffer his third UFC defeat—until, nearly nine minutes into the match, he reversed and mounted Varelans. He was able to do this because Varelans went unconscious for a few seconds when Kimo cut off the bigger man's circulation using his own shirt. As Varelans came out of it, Kimo landed 10 dead-on shots to his face that prompted Varelans' corner to throw in the towel. An exhausted Kimo had won an emotional, gutsy battle.

Everything was set up for the match of the night: Tank Abbott vs. Ken Shamrock—but once again, Shamrock had to pull out, this time due to a broken hand. For those in the know, this match was even more tantalizing given that the night before one of Tank's boys attacked Ken's adopted brother, Frank, who was eight years younger. En route to the hotel, Tank's goon crew approached Frank and taunted him as they had done earlier that week. The biggest one finally pushed the envelope, kicking what looked to be food from Frank's hand. "Frank just stood there in awe for a moment," said Kimo's training manager, Clint Santiago Dahl. "Then all of the sudden, Frank kicked the guy in the head and knocked him out like a sack of potatoes." Tank's boys just walked away into the darkness. The epic buildup for this fight was all for nothing, given the past. And for whatever reason, the emotionally complex Ken Shamrock, a man from a troubled background who could have been *the* star of MMA, could never quite rise to the occasion. He was not at a loss for words backstage, however, telling commentator Tony Blauer, "There is one person that I really dislike for some of the things he said about one of my fighters, and I take that personally. And I would like to say right here and right now, Tank Abbott—I want him. I want him and I'm making this challenge right now."

Abbott felt the same. Over the course of three interviews for this book, he could not stop talking about Shamrock, his claims ranging from him rigging the tournament to being the envy of SEG. Abbott's assumptions were incorrect on both counts. "In the ring, Ken Shamrock was a disappointment to me as a UFC booker and promoter," said Art Davie. "You are talking about a guy who was given more opportunities to be a star in the UFC [yet] every time someone handed him a spear and asked him to throw it, he figured a way to drop it and not throw it at all." While Shamrock was quick to say he didn't like Abbott, he did respect him as a fighter. Abbott wouldn't even give him that much: "He's a piece of trash. He is a poser of a warrior." Ken Shamrock moved back to his roots with pro wrestling when he signed with the WWF in 1997, but he eventually returned to MMA. Tank scoffed at Shamrock's pro wrestling reentry but joined up with the competition WCW. The two men never fought, and their rivalry became another UFC "what if?"

Shamrock did, however, meet up again with the Nasty Boys, the two wrestlers who had put him in a hospital in the late 1980s (see Chapter 4). In 1998, while on tour with the WWF, he saw his attackers in a Florida airport. "I confronted them. I was just furious. I never knew what I was going to say if I ever saw them face to face in a situation where I could do something. The blonde one ran away right there in the airport, and the other one came right over there with Billy Gunn standing next to me. I leaned over and said, 'I'm going to fucking kill you!' I guess he figured that because of where we were, nothing was going to happen, but I had no control. I was going to kill him.... I was going to literally beat the shit out of him until there was nothing left of his body. The guy just kept saying, 'Man, chill out. What's your problem? That was a long time ago.' Yeah, for you it was a long time ago; for me, it was yesterday. He went upstairs and then came back down where all the boys were sitting, but he couldn't see me because I went away to cool off. He said, 'Man, what's up with Shamrock? He needs to take a chill pill.' That's when I jumped over the seats and went right at him. I got right up in his face and said, 'This is where I fucking kill you. You think you're fuckin' tough? Let's do it right now.' He turned his shoulder and said, 'If you hit me, it will be a federal offense and I'll press charges.' I wanted to, but I knew that

I was not in the right frame of mind. At that point, I just turned away and walked."

• • •

FOR SOME REASON, Abbott got only one fight's rest before his next bout. The brackets were changed so that he would fight in the first semi-final match instead of Frye, who would get extra rest. This didn't help Shamrock's replacement, karate man Steve Nelmark. As Tank charged his beefy opponent, Nelmark circled to the left to draw away his power. Nelmark landed one punch, but Tank fired away with a big right hand at the same time, sending Nelmark across the Octagon and up against the fence. Abbott wasted little time in pressing the attack, swinging wild shots that his dazed foe could not defend. An uppercut sent Nelmark staggering before Abbott knocked him out with a right hand to the jaw that took his knees out from under him. It was a frightening sight, as Nelmark's folded body looked devoid of life. "Dave Meltzer and I were sitting right next to each other, and I swear to God, as soon as that punch landed, we turned to each other at the exact same time and said, 'Fuck! He's dead!'" said Joe Silva. "When Tank hit him, you just turned an off switch on him." It was all over within a minute. "I have to admit that I was always scared of seeing Tank in those early round matches; scared for the event, scared of what he might do," said play-by-play commentator Bruce Beck. Luckily, Nelmark was fine, and the fans cheered Abbott for a job well done. Just as in UFC VI, he was on his way to the finals and hardly the worse for wear.

Mark Hall sat in the dressing room, his mind cluttered by peer pressure. He had recently signed with Robert DePersia, believing the lawyer's lock on the UFC would earn him more money and better opportunities. His first match through DePersia had been at U Japan, where he fought Don Frye for a second time. "I was pissed off at myself for taking it easy on him the first time, and I felt wasting that time cost me the belt in the match against Coleman," said Frye. In the rematch, he pounded on Hall with little regard for his foe, but it still took him five and a half

minutes against an opponent with two broken ribs suffered in training two weeks before. Hall had taken the fight because he needed the
money. Now Frye was in bad shape; Goodridge had worn him out. He
sat there and contemplated pulling out of the semifinal, but an opportunity was about to arise.

In the week leading up to the fight, Kimo's training manager Clint
Dahl had weaned the fighter off of soft drinks, only wanting him to
drink water. Kimo not only wanted to have great cardio; he wanted to
look lean for the cameras, and he made good on that. But after giving
Kimo three gallons of water and seeing that he had finished all but half
a gallon, Dahl rewarded him with a requested Sprite. After the fight with
Paul Varelans, however, Dahl was perplexed as to why Kimo was not only
physically drained, but looked pale. After Art Davie seemed concerned
about his participation, Dahl had paramedics hook Kimo up with an IV
to simply hydrate him. It didn't work. Finally Kimo turned to Dahl and
said, "I fucked up bro. I didn't drink any water all week!" As it turned out,
Kimo gave the water to his dad, who was there in his corner. Eventually
Dahl could do no more, and Kimo had to be escorted to an ambulance
via stretcher. "To this day, nobody knows how close to death Kimo came
from dehydration from that fight. He had vertigo and was dizzy for two
and half months afterward." Davie finally broke the news to Don Frye
that his only option was fighting Mark Hall again in a rubber match.

Though it was unlikely he could beat Frye, Hall's "no quit" attitude
would almost certainly fatigue the Predator even further for the finals.
According to Hall, DePersia now intervened.

"Well, Mark, sometimes you do what you have to do, and we're a
team. This is Don's day...not yours. Your time's coming," said the lawyer.
"Mark, don't take this away from Don."

"No way," responded Hall. "I'm not going to do this [throw the fight]."

But, said Hall, it was made crystal clear that he should cooperate so
Frye would be fresh to take on Abbott in the final. "Robert kind of hinted
that my career would go nowhere if I didn't cooperate," he claimed. Hall
walked into the bathroom to think it over and Frye followed, lecturing

him about how his dream was to win the Ultimate Ultimate. He told Hall it wouldn't make any sense for them to fight for real a third time, as Frye had already beaten him twice. Hall contemplated firing DePersia but, in the end, decided to throw the match with Frye. He was promised a percentage of Frye's purse for doing the job.

As Hall entered the cage, he was all smiles and looked very relaxed, hardly the signs of someone about to be in a tough fight. McCarthy gave the go-ahead, and Frye ran right at Hall and took him down. The wrestler performed a heel hook and Hall tapped at 0:20. Hall sold the punishment to his ankle by wincing in pain, while Paul Varelans stepped in to help carry him backstage. Steve Owen, Frye's trainer, claimed Frye had been working with a Russian sambo expert on leg locks, but there was no doubt this match was worked. Stylistically, Frye had never taken such a quick and risky approach in any bout, not to mention having never gone for leg submissions before. In boxing, it's illegal to manage both corners, but DePersia knew there was no such UFC rule and didn't seem to care about the ethics of the situation.

Mark Hall continued to be managed by DePersia, who would get him a fight in Brazil months later, but he never fought in the UFC again. Nine months after the event, he divulged information about the fixed bout over the Internet. "I told [Frye] that I was going public with it, and he pretended like he didn't know what I was talking about," said Hall. He claimed Frye never paid him his share of the money. "I asked him again about giving me even half of the money, because my school wasn't doing well and I really needed it." DePersia contended he knew nothing about the setup and suggested Hall made the allegations only because he had lost his martial arts school, gone through a bad separation with his wife, and lost money in some other business deals with Frye. Frye said that he and Hall were supposed to hold a reality fighting seminar together (after UU '96); when he arrived, Hall was so poor that he was living in his own dojo, and the seminar only had a couple of dozen participants. Frye strongly refuted Hall's claim, saying he wouldn't need to work a fight to beat him.

In Hall's interview for this book, the subject got him so rattled that remnants of his old speech impediment resurfaced. He finished his thoughts on Frye by saying in 2000, "To this day I wake up at night thinking about that son of a bitch. I want to kill him. I not only did not get the money, but my UFC career was ruined. That dumb ass son of a bitch didn't even do the leg lock right." Hall later became a fight promoter in his own right of The Cobra Challenge in California. In 1999, Ken Shamrock beat him to within an inch of his life in a California casino, apparently over insulting words toward Shamrock's wife at the time.

Whatever the truth, Tank Abbott would be fighting in the finals for the second time against an opponent who, it seemed, had used a bit of funny business to get there. Undaunted, Abbott walked right toward Frye, who thought he could stand up with him. Frye quickly learned the meaning of heavy hands. With a single jab, Tank knocked him across the Octagon. Frye's wife Molly screamed out in fear. *Well, dummy, that's what you get for standing up with him*, thought Frye. "I took a step and was on my heels, and he caught me at the right time. I looked up and thought, *Shit, here he comes*." Remarkably, Frye was able to get back to his feet, and the two went toe to toe. Abbott bludgeoned Frye's face, blackening both eyes and drawing blood in seconds. "I remember David Isaacs was sitting next to me, and Dave was a big Tank fan," said Art Davie. "For a minute there it looked like Tank was going to pull it off. Deep down inside, SEG would have loved to have had Tank as their champion." Frye, however, moved on the offensive and stepped on Abbott's foot by mistake, sending him to the canvas. The Predator seized the moment, taking Tank's back. After sinking in his hooks and missing a punch, Frye went for the rear naked choke. Abbott was clearly exhausted and even though the choke had not sunk in all the way, he tapped.

Despite questions about how he got there, Don "The Predator" Frye truly earned the Ultimate Ultimate '96 championship. In one of the greatest matches in UFC history, he had shown he was a true warrior. Tears streamed down his battered face like Rocky Balboa as he delivered a heartfelt speech to the crowd. Even Scott Ferrozzo was so happy to see Frye win that he lost his composure and his eyes began to water.

Tank chalked up the defeat to the same politics he blamed for his other losses. Self-defense expert Tony Blauer interviewed him immediately after the match, and his replies left Blauer nearly speechless.

"You said every fight's a fight," said Blauer. "Are you disappointed?"

"Well, I'd like the 'W' [win], but I don't care....I'll go have a cocktail [and] maybe get in another fight tonight," said Abbott.

Blauer asked if Abbott respected Don Frye.

"No, I don't respect anybody, not even you!"

◆ ◆ ◆

DON FRYE WOULD NOT BE CHAMPION FOR LONG. He had broken his hand on Tank's head and had to have three pins inserted to hold the small, brittle bones together. He wouldn't fight in MMA again for five years. Frye interviewed with both the WWF and WCW but felt that his tough-guy, cowboy persona came off as too cocky even for pro wrestling. Jeff Blatnick recommended Frye to wrestling champion turned pro wrestler Brad Rheingans, who was the U.S. scout for New Japan Pro Wrestling. Frye jumped at the opportunity and soon became a "heel"—a bad guy in the organization. His first match was against New Japan owner Antonio Inoki (Frye lost), in Inoki's retirement appearance, held at the sold-out 75,000-seat Tokyo Dome. Fellow UFC vets Brian Johnston and David Beneteau both wrestled for New Japan and, with Frye, formed a group called Club 245. Johnston came up with the name from California penal code 245: "assault with intent to do major bodily harm." The trio walked out to the Japanese crowds wearing shirts that read, "A Group of Felonious Individuals Whose Purpose Is Best Served by Committing Violent, Unlawful Injury upon the Person of Another." The memory made Johnston laugh. "The Japanese didn't know what it was and thought it was a bar. They said, 'How do you get to Club 245? I'm dying to go there.'" The group eventually broke up and Beneteau returned to Canada, while Johnston became a "babyface" or good guy on the circuit.

On August 19, 2001, Johnston collapsed from a stroke while preparing another pro wrestler for action. Doctors told his wife Teiana, who he had married just one month before, that he had a 50 percent chance of surviving and even then would be a vegetable. Johnston had other plans. Today, given the new nickname "The Miracle," he is able to move around unassisted and is never at a loss for words. In the first quarter of 2002, he started a clothing line, Pain Inc., and has a bright future ahead. As for Frye, he returned to MMA in Japan's Pride while continuing to pro wrestle. On February 24, 2002, he faced off against Ken Shamrock and won a gutsy decision. Frye wanted to rematch Mark Coleman more than anything else, and the pair fought on June 6, 2003, but the result was pretty much the same as their first meeting.

Although the question had now been answered about how well different martial arts would fare against one another, the new question was how the drama would play out. In storybook fashion, there would be plot twists and turns, good guys, bad guys, and wolves in sheep's clothing. The UFC had finally bridged the gap between spectator sport and pro wrestling, leaving the audience guessing what would happen next.

16

A STRIKER'S VENGEANCE

From the first UFC, pure strikers from styles such as tae kwon do, karate, and kenpo had proven ineffective against groundfighters. While many claimed these competitors didn't truly represent their styles, it was apparent that a striker's tools could be taken from him once the fight went to the mat. Tank Abbott showed that striking could be dangerous, but against a wrestler like Dan Severn, he could do very little. Extreme Fighting also knew that grapplers would come out ahead and leaned toward the dominance of jiu-jitsu, creating stars out of Ralph Gracie, Conan Silveira, and John Lewis. For the third EF, matchmaker John Perretti landed undeniably the most experienced striker to fall victim to heavyweight Conan.

With over 15 years in kickboxing, Maurice Smith had worked his way up to become champion of the World Kickboxing Association (WKA), a European version of the PKA that allowed kicks below the waist. Smith had made martial arts his calling after seeing Bruce Lee on the big screen at age 13. He moved from tae kwon do to karate and wing chun and quickly realized that stepping into the ring was the only way to test himself. Smith competed in kickboxing at age 18 for the WKA as one of the few Americans to fight for the organization. He claimed his first championship at 21 and, after losing a decision to Don "The Dragon" Wilson, competed for over nine years without a single loss. At 6'2", Smith started out fighting at a slim 175 pounds, but he later moved to super-heavyweight to compete at 215.

The WKA led the way in popularizing kickboxing in Japan, and Smith made a name over there. As his popularity grew, he competed in pro wrestling in Japan for the Universal Wrestling Federation, his first match coming in November 1989 against Minoru Suzuki. Smith felt the Japanese wanted to leverage his kickboxing name to increase fans for the new shoot style of wrestling. From 1989 to 1995, he competed on and off for the UWF, Rings, and Pancrase, familiarizing himself with ground-work, even though some of the outcomes were predetermined. Smith eventually worked with Ken Shamrock, after meeting him in Pancrase, on stand-up in preparation for UFC VI. "We did more talking than training, and when he went into the WWF, I got pawned off to Frank [Shamrock]," said Smith. This turned out to be a blessing in disguise. Frank—the brother of Ken in name only, having been similarly adopted by Bob Shamrock—was if anything an even more talented fighter. He and Smith became fast friends and even better training partners.

Smith remembered being contacted for a slot in the first UFC, but without predetermined endings, he passed: "I was just a kickboxer, and my credibility would have helped their sport, but I would have got my butt kicked, more than likely." After turning down an opportunity at UFC VI while helping Ken Shamrock prepare for Severn, Smith talked everything over with Frank Shamrock, and both agreed that EF 3 was the best opportunity for his MMA debut. With the help of the Lion's Den, Smith trained specifically to combat a jiu-jitsu player. "We worked on defending the side, full mount on the ground, and [drilled] reversing the guy. If I did that, I worked to keep him against the fence and start punching him. I shouldn't worry about breaking the guard because that's not important." At 34 years old, Smith took on a whole new challenge against an opponent who seemed unbeatable: Conan Silveira.

EF was set up to have a four-man tournament to decide a definitive heavyweight champion in the fourth show. Smith and Silveira made up one bracket, Bart Vale and Murakami Kazunari the other. Vale had also started with the UWF in 1989, after 20 years of traditional martial arts, competing in point karate tournaments and local kickboxing shows in

Florida. In 1983, he met Sammy Soranaka, who introduced him to the shoot style of wrestling that Karl Gotch had perfected for the UWF group. Vale was hooked from the start. On whether UWF was real, Vale said, "People often asked me that. I wished they were [worked] because that would have saved my face from getting cracked and my shoulder from getting broken." Injuries did happen in the UWF, but the truth was that it was a pro wrestling organization with fixed endings. "All the throws and the grappling were basically real because we were shooting for position, and we were kicking each other hard and hitting each other hard," remembered Shamrock from his UWF match with Vale. "I had two black eyes, and he had a black eye and a broken nose." Unlike Smith or Shamrock, Vale built his career with the UWF and later Pro Wrestling Fujiwara Gumi. When shows were held in Florida, Bart Vale became the "champion of the world" by defeating founder Yoshiaki Fujiwara for the belt.

Vale was a tenacious businessman. After copyrighting the name Shootfighting, he created his own organization, the International Shoot Fighting Association. He looked like a true champion at 6'4" and 270 pounds and even convinced MTV that he was legit when it aired an entire segment on him in the early 1990s. As Vale was still under contract with the Japanese, "I remember telling Perretti that there were certain opponents that I was not allowed to fight. So he told me, 'Well, just get somebody from Japan that they would approve.'" The decision was made to bring in Murakami Kazunari, a 6'2" judo player with a solid physique. Kazunari was no stranger to MMA, as he had competed in the 1996 Lumax Cup (UFC rules except for no strikes to the face on the ground) in Japan just seven months earlier and had lost in the finals of the eight-man tournament.

In October 1996, EF 3 held its first sanctioned show in Oklahoma. For the first time since the original UFC, matches had three five-minute rounds (ridiculously called "phases") to keep the action moving. Ralph Gracie smoked karate man Ali Mihoubi, and John Lewis outmatched Brazilian Johil De Oliveira for a draw (EF didn't have judges, so any fight that went the distance became a draw). The event had its first major controversy when Carlson Gracie student Allan Goes defeated Oklahoma native Anthony Macias. Goes dominated Macias but head-butted him several times and fish-hooked (hooking an opponent's mouth with a finger much like a fish hook) him once. When the referee stopped Goes the first time for head-butting and tried to explain the foul to him, the Brazilian paid no attention, instead listening to Gracie in his corner. Nearly four minutes into the match, the ref stopped the action again for another butt, but Goes ended up with the win. Macias apparently was angry about Goes not getting off him when the ref stopped the action and appeared to verbally submit. Though Goes should have been disqualified, an error in communication gave the Brazilian the win. The ref frequently threatened disqualifications for the remainder of the night.

No one could predict who was going to win the Kazunari-Vale match since Vale had fought only one true MMA bout, against Mike Bitonio in the WCC, while Kazunari was an unknown. Vale was much larger, but that didn't stop Kazunari from rushing in, taking Vale's back in the clinch, and attempting a throw. Vale defended with a standing straight arm bar, the fight momentarily went to the ground, and then Vale landed two solid punches to a dazed Kazunari. What happened next was astonishing. The judo expert went into a frenzy, unleashing a plethora of lefts and rights that knocked Vale to the ground. Kazunari continued punching until the ref stopped the fight. "I was surprised that they ended it when they did; I gassed myself out," said Vale, who went on to open his own schools around the country. Despite his questionable fighting experience, he promoted Shootfighting and MMA the best he could. In the four years after EF 3, Vale would have one other legit match, against Dan Severn, who beat him soundly with punches in less than five minutes.

Maurice Smith came to the circular cage accompanied, as usual, by his 20-year manager Kirk Jenson—but this time he also had Frank Shamrock in his corner. The crowd bellowed their support for the underdog kickboxer. As the match got underway, Conan Silveira immediately went for the takedown and settled for being in Smith's half-guard. Smith kept the Brazilian at bay before surprisingly reversing the BJJ whiz and sitting in his guard for the rest of the round. Instead of exposing an arm trying to strike, Smith buried his head in Silveira's chest and punched the abdomen and head from the sides.

In Round 2, Smith kept Silveira away with solid Thai kicks to his thighs. The jiu-jitsu man eventually tied Smith up but, by grabbing him just under the arms, wasn't able to take him down. A frustrated Silveira tried to finish the fight standing, but his flailing arm punches did very little damage to such an experienced striker. Just as Vale had awakened Kazunari's punching, now Smith returned, connecting with four perfect punches that rocked the giant. Silveira, noticeably tired, managed to recover and tied the kickboxer up again to end the round.

Tying up Smith in the third round provided an opportunity for the kickboxer to throw a hard knee to separate them. Whack! Smith landed a devastating kick to Silveira's left thigh that echoed throughout the venue. A wobbly Silveira couldn't react quickly enough before getting kicked again. Muay Thai fighters often bait their opponents with leg kicks that over time make them drop their guard for protection; the opponent's reflexive action then sets up the finishing blow. Just 90 seconds into the round, Maurice Smith made his move by landing a perfect high kick to the side of Conan's neck, which sent him reeling. "What ended up happening—and this has happened to me twice—was you don't feel it," said Smith. "You don't go down, but it's like the blood stops flowing to your brain for a second." The referee stopped the bout before Smith could do anything else. Silveira claimed his knee had been injured just days before the match, but there was no sign of this. "I wasn't getting away from him and wasn't in my game plan," said Silveira. "He did hurt me because he was throwing all these kicks and punches and I wasn't stepping out." The match became a benchmark for the sport: a kickboxer with basic grappling skills had claimed a knockout victory over a Carlson Gracie jiu-jitsu black belt.

◆ ◆ ◆

SEG MADE TWO MAJOR CHANGES to its tournament format for UFC XII
four months later. UFC XI had seen a few injuries, so the eight-man tournament was disbanded in favor of a less-punishing four-man tournament,
and weight classes were instituted for lightweight (under 200 pounds) and
heavyweight (over 200 pounds), allowing smaller fighters to take on opponents their own size and so lend more credibility to the sport. In the first-
ever lightweight tournament, Lion's Den fighter Jerry Bohlander emerged
the victor by scoring two easy wins in under two minutes combined.

Bohlander's only real competition would have been the victor between
Carlson Gracie student Wallid Ismail and Pancrase fighter Yoshiki
Takahashi. Unfamiliar with the rules, Takahashi used the fence to subdue
Ismail's takedown attempts and utilize his better stand-up skills. Ismail,
a native of the Amazon, had beaten both Renzo and Ralph Gracie in jiu-
jitsu matches, but he couldn't put anything together to beat Takahashi. "I
expended a lot of energy trying to put Takahashi down, but he held the
fence and I lost all my power," he said. "I knew if I put him on the floor,
I'd beat him in one minute." Takahashi won by decision but was unable to
fight Bohlander due to an injury. The young Lion's Den standout fought
an easy final against alternate Nick Sanzo, who was submitted with a
neck crank variation called a crucifix. Ismail would go on to choke out
Royce Gracie unconscious in a jiu-jitsu match the following year. "Royce
went to Brazil and said in a magazine, 'I challenge everybody to jiu-jitsu,
but I want no time and no points—just submission,'" said Ismail. "After
the fight, Royce said a lot of bullshit. Royce said that I beat him because
of luck. If we fought 100 times, he would lose 99."

For the heavyweight tournament, Scott "The Pitbull" Ferrozzo was
the only veteran among newcomers Jim Mullen, Tra Telligman, and
Vitor Belfort. All eyes turned to 19-year-old Belfort, who came into the
Octagon with an Adonis-like body and choirboy face. Born in Brazil,
Belfort had trained in jiu-jitsu from the age of six and dabbled in boxing
and other sports. At 17, he moved to Los Angeles and stayed with his

adoptive father, Carlson Gracie, who stepped up his jiu-jitsu training. Belfort was going to adopt the Gracie name, but pressure from the rest of the family, who were unsure of his skills, put a stop to it. After two years, Carlson gave Belfort his jiu-jitsu black belt and put him in his first fight in the Hawaiian promotion, Superbrawl. Belfort beat UFC veteran John Hess to a pulp in 15 seconds without even using any jiu-jitsu.

The UFC presented a more difficult test: Belfort's first opponent would be Lion's Den member and Superbrawl champion Tra "Trauma" Telligman. Telligman hailed from a rough neighborhood in Dallas, Texas, and took up martial arts for self-protection. He had already survived a terrible car accident as a 17-month-old toddler; the impact crushed his sternum and ribs and destroyed his right pectoral muscle. He never saw it as a handicap and excelled in sports as he grew older. After training in martial arts, Telligman met Guy Mezger and joined the Lion's Den. He went on to win several fights in Russia and Hawaii before getting a slot in the UFC on two weeks' notice. Telligman was out of shape but knew his opponent's only skills were jiu-jitsu. "The biggest fear in my mind was that I was getting out there with this kid that didn't belong in the ring with me, and if I don't blast him out of there in six or seven minutes, I'm going to get beat by some kid," said Telligman. Color commentator Jeff Blatnick also predicted Belfort would try to take the fight to the ground. Both observations could not have been more incorrect.

In the first semifinal, Telligman circled to the left of Belfort, who bounced back and forth as if waiting for a signal. Telligman wanted him to shoot for the takedown, but Belfort had other plans. "He kind of winked at me, and then he lit me up," said Telligman. Belfort swarmed him with lightning-fast punches to close the distance and try for a take-down. Up against the fence, the Lion's Den fighter stopped the takedown, forcing the Brazilian to unload a series of accurate crosses and straight punches right out of a comic book, his back muscles flexing wildly with each punch thrown. "He was landing everything that he was throwing; he has very good timing with the distance of his punches," remarked

Telligman later. Moving away from the fence, Belfort continued his attack, eventually sending the Texan to the mat. Telligman held Belfort in an open guard, but could do very little as his opponent quickly moved his leg out of the way and took side mount. After landing several elbows to the neck, Belfort looked up to John McCarthy and motioned that his opponent had sustained enough damage. McCarthy stopped the bout. Tank Abbott, watching from the sidelines, was miffed at Jeff Blatnick's praise of Belfort's hand speed.

Scott Ferrozzo's semi against kickboxer Jim Mullen was a one-sided beating. The rotund pitfighter worked on Mullen against the fence with uppercuts, knees, and punches. He seemed to enjoy hurting Mullen, who, according to Ferrozzo, had been trash-talking him the week of the fight. After one stoppage to check for a cut, the match was finally over when McCarthy realized Mullen could no longer defend himself; his face looked like a pepperoni pizza. Before the match, Ferrozzo had said, "The rule is not to get hit at all in the face," and he showed why in this match.

Ferrozzo, who had dropped 30 pounds since his UFC debut thanks to Becky Levi, didn't know anything about Belfort and approached the final cautiously. So did the Brazilian. After feeling each other out, Belfort landed a solid left hand flush on Ferrozzo's chin that shook him. Taking a step back to insure he didn't get trapped, Belfort fired another left. This time it dropped Ferrozzo, who fell into his arms. Belfort scooped him up and dumped him to the mat. The big man got to his knees for an escape before Belfort could do any significant damage. Holding on to Ferrozzo with his left hand, Belfort threw five hard rights to the side of his head, then two equally hard lefts. Ferrozzo protected his head with both hands, but McCarthy moved in to stop the fight at 0:45. "I thought that he would try and mount me, and I was going to try and get him up close," said Ferrozzo. "All of a sudden I felt the pressure let up, so [after the match was stopped], I got him up against the fence and then I'm accosted by the refs." The melee brought in fellow ref Joe Hamilton to calm Ferrozzo down. Later, Ferrozzo claimed he hadn't been hurt, though he admitted, "He did crack me pretty good."

◆ ◆ ◆

ON THE DAY THAT UFC XII AIRED, Leo J. Hindery Jr. was named president of TCI Cable. It was the worst possible news for SEG. Cable was their lifeblood, sustaining the sport financially and helping to build its audience. But Hindery was an implacable opponent of MMA events and had refused to carry them when he ran a small cable network in San Francisco. Now he was in charge of an industry giant that could reach 14 million viewers in 46 states.

It wasn't long before Bob Meyrowitz, John McCarthy, and Art Davie were flying down to meet Hindery to discuss his stance on the UFC. Meyrowitz told Hindery there would be additions to the rules: no headbutts, no groin shots, and mandatory gloves. "The whole reason we didn't use gloves was because the fighter couldn't hit the person as much because it hurt their hand," noted McCarthy. "[Mandatory gloves] went against what we had been saying the whole time." Still, in order to appease the ignorance and misinformation that had painted a negative picture for the sport, all UFC fighters were now required to wear four-to-six-ounce gloves (most gloves are four ounces, but depending on the size can vary). These are much smaller than boxing gloves, allowing the fighter to hit harder without hurting his hand but still able to grapple. Because of the politicians, the sport actually became more dangerous. Gloves became required in every MMA event in the U.S. that employed closed-fist strikes. The number of knockouts rose, though the risk of brain damage was minimized due to the grappling-oriented nature of these fights.

The SEG team was wasting their efforts. Hindery wouldn't budge; there was no way he was going to distribute the UFC. "I came here, found out where the bathrooms are, and I cancelled [Ultimate Fighting]," he later bragged to the *Los Angeles Times*. Worse was to follow. Time Warner followed Hindery's lead and dropped the sport. With TCI and Time Warner jointly acquiring a controlling stake in Viewers Choice, the biggest pay-per-view distributor, it effectively meant the UFC was off the small screen. The picture looked bleak. Though Meyrowitz vowed to soldier on, many muttered that this was the beginning of the end for MMA's chance to crack the mainstream.

• • •

FOR UFC XIII: ULTIMATE FORCE, Vitor Belfort tested himself against Tank Abbott in the superfight. Abbott and training partner Tito Ortiz put all their energies into getting him ready for the match. "We worked so damn hard for that fight. We lifted, ran, wrestled, and boxed everyday," said Ortiz. "Dave was in such good shape; he could go for 20 minutes." While Abbott's prefight interview followed the standard "no respect" mode, Belfort admitted his opponent was dangerous and that he had everything to lose by falling victim to him.

The fight got off to a quick start. Without wasting any time, Abbott charged Belfort and missed with a big right hand, allowing the Brazilian to go for a takedown. Abbott, pushed up against the fence, attempted a hip toss but ended up underneath his opponent. Belfort wrapped up Abbott's left arm for a submission, but the streetfighter twirled around and drove him to the mat. Abbott then allowed him to stand, later saying he wanted to trade punches, but trainer Ortiz said he respected the Brazilian's ground skills too much. Both men tied up and started slugging away at each other's midsections until Belfort pushed Tank away and opened up with his incredible hand speed. Belfort was far too fast for Abbott and finally decked him with a punch.

As in his match against Ferrozzo, Belfort maintained top position and dropped bombs. Ref McCarthy repeatedly yelled, "Get outta there, Tank!" Belfort moved around the back and continued his onslaught as Abbott put both hands over his head for protection. After a couple more punches, McCarthy stopped the bout at 0:53. "I go over to him [Tank], and he's sitting on the ground, and he looks up to me and says, 'That kid rocked my world!' That was his exact statement," said McCarthy. "Tank doesn't even remember that he was rattled; he was on queer street." Abbott had quite a different take on the matter later, claiming that McCarthy stopped the fight too soon, as he was just waiting for a chance to escape Belfort's trap. That said, Abbott went out of his way to shake Belfort's hand. The UFC had found a powerful new striker to take the attention away from the grapplers—a strange irony, given Belfort's BJJ background.

That evening, as Abbott and company tanked it up at a bar inside their hotel, Belfort's coach Al Stankie approached Abbott and shook his hand. Stankie wouldn't let go, and the two exchanged words before Abbott pulled away, cautioning Stankie. Later that night at the after fight party, Tank took retribution, slapping Stankie and starting an old-fashioned barroom brawl. "Wallid [Ismail] kind of came around from the side and cold-cocked [Tank]," said Paul Herrera. "Eddie [Ruiz] tackled Wallid and got him under the table and started fucking him up. My brother jumped on another guy. It was a fun little go, a melee. Dave didn't even get into it." Abbott never got his licks in on Ismail, while Belfort was nowhere to be found and didn't get involved. But Abbott couldn't resist some parting words for Ismail: "He's still on the roost...if he crosses my path the wrong time, you'll find him in the hospital. I'll catch that fucker." As in the UFC, Tank's best fights will forever be tossed back and forth in fandom rather than in real life.

UFC XIII also made Bruce Buffer its staple announcer. He has introduced the event ever since, becoming as much a fixture as his brother Michael is at boxing title fights. "Pat Miletich came up to me after a fight and said that he loves the way I announce him because it gets him so juiced up for a fight," said Buffer. "That means everything to me, when fighters praise my work and tell me this." Now known as the "Voice of the Octagon," he has announced other shows as well, including King of the Cage and the Abu Dhabi Combat Championships. For the UFC, Bruce coined a slogan to match his brother's, starting off each show with, "It's time...to begin." His likeness even appeared in the UFC video game. Managing Michael and doing motivational speaking engagements hasn't taken away Bruce's passion and dedication to promoting the sport he holds so dear. But over the years he has also carved out his own legacy as a world-class poker player.

17

FROM ONE EXTREME TO ANOTHER

I mitators continued to proliferate. The UFC was still going despite all of the political pressure and the collapsing cable television deals, and yet others vied to come onto the scene. They included Martial Arts Reality Superfighting (MARS), one of a select few big-budget shows with the ingredients to be a hit. Dr. John Keating, a prominent surgeon in Atlanta, Georgia, was a lifelong martial artist who had served as a ring physician for UFC VII and numerous pro karate events. First-time fight promoter Keating learned that a great idea and a lot of money can quickly be wasted by incompetence and seedy business practices. His first mistake was partnering up with William Sieglen. "He would talk about being married to Victoria's Secret models, and owning all these businesses and houses, but he lived in a little apartment here," said Keating. The list of Sieglen's unbelievable tales as a conman is lengthy, according to Keating. Despite Sieglen's questionable credentials, he and Keating staged underground pit fights in Atlanta dojos (where Don Frye and Jeremy Horn made their unofficial debuts), which strongly resembled the unrefined skirmishes in the UFC's early days. Few of the participants were paid, but that didn't stop one fight from lasting 90 minutes. There was, however, plenty of side betting by businessmen thirsty for action.

Using his contacts, Keating arranged a meeting with TVKO, which supplied top-notch boxing matches for pay-per-view. They responded with interest, to the point of wanting to sign a contract to promote shows in Atlantic City. Keating (who now claims to be a fool for not signing) and his lawyer felt they could make more money on their own. Keating began working with a young networker named Tom Huggins who had connections with several Brazilian fighters. Having previously failed to set up shows with both Howard Petschler and John Perretti, he felt this was the perfect time for MARS. He worked with investors and "raised enough money to produce three full-fledged fights and make them better-paid fights than anyone has ever had." His vision was a show that had as few rules as possible, save for no biting or eye gouging. Lacking experience in fight promotion, he hired a showrunner in the television industry to land a quick deal with the pay-per-view companies in New York. The deal was shoddy at best, but at least MARS had a chance.

MARS was held on November 22, 1996, in Birmingham, Alabama, but despite best intentions, everything went wrong. Keating arrived at the venue to find dozens of people there, flown in by Huggins (according to Keating), who had nothing to do with the fight. Thousands of dollars were wasted treating these people like kings while the show suffered. Keating hired a high-priced public relations team to market the show in Alabama, but the turnout was pathetic; fewer than 2,000 people showed up. "It's almost impossible to have a fight in Alabama and not have a good crowd; we managed to do it," said Keating. Apparently, the PR firm had no idea how to promote a fight like this. On top of that, Keating promoted another MMA show called Shooting Stars earlier the same day, before MARS. Hardly anyone watched it. Nearly $100,000 was spent on a state-of-the-art sound system in the auditorium, but this was a fight, not a rock concert.

The theme for MARS, Russia vs. Brazil, was also problematic. Keating has since fought hard to dispel rumors that his group wanted the Brazilians to win. "A lot of people complained that the Russians weren't well-matched for the Brazilians. That may be so, but it was not our fault. We spent a fortune trying to get the best Russians to come up and fight. There was always one excuse or another." Oleg Taktarov vs.

Renzo Gracie was the headliner, but even that was in jeopardy. Taktarov's management created numerous problems by trying to stage his rematch with Marco Ruas 12 days before MARS. They wanted $50,000 more to nix the rematch, but Keating emphatically refused; Taktarov had already signed a contract. Taktarov went ahead anyway, fought Ruas for 31 minutes (World Vale Tudo Championships 2), and broke his hand in the process. "My manager kept telling me, 'We got to take this fight?'" remembered Taktarov. "I said how can I take this fight if I have a broken hand and I'm tired. He told me this fight was not going to be seen by anyone because it was for a new company, and they weren't going to be on pay-per-view. I wanted to hold out for a bigger fight, but I took the $20,000 [show purse]."

Shooting Stars (featuring fighters like Anthony Macias and John Dixson) went off without a hitch, despite the sparse attendance, and MARS followed with an above-average show. Olympic wrestling contender Tom Erikson, one of the few Americans in the event, made his debut by pummeling a lethargic but never-say-die Russian, while Brazilian Murilo Bustamante, a Carlson Gracie protégé, enlivened the small crowd with his submission and stand-up skills. Bustamante was a highly decorated BJJ black belt who had actually competed in vale tudo as early as 1991. After taking out their first- and second-round opponents, Erikson and Bustamante met in the finals: the proverbial David vs. Goliath.

With nothing but power and wrestling skill, the 6'3", 280-pound Erikson had difficulty putting away Bustamante, who weighed 100 pounds less. Since the event had no time limits, the Brazilian repeatedly fell on his back in an effort to bait Erikson into a ground attack. The confused and frustrated wrestler didn't know what to make of the situation, and the two ended up fighting a slow, 40-minute battle with infrequent action. At the 30-minute mark, Keating, who was friends with many of the Brazilians, allowed the fight to continue for another 10 minutes, pushing for a decisive winner since there would be no judge's decision. "The Brazilians at ringside started shrieking at me that I was an asshole for giving them another 10 minutes, and at this point, I'm completely puzzled," said Keating. "I thought they wanted more time, and they're screaming at me that I'm giving them too much time. They were claiming that I was trying to fuck Murilo by extending the time." Both men fought their hearts out to a draw, only to share the loser's purse. Carlson Gracie students Carlos Barretto and Ze Mario Sperry both walked over their respective Russian opponents in their superfights leading up to the headliner.

Five minutes before he was scheduled to appear, Oleg Taktarov announced he was pulling out. He wanted more money and felt the promoters owed it to him. "I cannot remember his [exact] reason for demanding that money, but it may in fact have been money to buy him out of his SEG contract," said Keating. "Whatever it was, this was money we categorically did not owe him." In a last-ditch effort, Keating walked into Taktarov's dressing room and told him that he had extended his hospitality to both Taktarov and his manager, from treating them to dinner to housing them for a stay during the 1996 Olympics. "We had an agreement, and if you don't want to come out, that's entirely up to you," Keating told Taktarov. "But I'm telling you right now, we will go on international television and announce to the world that you are afraid to fight a man that you outweigh by 25 pounds." The Russian finally agreed to fight. He pressed the attack early by putting Gracie down with a quick flurry, but from the bottom the Brazilian came back with a well-placed kick to Taktarov's chin that knocked him out cold. Taktarov said he was trying to go for the ankle but couldn't get a grip due to the broken hand. The unconscious Russian instinctively sat upright as Gracie got in some licks before the match was stopped at 1:03.

It was sweet irony for Keating and MARS after all of the alleged problems with Taktarov. On the flip side, "Renzo Gracie was a total and complete gentleman, and he is without question the most honorable man in the martial arts today," said Keating in 2000. Taktarov said later that he fired his manager after this match and that part of the reason he took the fight was because his manager was broke and needed the money more than him. "Oleg's manager, Mike Flynt, made a big scene at the afterfight party," said Brett Moses, who worked with Keating the night of the show. Apparently, there was some debate over Taktarov having to pay back $5,000 for being released from his SEG contract. "He tried to allege that the contract said that Oleg only had to pay back his share from the winner's purse and that since he lost, MARS had no right to deduct the $5,000. His interpretation of the contract proved to be incorrect."

Although the show had some great moments, large parts of the auditorium appeared deserted. "At the end of the day we spent all the money for three [events] on the one [MARS], and all of that money was wasted," admitted Keating. "It was not wasted as much on the fight as it was for flying people in who had no business being flown in, paying outrageous amounts of money on hotel rooms and airplane tickets, and spending money on public relations people who didn't do the work." For years Keating continued to work in the scene as a ringside physician, helping local promoters when he could.

◆ ◆ ◆

WITH EF AND UFC TRYING TO TAP INTO a dwindling pay-per-view market, regional promotions like Iowa's Extreme Challenge evolved to capitalize on local demand. Enter Monte Cox, Quad City newspaper editor and former pro boxer, who turned his knack for marketing into a career as a boxing promoter. After working with ESPN and TVKO on numerous shows, Cox felt he couldn't go any further with them. He wasn't making much money anyway, and the thrill was turning into a routine. But when he heard of local hero Pat Miletich's upcoming MMA match in Chicago, he contacted him for a story. Cox journeyed to Miletich's gym to understand what he did and actually rolled around with him to get a feel for submission fighting.

Miletich was a two-time All-American in high school football and wrestling and was on his way to college when he had to return home to Iowa because his mother had fallen ill. Out of shape and bored, the 21-year-old was invited to a local gym to check out traditional karate.

Martial arts wasn't really his thing, but Miletich wanted to learn how to fight, and the gym taught boxing and Muay Thai. Before long, he had earned a black belt and won a Muay Thai kickboxing title. He also saw the UFC and felt the early competitors were unskilled. Invited to a Renzo Gracie seminar, he decided to see what jiu-jitsu was all about. "Renzo was just going through everybody and tapping everyone out, and I knew right then that this was the real stuff," said Miletich. "I was very impressed with Renzo. That convinced me to start training in it. I knew if I could combine the Muay Thai with the wrestling takedowns I knew, and match that with good groundfighting skills, I would be tough to beat." Without anyone to further his training, Miletich bought an 11-tape Brazilian jiu-jitsu instructional series by Renzo Gracie and studied it for over a year: picture a television next to a wrestling mat and a very worn-out remote control. Miletich's kickboxing success also led him to compete in a July 1995 MMA tournament called Battle of the Masters in Chicago.

After winning the first and second Battle of the Masters, Miletich asked Cox if he would be willing to give this sport a shot. Though the boxing promoter was reluctant, he held the Quad City Ultimate to play on the "ultimate" angle initiated by the UFC. The show brought in 8,000 people, and Cox had found a new outlet for his energies. Though he still dabbled in boxing, Cox continued promoting smaller events and saw Miletich as the star. "There is no other person in this sport who can bring out that many people here in Iowa," said Cox. The two worked together to promote events until things got too hot for the renegade sport and it faced a ban in Iowa. Using his relationships with the boxing commission, Cox was able to get MMA regulated in the state, by doing away with certain strikes that might be considered a little too much (headbutts, kicking a downed opponent). He also made it clear that if anyone wanted to promote a show in Iowa, they had to adhere to those rules, which kept out people who didn't know what they were doing. After the first two Quad City Ultimates, Cox changed the name to Extreme Challenge. He put on four shows, then got a call from Donald Zuckerman, who needed a safe haven for the fourth Extreme Fighting event.

Though Zuckerman and his team had lost ground with pay-per-view as a result of the first two EF shows, they had come back strongly for the third. The fourth promised to be their finest hour. Taking a cue from the UFC, they added world-class wrestlers Kenny Monday and Kevin Jackson to the card. While Dan Severn and Mark Coleman had won their share of amateur wrestling accolades, their achievements paled compared to Monday's and Jackson's. Each had won Olympic gold medals in freestyle wrestling, in 1988 and 1992, respectively. Like Coleman, they ventured into the fighting sports because they could use their wrestling backgrounds and make substantially more money than any coaching job could pay. Monday faced John Lewis while Jackson squared off against John Lober. Could two great wrestlers defeat two submission fighters on wrestling skills alone?

While terms like *jiu-jitsu, submission fighting,* and every variation thereof became commonplace in describing an MMA fighter's skills, Seattle-based Matt Hume perhaps claimed the most accurate style of all: pankration. Hume's introduction to martial arts was a given, as his policeman father had actually trained under Bruce Lee for a short period of time and had taught his son boxing at the age of four. Though his father laid out a practical foundation of grappling and submission, Hume also studied traditional martial arts. If he found something that worked, he wanted that knowledge. So when a wrestler friend told him about the ancient Greek sport of pankration, Hume adopted the name and belief system. According to Hume, pankration is "the positioning of a great jiu-jitsu player, the takedowns of a great freestyle wrestler, the stand-up of a great Muay Thai fighter and boxer, and the lower body submissions of a Pancrase guy or a sambo guy, as well as being able to switch those up and go to the upper body and capitalize on everything." The powerful combination was a discipline that required intensive training and extensive study of the various styles involved.

Hume set up his own school and competed in Pancrase on the recommendation of fellow Washington native and kickboxing champ Maurice Smith. Like Monte Cox, Hume also moved into fight promotion and started United Full Contact Fighting, producing events in Seattle and Hawaii as early as 1991. John Perretti invited Hume to compete in the third EF. After two years away from serious competition, he had trouble with shootfighter Erik Paulson, but he won the fight by opening up a cut on Paulson's head with a knee. For the fourth show, he took on hometown favorite Pat Miletich, who had more fighting experience. Miletich predicted he would have to stop Hume from getting out of the match too early by forcing a cut. His words could not have been more ironic.

Hume whacked away at Miletich's legs with a couple of hard kicks to start off Round 1, but Miletich would get the takedown. Hume pulled guard and kept Miletich in tight to keep him from striking. After a brief melee to bring the fight back upstairs, Hume caught Miletich in a guillotine choke, but the Iowan escaped. Hume pressed the action for the last 30 seconds of the round. "I wanted to see where his conditioning was...when I felt I was ready on the second stand-up, I went after him with punches and kicks," recalled Hume. Miletich acknowledged their effectiveness: "He threw a right hand to make me duck. That was the way I was taught in Muay Thai too—you throw a right hand and make them duck, plum their head, and start throwing knees, and he did it perfect." After Hume landed four solid knees, Miletich didn't want to risk being cut so he fell to his back. Hume launched a flurry of punches until the end of the round.

As Miletich walked back to his corner, he felt his nose. Hume had broken loose some cartilage busted in an earlier training session with a boxer. The doctor examined it and ended the fight. Although a great technical match was stopped short of becoming a classic, both men have nothing but the highest admiration for one another. "To this day, Matt is the smartest fighter I've ever fought. I respect Matt a great deal because he's a Christian and a great guy, and he's just an awesome athlete," said Miletich. Though it was his first loss, he later became the UFC's first lightweight (at that time under 200 pounds) champion and the first welterweight (170 pounds) champion. As Iowa's pride and joy, he has served as mentor and trainer to a whole class of upcoming fighters competing under the banner of Miletich Fighting Systems. Many (Matt Hughes, Jens Pulver, and Tim Sylvia) would go on to become champions themselves.

Amateur wrestlers typically had a difficult time defending submissions when they crossed over into MMA, and Olympic wrestlers Kevin Jackson and Kenny Monday faced jiu-jitsu players in their inaugural matches. After drawing with Igor Zinoviev at EF 3, Jackson's foe, John Lober, exemplified a tough opponent. It took all of 30 seconds for Jackson to gain side mount, but his inexperience allowed Lober to spin underneath and attempt both an arm bar and a leg submission, without success. Lober pulled guard, but the wrestler broke free to dominate on the mat. In Round 2, the wrestler took Lober down again and eventually trapped one arm and sunk in an arm triangle choke. Lober's grimaced face turned purple before he finally capitulated at 1:12 of the round. The battered and beaten Lober said later that he had fought with a fever, not wanting to let Perretti down by pulling out. It's doubtful it made much of a difference. Jackson claimed his first MMA victory. He said he "didn't like the brutality of it," but that was what it took to get the submission.

EF had created a personality with John Lewis, who had become the sport's poster boy by speaking up in its defense on talk shows like *Jerry Springer*. In an attempt to make Lewis look bad, one of Springer's goons jumped the gun on a planned grappling demonstration and shot in on Lewis while he was off guard. Lewis impressed the crowd by making him tap seconds later. After drawing with Carlson Gracie Jr. and beating two worthy opponents, Lewis fought Kenny Monday to cement his status. Far more aggressive than Jackson, Monday shot on Lewis as the match began and was soon in the guard position. Lewis instantly sunk in a textbook arm bar on the overzealous Monday that should have made him tap, but the wrestler seemed only irritated. He pulled out of it with his incredible strength and unloaded on Lewis as payback. After missing another arm bar and an ankle lock, Monday crushed Lewis up against the fence and landed several shots to his face. "Overall, you can't really train to have a chin, you just have to be a tough guy going in," said Lewis later. "I was knocked out on my feet. I got rocked." Near the end of the first round, Monday went head to head in Lewis's guard to keep from being arm-barred again.

In the second round, Monday and Lewis returned to the same position. Monday wore Lewis down with punches until he could no longer keep the guard. The wrestler machine-gunned more than 20 right hands to Lewis's head. With just under a minute left, the referee stopped the fight, since Lewis could not properly defend himself. It was another incredible victory for the wrestlers. "By the time the fight happened, he [Monday] was 200-plus pounds already," said Lewis. "I was 179 pounds and pushing it, and I still fought him the way I wanted to. My problem in that fight was underestimating what it takes to be an Olympian." Monday never fought in MMA again, while Lewis took the loss in stride and carved his future in the sport as a fighter, trainer, gym owner, and fight promoter.

The final match in EF 4 pitted Maurice Smith against Murakami Kazunari, still a relative unknown even after soundly defeating Bart Vale in the previous show. He showed no fear of Smith and landed a clean palm strike that dropped the kickboxer in the opening seconds. "When he hit me, I didn't know where I was," recalled Smith. "When he was punching at me, I still wasn't absolutely coherent. If I hadn't held on out of instinct, he might have kicked my ass." Kazunari's mistake was letting Smith regain his composure enough to get back to his feet. The two circled each other for a moment before the kickboxer landed one of the hardest right hands in MMA history up to that point. WHAM! Kazunari spun all the way around and collapsed to the ground, lights out. Smith had demonstrated that an experienced striker could never be underestimated. EF 4 could not have ended on a more exciting note, but backstage, Smith's opponent wasn't looking too good. "When he went down, I was really concerned," said Smith. "I didn't find out until later that he was paralyzed for almost two hours, and I was kind of nervous about it." Kazunari fully recovered and eventually moved into pro wrestling in Japan but still dabbled in MMA.

• • •

DESPITE A TREMENDOUS FOURTH SHOW that earned the respect of the fans and the critics, Extreme Fighting was in dire straits. The damage done by the Canadian debacle proved to be terminal. "Donald did the math with me, and we had been taken off a lot of the pay-per-view universe that the UFC was still on," said John Perretti. "So they still had buy rates for half the nation that we weren't allowed to be on because we weren't pushing enough numbers." The last show had been seen in only 45,000 homes, nowhere near enough to keep going. Another massive blow came when Request TV, the second-largest pay-per-view distributor at the time, decided not to carry another EF show because of opposition from TCI and some other cable companies. Zuckerman and Perretti almost matched the UFC's success with half the staff, but the pressure was too much. Zuckerman was also quick to say that financial troubles at *Penthouse* (owned by his backer General Media) and Time Warner's ban on the sport made sure there was no EF 5.

Within days of EF 4, Battlecade folded. Zuckerman became a film producer in Hollywood; Perretti stuck with the fight game, working with Igor Zinoviev in Japan. But months after EF called it quits, Perretti had a new idea: staging a submission-only competition with wrestlers vs. submission experts. Perretti and Zuckerman knew that politicians would leave them alone, but this time they had to bankroll the project themselves. The two met with USA Wrestling to get them onboard, and after several meetings, they agreed to support The Contenders. Held on July 14, 1997, the event showcased many great athletes, including wrestlers Tom Erikson, Dan Henderson, and Kenny Monday, and submission fighters Matt Hume, Carlos Newton, and Frank Shamrock. Hume was especially excited to face Monday, whom he saw as the "epitome of wrestling" and an opponent he would have faced in MMA had EF continued.

With wrestling's legendary coach Dan Gable representing wrestling and "Judo" Gene LeBell representing submission, the show had promise, but it failed to ignite much interest from fans of either genre. The lackluster marketing campaign featured none of the competitors, and a horrible rendition of the song *Simply the Best* didn't help either. While some of the matches were interesting, the fuzzy rules didn't give much direction on how to judge a submission-only event. Frank Shamrock and Matt Hume provided the only flashes of excitement, each man finishing his opponent in under a minute.

Before the show, a wrestling-biased female reporter, who couldn't understand how a submission fighter could possibly defeat a wrestler, taunted Shamrock. Shamrock laughed it off, then tapped out Dan Henderson by heel hook at 0:54. Hume wanted to beat that time when he faced the event's best wrestler, Kenny Monday. He engaged the Olympian and fell to his back to get things moving. "I put my leg in front of him to bait him, since he practices this technique that is basically a half Boston crab," said Hume. "I put my leg up for him and he went for it. I went up around his back and put the figure four on him." Monday tapped out in less than 30 seconds. As Hume went to shake his hand, Monday pushed him away and asked for a real fight. "I told him that he was still one of my heroes regardless of what he thought of me," said Hume. "He just had a bad attitude about it." Monday never competed again. Hume won in another submission-only tournament in Abu Dhabi but, riddled with injuries, moved behind the scenes as a prominent manager, trainer, and judge. On December 13, 2002, he resurfaced in the ring for indie-based Hook n' Shoot, arm-barring Canadian Shawn "Pain" Peters in less than two minutes.

The Contenders ended up being a one-time event due to a lack of interest. "I think USA Wrestling bullshitted us into believing they were going to promote it harder than they did," said Perretti. "No wrestlers watched it; no martial artists watched it. It was the worst buy rate in history, but a terrific show. If we had done four [shows], ESPN2 was going to buy it, and I was going to make all my money back." Extreme Fighting was the only stateside MMA promotion that ever came close to matching the UFC's early success. But countless promoters try and have taken on similar political battles in their respective states to cement MMA as a bona fide sport. Local businessmen like Denver's Sven Bean have taken it upon themselves to educate commissions and properly sell them on what the sport is all about; like Monte Cox, he met with the Colorado commission and got the sport legalized on July 1, 2000. His Ring of Fire promotion is the biggest in the state. The age of old boxing promoters with decades of experience has been replaced by ordinary people who have turned their passion for the sport into a cause worth fighting for.

18

GROWING
PAINS

The battle waged by SEG in New York nearly cancelled UFC XII, but the show somehow managed to live up to its potential after moving to the comparative backwater of Alabama. It would be SEG's final event to reach the masses: TCI, Cablevision, and Time Warner collectively put an end to MMA on pay-per-view. Canada had been a lucrative market for the UFC, with the highest per-capita viewership, but not anymore; TCI Canada also censored the event. Pay-per-view had created the UFC's appeal, but to survive SEG now had to decrease fighter purses, concentrate more on gate receipts, and remarket the show to satellite cable systems, a minuscule audience compared to the major cable players. Though the show could still be watched on a dozen or more smaller cable providers, the controversy and the media hype had come to a screeching halt. Politics had managed to bury it—for now.

But this was a sport that had no intention of dying. UFC XIII: Ultimate Force, held on May 30, 1997, at the Augusta-Richmond Civic Center, played to a capacity crowd—but penetrated less than one-tenth of its former cable reach. It was structured like the previous show, with two four-man tourneys to crown heavyweight and lightweight champions. The UFC was accumulating too many champions with little variance between them. There were tournament champions crowned at each show, and there were superfight champions crowned at each show, but no official rankings as in boxing. The confusion didn't increase fan interest. For the lightweight tourney, Christophe Leininger returned after losing to Ken Shamrock in UFC III. Leininger, who had worked with Kevin Jackson and other wrestlers in Arizona, had won an eight-man tournament as a tune-up for his UFC comeback.

Enson Inoue came into the tournament with highly touted jiu-jitsu skills and a 6–2 record while fighting for the Shooto organization in Japan. Born in Hawaii, Inoue had studied jiu-jitsu under Relson Gracie while in college. On a chance trip to Japan, Inoue, who was part Japanese, decided to stay in the country. A Shooto promoter discovered him after Inoue wandered into a local gym to polish his jiu-jitsu training. He would become one of Japan's most celebrated stars.

Guy Mezger, who had fought in two alternate matches in the UFC, also got his chance to compete for the lightweight title. Mezger looked more like a model than a fighter, but his extensive background said otherwise. Born in Dallas, Texas, he had wrestled since the age of 14 and studied different martial arts, including chung moo kwan. Mezger blew out his knee while on a wrestling scholarship in college, ending any chance of making a career on the mat, but started competing in point karate and full-contact matches, though he didn't make much money or get a title shot. Mezger's first sight of the UFC showed him the Promised Land. He had great admiration for Ken Shamrock, identifying his marketability and athleticism. Shamrock prepared Mezger for his UFC IV debut. The two became friends, and Mezger eventually joined the Lion's Den. On the advice of Shamrock, he ventured to Japan and fought in Pancrase, since it was a more reliable paycheck and the UFC's future was in question at the time. He returned to UFC XIII with a sharper set of tools that he hoped would net him the title.

The heavyweight tournament featured four newcomers: kickboxer Dmitri Stepanov, pro wrestler Tony "The Viking" Halme (also known as Ludwig Borga from WWF), hybrid fighter Steven Graham, and wrestler Randy Couture. Born in Littlewood, Washington, the favored Couture had made wrestling his sport of choice throughout junior high and high school, though he also played football and boxed. His collegiate honors included being a three-time wrestling All-American for Oklahoma State

University and four-time Greco Roman in the Nationals. After earning a degree in German, Couture hoped to compete in the Olympics. Then he saw an old college chum fight in the UFC.

In February 1996, Couture watched Don Frye at UFC VIII and thought it might be a new outlet for his wrestling abilities. He sent in an application to SEG, who put him on standby since they'd reached their quota for wrestlers. Couture blew off the opportunity and signed on with Real American Wrestling (RAW), an organization designed to bring national attention to amateur wrestling. Two months after signing with RAW, Couture trained with the U.S. team in Puerto Rico in preparation for the Pan American Games. When RAW co-founder Ricco Chapirelli informed Couture that a slot had opened for UFC XIII, Couture jumped at the chance despite the event being only two weeks away. Couture spent another five days in Puerto Rico, then trained with Chapirelli in Atlanta for one week prior to the show. "Ricco showed me what the guard was and how to pass it and what an arm lock was and how to defend against it," said Couture. With only his grappling background and some boxing (which he had done 10 years before in the Army), Couture entered the event as a true greenhorn.

The lightweight semis started with Guy Mezger against Christophe Leininger. The match went the distance, with uninspiring performances by both fighters. Mezger fought cautiously, throwing jabs instead of combinations, and couldn't put Leininger away. Leininger fought in a gi and looked sloppy and uncomfortable while standing up with Mezger. The only highlight came when Leininger lifted Mezger over him, but the Lion's Den member quickly recovered and took full mount. After a 12-minute regulation and a three-minute overtime period, Mezger won by unanimous decision. "When McCarthy pulled me off of him," said Mezger, "Leininger said, 'I didn't quit! Don't stop it!' Jokingly, I said, 'Don't worry Chris; I quit. I'm tired of hitting you.'"

Enson Inoue made quick work of wrestler Royce "The Farmer" Alger, who took Inoue down and laid in his closed guard. Inoue was the only one with a game plan. While trading strikes, he moved into position by throwing one leg over Alger's head and locked out his arm. The best way to escape from an arm bar is to close the distance and try to finagle out of it. Alger did just the opposite by trying to pull straight out of it, thus making the submission tighter. With his arm fully extended, Alger didn't last long. He tapped the mat at 1:40.

Inoue–Mezger would have made a great match, but Inoue suffered a broken orbital bone and had to withdraw from the tournament. Alternate Tito Ortiz took his place. Ortiz was 6'2", lean and muscular, and his bleached blond hair marked him out. Born and raised in Huntington Beach, Jacob Christopher Ortiz was nicknamed "Tito" by his father because he was a troublemaker. The name stuck and so did the reason it was given to him. While in high school, wrestling coach and Tank Abbott cohort Paul Herrera introduced Ortiz to wrestling. He was a natural and saw the sport as a way to stay on the straight and narrow. His success continued through college where, as a sophomore, Ortiz racked up a 36–0 record, with 34 by pin. Ortiz prepared Tank Abbott for his UFC XI appearance, so Abbott returned the favor and got him an alternate slot at UFC XIII. Ortiz wrecked Wes Albritton with punches in 31 seconds.

Sitting backstage was Mezger, who had also broken his hand on Leninger's head. "I was looking at everybody and thought, *I can fight with this hand even though I'll look like Michael Jackson*," said Mezger, who would fight in the lightweight finale with only one glove. Ortiz showed little respect for Mezger, charging him and throwing heavy leather. Mezger eventually shot for the single-leg takedown, but Ortiz sprawled and took side mount. He used his favorite wrestling move, the inside cradle, to set up a series of devastating knees to Mezger's head. Mezger appeared to be tapping out from the damage and was trying to defend the knees when referee McCarthy stopped the action. The referee noticed two arterial cuts to Mezger's head that spurted blood every time his heart pounded. Mezger was taken over to cutman Leon Tabbs and doctor Richard Istrico. Ortiz naturally thought he had become the lightweight champion. But the match continued after Tabbs and Istrico momentarily stopped the bleeding and gave the okay to restart.

Mezger and Ortiz resumed from opposite ends of the Octagon. Ortiz scrambled with Mezger for a few seconds before shooting in for the double-leg takedown. He kept his head on the outside, allowing Mezger to sink in a guillotine choke, just as Severn had done to Shamrock in their first meeting. Mezger fell to the mat and put Ortiz in a closed guard for leverage, squeezing his opponent's neck. Ortiz could barely move and had no choice but to tap out. Mezger was the lightweight champion.

For the heavyweight semis, 290-pound Steven Graham manhandled 217-pound Dmitri Stephanov and tapped him out with a key lock at 1:30. Tony Halme's shootfighting background was questionable, but he was an amusing prefight interview prior to his bout against Randy Couture: "My greatest strength is I'm not afraid of anybody. I have balls of iron. I go in there to rip the head off or die trying." As the match began, Halme dashed toward Couture (age 33, 6'1", and 225 pounds), missed a punch, and was taken down immediately. The 6'4", 300-pound Halme kept a tight grip, but Couture rolled him to his stomach, submitting him via choke in just short of a minute.

Couture had a harder time with 23-year-old Steven Graham. The wrestler took Graham down during the opening seconds of the match, but he couldn't finish him with the choke. Couture moved to a front headlock, then spun around for a second choke attempt. With his opponent completely down, Couture flailed away at Graham's head until McCarthy intervened. Couture, with no professional experience, had won the heavyweight championship. "I wasn't thinking too much about fighting other than it was nice to get paid for it," said Couture. He found the experience exhilarating, partially because his interest in wrestling had grown somewhat stagnant and he'd needed a change of pace.

◆ ◆ ◆

UFC XIV: SHOWDOWN was held in Birmingham, Alabama, at the Boutwell Arena with 4,800 in attendance. EF champions Maurice Smith and Kevin Jackson had both been aching to get back into the mix. Smith fought for the UFC heavyweight championship by taking on Mark

Coleman. Jackson competed in a four-man middleweight tournament. Beginning with this show, the classifications were as follows: lightweights (169 pounds and below), middleweights (170 to 199 pounds), and heavyweights (200 pounds and over). For the first time, four- to six-ounce grappling gloves were mandatory for all fighters. There would also be a heavyweight tournament featuring UFC vets Brian Johnston and Moti Horenstein and newcomers Dan "The Bull" Bobish and Mark Kerr. Kerr stood out as the darkhorse contender, and it wasn't difficult to see why.

At 6'1" and 255 pounds, Mark Kerr had earned the moniker "The Smashing Machine" while fighting at the World Vale Tudo Championships 3 in January 1997 in Brazil. With a bodybuilder physique, he destroyed Paul Varelans and Fabio Gurgel with his wrestling prowess, powerful knees, and punches. Kerr had wrestled from the age of four but, incredible as it now seems, was so small that it led to high school bullying in Iowa. Luckily, upperclassman Pat Miletich was there to stick up for him. By the time he graduated from Syracuse University, his wrestling record was 98–20–2, and the university named him its 1992 Athlete of the Year. He made it to the Olympic qualifiers but lost in the first round. In 1994, Kerr won 16 straight matches without giving up a single point and, by 1996, was one of the best wrestlers around. A series of injuries kept him out of the 1996 Summer Games, so he followed his wrestling brethren and turned to MMA as his new combative outlet.

The middleweight tournament was not as strong as previous shows. Art Davie matched two one-dimensional fighters (boxer Yuri Vaulin and karate champ Todd Butler) against jiu-jitsu's Joe Moreira and wrestler Kevin Jackson. Vaulin was clueless and defenseless against Moreira, but all Moreira could do was get the takedown. He won by decision but dropped out of the event due to a concussion. Jackson wasted little time in taking Butler down; he tapped him out with head shots. Jiu-jitsu exponent Anthony Fryklund replaced Moreira and couldn't mount much of an offense; Jackson forced the tap out by rear naked choke at 0:44. Unfortunately the action wasn't quite over. As the Internet started to take shape with forums and news lists, arm chair warriors often fought their own cyber space battles, and one calling himself "Dick Rude" infuriated ref John McCarthy who vowed never to get on MMA sites again. The week of the event, martial artist and frequent UFC judge Michael DePasquale Jr. joked to McCarthy that his fighter, Fryklund, was the infamous Rude. Though the ref brushed it off, Fryklund's in-cage behavior began to wear thin. He stormed the Octagon during Fryklund's first match after the fighter delivered a late blow. After Jackson finished Fryklund and he had to break them apart, McCarthy went into a rage. "I go and pick him up and as I do, he shoves me off of my chest and shoulder area. I got mad! I said, 'You acted like an ass before,' so I thought I would play into it. I pick him up, and his feet are dangling off the ground. I say, 'Who the fuck do you think you're pushing on?' I got mad and I was wrong," said McCarthy. In the Octagon, rarely did anyone challenge "Big" John.

In the heavyweights, Mark Kerr took on karate practitioner Moti Horenstein. Kerr made his Octagon debut to the sound of screaming fans marveling at his hulking frame. Horenstein had said he was ready for wrestlers, but Kerr quickly closed the distance and took him down without a single punch or kick. After gaining side mount, Kerr delivered four knees to Horenstein's face before McCarthy stopped the punishment at 2:22.

Brian Johnston and Dan Bobish both bombed away with fast and furious head punches in their semifinal. Bobish, 310 pounds of solid beef, was much too powerful for the less bulky Johnston. "I remember hitting him and getting no response," said Johnston. "That kind of worried me." Just as Ken Shamrock had done in Ultimate Ultimate '96, Bobish took Johnston down and applied pressure on his head up against the fence. "He was so heavy, and he was just leaning into me. I was almost ready to pass out," said Johnston, who eventually tapped to a forearm choke after Bobish landed elbows, headbutts, and punches.

The heavyweight final between Kerr and Bobish should have been exciting, but a loophole in the rules brought it to a premature end. Kerr threw two leg kicks at Bobish, who was on the attack during the opening seconds of the round. Without any setup, Kerr then made a risky move and shot in for the double-leg takedown on Bobish, a 1992 NCAA wrestling champion in his own right. Using all of his momentum, Kerr put Bobish on his back and crowded him up against the fence. Bobish landed some small shots while Kerr tried for an arm triangle choke. Just as he was in position, Bobish moved his arm out of the way, and Kerr pressed his chin down into Bobish's right eye socket. After a few seconds, the pain was too unbearable and Bobish tapped. Though the rules forbade eye gouging, a chin to the eye was never covered. "I used to talk about how great a technique it was," said McCarthy, who confirmed it was not against the rules at that time. After this match, however, the eye-gouging rule was amended.

For Kerr, who had reeled off two bloodbath wins in Brazil and dispatched two opponents in the UFC just as easily, it would be hard to predict his emotional state after that first UFC experience. "Wrestling was never a do-or-die thing, and you were never faced with the extremes that you are faced with when you fight. If you are emotionally flat for a wrestling match, you might get pinned, but if you do that in a fight, the consequences are a lot bigger. The amount of extremes between this and wrestling is way different."

Intense heat had been created for the superfight between Maurice Smith, who needed a home after the defunct EF, and Mark Coleman. It would be the classic contrast in styles: the striker vs. the grappler. Smith, during his prefight interview, even said Coleman punched like a girl. "I knew wrestlers and they weren't punching like fighters," said Smith later. "It was more of a criticism than something to tear him down." Coleman had notched two straight tournament victories and a quick submission over Dan Severn. Few people believed a kickboxer could do anything against Coleman. The buzz for this match even championed the rematch between Royce Gracie and Ken Shamrock at UFC V.

While Smith entered the cage with a small crew, Coleman's entourage was an army of over 20 people. The 245-pound, 32-year-old Coleman outweighed Smith by 25 pounds and was three years younger, but Smith had been working with Lion's Den trainer Frank Shamrock on guarding against the neck crank that Coleman had used so successfully in past fights. Coleman's strategy was different: "I was going out drinking—not training—and watching Maurice Smith on film. To me, it looked like a guy that I was going to take down, punch a few times, slide off to my side headlock, and walk out of there."

Twenty-two seconds into the match, Coleman faked a left jab and shot in on Smith, taking him down with ease. In Smith's open guard, Coleman became a man possessed. For over a minute, he fired away with punches, elbows, and countless headbutts as Smith tried his best to defend. "When he came into the fight, he was so pissed off [because of the punch-like-a-girl comment] that his game plan was to kick my ass," said Smith. "He hit me about four times really hard that totally rocked me, but it took a lot out of him." For the first four minutes, Smith frustrated Coleman by preventing him from gaining side mount, while delivering several punches and elbows to Coleman's head. "After the two-minute mark, everything fell into place, and I realized how dumb I was for taking on a championship fighter of Maurice Smith's caliber and just absolutely showing him no respect," said Coleman.

Just before the five-minute mark, Coleman finally got side mount, but Smith rolled over to his stomach, opening himself up for a rear naked choke. Coleman couldn't finish; Smith escaped, but the wrestler took full mount and fired more head punches. Smith kept his composure, and volleyed from side and side, tiring the wrestler out in the process. Then he rolled back over, with Coleman attempting another choke. The kickboxer defended well from this position. "I didn't quit," said Coleman. "I was still going for the win. Everything in my whole body just seized up, and I was just hoping to get that side headlock choke on him, but he had studied it and was very slippery." At 7:30, the Coleman-heavy crowd had changed its tune, and a chant of "Maurice" echoed through the auditorium.

At 9:00, Coleman missed an arm triangle attempt, and the kickboxer seized the opportunity to bring the fight back upstairs. Coleman, resting his hands on his knees, was gassed. He attempted a takedown but was so tired he slipped to the ground. As he rose, Smith attempted a head kick that looked close to being a foul; it was unclear whether Coleman had more than two points of contact on the ground (to appease politicians, kicking an opponent's head on the ground had been made an infraction of the rules). The fight was stopped momentarily to warn Smith, while Coleman got a few seconds rest.

At the restart, Coleman was so tired he couldn't even budge from his corner, so Smith pressed the attack. A missed leg kick led to another takedown by Coleman, but the kickboxer controlled by connecting with elbow strikes to the head. No matter what Coleman did to move from that position, Smith worked the open guard with proficiency. "I didn't want to use the closed guard like I did with Conan Silveira because a wrestler is not going to play the same game," said Smith. At just under 13 minutes, Coleman finally got the patented side mount choke that had put Severn away, but Smith slipped right out and continued throwing elbows. With 45 seconds to go in the 15-minute regulation, Smith reversed Coleman, took his back, and landed two punches before bringing the fight back standing.

In the rest period before the first of two three-minute overtimes, Frank Shamrock coached Smith, while Kevin Jackson yelled at Coleman to get working. "Just six more minutes," said Jackson, but Coleman was too busy catching his breath. When the overtime period started, Smith attacked with leg kicks and taunted Coleman to engage. Coleman was completely wasted and kept checking the clock to see when the punishment would end. In an act of desperation, he finally attempted a takedown, but Smith just moved out of the way. At 2:14 into the first overtime, Smith landed four hard punches and one head kick, but Coleman held on until the end of the period. Smith raised his hands victoriously before walking to his corner.

McCarthy walked over to Coleman and told him, "You gotta fight back." On resumption, Smith was even more confident and chased Coleman to chop him down. Smith even slipped and fell after missing a head kick, but Coleman was too worn out to capitalize. At 1:30 of the final period, the overhead lights momentarily went out, but McCarthy pushed the action and asked the wrestler if he wanted out. Despite the fatigue and the bruises on his thighs from kicks, Coleman did not quit. Smith played cautious as the final seconds wound down. "If I would have pressed it, I might have got caught on the ground again. I would have lost that fight because one judge had me losing all the way to the last minute," explained Smith.

The epic battle went to the judges, with a unanimous decision going to Maurice Smith. It was the most exciting fight of 1997 and the biggest upset in the history of MMA up until that point. Smith now claimed championships in both EF and UFC. "Winning the title was not as important to me as knowing that I could fight anyone in any style," said Smith. For the second time, a striker had defeated a well-known grappler, but conditioning won the fight. No matter how powerful, how strong, or how knowledgeable a fighter is, he must be conditioned enough to go the distance. With his kickboxing background and training routines, Smith was able to pull off a major victory.

For Mark Coleman, there was a new test: to move past his one-dimensional view of a sport he felt had been tamed. "After that fight, it totally changed everything," said Coleman. "It was humbling and brought me back to the ground. It took at least two weeks before I could start using my left leg, but as soon as I was able to start working out, I was on a mission to come back."

◆ ◆ ◆

UFC XV: COLLISION COURSE, held at the Casino Magic Dome in Bay St. Louis, Missouri, on October 17, 1997, was another showcase for the monstrous Mark Kerr. Randy Couture took on Vitor Belfort in a heavyweight elimination superfight to decide Maurice Smith's opponent in a future event. Smith was originally slated to defend his title against Dan Severn, but Severn pulled out due to injury.

Six days before the event, a lavishly produced Japanese MMA show called Pride made its debut. Pride was created to segue between pro wrestling and MMA and spotlighted Rickson Gracie against pro wrestler Nobuhiko Takada as the headliner. Tank Abbott was set to fight Kimo, but some trouble with the law kept Abbott from leaving the country. Severn took his place, despite his commitment with the UFC, and fought Kimo to a boring 30-minute decision. A desperate SEG had contacted Abbott even before Pride but called off his participation believing Severn would be fine. With less than a week, they asked for Abbott again when Severn could not make it. "I told them that I had not been training and that I had been drinking," said Abbott, who tipped the scales at 277 pounds. He accepted their offer anyway.

UFC XV started with two heavyweight alternate matches to decide a replacement if one was needed. Then Mark Kerr stepped in to take on Airborne Army Ranger Greg Stott. Stott talked a good game and pestered matchmaker Art Davie at every UFC with photos and business cards, trying to get a shot in the show. Davie finally gave in just to shut him up. Stott claimed to represent R.I.P.—Ranger International Performance— which he called "the most expeditious form of combat." Unfortunately, one knee from Kerr knocked him out in 20 seconds; Stott's UFC career would Rest In Peace.

By all accounts, David Beneteau was brought in to lose against Carlos Barretto. Beneteau was a solid wrestler, but with his 2–3 UFC record, most felt he hardly stood a chance against the veteran Brazilian jiu-jitsu champion. Nicknamed Carlao (meaning Big Carlos), Barretto stood 6'4" and weighed 235 pounds of solid muscle. He was also undefeated in MMA, having bested three grapplers to win the Universal Vale Tudo Fighting Championship 6 in March 1997.

Barretto had a difficult time with Beneteau, who was able to take down the Brazilian at will; he had been training with jiu-jitsu champ Pedro Sauer. Five minutes into the match, Barretto had the wrestler against the fence and tried everything to get him down. He succeeded, but Beneteau was on top, and the Carlson Gracie student paid the price with over a dozen punches to the head. As the match continued, the Brazilian became frustrated for having to fight standing up. After the 12-minute regulation period, Barretto scored a takedown, but he couldn't do anything in the three-minute overtime. In one of the closest matches in UFC history up to that point, Beneteau won by unanimous decision.

Beneteau should have faced Kerr in the finals but pulled out with no explanation other than to say he would lose. "He [Beneteau] knew he wasn't hurt; he just didn't want to get his ass kicked," remembered SEG's David Isaacs. "I said to him, 'You know, I probably would have made the same decision, but I'm not a fighter.'" Beneteau thought it was the most "intelligent thing considering what I was up against," but the way he did it effectively ended his MMA career. Although other fighters have feigned injuries to keep from losing a fight, Beneteau told the truth and was shunned for it. He made a brief comeback after attending law school but failed to gain much attention. "After I beat Carlos, I was ranked eighth in the world and was never called again for a fight," said Beneteau, who knew pulling out from the Kerr match was the sole reason.

The heavyweight final for UFC XV was no crowd-pleaser: Kerr choked out alternate Dwane Cason, nephew of ex-boxer Leon Spinks, in 54 seconds to win his second tournament.

Vitor Belfort vs. Randy Couture turned out to be the most exciting match of the event. Couture watched tapes of Belfort and studied with boxing trainers to maximize his footwork, combinations, and defense. His game plan was to use his Greco Roman wrestling to tie Belfort up and keep him from striking. Before their match, however, it was difficult to get Belfort out of his trailer due to a mysterious intestinal virus that made him nauseated. Rumors also surfaced that he was having problems with both his girlfriend and Carlson Gracie.

When Belfort finally came out, he fought Couture in a very low stance, anticipating a takedown attempt, but the wrestler felt comfortable standing up. He circled away from Belfort, who had positioned himself as a southpaw, and stayed clear of his onslaught of punches. "I kind of had some reach and height over him, so with that lower stance, he was right there to hit," said Couture, who landed a left jab less than a minute into regulation. After a brief exchange, Belfort crowded Couture up against the fence and clutched his left leg for a takedown. The wrestler remained calm and worked through it before going on the offensive. Couture tied up with Belfort to shut down his striking game and, at 2:41, took the Brazilian down with a double leg.

Couture latched on a front head lock, opening Belfort up with punches before the Brazilian pulled out. Pulling Couture into his guard, Belfort kept Couture out of punching range, but the wrestler was able to break free, finagling another front head lock. At 6:40, Couture launched his knees at Belfort's head and followed up with strikes that stung his opponent. The Brazilian was tired but fired back as best he could. Couture wouldn't give him a target. At 7:32, the wrestler moved in for the kill and slugged away at Belfort with uppercuts that eventually sent him to the mat. Couture followed up with knees and more punches until referee McCarthy stopped the match at 8:17. Randy Couture had a smart game plan that outmatched Vitor Belfort on every level. "Vitor is a single-dimension fighter who got outboxed by a wrestler because he didn't have a basic background in boxing," commented Maurice Smith.

For the heavyweight title, Tank Abbott, who had failed to win a tournament or a superfight coming off the dizzying loss to Belfort, faced Maurice Smith. Smith played it smart and chose not to meet the bloated Abbott head-on, instead making him expend energy. He landed a leg kick, but Abbott took him up against the fence and clobbered him with punches that dropped the kickboxer. "He hit me in the back of the head, and I had a pain there for at least another week," said Smith. On the ground, Smith regained his composure and pulled Abbott into his guard. Much like Coleman, Abbott swatted at Smith, but few of his punches landed and he became tired. At 3:30, Abbott gained side mount but lost it immediately when he tried to strike.

Both men worked on the ground with little success. Abbott landed some punches; Smith rained down elbows to Abbott's head and missed two arm locks. At 7:32, McCarthy stood them up. Abbott was completely out of gas, with both hands on his knees. Smith calmly walked toward Abbott, who hardly looked as if he was in the fight anymore. Whack! Abbott took a solid leg kick from Smith that nearly spun him around. A second leg kick resounded throughout the venue; the crowd could almost feel Abbott's pain. "Do you want out?" asked McCarthy. As Smith landed the third one, Abbott verbally submitted and flopped down on the mat to catch his breath.

Smith had earned a shot at Couture at UFC Japan, but Abbott ended the show with his usual honest banter. "As of last Saturday, I stepped off the bar stool and stepped into the Octagon," he said. "I haven't been training; I've been partying. I came out here and went for it." Abbott later charged McCarthy with an unfair stand-up, noting that he was too gassed to continue. He said that McCarthy stood them up right after Abbott moved out of Smith's guard. But the videotape clearly showed that the match had been a stalemate on the ground with neither man getting the better of the other.

A kickboxer beat a wrestler. A wrestler outstruck a jiu-jitsu player. Another wrestler defeated a jiu-jitsu champion by staving off his take-down attempts. The ever-evolving playing field of MMA had blurred the lines between singular styles. Grappling, submission, and striking had each proven dominant alone, but now a blended system with conditioning and strategy became the next logical step. As the matchmaking improved to keep out one-dimensional styles like karate and boxing and examine true cross-trained fighters, the crowds were also becoming more educated. Their eyes were now open to what the sport should have been all along.

19

ULTIMATE BETRAYAL

The third Ultimate Fighting Championship was originally to have been held in Japan, a country in tune with the sport, but plans fell through. It would take SEG another three years to get there, when the company landed a deal with some of the people involved with a Japanese pro wrestling group, Kingdom, to set the stage for the last show of the year in December 1997: Ultimate Japan. Superstars Ken Shamrock, Mark Kerr, Randy Couture, Vitor Belfort, Tank Abbott, and Maurice Smith headlined the card to make UFC's debut in the Land of the Rising Sun a memorable one.

Kingdom was an offshoot of the Universal Wrestling Federation International, pro wrestler Nobuhiko Takada's group, which emerged after the original UWF. Unlike other shoot-style pro wrestling shows, Kingdom permitted closed-fist strikes to the face rather than open-hand slaps, but most of the matches were worked. That said, they really hit each other, and only the trained eye could tell something was amiss. UFC Japan's main event pitted Shamrock against Takada, but the latter dropped out because Shamrock refused to do a work. Officially, Takada's omission from the card stemmed from a knee injury suffered in his legit match against Rickson Gracie in Pride two months earlier.

Shamrock moved on to the WWF, and Pride claimed another casualty for Ultimate Japan when Mark Kerr pulled out of the show. A press release issued by SEG announced that Kerr was enjoined from fighting in other events because of his exclusive participation agreement with the UFC. SEG's old nemesis, Robert DePersia, managed Kerr and believed there had to be a time limit on exclusivity. But Kerr was legally bound by his contract, according to SEG exec David Isaacs: "In the middle of his contract, after we had spent time and money building him up, he decided that he was just going to fight for someone else." According to Isaacs, Kerr argued in court that the UFC was not a real sport, so how could he be held in an enforceable agreement? A court battle ensued. Kerr won a release from his contract and fought in Pride's second show. Though DePersia claimed SEG lost the court case, Kerr was required to pay a steep but undisclosed price to the company so he could fight for the Japanese organization.

Kerr ultimately became one of the biggest stars in the sport, and Pride had more money to keep him happy. He would be thrust into the limelight not for his fights, but for being the subject of an intense 2003 documentary called *The Smashing Machine*. Filmmakers traveled with Kerr for over a year, expecting to see the rise of a modern-day warrior. Instead they found a man struggling with drug addiction (painkillers), bad relationships, and fighting itself. The program drew controversy from an MMA community unwilling to see its merits, while mainstream critics praised it for capturing the demons that haunt many athletes. People wanted to see Kerr return to the ring in tiptop shape, but he was never able to reach the level of his former self.

With Shamrock and Kerr gone, all it took was Vitor Belfort dropping out of the show to prompt a Japanese ultimatum to the UFC. After his loss to Randy Couture, Belfort was no longer the fighter who had taken the MMA world by storm with his supersonic hand speed. He was still recuperating from his "worm intestinal virus" and was not feeling up to snuff for the Japan show. But SEG had no choice: either Belfort fought or the show would be cancelled. SEG secured wrestler Brad Kohler to tangle with the Brazilian phenom in Japan, believing he would be an easy opponent, but with one week to go before the show, Belfort told SEG he didn't want to fight Kohler, especially since the wrestler had lasted an hour against Travis Fulton in Hook n' Shoot, an ambitious indie show held in a dojo in Indiana—both fighters punched and grappled in a pool of their own sweat before Kohler pulled out the victory. SEG caved in and let Belfort pick his opponent—occasional training partner Joe Charles. "If we wanted Vitor in the Octagon, that was the only way to do it," said Isaacs. "It wasn't a perfect solution, but sometimes there is not a perfect solution." Kohler now faced Tra "Trauma" Telligman, who had lost to Belfort in his UFC debut.

Ultimate Japan was also a double header: the first-ever middleweight champ would be crowned, and Maurice Smith would defend his heavyweight belt against Randy Couture. The middleweight championship was difficult to schedule, as fellow Lion's Den fighters Guy Mezger and Jerry Bohlander obviously could not face one other. Olympic gold medalist wrestler, EF champ, and UFC winner Kevin Jackson took one slot, and fight consultant Joe Silva devised a plan for his opponent. Though Art Davie had picked Frank Shamrock for the shot, Silva pushed for the winner of Shamrock's match with Enson Inoue. The two were fighting in Japan Vale Tudo '97, held in November, and the winner would face Jackson the following month.

Frank Juarez Shamrock, the "brother" of Ken, had lived with Bob during his youth and was legally adopted at age 21. Though not related by blood, Frank had a physique and marketable face similar to Ken and had also spent time moving from group home to group home before settling with the disciplinarian Bob. As part of the Lion's Den, Frank had walked down the aisle to the Octagon on many occasions with Ken, Guy Mezger, and Jerry Bohlander but was not a recognizable name in the U.S., as he had been competing in Japan's Pancrase. After becoming the provisional King of Pancrase due to an injury to Bas Rutten, Frank fought his first MMA match on January 17, 1997, against John Lober in a Hawaiian event called Superbrawl, promoted by ex-Chippendales dancer T.J. Thompson. Lober hit Shamrock with everything he had and won the match by decision, though Shamrock knocked Lober's teeth out in the process.

Bob never felt Frank was the right kind of fighter for MMA; Frank was too nice a guy and didn't have Ken's killer instinct. "I was used to finessing holds out of people [working with the Pancrase fighters for years] and making them work and expend energy, but when you add punching, a lot of your holds become obsolete," said Frank. "If you go for different holds, you get punched, and I wasn't prepared for that." Frank had nowhere else to turn; he couldn't go back to Pancrase, which had legal problems with Ken and didn't care about having another Shamrock in its ranks. "I hiked up on Diamond Head in Hawaii, and I sat down and thought, *Am I going to do this or not?* I decided that if I was going to do it, then I was going to do it 100 percent and be 100 percent honest with myself."

While in Hawaii, Frank met Angelina Brown, who had been fired by T.J. Thompson after working for the Superbrawl promotion. The two fell instantly in love and later married. Angelina became a driving force behind her husband's career, something that threatened the fabric of the male-dominated Lion's Den. Ken Shamrock admitted he never wanted to train Frank but, out of respect for Bob, agreed to take him in and teach him submission fighting. "What you have to understand is that Frank was not my best student," said Ken, "and that's why I held him back from MMA for a long time. Jerry Bohlander and Guy Mezger were handling him, and those guys had the opportunity in the UFC." While Frank was still living with Bob and sharing a room with Jerry, he made the decision to become his own man and make his mark. He contacted SEG about the slot against Jackson, leapfrogging Mezger and Bohlander. "It wouldn't have been such a big deal, but he was doing it behind my back," said Bohlander. "I was loyal to the UFC, but they weren't loyal to me. I felt betrayed on two ends: by the company that I worked so hard for and by one of my best friends." It did make business sense for Shamrock to get the nod, as he had already established himself in Japan, though Mezger would win the King of Pancrase title in April 1998.

Frank Shamrock was a determined individual and felt he had to break loose of the nest that had kept him safe for several years. Without warning, he moved out. He wanted to see if "the system that we were using really worked. So I decided to put it to the test. I just called up organizations and said, 'I want to fight. I want to fight your best guy.'" In October, Shamrock quickly submitted wrestler Dan Henderson in a submission-only match in The Contenders. The match with Enson Inoue came the following month. In front of a capacity crowd in Japan, the two fought a true brawl, with neither willing to give up. Just past the 15-minute mark,

Shamrock floored Inoue with a hard knee to the chin, forcing Enson's older brother Egan to enter the ring to stop any further punishment. The match was ruled a disqualification in favor of Shamrock. There was no doubt he was a much different fighter from the one who had lost in Hawaii. Fighting in the UFC, albeit in Japan, meant audiences back home would see the other Shamrock live in action for the first time, since neither Superbrawl nor Japan Vale Tudo '97 were shown on U.S. cable. Some of Frank's older Pancrase fights were shown, however, after SEG acquired the licensing rights for pay-per-view specials.

As well as last-minute changes to the card, there were changes at SEG. Mike Goldberg replaced Bruce Beck as the play-by-play commentator, as Beck had moved on to news and other projects. More significantly, Art Davie was abruptly fired for trying to start another show behind SEG's back. Though Davie was fairly tight-lipped about the project, known as Thunderdome, he did comment on the UFC: "The show was going down. By having more rules, we were losing a big part of the audience that wasn't into martial arts and just wanted to see a good fight. And the more it would go to the ground and become a grappler's game, the more difficult it was for the core market to stay with the show." Davie also felt there was no future for the UFC, since cable had left the picture. So why would he want to start up a similar show?

Joe Silva was the one who first got wind of the project. He brought it to the attention of David Isaacs, who was shocked that his friend and co-worker would do such a thing. Bob Meyrowitz learned about it when longtime friend Andy Anderson was approached by Davie to finance Thunderdome. Meyrowitz called Davie into his office and confronted him. "I was shocked by Art's participation in Thunderdome, both that he was involved and at the deception he used to cover up what he had done, all the while acting like a member of the SEG/UFC 'team,'" said Isaacs. "Professionally and personally, he crossed the line. In the past, I had defended Art when others criticized his character or his lack of matchmaking skills. Others at SEG and I had taken over various aspects of his job and/or assisted him when deficiencies became clear. Perhaps we should have taken more seriously some of the charges, but we found them so hard to believe that we did not do so until we had hard evidence: a copy of the Thunderdome proposal." Meyrowitz phoned Davie just before he was to depart for Japan, ticket in hand, and fired him.

◆ ◆ ◆

A CAPACITY CROWD IN YOKOHOMA, Japan's second-largest city, was treated to hometown favorite Yoji Anjo against the ever-colorful Tank Abbott in the first bracket of the heavyweight tournament. Just a week before, Abbott had entered stablemates Paul Herrera and Eddie Ruiz in Kingdom, and both had lost in apparently real matches, so this was a chance for Abbott to set things straight. Squeezing Anjo's face against the fence, he resembled Playdoh as Abbott worked him over with big shots. The Japanese pro wrestler had one chance with an arm bar, but Abbott was far too strong and kept pounding away until the two were stood up at the nine-minute mark. Abbott was so gassed that he rested his hands on his knees, but while Anjo raised the ante by throwing Thai kicks, none of them had the sting of a Maurice Smith. The match went to a decision, with Abbott getting the nod. Rare as it was for Abbott to praise an opponent, he said of Anjo, "The man has heart and honor like no tomorrow."

Originally, Conan Silveira was to face UFC XV competitor Alex Hunter for the second bracket, but Kazushi Sakuraba took Hunter's place, forcing the American to take an alternate slot. Sakuraba had beaten Herrera in the Kingdom match in just three minutes, and Herrera was impressed. "He really helped me to increase my training to the way they were training," he said, "and I've come light years." Sakuraba was Nobuhiko Takada's pupil and known for his hard work ethic, as in he could "work" a fight so well that it looked real. In 1996, Sakuraba fought his first supposed MMA match against Kimo, but due to his pro wrestling background from Kingdom, it looked like a questionably worked match. For the UFC, however, he would get a chance to prove his skills beyond doubt in a complete shoot.

The Brazilian started things off by catching the 5'9" Sakuraba in a guillotine choke as they went to the ground. The Japanese wrestler pulled out and shot for an ankle lock, but Silveira fired back with strikes. At two minutes, Silveira moved back to his feet and threw wild punches at Sakuraba up against the fence. Silveira landed one solid shot as his opponent covered up before dropping down for a shot at Silveira's leg. Believing Sakuraba was injured, McCarthy stopped the match as soon as Sakuraba went to the ground. "That's it. No more fight," he said to the stunned Japanese, who didn't seem hurt at all. The scene turned ugly, as the normally respectful Japanese crowd erupted in boos. Sakuraba threw down his mouthpiece in disgust and even tried to take the microphone from announcer Bruce Buffer to voice his disapproval to the crowd. He would not leave the Octagon for over 45 minutes. McCarthy said later: "I really thought he was hurt. At the time, when I made that call, I would have bet my life that he was hurt and was going down. It wasn't a good shoot that Sakuraba made, but when I looked at the tape, I made the wrong call."

It was time for Frank Shamrock to make his debut in the UFC, against Kevin Jackson for the middleweight crown. Wrestlers were back on the upswing, as both Mark Kerr and Randy Couture had won in the UFC after Mark Coleman's loss to Maurice Smith. Since his win in The Contenders, Shamrock trained with wrestlers at Stanford University and knew he had found a wrestler's weakness. But Jackson came out smoking, flailing punches before taking Shamrock down. With the wrestler in his guard, Shamrock grasped Jackson's right arm, pushed out his hips, and pulled his leg over Jackson's head. Shamrock quickly extended Jackson's arm and the wrestler tapped out. Frank Shamrock had just won the middleweight championship in an unbelievable 16 seconds (SEG wrongly timed the bout at 22 seconds). A paradigm shift had once again occurred in MMA. The balance between wrestling, submission, and stand-up had been altered yet again. It now came down to an understanding of how a fighter can use his natural skills to systematically mesh these elements together without missing a beat.

In Shamrock, the sport had a new hero. "I have more respect for Frank Shamrock than anyone else who has ever entered the Octagon," said commentator and MMA Commissioner Jeff Blatnick back in 2000. "To watch him be part of an entourage, break away from a shadow, create his own image, be his own man in the face of other people's criticisms, and then to display the athletic prowess and just pure sportsmanship he has and continues to have...that's probably the brightest spot I've seen in all the UFC. If you want to legitimize this thing we call MMA, then look at Frank Shamrock."

In contrast, Vitor Belfort gave a lackluster performance in what appeared to be a straight grappling match with Joe Charles. No strikes of any kind were thrown in the exhibition-like fray, though it appeared they were shooting for position. Belfort finally tapped out Charles with an arm bar. The finals of the heavyweight tournament also appeared suspect as Conan Silveira took on Kazushi Sakuraba for the second time. SEG had been slow to label their first fight; it was later ruled a no-contest. Abbott pulled out of the finals, claiming a broken hand, but modified that decision in a later interview: "It was the hand, but I can always fight. I'll fight one-handed! They [SEG] thought they were going to work me, and I fucked the whole show up and I did it very well."

Though he felt in his mind that he'd won the first fight, Conan Silveira sat in his dressing room with several conflicting thoughts running through his mind. Dozens of Japanese press members and other people were pounding on his door and stressing him out. "Imagine yourself in a foreign country, where you don't speak the language and don't know what is going on," said Silveira. "Besides that, I had everyone telling me that the [fate of] the UFC was in my hands. As a fighter, you don't want to have that in your mind."

Sakuraba attacked Silveira much like he had in their first meeting, but this time the Brazilian didn't mount much of a defense. "My body went out there the second time, but my mind wasn't there," he said. After missing a key lock, Sakuraba got side mount and immediately executed an arm bar; Silveira tapped right away. Though the Brazilian insisted that no one "told me anything," the whole episode looked suspicious. "For whatever reason, SEG came up with a rematch decision, and one fighter changed the way he fought and the other ended up winning easily," said Jeff Blatnick. The Japanese crowd signed off with approval at the Kingdom fighter's victory. Conan Silveira felt disgusted by the whole turn of events. "I didn't think that I wanted to fight anymore, because it didn't matter how hard you trained if people had the power to manipulate the situation." Silveira avenged his loss to Smith in 1999, but his comeback was short-lived. On June 20, 2003, Conan and 15 others were arrested and convicted in connection with a smuggling ring importing the party drug Ecstasy. He came back one more time in 2007 and subsequently hung it up to be a full-time trainer and co-founder of the famed American Top Team.

For many, Maurice Smith had taken the sport to a higher plain as a striker, first by beating a jiu-jitsu man and then by defeating a powerful wrestler. He had won the heavyweight championship from Coleman and successfully defended against last-minute replacement Abbott. But Couture and the RAW team had worked out a game plan for Smith: to evade his kicks and use those techniques as setups for takedowns. They knew Smith had been working with Frank Shamrock on the ground and that he was a very experienced competitor who was comfortable in that position. Unlike Belfort, Couture didn't want any part of Smith's stand-up game, so after a few leg kicks, the wrestler took him to the ground much the same way that Coleman had.

After attempting a key lock, Couture gained half mount, and the two remained in that position during the 15-minute regulation. "I thought he was going to tie me up and frustrate me so that I would expend energy," said Couture. "He would try to get me tired in the hope that he would get me back on my feet where I would not be able to protect myself." During two overtime periods, Smith landed several good Thai kicks, but Couture kept his hands up and shut the kickboxer's game down by taking him to the mat. "[During the] last overtime, he was on top of me and had his chest across me in the choke position; he almost submitted me," said Smith. "It was really close, but I thought, *man, if I get submitted by a wrestler, that's going to be bad.* I thought of what the Lion's Den would say, so I just got lucky and got out."

The fight went to a decision. "I should have risked more to try and be more dominant instead of being so controlling," said Couture, who felt he had done more than enough to win the fight at the time. Former EF matchmaker John Perretti was one of the judges and ruled the match a draw, which he was not actually allowed to do. The other two judges gave it to Couture. He was now the UFC heavyweight champion.

Meanwhile John Perretti, after berating the UFC for its matches and publicly denouncing commentator Jeff Blatnick and ref John McCarthy in a webzine interview, was somewhat surprisingly hired by SEG as matchmaker through David Isaacs. Even though riddled with problems, UFC Japan was an important step forward for the UFC and for MMA in general.

With all the controversy and intrigue, UFC Japan couldn't end without a Tank-related incident. It happened at a ritzy Japanese bar called Lexington Queen. Sitting in the VIP lounge was Andy Anderson, who had shelled out over $3,000 for liquor and wine to entertain guests at a private party. Tank, Paul Herrera, and Eddie Ruiz felt they were deserving of VIP status and created a ruckus near the entrance when the manager felt uneasy about letting them in. Tank promised everyone would behave, but he wouldn't sit where he was instructed, finding solace in some women who joined him at his table. "I had four or five bottles of liquor, two bottles of champagne, and a bottle of wine," said Andy Anderson, "and out of the blue, Paul Herrera comes over and for no reason whatsoever tackles me and runs me to the end of the table against the wall and breaks all these bottles of liquor everywhere and just makes a huge mess. So I got up and dropped Paul." Tank paid no attention, as he knew his boys had caused the skirmish and should finish it. As things began to get out of hand, Anderson walked over to David Isaacs, who seemed out of it and wanted to know if the party was over. "Yes David, that means the party is over," said Anderson, who knew that fighting in a public place in Japan meant considerable trouble with the law. Luckily, everyone got out okay. Herrera apologized to Anderson three years later.

20

DARK AGES

B y 1998, the UFC had a love-hate relationship with fans, fighters, and competing promoters. The big venues were gone, some shows didn't even sell merchandise, and the cards featured few marquee names. A new crop of young fighters competed at a fraction of what their predecessors made, as SEG struggled to stay afloat. But there was still no other brand name like the UFC, and like it or not, it held the main key to the sport's salvation in America.

After holding as many as five shows a year, SEG produced only three UFCs during 1998 as they tried to build Frank Shamrock as the future of the sport. With pay-per-view out of the picture, save for emerging satellite systems, the majority of fans thought the UFC was dead. On March 13, 1998, UFC XVI held its first-ever lightweight tournament (under 170 pounds at that time) where UFC-debuting Pat Miletich swept the competition. Miletich became SEG's star lightweight fighter. As for Shamrock, he was coming off the best win of his career and now had to face another Extreme Fighting champion in Igor Zinoviev. The fight didn't last long; Shamrock picked Zinoviev up and dropped him on his head, knocking him out cold in 22 seconds. "I thought it was going to be a stand-up fight like he did against Inoue," admitted Zinoviev. "He broke my collarbone along the same shoulder that I had surgery on. It took eight months for me to recover from that fight, and that was it…my career was over." Zinoviev lives in New Jersey, still trains people, and was a coach on the now-defunct International Fight League for a short while.

The Dedge Incident

As if being kicked off cable with little to no fanfare was bad enough, American fighter Douglas Dedge passed away on March 18, 1998, after competing in an unregulated match in Kiev, Ukraine, two days earlier. Fox News picked it up as "UFC fighter dies" and called Joel Gold of *Full Contact Fighter* for an interview. Skeptical at first, Gold went to the studio, saw the actual tape, and made his best case for why this unfortunate accident was certainly not representative of the UFC's safety standards. The newscaster was shocked when Gold professed that MMA was safer than boxing, but he could back it up. After being called for a second taped interview, he felt fine about it until he saw the feed that night.

Gold would not be the only person on the news segment. "I never would have done this interview in this manner if I knew of the plan they had to have Art [Davie] on live trying to get even with the UFC on TV," said Gold. Sure enough, Davie's segment would be live while Gold's comments would be edited. Years later, Davie commented on that interview, saying, "it's always been a potentially dangerous event. We haven't done a lot of these bouts, but like any full-contact event, the potential for injury and death does exist." To Gold's recollection, Davie said that MMA was not a sport, going far deeper than just saying the event was "dangerous."

Bob Meyrowitz called up Davie shortly thereafter and the two argued over the phone. Davie contended that Meyrowitz would not admit there was a "potential" for injury. "I asked what on earth he was thinking to possess him to do something like that," exclaimed Meyrowitz. "You were going behind my back trying to start another organization. We had a friendly relationship, and instead of leaving on good terms, he gets upset that he got fired and then shows what kind of individual he is by trying to slam everybody involved in causing a big problem. Fortunately, the Nevada State Athletic Commission knew every facet of what had gone on with Art Davie so it was no problem."

In a letter dated March 19, 1998, to Bob Meyrowitz with a copy to John McCain, Davie wrote, "I'm writing to urge you, as the owner of THE ULTIMATE FIGHTING CHAMPIONSHIP (UFC), to reconsider promoting these tournaments in light of the untimely death of American Douglas Dedge." He went on to say, "When I brought this event to you, I advised you that this was hand-to-hand combat and not a sport." The grassroots MMA media called him Benedict Arthur, but the damage had been done. While no one could argue that MMA had the potential for injury, all of the legal battles and Davie's rulebooks showing and proving the sport wasn't as dangerous as boxing became moot. "I was pissed off at Art because he was one of us and he knew the truth, and after he gets fired, he comes back and does this," said Gold.

Davie later admitted in the interview for this book that he wrote the letter to piss off Meyrowitz and to draw him into another argument, but the SEG boss never called. "I kind of resented the way the whole thing went down because I wasn't trying to damage the UFC—I wasn't trying to damage MMA particularly—but quite frankly, I felt bad about the Dedge incident and knew the potential was there for something to happen with all the promoters getting on the scene." Davie tried to clear the air with a letter in the Spring 1998 issue of *Full Contact Fighter*, but Gold's rebuttal and letters from fighters just made it worse. Davie would try to bring K-1 to the states, and despite getting it sanctioned in Nevada, it failed to take off.

AT UFC XVII, HELD MAY 15, 1998, Mark Coleman would look to rebound after the loss to Maurice Smith, but the prelims would introduce a figure that would ultimately become the face of the UFC: Chuck Liddell. The California native took up martial arts at age 12 and trained for several years, but wrestling would be his calling and one of his motivations for entering California Polytechnic State University, where he earned a degree in accounting.

After college, like many would-be fighters, the desire to compete was still very much alive, so he hooked up with San Luis Obispo trainer John Hackleman and took up kickboxing. Instead of getting a desk job, Liddell tended bar and taught kickboxing classes at the local YMCA. After a friend from Las Vegas got him into a quasi-MMA match with open-hand strikes to the face, he got a prelim shot at the UFC. "The way I thought about it was to stay on my feet," said Liddell. "If I stayed on my feet and made it exciting, I'd get invited back." Against fellow striker Noe Hernandez, the fight looked more like a kickboxing bout; Liddell won by decision.

While Tank Abbott quickly disposed of Brazilian jiu-jitsu exponent Hugo Duarte, Mark Coleman needed an impressive win to show people that he was back. "I was on a mission that I was going to come back, and I was going to be in the best shape of my life and get my revenge on Maurice Smith," said Coleman, "but I blew my knee out two weeks later about the third practice into it. I was so frustrated, depressed, and disappointed at that time because I worked really hard, and then I took the Pete Williams fight." Williams was a handsome, clean-cut Lion's Den fighter who made his Octagon debut after competing in Hawaii and Japan. Though Coleman managed to slightly edge Williams during the 12-minute regulation, he was spent going into the overtime period. "I remember getting to my corner to go into overtime, and all I could see was a big cloud of smoke," said Coleman. "I just kept telling myself to get him on the ground and the fight was mine...but we all know what happened after that." Coleman was exhausted, and 22-year-old Williams took control, pelting him with lefts and rights and leg kicks. Just 38 seconds into overtime, Williams delivered a head kick that crumbled Coleman; it would become one of the UFC's best highlight reel knockouts.

◆ ◆ ◆

THANKS TO BRAZILIAN PROMOTER SERGIO BATARELLI, SEG moved its final 1998 show to Sao Paulo for Ultimate Brazil, which introduced two major stars to American fans: Pedro Rizzo and Wanderlei Silva. Rizzo was a student of Marco Ruas, who even considered the striker to be like his very own son. Silva was a rough-and-tumble vale tudo fighter with a bald, tattoo-laden head and a menacing scowl. Their performances couldn't have been more different. Rizzo faced off against Tank Abbott, but this time, the rotund striker got more than he bargained for. After barreling toward Rizzo throwing bombs, Abbott was floored by a right hand from the Brazilian, who proceeded to chop him down with leg kicks and accurate punches. The pit fighter got the takedown but was too spent to do much about it. Back on their feet, Rizzo went on the attack, delivering a right-left combo that knocked Abbott out. "He kicked my ass," said Abbott. "Those leg kicks hit me so hard I thought he broke my leg. He was whacking the shit out of me."

As for Silva, he faced Vitor Belfort in a match that consultant Joe Silva put together. Belfort may have had all the physical skills, but his mind was elsewhere. Joe Silva had to talk to his mother and him several times to get him mentally focused for the fight. Matchmaker John Perretti did just the opposite, almost apologizing to Belfort for taking the bout. Perretti nicknamed Wanderlei Silva the Axe Murderer, a moniker that would stick with him for his entire career. But on this night, after a half minute of posturing, Belfort clocked Silva and made a beeline toward him, machine-gunning lefts and rights. Silva had zero defense and collapsed next to the cage until "Big" John McCarthy called the fight in just 44 seconds!

The main event rematched Frank Shamrock against the man who handed him his first MMA loss, John Lober. Shamrock had actually fought in the previous event against Jeremy Horn, but the match would be shown for a "best of" pay-per-view event called Night of the Champions; it was a way for SEG to save money, produce a new UFC, and still have a fresh main event. Shamrock was told that Horn was a B-level fighter and hardly trained. It took him 16 minutes to wear Horn down and frustrate him enough to catch him with a knee bar submission. Lober was an entirely different story.

Though he was recovering from a broken leg, the Huntington Beach native wanted the Shamrock fight and decided to play mind games. He sent him threatening emails telling him how much he was going to destroy him in the Octagon. "During the fight, I got him down on the ground and I was on top of him and I had him in a half-guard position and said, 'Is that all you got?'" said Lober. Shamrock did have a lot, reversed that position, and though he could have cranked a guillotine earlier in the fight, he wanted to punish him. "I was really working on my striking, and I felt like I just wanted to beat him down," exclaimed Shamrock. "When he got me up to the fence, I said to Frank, 'Okay, that's enough!'" according to Lober. "And he said, 'I want you to say it!' I just tapped [at 7:40] and said, 'That's enough dude.'" For the third straight time in 1998, Shamrock was the victor and still the UFC middleweight champion. But there would be a new star on the horizon.

• • •

TITO ORTIZ RETURNED TO HIS OLD STOMPING GROUNDS of Huntington Beach, California, between semesters of physical education classes at Cal State-Bakersfield. A night of partying with old friends led to a fight when someone broke a bottle over the head of one of Ortiz's friends. The once-UFC fighter moved into action, choking out one guy and knocking out another, but for his troubles, he was arrested on assault charges. Broke and in need of a good lawyer, Ortiz turned to his friend and training partner Tank Abbott for help. Abbott agreed to hook Ortiz up with a lawyer, but that's where the story gets fuzzy. Abbott proclaimed that Ortiz called up two days later saying he was not going to pay for it at all. Ortiz said Abbott wanted him to pony up for the lawyer right then when he didn't have the money. "Dave said, 'No, I'm not going to be your dad.'" remembered Ortiz. "So I go, 'Okay, you just screwed one of your best partners over.' From then on, I have never talked to him."

Down on his luck, Ortiz ventured into a local club in Bakersfield while he was back in college. He didn't really want to be in school and was looking for an alternative. That's where he met Sal Garcia, a budding club owner who had trained in BJJ with Carlson Gracie, who thought he could do something for him. The duo hatched a plan to crash the UFC Brazil scene and put SEG on notice that Tito Ortiz was back and better than ever. "It was like the movie *Jerry Maguire* when he walked the room with Cuba Gooding Jr.," laughed Garcia. "We made up cards and made sure that people took notice. Joe Silva was instrumental in getting Ortiz back into the show." Ortiz also cornered Lober for his match against Shamrock. While 1998 was the year of Frank Shamrock, 1999 would be the year of Tito Ortiz.

On January 8, 1999, the main event of UFC XVIII was supposed to be Randy Couture vs. Bas Rutten, but Couture vacated his heavyweight title over a contract dispute. The wrestler had negotiated a nice six-figure deal with SEG a month before his fight with Maurice Smith, but when it came time to execute against Rutten, things had changed. "Oh, we're not going to pay you," remarked Couture of SEG. "They told me, 'We are not going to honor that contract; this is what we can afford to pay you, so take it or leave it!' This was just one more instance of disrespect toward me, which was the way I felt so we ended up sitting on it. I went from having a $300,000 contract with the UFC for that year to nothing...not having a relationship with them at all." Couture fought in Japan four times, losing twice, until his eventual return to the UFC in November 2000. The cash-strapped SEG now had an easy way to name the show—Road to the Heavyweight Title—and John Perretti wanted to make Bas Rutten the star attraction. Posters called him the World's Greatest Martial Artist. "See, they screwed up on that...they were supposed to say the World's Greatest Looking Martial Artist," laughed Rutten. His fight against Tsuyoshi Kosaka was no laughing matter, and after a tough, grueling contest, Rutten knocked out the Japanese star just after 14 minutes.

Meanwhile Tito Ortiz would get another shot in the UFC, this time against a former wrestling opponent in Jerry Bohlander. Ortiz wasn't favored to win, but that didn't seem to bother him. "I was like, 'I'm going to overpower this guy, and I'm going to outpunch him,'" said Ortiz, who manhandled the Lion's Den student before the fight was stopped on a cut just after 14 minutes. Bohlander said later that the Lion's Den had begun to fall apart and that he shouldn't have been in there at all. Ortiz showboated a bit in the Octagon and put on a shirt from porno company Xtreme Associates. Back then, there were few sponsors who wanted anything to do with MMA. A couple of grand from a porn company wasn't exactly going to be turned down.

UFC XIX: Young Guns, held March 5, 1999, was headlined with Vitor Belfort, whose picture was the only one featured on the poster, vs. Guy Mezger, but the Brazilian dropped out due to injury. Needing a late replacement, SEG contacted Tito Ortiz for the slot on two weeks' notice. Ortiz hadn't trained and spent all of his time drinking and partying with his fiancée Kristin and friends. Manager Garcia and Ortiz talked it over and agreed to take the fight. By this time, Mezger had become the seventh King of Pancrase and sported a 22–7–2 record. "I had the flu really bad and couldn't train that hard, but to be honest, my ego got to me a little bit because I didn't think Tito could beat me," remembered Mezger. Garcia admitted seeing Mezger before the fight and knew he was sick.

Ortiz used his wrestling ability to control Mezger and stayed out of the Lion's Den fighter's submission traps. Finally Ortiz took his back and rained down punches. "He wasn't hurting me; I was just exhausted," said Mezger. "To be honest, he's just not a hard puncher, so it was easier for me to let him punch me and tire himself out than it was to block that shit." John McCarthy felt otherwise, and just four seconds shy of the 10-minute mark, the fight was stopped and Ortiz emerged the victor. With the Lion's Den watching, Ortiz put on a new shirt, but this time it was personal. Ortiz believed that Mezger had talked trash before the fight; his shirt read, "GAY Mezger is my Bitch!" Though Mezger didn't see the shirt, Ken Shamrock certainly did and hopped up on the Octagon apron, shouting some choice words. Ortiz walked toward him laughing and had to be pulled away by McCarthy. "I was laughing so hard because I ruffled his feathers," exclaimed Ortiz. The Ortiz vs. Lion's Den rivalry was far from over.

◆ ◆ ◆

WHILE ORTIZ BROUGHT SOME FIREWORKS back to the UFC, SEG boss Bob Meyrowitz prepared for his own show. Meyrowitz, Dr. Richard Istrico, and John McCarthy flew to Nevada for a formalized meeting with the athletic commission to be held on April 23, 1999. Meyrowitz felt he had the support and the votes to legally sanction MMA in Nevada, the holy grail of combative sports. The lobbyist who had worked so hard to ensure that the NSAC would pass the sport unfortunately had a plane delay and would not be able to make the meeting that was set for 9:00 AM that morning. "To my recollection it was about midnight, and I was asleep in my room when I got a call from the lobbyist saying that one of the commission members had changed their mind," said Meyrowitz. "He, the lobbyist, apologized for not being there but recommended that we didn't go before the commission. That way, we won't have the 'no' vote, and when he gets back, he will see what the problem is and take care of it." Meyrowitz was perplexed as to how a 3–2 vote, as he believed, would all of the sudden become a 2–3 vote. To this day, no one knows who on the commission changed their mind.

At UFC XX On May 7, 1999, SEG would finally crown a new heavyweight champion between Bas Rutten and Kevin Randleman, who had been a two-time Division I NCAA wrestling champion for Ohio State. Randleman had been Mark Coleman's friend and protégé for years and only had 30 days of training to defeat Maurice Smith at UFC XIX. This time around, he would be ready. Randleman had an incredibly muscular physique, dyed blonde hair, and a wild, spastic ring prowess. For the first four minutes of the fight, Randleman tore through Rutten and battered his face with vicious ground and pound. Stopping the fight to look at Rutten's face, the Dutchman's nose looked broken. Nobody knew that he had plastic surgery years earlier and that part of his nose was silicon, so it looked out of place. At the restart, Randleman got him down again, but his fire was gone. "I struck him and tried for three arm bars," said Rutten. "I went for something; he didn't do anything anymore. He threw like four punches during the whole fight after that." At the end of the match, Rutten looked like he had been fed through a shredder, while Randleman's face was untouched.

After 21 minutes of combat, Rutten was ruled the winner by split decision, much to the disappointment of Randleman and much of the crowd. Because of this match and the way it was scored, the longer 10-plus-minute rounds and overtimes were changed to the conventional three five-minute rounds for nontitle fights and five five-minute rounds for championship bouts. Riddled with injuries, Rutten vacated the heavyweight title shortly thereafter and continued his career in television and film, writing, fitness, and other endeavors. Seven months later, Randleman got a second chance at the title, this time winning by decision over Pete Williams at UFC XXIII: Ultimate Japan 2.

♦ ♦ ♦

FRANK SHAMROCK HAD NOT STEPPED into the Octagon for nearly a year by the time he faced Tito Ortiz for the title at UFC XXII: There Can Be Only One Champion on September 24, 1999. He had taken one token fight against Japanese star Kiyoshi Tamura for Rings that went to a draw. Ortiz would be bigger, younger, and stronger, while Shamrock would have experience and heart on his side. "I figured that I could either get him really quick with that arm bar, or it was going to be a long fight and I was going to beat him down," said Shamrock. Unfortunately it would be the latter. Over the course of four rounds, Ortiz and Shamrock mixed it up, but Ortiz controlled the fight with his wrestling and stayed busy topside. "He never stopped no matter what I did to him," said Ortiz. "I don't think I've ever given anybody a worse beating than that, and he took it."

With 54 seconds left in Round 4, Shamrock reversed his opponent and went on a supersonic tear of punches and kicks that dazed Ortiz. The wrestler shot in for the takedown, but Shamrock, blood trickling from his forehead, caught him in a guillotine choke. Unable to lock it in, Shamrock moved to his feet and pounded on Ortiz, who was on all fours. With 11 seconds left, Ortiz tapped out. "I mentally broke him," remarked Shamrock, who announced his retirement from the UFC after what many have called one of the best UFC fights of all time.

John Lober was in Ortiz's corner, but didn't say much during the match. When Lober had fought Shamrock, Ortiz had cornered him and made a later comment that he could have beaten Shamrock. Lober didn't like that very much. "He didn't give me the respect that I thought I should get from him," said Lober. "And so, what I did to him is like I'm going to show him what a fight is all about." When Ortiz heard this from this author, he was not at a loss for words. "I was wondering why those motherfuckers never told me how much time I had left!" exclaimed Ortiz. "I busted my ass for Frank too." Much like Randleman, Ortiz got another crack at the middleweight title by facing Wanderlei Silva at UFC

XXV: Ultimate Japan 3 on April 14, 2000. Silva had rebounded from his loss against Belfort by winning six straight fights, though the competition wasn't worthy of a championship run. Ortiz controlled Silva on the ground and won via unanimous decision; the "Huntington Beach Bad Boy" was the UFC middleweight champ.

As for Shamrock, the nest egg he had built for himself was already starting to crack by the time he walked down the ramp to fight Tito. "I loved Angie to death and never saw anything wrong with her until I was walking out to fight Tito," said Shamrock. "I stepped out and she stuck her arm out in front of me, and she was wearing that beautiful red dress with those ruby red lips and said, 'Hold on honey. Let me get out in front of you so the cameras can see me.' At that point, I had my moment of clarity. She just wants to be famous!" Shortly after the fight, their marriage began to crumble as Shamrock could not get that image out of his mind. "We eventually had a big fight, she locked me out of the house, and took $180,000 out of my bank account and all of my savings—everything that I had built up from fighting. And I was like, *Ahh, I think I get it!* I ended up sleeping on my sister's couch." After getting a divorce and being left high and dry, he met his current wife Amy; the couple has one daughter, Nicolette. Shamrock retired from competition on June 26, 2010, after losing two straight matches. He gave a farewell speech and would pass the torch to a new class of mixed martial artists.

At UFC XXIV: First Defense on March 10, 2000, Kevin Randleman was scheduled to defend his heavyweight title against Pedro Rizzo, but it was not to be. Before the matches even started, there were several brawls in the audience; the fans in Louisiana were restless for action. At one point, two females got into it and almost tumbled backstage. The entire card was excessively watered down compared to prior events, though SEG had been running on fumes for months. In fact many of the cards started to look more like Monte Cox's Extreme Challenge since Cox himself had turned into an elite manager of many fighters. SEG couldn't hold on to top talent because fighters were finding better paychecks in Japan. With the main event looming, this author wandered backstage

Up-Close Perspective

I was given a rare opportunity to be in Tito's entourage when he walked out to fight Frank Shamrock. I remember sitting in this little room with metal music playing in the background and Ortiz's corner men walking around him in a circle, shouting and getting him pumped up. Finally his manager Sal walked through the circle and placed his hands on Tito's shoulders. "This is your time!" he said. Walking out to all the fans and seeing the UFC from that perspective was a truly emotional high. When the fight started, to tempt fate a little further, I sat cageside next to Tank Abbott and Paul Herrera. Tank had a bottle of vodka and was pouring drinks for himself and Paul. To really push it, every time Paul looked away, I'd take his drink and then tell him he must have drank it all. That went back and forth a few times. Tank shouted in support of Shamrock, but at the same time, deep down inside he wanted Tito to win. After the fight we went to a dive bar of a strip club where I drank and partied with these guys all night long. It was a crazy scene, but a great memory.

only to find Kevin Randleman knocked out on the floor. Apparently, with all the drapery, he slipped on a bunch of metal pipes and knocked himself out. With the crowd as unruly as they were, people in the know were told to escape before the announcement was made.

On June 9, 2000, Randleman and Rizzo finally met again at UFC XXVI: Field of Dreams that took place in Cox's backyard in Iowa. On the night before the fight, this author remembered having drinks with UFC V vet Andy Anderson in his room along with Dan Caldwell, better known as TapouT's Punkass. For some reason, Randleman wanted to join in the fun. Downing several shots, he proceeded to hop over the twin beds, one by one, going back and forth like a super-muscled Jack Be Nimble. Knock! Knock! Mark Coleman finally entered the room and said, "C'mon Kev, we got a championship fight tomorrow!" Randleman was a very hyper fighter who was always jumping up and down, even before his fights. It was questionable as to whether he would stay within the rules, as kicking with shoes was now illegal. Before Randleman's match, Dallas-based Lion's Den fighter Alex Andrade became the first fighter in UFC history to be disqualified for kicking Amaury Bitetti with shoes on after being warned several times. Randleman thankfully stayed in line and grounded out a unanimous, boring decision victory, much to the disappointment of the crowd. Randleman won, but he was kicked so hard he had to have surgery to reattach part of his quadriceps muscle.

After a lackluster UFC XXVII card where Rizzo dispatched former UFC champion Dan Severn, who had no business being there, Bob Meyrowitz hoped SEG had finally turned a corner. Thanks to the efforts of the IFC, Larry Hazzard of the New Jersey State Athletic Commission had officially passed the unified rules that became the benchmark by which other commissions patterned their sanctioning of MMA. The biggest rule change would be the omission of knees to the head. "We were struggling on just a few satellite stations, and there was a whole belief that, and we were told by cable, that if we were approved by a major sanctioning body that they would put us back on," said Meyrowitz. "We were approved by the NJSAC, and when we went back to cable, they said, 'No, although we mean major, we mean Nevada.'" Meyrowitz's business would not survive without cable, as attendance for several shows had dipped below 2,000.

UFC 28: High Stakes (SEG started losing the Roman numerals in telecasts and on posters), held November 17, 2000, brought back some respect to the UFC as the show was held at the Trump Taj Mahal in New Jersey in front of 5,000 fans. Randy Couture came back into the fold, vying to retake the UFC heavyweight championship from Randleman. After a highlight reel knockout delivered by upstart and eventual light-weight champion Jens Pulver over John Lewis, who had moved on to trainer, it was freestyle wrestling champion Randleman vs. Greco Roman wrestling champion Couture. Randleman was too fast and too strong, and though he was able to get the takedown, Couture frustrated him from the bottom. "While most wrestlers were working on shoots, I started training from the bottom and fighting from the bottom," said Couture. "I wanted to frustrate him." Down on points going into Round 3, Couture finally tied up with Randleman and got his own takedown,

Greco-Roman style. "Working topside, Randleman had not been down there at all, and he was basically like a dying cockroach with the arms and feet up in the air. He didn't have any idea on how to fight from his back." Couture turned up the heat, dropping bombs and forcing the fight to be stopped at 4:13. "The Natural" was now back on top as the UFC heavyweight champion.

Going into the last show of 2000, Meyrowitz had his champion back, was sanctioned by a major state, got a DVD deal to release two "best of" compilations, and had the first UFC video game released back in June on the new Sega Dreamcast. He was also riding high with his radio-streamed talk radio platform, eYada.com, which was launched the year before. But nothing was going to change until the UFC got back on cable; the numbers from satellite were negligible at best. Something needed to change, and moving into the new millennium, there was a light at the end of the dark ages.

Renzo Gracie readying the finishing blow on Oleg Taktarov at MARS. *(Courtesy of Robin Postell)*

Left: Mark Coleman pounds on Maurice Smith at UFC XIV. *(Courtesy of Cal Cooper)*

Right: Randy Couture goes on the warpath against Vitor Belfort. *(Courtesy of Robin Postell)*

Kevin Randleman works on a bloodied Bas Rutten at UFC XX. *(Courtesy of Joel Gold/Full Contact Fighter)*

Kevin Randleman displays anger and frustration over his decision loss to Bas Rutten at UFC XX. *(Courtesy of Joel Gold/Full Contact Fighter)*

Left: Jon Fitch performs a suplex on Kengo Ura at Venom. *(Courtesy of Peter Lockley)*

Right: Eddie Bravo shows off his invention of the rubber guard with invisible collar. *(Courtesy of Eddie Bravo)*

Frank Shamrock lands a knee on Enson Inoue at Japan Vale Tudo '97. *(Courtesy of Frank Shamrock)*

Frank Juarez Shamrock lands an elbow on Tito Ortiz during their epic duel at UFC XXII and celebrates after the fight. Shamrock would have one of the best come-from-behind victories ever in the UFC. *(Courtesy of Joel Gold/Full Contact Fighter)*

High-flying Kazushi Sakuraba goes on the attack during his 90-minute match with Royce Gracie at Pride Grand Prix 2000. *(Courtesy of Susumu Nagao)*

Tito Ortiz slugs it out with Ken Shamrock at UFC 40: Vendetta. *(Courtesy of Susumu Nagao)*

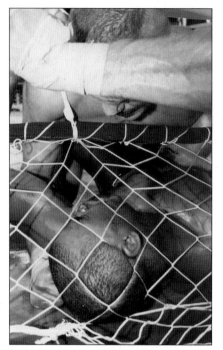

Left: Chuck Liddell hammers down on Jose "Pele" Landi-jons during their old school vale tudo bout at IVC 6. *(Courtesy of Joel Gold/Full Contact Fighter)*

Right: A young Georges St. Pierre wins the UCC welterweight title over Justin Bruckmann in only his second fight in 2002. He would go on to become one of the best pound-for-pound fighters in the world. *(Courtesy of Mike McNeil)*

Gina Carano lands a punch on Cristiane "Cyborg" Santos during their Strikeforce 145-pound championship fight. *(Courtesy of Strikeforce)*

Fedor Emelianenko swings for the fences at Fabricio Werdum at Strikeforce. *(Courtesy of Strikeforce)*

Brock Lesnar gets his revenge on Frank Mir at UFC 100. *(Courtesy of Susumu Nagao)*

Left: John Marsh trades blows with Vladimir Matyushenko at the IFC. *(Courtesy of IFC)*

Right: Rumina Sato performs a flying arm bar at Shooto. *(Courtesy of Shooto)*

Author Clyde Gentry III flanked by Shooto superstars Rumina Sato (left) and Hayato Sakurai (right). *(Courtesy of Cal Cooper)*

21

2001: A ZUFFA
ODYSSEY

SEG returned to Japan for the fourth time to hold its final show of 2000, UFC 29, on December 16. Tito Ortiz successfully defended his middleweight belt against Pancrase star Yuki Kondo. As fake snow started to fall down from the rafters, Ortiz was all smiles with friend and sometimes sparring partner Chuck Liddell, but there was an unfamiliar face in their midst. After Ortiz's fight with Wanderlei Silva, Sal Garcia no longer managed Ortiz or Liddell; that task now belonged to Dana White. White was born in Manchester, Connecticut, and grew up in Las Vegas. He had a boxing background, even boxing in the amateur leagues, and had popularized a boxing/aerobics program in Las Vegas. On June 11, 2000, White got Liddell a fight on a July IFC card and had also signed an agreement with the IFC to sell sponsorships, according to IFC head honcho Paul Smith. The fight manager would soon have a lot more than that on his plate.

The reason the UFC kept returning to Japan was because Meyrowitz wasn't flipping the bill for all of it. That said, SEG couldn't even afford to send commentators Mike Goldberg and Jeff Blatnick to the show; they had to settle for watching the tape. "I ran [the UFC] all out of my own pocket," said Meyrowitz. "The budgets really hadn't dropped very much, but the amount of money we were losing on each show was increasing. I was taking millions of dollars in losses...in real losses, not paper losses." After spending all the money on Nevada and failing to get the commission on board, it became an untenable situation whereby Meyrowitz pondered how long he could keep it going. "At this point, there have been so many things that have gone wrong that nothing brings tears to my eyes anymore. I just look at it and wonder what went wrong; what got so out of hand? But it was just an injustice [the political persecution], and it was just wrong on how it played out. I really just couldn't end it like that...you couldn't let it end wrong."

According to the UFC president, he never put the UFC up for sale, nor did he actively make calls to get anyone to buy it. "My recollection of it was that I was approached by Dana White, and he asked if I would be interested in selling." Months earlier Meyrowitz thought something was amiss when he got a fax from Tito Ortiz stating he would no longer be managed by Sal Garcia. "As you might remember about faxes, at the very top of the page it would say where it came from, and it said that it came from the 'Office of Lorenzo Fertitta,'" remembered Meyrowitz. "So at that point I found it somewhat amusing that someone who was from the [Nevada State Athletic Commission] would be working with an athlete." According to Fertitta, he began a dialogue with Meyrowitz in November 2000 about purchasing the UFC through his longtime friend, Dana White. At UFC 29, both Ortiz and Liddell sported the sponsor of Gordon Biersch Brewing Company, which the Fertitta family had bought controlling interest in back in November 1995. Liddell also thanked Station Casinos, which was owned by Lorenzo and his brother Frank Fertitta III.

As natives of Las Vegas, the Fertitta brothers grew up in the casino business. In 1976, their father Frank Fertitta Jr. started Bingo Palace, which catered to locals off the strip. The company took off more than 10 years later when Lorenzo and Frank exploited that model by building a string of branded casinos that became collectively known as Station Casinos. The overlooked market made the family very prosperous; in 2001, Fertitta Enterprises was the fifth-largest publicly traded gaming company.

Since there weren't many organized sporting events in the state, Fertitta's father took his young son to boxing matches, a passion both shared. In November 1996, Lorenzo took a post on the Nevada State Athletic Commission (NSAC) but was also becoming a closet fan of the

UFC. "I thought it was very interesting, but I was also a little uncomfortable with some of the brutality of it," said Fertitta. The failed "vote" to get MMA sanctioned in Nevada in April 1999 was not a vote at all according to Fertitta; it was merely an item on the agenda up for discussion. Meyrowitz contends that he would have never hired a lobbyist and spent that much money just to see it become an item for discussion. Many others in the MMA community also say it was going to be an item up for "vote" until Meyrowitz pulled it off the table. Lorenzo Fertitta's mind-set about the UFC didn't change until he saw a live event. The NSAC was invited by Meyrowitz to observe a UFC, so Lorenzo flew to Iowa and watched UFC XXI live on July 17, 1999.

Fertitta's eyes were opened for the first time to what the UFC was truly about when he spoke to some of the fighters that night. "After meeting [Frank Shamrock] and talking with him for a few minutes, I realized that these were not guys stepping out of a bar trying to hurt each other; they were professional athletes," he said. One snafu that might have hurt that perception was allowing a match to go on between 200-pound Jeremy Horn and 170-pound Daiju Takase, an obvious mismatch. When Fertitta learned that John Lewis, who was cornering fighter Andre Pederneiras, lived in Las Vegas, the two agreed to meet on their return. Before long, Fertitta took private Brazilian jiu-jitsu lessons from Lewis and loved every minute of it. From May 14 to May 18, 2000, according to IFC head honcho Paul Smith, he and Andy Anderson flew to Las Vegas on an invitation from Dana White to talk about MMA and the IFC. Smith met with Fertitta, who asked questions about the sport. After leaving the NSAC to take over as president of Station Casinos in July 2000, Fertitta got wind that the UFC might be for sale. According to Lorenzo, White had spoken with David Meyrowitz (Bob's brother) and thought there might be an opportunity. After talking things over with his brother Frank, Lorenzo approached Meyrowitz. The SEG president only wanted an investor, but Fertitta insisted that a 100 percent buyout was the only deal he'd consider.

On January 9, 2001, Zuffa Entertainment (*zuffa* means "to fight" or "to scrap" in Italian) bought the Ultimate Fighting Championship lock, stock, and Octagon for $2 million. "It was all very quick and straight-forward," said Meyrowitz of the sale. "As I say, at that point, I really was tired of the fight. Nevada had been very, very upsetting to me, and I was kind of happy. And people would say to me, 'Don't you regret selling it?' My grandson says it to me all the time. No, I don't." Lorenzo and Frank Fertitta were co-owners, while Dana White would serve as president. A consummate businessman, Lorenzo Fertitta became a die-hard fan of the sport. Both Fertitta brothers and White are so competitive that they grapple with several fighters and keep what they learn to themselves. The Zuffa office even had a boxing ring set up where the three would spar one another.

Lorenzo Fertitta and Dana White immediately began overhauling the UFC to make SEG's original date of February 23, 2001, for UFC 30 back in Atlantic City at Trump Taj Mahal. "Without Larry Hazzard and the New Jersey State Athletic Commission, this sport would still be dying a slow death," said Fertitta. Hazzard was once considered the man who ran boxing out of New Jersey, since he had been known for frequently changing the rules. By Hazzard taking a chance on the sport, other commissions and former naysayers were looking at the UFC with interest. Rebranded as "The All New" Ultimate Fighting Championship, the show's new look and energy were hard to dismiss; the famed Ultiman was replaced with a shiny, golden UFC logo. SEG had become lax in many areas, from weak merchandizing to failing to treat the show as entertainment. "When I went to a show in New Orleans, I wanted to buy something; I wanted to buy a T-shirt," said Fertitta. "I couldn't find anything anywhere. I was blown away that there was this unbelievably strong brand, and they [SEG] weren't taking advantage of all the items that could generate revenue." Zuffa offered full-color programs and different styles of T-shirts and posters, and the main event fight between Tito Ortiz and Evan Tanner showcased all the glitz and laser light shows of a scaled-down WWE. The fans appreciated it, and, for the first time, it appeared as if the company understood that delicate balance between reality and show business. "There is a considerable consumer demand for reality-based sports," said Fertitta. "This sport has the opportunity to become as big as boxing one day because it's shown it has a tremendous following," he said in April 2001.

• • •

JOHN PERRETTI WAS RELIEVED of his matchmaking duties after Zuffa took control. The brothers set a meeting with all former SEG employees but Perretti was unavailable while shooting a film in Japan. Even Art Davie threw his hat into the ring. After Tito Ortiz talked him up, "I was convinced in five minutes that Joe [Silva] was going to play a key role moving forward with building the new UFC," said Fertitta. Silva wasn't a former karate champion, but his years of dedication to the UFC and insight into MMA were second to none. He has an innate talent for looking at the whole picture and evaluating a host of variables to put together smart matches. Silva became vice president of talent relations, a position he holds to this day. "Joe, Dana, and I get into arguments on a daily basis and he always wins," confessed Fertitta.

Zuffa launched a multimillion dollar ad campaign, placing ads in *Playboy*, *Maxim*, *Stuff*, and other magazines focused on the 18-34 male. Using Carmen Electra as their spokesperson, they did model-like photo shoots with the UFC's top stars. The new UFC wouldn't rely on old gimmicks; it would be sold as the sport of the future. Tito Ortiz assumed his poster boy image. Randy Couture also garnered a strong fan base due to his smart strategies in the Octagon that netted him victory after victory. His match with Pedro Rizzo at UFC 31 will go down as one of the best back-and-forth matches in the promotion's history; Couture decisioned him but returned and beat him via TKO at UFC 34. New weight classes produced more champions beginning with UFC 31. In addition to light-heavyweight (186 to 205 pounds) and heavyweight (206 to 265 pounds), three other weight classes became permanent fixtures: lightweight (146 to 155 pounds), welterweight (156 to 170 pounds), and middleweight (171 to 185 pounds). Nontitle bouts would also be permanently marked at three rounds; before this, some bouts were two rounds and led to unnecessary draws.

At UFC 32, Zuffa packed over 12,500 fans into New Jersey's Continental Airlines Arena (formerly known as the Meadowlands). This topped the previous attendance records of 9,000 for UFC IX in Buffalo, New York. "The UFC events in the past were never promoted; they never went out and did advertising or promotion," said Fertitta. "I'm not going to go from having shows at the Taj Mahal in the state of New Jersey to some very small community. Every show either needs to be a step up or a parallel step. It gives us the opportunity to show that this is the new UFC."

In July 2001, MMA won its biggest battle when Zuffa won approval to hold UFC 33 in Las Vegas at the $950 million Mandalay Bay megaresort, sanctioned by the NSAC. Roughly seven years later, Meyrowitz talked about the sale of the UFC to Zuffa for a documentary on CNBC and spun a little different story, giving the perception that Lorenzo Fertitta was the one who held up the UFC from originally being sanctioned in Nevada for his own self-serving needs. Zuffa issued a 10-point retraction to correct the program showing that the April 1999 meeting with the NSAC was never intended to elicit a vote of any kind, and between the time of that meeting and sanctioning in Nevada, 18 months had passed.

While no one will ever know the truth, the ties between Dana White and the fighters in July 2000, Fertitta leaving the commission in July 2000, and the subsequent sale of the UFC and sanctioning in Nevada appeared terribly coincidental. True it took 18 months, but one also has to consider that any member of the NSAC cannot participate in any form of combative sports. Question was, did Fertitta's new role preclude him from doing anything in the state as a commission member sooner? According to an attorney for the NSAC, there is no waiting period after a commission member leaves his post to become actively involved in combat sports, while several other states do have waiting periods. Nonetheless, it took roughly a year (July 2000 to July 2001) from the time Fertitta left his post to the time the sport got passed in Nevada. "When I first heard about the UFC being sold to Fertitta, I thought 'Oh my God, now it all makes sense!'" exclaimed Joel Gold, who started *Full Contact Fighter* after UFC XIII. "But I didn't care...my sport was going to get passed in Nevada, so I didn't care to look at the injustice of it."

UFC 33: Victory in Vegas was held on September 28, 2001, with the headliner of Tito Ortiz vs. Vitor Belfort, who had to be replaced on late notice by wrestler Vladimir Matyushenko. Zuffa spent millions pushing the show because In Demand cable agreed to air the event. The UFC had regained access to millions of homes it had lost in 1997. With three titles up for grabs, this was to be the show to put the UFC and MMA back on the map. Everyone watched in anticipation, hoping for the best. Unfortunately, not everything went to plan. Every match on the card went to a decision, save for two dark (unaired) matches that had decisive endings. The showy entrances and subpar matches—though solid on paper—pushed the show past the three-hour mark, a setback the UFC and the sport could not afford. Zuffa's In Demand deal said the UFC had to generate at least 75,000 buy rates before turning a profit, otherwise a penalty would be assessed. The show came close, but it didn't hit that number. "UFC 33 probably hurt them really, really bad," said Dave Meltzer. "They had no TV, and they spent all that money publicizing that show, and it was terrible." The athletes looked as if they didn't want to put themselves out there to win; they just didn't want to lose. At a press conference at UFC 111, Dana White proclaimed, "UFC 33 is the only one I can remember where every fight sucked."

Zuffa redeemed itself two months later at the MGM Grand in Las Vegas, when UFC 34 brought back the kind of dramatic action missing from the previous show. All of the matches provided surprises, knockouts, and submissions. Because of the previous show, Zuffa stepped up educating judges (namely over UFC 33's Liddell vs. Bustamante match) and also instituted a new rule allowing the referee to stand up fighters if they remained inactive on the ground. At UFC 33, Tony DeSouza laid on the ground with Jutaro Nakao with neither man doing anything.

Nakao delivered the only KO of the night 15 seconds into Round 2, but it was too late. For the sake of the audience, the referee now had some authority to keep the action moving. Buy rates dropped considerably because of UFC 33, however, and Zuffa spent even more money trying to recapture the audience.

Zuffa finally won the attention of the mainstream sports media when Fox Sports Net's *The Best Damn Sports Show...Period!* wanted to air a complete match. On June 22, 2002, UFC 37.5 took place in a smaller venue site at the Bellagio in Las Vegas, decked out with *BDSSP* logos. The show headlined a contender bout for the light-heavyweight title between Chuck Liddell and Vitor Belfort. Liddell won a close decision, but three days later, *BDSSP* broadcast Robbie Lawler vs. Steve Berger in its entirety. It wasn't anything special, but it was the first time a UFC match had been shown on a network hitting over 50 million homes. The show went through the roof, and *BDSSP* continued to cover the UFC, often generating heat for the franchise's main events.

Liddell wouldn't get the chance to face poster boy Ortiz right away, since Zuffa had a potential blockbuster on its hands: Ortiz vs. Ken Shamrock at UFC 40: Vendetta. It was the continuation of the Ortiz/ Lion's Den saga that spilled over from the two almost going at it during UFC XIX. It was old versus new, respect versus rebellion, and big dollar signs for Zuffa. This would be the most celebrated match in UFC history at the time. Ken Shamrock was still one of the UFC's most marketable names, and with his stint as a WWF pro wrestler, there was something for the fans to talk about.

Held at the MGM Grand on November 22, 2002, UFC 40 hosted the largest audience ever assembled for an MMA event in the U.S. and the largest attendance that year for an event in Las Vegas: 13,770. People were split down the middle, and this would be the litmus test as to whether 26-year-old Ortiz could cement his success by taking the torch from the 38-year-old Shamrock. In a one-sided beatdown, Ortiz mangled Shamrock's face with elbows and forearm strikes. Shamrock never gave up, but his corner threw in the towel after three grueling rounds.

Shamrock would never be the same after this match. After rallying back in 2004 with a quick win over a worn-out Kimo Leopoldo, he would lose five straight matches by KO or TKO, two of those to Ortiz. Shamrock retired in October 2006 but wanted to return to the Octagon in June 2007; Zuffa wasn't interested. In 2010, Shamrock sued Zuffa, who had released him from his contract for what would have been two more fights. Zuffa won the lawsuit, and Shamrock was ordered to pay for Zuffa's legal bills in the amount of $175,000—money he did not have. Shamrock has four children with his former wife Tina and three stepchildren with his current wife Tonya. Like so many fighters, he has had to continue competing the only way he knows how, and as of this writing, he plans to keep on doing so. Two of Shamrock's biological sons, Sean and Ryan, both fought professionally in MMA.

On January 14, 2010, Ken and Frank's adoptive father Bob passed away due to health complications from diabetes; he was 68 years old. Though all three were on the outs in 2000, Ken had made his amends, and Frank did too. "I saw him I believe after his second or third heart attack," said Frank. "Bob was a wonderful man who loved so much that if he couldn't love you, he had to remove you. You are either with someone or you aren't. It hurt him too badly." Ken and Frank actually tried over a couple of years to set up a money fight between each other, but it was not to be.

As for Tito Ortiz, he became the people's champion, especially for the UFC's core market. UFC 40 also drew pay-per-view buys of 150,000, the most since the early days of the promotion. That show also boasted the most extravagant live production with fireworks, but many felt the fighter vignettes pushed the UFC further into WWE (WWF became World Wrestling Entertainment over a trademark dispute in May 2002) territory, instead of treating it as a sport. Not stopping there, UFC President Dana White announced the return of Tank Abbott, who signed a three-fight deal; matchmaker Joe Silva knew nothing of it, and Tank ended up losing all three matches, fading into the shadows of B-shows.

Zuffa thought it had found its stride, building an action-packed event off a great headliner and a bevy of up-and-comers to develop new rivalries down the road. Unfortunately, they couldn't repeat that success. "I remember thinking this was a turning point; it was a great show with a good main event, but then the next show returned right back to where they were at," said Dave Meltzer. UFC 41 did a paltry 60,000 buys, and UFC 42 dropped to 35,000. With five weight classes and only a handful of memorable showmen, the UFC had great athletes but not marketable stars.

UFC 42's main event pitting Matt Hughes against Sean Sherk failed to move people. Hughes was a formidable welterweight champion but didn't have much of a personality. His opponent had fought for the UFC in dark matches; no one had ever seen him on pay-per-view, and now he was fighting the champ. More than half of the crowd had dispersed by the time Hughes gave his victory speech after decisioning Sherk, the sound sweetened a la pro wrestling for extra effect. Despite Zuffa's efforts to push Hughes, it took some time for the audience to embrace him as a star, though he was a worthy champion. At UFC 60, on May 27, 2006, Zuffa brought back Royce Gracie to fight Hughes in a nontitle fight. Hughes almost submitted Gracie but instead won by TKO at 4:39. Hughes found an audience that liked his good ole boy, no-nonsense personality; it just took a little time to get there.

If every event couldn't be headlined by two characters like Shamrock and Ortiz, how could Zuffa build a sport but also provide entertainment? "Some fans like technical matches while others like brawlers," said Joe Silva. "It's hard to bridge the gap between sport and entertainment without alienating someone." Even with the success of UFC 40, Zuffa was losing money and was conflicted on whether to ham it up like the WWE or focus on building a sport.

On July 17, 2003, Zuffa issued a press release announcing a new format for the show. Dana White stated, "We listened to sports media experts, the analysts, and handicappers who were telling us some of the over-the-top spectacle was preventing us from being taken seriously." But in reality, the fireworks and glitz cost money, and Zuffa needed to cut its budgets. Perception about the UFC being a sport would hardly change by omitting the souped-up production. The one thing it did accomplish was putting any hype in the hands of the fight itself. The fighter vignettes were clipped, so people really didn't know who they were watching or why. At UFC 44 that September, the changes took effect without much opposition as Randy Couture, who had dropped down to light heavyweight, battled Tito Ortiz for the championship. Couture had already defeated Chuck Liddell at UFC 43, and Ortiz was ready to show the world he was the undisputed champion. Over the course of five rounds, Couture battered Ortiz at will, even spanking him for good measure with seconds remaining in the bout. Couture won by unanimous decision.

UFC 45: Revolution was billed as the 10th anniversary show, and Zuffa flew in champions old and new for the occasion, awarding Royce Gracie and Ken Shamrock UFC Hall of Fame plaques for their dedication to the sport. Shamrock gave a heartfelt speech about the UFC and how the fans have kept MMA alive for so long. The light heavyweight division had become the cream of the crop for Zuffa, with Ortiz, Liddell, Couture, and Belfort, while Japan's Pride still had the lion's share of top heavyweights. Rivalries and rematches created a virtual round robin of worthy matchups. A match nearly two years in the making, Ortiz vs. Liddell, took center stage at UFC 47: It's On, which took place on April 4, 2004. Both men had been trash-talking and hyping it up every chance they got on radio, TV, and even in a featured documentary. With both coming off losses and with no belt on the line, it was a personal fight that generated a lot of interest, much like Ortiz vs. Shamrock. Just 38 seconds into the second round, Liddell pummeled Ortiz with punches to claim the victory.

• • •

ON THE OUTSIDE, it looked like Zuffa was well on its way to mainstreaming the sport of MMA, something that SEG could never do. But according to an article that made the cover of *Forbes* on May 5, 2008, Zuffa had lost over $44 million during the first three years of operation. As told to writer Matthew Miller, "One morning in 2004 I called Dana and said we wanted out," said Lorenzo Fertitta. "We were spending our family fortune. Dana called back and said he had found a buyer offering $4 million." The pay-per-view model that had worked so well for the UFC was no longer the same, just as getting into Vegas, as it turned out, really didn't mean that much in the grand scheme of things. "For whatever reason, the UFC from 1994 to 1996 was very strong on pay-per-view, and I don't think that will ever happen again," said Dave Meltzer. "Nobody had ever succeeded on PPV without television."

After trying for two years to get a television deal, Zuffa signed a 13-week series for upstart cable broadcaster Spike TV. The American boob tube wasn't ready for conventional MMA programming, but it was geared for reality TV. The deal was less than perfect. Zuffa had to pay for the air time and for production of the show. *The Ultimate Fighter* gave up-and-coming fighters a chance to prove themselves all in the hopes of winning a six-figure contract; it also gave audiences 13 weeks to familiarize themselves with athletes who would ultimately become pay-per-view moneymakers. "I remember Dana saying that no one wanted to touch the show with a 10-foot pole, and Spike was the only network with a nut sack," said Season 1 finalist Stephan Bonnar. "Even Spike, he said, was reluctant and knew it was a huge gamble. I remember thinking, *What, are they stupid?* This show is going to totally kick ass. There wasn't a doubt in my mind." *The Ultimate Fighter* debuted on January 17, 2005, and backed by a Zuffa multimillion dollar campaign, it became a huge hit for Spike TV and the UFC owners.

The Ultimate Fighter Season 1 finale would become the turning point for the entire sport in the eyes of the audience. The two finalists weren't bulking, muscular prospects; neither had any tattoos, and both looked like a couple of kids fresh out of college. There wasn't any rivalry, but with both men smiling ear to ear, their match on April 9, 2005, can only be described as the gutsiest contest of heart and courage. No takedowns or submissions, these men set out to knock each other's heads off. "I got punched in the face about 100 times, so looking back, it's kind of a blur," said Bonnar. New and old UFC fans began calling each other to get them to tune in, and the ratings soared. When it was all over with, both men were given the coveted six-figure contract, and the audience agreed wholeheartedly. Dana White said it was "the most important fight in UFC history," and the match was voted the greatest fight in UFC history in 2009.

When Zuffa first took over the UFC, their only sponsor was the Fertitta-owned Gordon Biersch Brewing Company. After *The Ultimate Fighter* debuted, major sponsors started pouring in and Zuffa had to start turning companies away for valuable mat space. The show created numerous stars for the promotion—even the ones who didn't win—and even gave way to a new fandom term: TUF noob (fans who started watching the UFC post *The Ultimate Fighter*). The show also did the one thing that Zuffa needed to stay in business: increase pay-per-view buy rates. UFC 40's 150,000 buy rates would be quickly squashed by the first PPV to air after the first *Ultimate Fighter* series ended; UFC 52, where Chuck Liddell became the champion by defeating Randy Couture, pulled in 280,000 buys. The pay-per-view model that Zuffa desperately needed to take effect was now in full swing. It wasn't an issue of hitting mid-six figures; it was how the promotion would hit seven.

Spike TV also gave the UFC two other shows, a clip show called *UFC Unleashed* and a live show, *Ultimate Fight Night Live*. Two years after the first season, Spike TV reportedly paid Zuffa over $100 million for the rights to the series and the network now picked up production costs. Liddell became the new face of Zuffa's UFC, becoming the first MMA athlete on the cover of *Sports Illustrated* and knocking out countless opponents in his wake. Zuffa now had a formula for their success: build up the two pay-per-view headliners by having them coach a season of *TUF* and also develop an endless amount of new stars who will eventually take over for the old guard. *TUF* Season 1 winner Forrest Griffin returned to coach the seventh season.

Although *The Ultimate Fighter* did exactly what it was supposed to do, producers of the show needed a little more zip from one-time host Willa Ford and coaches Randy Couture and Chuck Liddell. They found what they were looking for in the f-bomb-dropping Dana White, who was never afraid to speak his mind and became something of a real Vince McMahon for the sport. "The only star they really created, and it tuned out to be a very good one by the way—a very shrewd move—was Dana White," said Meyrowitz. Chuck Liddell may have been the face, but Dana White was the mouth. Shaving his head bald, he became something of a Lex Luthor for many—especially in the media—when in late 2005 Zuffa banned much of the Internet media that had kept the sport going for so long. Sherdog.com, the largest independent MMA media website, had its credentials pulled in 2005 (later restored four years later). *Full Contact Fighter*, which was a website, monthly newspaper, and clothing line, also went by the wayside. "Every time [Dana] saw the paper, if there was something he didn't like, Oh boy!" exclaimed Joel Gold. "He'd call me up and start yelling, and I'd tell him, 'You don't own my publication! I don't bend over.' I still don't know to this day why I got blacklisted. The only answer I got from him was that I gave Pride too many covers! Not one fighter or promoter stood up for the MMA community that for all those years we stood up for them. That was sad." Despite the MMA media's grassroots movement that kept the UFC alive for so many years, White and the UFC have become almost antagonistic toward the MMA media, preferring to work with mainstream sports media.

In Lorenzo Fertitta's interview for this book, which was done months after Zuffa took control of the UFC, he professed to unify the sport. "The problem has been that everyone has traditionally played in their own sandbox," said Fertitta. "That's like saying, 'I'm the UFC, and I'm not going to recognize anyone else.' It's important for all the promoters to communicate so that we can all move in the same direction rather than fight each other." He told everyone at an April 2001 New Jersey rules meeting that the Octagon format was not off-limits, pushing to keep MMA safe inside of a cage, rather than the ring. But that tune changed fairly quickly when Zuffa later trademarked the Octagon name and sent out "cease and desist" letters to anyone who even came close to something eight-sided. Even Greg "Kazja" Patschull has been inundated with threats of legal action but has paid no mind since he used an octagonal cage prior to the first UFC. From a marketing perspective it's clear why Zuffa did this, but from a sport perspective it meant there wouldn't be any uniformity in reference to what surface the fighters would be competing on.

The Zuffa empire now had a king who wasn't afraid of anything. If a rival promotion overstepped its bounds, White would counterprogram using Spike TV as his weapon. He would frequently call out other promotions, lambasting their events and athletes. As long as the promotion stayed under the wire—out of sight and out of mind—it was safe. When Tito Ortiz came back into the fold after being on the outs with White, his only condition was that White fight him in a boxing match. The bout never happened as proposed in March 2007, but it wasn't because of White, who was the center of a Spike TV documentary on the bit. Of course, that match would have been a disaster either way. White started doing video blogs before shows and developed a following on Twitter. But sometimes the UFC head honcho didn't know when to hold back. In one of White's video blogs directed at MMA journalist Loretta Hunt, White managed to not only use derogatory remarks against women, but also homosexuals; GLAAD asked for an apology on April 2, 2009. White quit doing video blogs, but that wouldn't last long.

White has no doubt turned many fighters into millionaires and can be classified as the best person you would want on your side. When certain fighters have been in trouble or have needed help, White would be the first one on the scene. When Chuck Liddell lost three straight fights by knockout, one could see that White genuinely cared for his friend and vowed to always have a place for him in the UFC—just not in the Octagon. But White has also done some things that truly show where the UFC is in the grand scheme of things. In late November 2008, White released 8–1 welterweight Jon Fitch, reportedly over Fitch's unwillingness to sign a contract stating he was giving up his likeness rights into perpetuity for use in the UFC video game, etc. In an interview with *Fight Network Radio*, Fitch said it was "100 percent a power play...They are trying to send a message to the rest of the [fighters] out there." Not only was Fitch out, but White threatened that any of Fitch's American Kickboxing Academy teammates were on thin ice as well. It took all of 24 hours before Fitch returned to the UFC and signed that agreement. Fitch claimed it was never about the agreement in the first place, but about White's tactics. Even Randy Couture, who had left SEG prior and then Zuffa over a contract dispute, couldn't mount much of a defense in a case against Zuffa, the company reportedly worth over $1 billion in 2008. Rather than face more financial losses, Couture came back too. As the old saying goes, "He who has the money calls the shots."

The aforementioned *Forbes* article said that the UFC controlled 90 percent of the MMA industry, and this was back in 2008. Fertitta was quoted as saying, "We are like football and the NFL. The sport of mixed martial arts is known by one name: UFC." While it's fair to call the UFC a monopoly, Zuffa and Dana White have done more for MMA than anyone else, bringing the sport to millions of people worldwide. On June 19, 2008, Lorenzo Fertitta stepped down as president of Station Casinos, which filed for Chapter 11 bankruptcy the following year, to work full time on Zuffa. The company has made tremendous inroads, especially in sanctioning. After leaving his post with the NSAC, once-enemy of the UFC Marc Ratner became vice president of regulatory affairs. He, along with Randy Couture and others, have traveled throughout the U.S. to get the UFC and MMA sanctioned in as many states as possible. But still, one can't help but look at Zuffa's immense power. Former California State Athletic Commissioner Armando Garcia, after leaving his post, became head of security for Station Casinos. With the amount of money and power that Zuffa wields, opportunities are limitless. On January 12, 2010, Zuffa sold a 10 percent interest in the company to Abu Dhabi government-owned Flash Entertainment. Lorenzo and Frank Fertitta III would now hold 40.5 percent ownership each, Dana White would hold 9 percent, and Flash 10 percent. This is part of a worldwide footprint for the company, which already had opened offices in the United Kingdom (2006), China, and Canada (both 2010). UFC 122, a minor event that took place in Germany on November 13, 2010, was reportedly broadcast to over a half billion homes. The goal, quite simply, is to tap out the world via the UFC. And so far, they've done a stellar job.

On July 11, 2009, the UFC broke even more new ground when it staged UFC 100 at the Mandalay Events Center in Las Vegas, Nevada. The show garnered the second-largest MMA gate in Nevada with $5.1 million, just short of the $5.3 million made by the rematch between Chuck Liddell and Tito Ortiz in December 2006. That said, UFC 100 set a pay-per-view record that is reportedly 1.6 million buys at $45 a pop. This benchmark in pay-per-views can be attributed to amateur wrestler-turned-pro wrestler-turned-UFC star Brock Lesnar. "When Brock Lesnar came into pro wrestling in 2004, I know for a fact the UFC wanted his number," said Dave Meltzer. "Brock had the size thing and he wasn't sloppy; he was genuinely a fantastic athlete and he could really wrestle. He was also famous. MMA fans wanted him to lose really bad, but the pro wrestling fans wanted him to lose really bad as well because he deserted them. He was not popular for leaving pro wrestling in his prime, but when he started winning, pro wrestling fans got really behind him." Standing 6'3" and having to cut weight to make the 265-pound cutoff, Lesnar lost his first UFC bout to Frank Mir but went on a tear after that, racking up wins and becoming a major superstar for the promotion. At UFC 121, Mexican American heavyweight prodigy Cain Velasquez quickly dispatched Lesnar to become the new champion. The UFC has prided itself as being a very culturally and ethnically diverse promotion with the champions to prove it: Georges St. Pierre (French Canadian), B.J. Penn (Hawaiian), Rashad Evans, Quinton Jackson (African American), and Anderson Silva (Brazilian). But the promotion has been slow to draw the attention of Latino viewers, and with Cain Velasquez, they finally have a vehicle to drive that audience. With Latinos comprising the largest fan segment for boxing, the UFC intends on attracting them to MMA. Zuffa showed UFC 100 for free on Televisa in Mexico; they have started a Spanish-language MMA website and have lent out the Octagon to Mexican promotions. Whether Velasquez remains the UFC champion—the division is plagued by frequent injuries and turnover—or not, Zuffa has stepped up its efforts to win over the Latino fan base.

◆ ◆ ◆

ZUFFA'S UFC, for all the talk of being a monopoly under White's dictatorship, is a true success story financially. And while the promotion can pretty much do whatever it wants unabated, fans have been assaulted by a plethora of tremendous fights, dramatic but true storylines, and an evolving experience of seeing some of the greatest athletes in the world perform at their very best. The UFC's success has spawned other promotions, multimedia outlets, hordes of memorabilia and collectibles, and now even fan expos that bring in hundreds of thousands of people all over the world. While Lorenzo Fertitta's comment about the sport "being the UFC" is categorically untrue, perception is greater than reality, and for fans that perception is pretty amazing considering what the promotion has been through after nearly 20 years of mixed martial arts glory.

22

FIGHTING THE
800-POUND GORILLA

Countless MMA promotions have come and gone from the sport, much like kickboxing's early days. Champions were crowned one night, then their belts were worth nothing the next. In lieu of originality, most of these promotions combined any of the following words to create a name: *ultimate, extreme, rage, world, cagefighting, international,* and *championship.* Sherdog.com has the best record of fight statistics anywhere, and from an analysis conducted in 2001, 400 MMA promotions from around the world provided some interesting results. Only 145 promotions were still active at the time of this writing, compared to 255 that had not produced any event within the eight months prior to the analysis. Of those inactive promotions, 50 percent promoted only one show before folding.

So many inexperienced promoters have come onto the scene, spent thousands of dollars, lost thousands of dollars, and vanished from sight. But since the days of Zuffa, some well-financed promotions have roared onto the scene hoping to chip away at the UFC's market share. "These guys sit around saying that if the UFC does like 700,000 buys and some over a million, and the sport is so popular, that all I have to do is 10 percent of that and do 70,000 buys and break even," said pro wrestling and MMA expert Dave Meltzer. "But the reality is they would be lucky to get 7,000. They don't think of it that way. They don't realize just how big the UFC is and that those stars were on television and heavily promoted over a long stretch of time." Some shows experimented with format, some shows had a unique theme, and some even had television. But the monster known as the UFC would not be easy to topple, and these 10 promotions all have their own intriguing stories about fighting that 800-pound gorilla...some even made it out alive. (The dates listed below each promotion signify the dates from first to last event, which doesn't include the genesis of each company, or its demise in come cases.)

World Extreme Cagefighting
(June 30, 2001 to December 16, 2010)

Southern California had the International Fighting Championships and King of the Cage, while Central California had World Extreme Cagefighting. San Luis Obispo was the home of Scott Adams, who wrestled for California Polytechnic alongside Chuck Liddell. After college the two men started up a place to train called S.L.O. Kickboxing in their college hometown. Adams was a groundfighter and marketer, while Liddell was a stand-up fighter and accountant, so they equaled each other out. When traditional martial artist Reed Harris walked into the gym, he was blown away by the groundfighting techniques and befriended Adams.

With the MMA craze hitting the California scene down south, Harris and Reed formulated a plan to meet with one of Reed's contacts at The Palace (which became known as Tachi Palace), an Indian casino in Lemoore, California. Eventually the duo took some members of the tribe to see one of Paul Smith's IFC events, and World Extreme Cagefighting was born in 2001. "We had 6,000 people for that first show," said Adams. "It was like lightning in a bottle because so many people in the area were thirsting for MMA." Using his on-site fee from The Palace, Adams handled the matchmaking and didn't want to be just another regional promotion, so he flew in talent when he could. "I always knew that lighter weight boxers were a draw, and I just couldn't figure out why there was not a showcase here in the states for the lighter weights in MMA." The WEC started to shift toward lighter fighters, building stars like Fresno native Cole Escovedo, Cesar Gracie Academy's Gilbert Melendez, and American Kickboxing Academy's Richard Crunkilton. According to Adams, the fight that really put the promotion on the map for the lighter weights was a WEC 19 featherweight (145 pounds) contest between champion Escovedo and Urijah Faber, who would take the title after two hard-fought rounds.

In 2006, Adams and Reed felt like they were stuck in Lemoore. During the five years of running the WEC, the promotion had only been out of Lemoore one time for WEC 4 at Mohegan Sun Casino in Connecticut. The WEC needed capital if it was to expand, and both men knew they had a great product on their hands. "We tested the waters, and Zuffa made us the best offer," said Adams, who along with Reed stayed on with the WEC as co-general managers when it was sold in December 2006. A lot of the fighters who were part of the pre-Zuffa WEC now were part of the post-Zuffa era. Zuffa had its own feeder show, far removed from when SEG had to rely on other promotions alone. The new WEC would also have more eyeballs on screens when Zuffa secured a deal with the upstart Versus network to air two-hour live events and, similar to *UFC Unleashed*, clip shows of prior WEC fights.

After nearly two years, Zuffa wanted a change in guard. In November 2008, Adams was made an offer to leave the WEC on very favorable terms, and the WEC co-creator couldn't have been happier. He was replaced by Sean Shelby, a protégé of UFC matchmaker Joe Silva. Though Zuffa could pluck talent from anywhere, it became clear that the WEC wasn't just a feeder show; it had its own weight divisions that didn't interfere with the UFC. The decision was finally made to make the WEC strictly a lighter-weight promotion, anything 155 pounds and down. Fighters like Brian Stann, who had impressed as a light heavyweight, got moved up to the UFC, as did Chael Sonnen, who had unofficially won the 185-pound belt in one of the WEC's events prior to the changeover. The final WEC with heavier weight classes took place on December 3, 2008, after which 170 pounds and up would be dissolved, and a new weight class (flyweight at 125 pounds) was added. The lightweight division at 155 pounds would be shared between the two promotions.

The promotion lured top fighters, not only from the U.S. and Brazil, but from China, Korea, and Mexico. On October 28, 2010, Dana White sent shockwaves through the MMA community when he announced that the WEC would cease operations in favor of merging the two companies under the UFC banner. Beginning in 2011, the UFC would now include both the featherweight and bantamweight classes, with the flyweight class to be added later. From a branding perspective, the merge is a good move because it expands the UFC universe with network Versus in tow, but now fans have to keep track of two more weight classes, many more stars, and could a breaking point be on the horizon for too many shows to showcase too many stars? "It is going to be more difficult for the UFC to feature seven weight divisions instead of five and develop contenders," said Dave Meltzer. "But the champions in the lighter divisions over the long haul will have so much more income potential and a lot higher ceiling." Going back to the pro wrestling model where stables were kept manageable so that fans can stay connected to their favorites, it will be interesting to see how the UFC pulls off the merger. Already the promotion is narrowing its current stable to make room for the two weight classes, but will that be enough? The only logical answer lies in a long bandied-about rumor of the UFC starting its own network, which given the promotion's momentum, most likely won't be a rumor much longer.

World Fighting Alliance
(November 3, 2001 to November 23, 2002; July 22, 2006)

After his fighting career started to wane, John Lewis set up shop in Las Vegas, Nevada, and carved out a pretty strong Brazilian jiu-jitsu school. After Lorenzo Fertitta met him at an Iowa UFC, he started working out with both Fertitta brothers and Dana White. Though complimentary about Zuffa's emergence, Lewis wanted to get in on the action and applied for a Nevada MMA license in 2000. He wanted to do something different and hooked up with John Huntington, who regularly sold out the Mandalay Bay Events Center for some of the biggest club parties in the world. "These are the Pimp n' Ho and Club Rubber parties," said Lewis. "These are big, traveling theme shows that's just an ocean of people." Lewis and Huntington hooked up with Nevada-based lawyer Louis Palazzo to invest in their creation called World Fighting Alliance, "Where the Night Club Meets the Fight Club." The first show took place on November 3, 2001, piggybacking off UFC 34, which was held the night before. It almost didn't come off when a production snag forced the cage not being ready until an hour after the show was supposed to begin. With techno music pounding the 2,000-seat auditorium called The Joint at the Hard Rock Hotel and go-go dancers galore, the first event had its share of great fights, introducing Rich "Ace" Franklin to a bigger crowd. Franklin, a school teacher, would end up becoming one of the UFC's bigger stars. Lewis said they only accomplished 40 percent of what they wanted to do with the first show and returned eight months later with a second installment. The promotion improved upon its concept and certainly had more of a club vibe. Ice-T even rapped to kick off the third event, held the day after UFC 40. With fight cards that were just below the UFC level, no television, no pay-per-view, and a limited audience, the WFA ceased operations as there was no way the investor could turn a profit.

Jump ahead to 2005, when after the success of *The Ultimate Fighter*, investors Palazzo and fellow lawyer Ross Goodman began picking up top-tier talent to relaunch the WFA. Led by CEO Jeremy Lappen, an entertainment attorney and former partner of the early MMA management company, Battle Management, the new WFA took place at The Forum in Los Angeles on July 22, 2006, with a star-studded card that included the return of Bas Rutten, Quinton Jackson, Matt Lindland, Lyoto Machida, and Urijah Faber. Rutten was originally going to face Kimo Leopoldo, but he was nixed from the card over testing positive for steroids. His replacement, Ruben "Warpath" Villareal, was a C-level fighter who would take on anybody for a price, and Rutten chopped him down quickly with leg kicks. The show aired on pay-per-view, but despite the hype, only 2,300 tickets were sold, and buy rates didn't eclipse 50,000.

The promotion touted big paydays, fighter training per diems, and iron-clad contracts and said it would return in December of that year. When that show got pushed back, Lappen sued Palazzo and Goodman on November 15, 2006, for breach of contract as he had not been paid. The two parties settled out of court for an undisclosed sum, and Lappen had already been on Dana White's bad side after reportedly being removed from his seat and escorted out of UFC 61. Lappen would end up serving with doomed EliteXC heading up fight operations, only to move over and run CAMO (California Amateur Mixed Martial Arts Organization), much to the chagrin of Ryan Chenoweth, who started promoting amateur shows back in 1994 and had championed the rules in the late 1990s. "From everything I have seen, something fishy has happened here," said Paul Smith of the IFC, a former sanctioning body for indie MMA events. "How can the CSAC put someone in a sole position or monopoly over all amateur MMA [in the state] that has zero experience in sanctioning any MMA shows ever?" Lappen runs CAMO with former EliteXC matchmaker JT Steele.

With the WFA holding contracts of some pretty significant talent, Zuffa moved in for the kill. On December 11, 2006, Dave Meltzer's *The Wrestling Observer* made the announcement that Zuffa had purchased certain assets (read: fighter contracts) from the WFA. It would add a dozen fighters to the promotion, and its new sister show, the WEC. "With the exception of that one period of the early UFCs, no one has ever made money on pay-per-view without television," said Meltzer. "There's no guarantee that you'll make money with television on pay-per-view, but without it, there is no way you make money on pay-per-view." Call it vanity or delusions of grandeur, but time and time again people seem to forget this fact, even after seeing the UFC fail at drawing numbers before Zuffa hit its stride with *The Ultimate Fighter*.

BodogFIGHT
(August 22, 2006 to November 30, 2007)

Canadian billionaire Calvin Ayre created Bodog in 1994 with $10,000 to his name. Bodog first became an online gambling website, which grew to serve as an umbrella for numerous other enterprises. By 2006, he had made the cover of *Forbes'* "Billionaires" edition, but his online gambling activities got him in hot water. In March 2006, his Costa Rican house was raided by authorities, and he supposedly can't set foot into the U.S. After shooting shows beginning on August 22, 2006, BodogFIGHT was launched on the upstart ION television network on February 7, 2007, with Ayre front and center as the playboy host surrounded by bikini-clad women and first-class everything. The billionaire liked MMA and thought it would be a great fit for the Bodog brand. Fights were held in a ring with the audience comprised of other fighters and friends; events took place in Costa Rica, Russia, British Columbia, and one lone event in New Jersey. Staging for the fights lacked any originality, but each program spent considerable time building up the fighters in some of the most in-depth MMA character pieces ever committed to celluloid, save for some high-dollar UFC specials. "Showing that these fighters had lives outside the ring helped make them more relatable to the viewer at home, and if viewers can establish some kind of personal connection to a particular fighter, they'll have one extra reason to tune in next week to cheer him on," said Ayre. Some of the fighters that graced the organization included Chael Sonnen, Cain Velasquez, Tara LaRosa, and Amanda Buckner, with former Hook n' Shoot promoter Jeff Osborne running a lot of the day-to-day fight operations.

With a fledgling network; spending millions of dollars on fighters, flights, and particulars; and a brand name that fans could hardly identify with, it was difficult to see how BodogFIGHT could turn a profit. "The main consideration in launching BodogFIGHT (or BodogMUSIC, BodogTV, etc.) was to build brand awareness, to positively associate the Bodog name with different forms of entertainment that resonated in the minds of our target audience. If any of these individual ventures turned a profit, great, but that was very much a secondary consideration." Barely on American television for a few months, Ayre promoted a token pay-per-view on April 14, 2007, with Russian Fedor Emelianenko headlining. It barely got noticed, save for then-Russian president Vladimir Putin being in attendance. In mid-2008, BodogFIGHT closed down, losing a reported $38 million in the process according to MMA business site

MMApayout.com. "Contrary to popular mythology, BodogFIGHT wasn't shut down based on some bean-counting 'failsafe' lever being tripped or anything," said Ayre, who claimed he wanted to devote his time to restructuring the overall Bodog business model. "And hey, enduring many long hours of video shoots (and subsequent wrap parties) surrounded by beautiful girls in bikinis ain't exactly a bad way to earn a living."

International Fight League
(April 29, 2006 to May 16, 2008)

Inspired by the Mark Kerr documentary *The Smashing Machine*, Wizard comic book magazine founder Gareb Shamus and real estate developer Kurt Otto formed the International Fight League in January 2006. Instead of single events and single fights, the IFL was comprised of five-man teams representing different cities that would clash against one another, building to a final team championship each year. "It was a really neat thing to see this happen in the sport with these professional teams," said Frank Shamrock, who coached the San Jose Razorclaws. "I thought it was a great thing that added a lot of flavor to the martial arts." The IFL became the first MMA series to be featured on broadcast television, on Fox Sports Net and MyNetwork TV. Problem was, with so many teams in so many conventional mainstream sports, it was difficult for fans to keep track of who was who, and the fighters themselves got lost amid team names that nobody knew. Broadcast fights were also taped, which took out the "live" real experience.

As the first publicly traded MMA company, the IFL had a market capitalization in 2006 of $150 million, and many an MMA pundit made money off the IFL stock that shot up to $17 per share in January 2007. With television and word that the IFL might be a real contender against the UFC, lawsuits started flying, first by Zuffa alleging the company was using proprietary information from former Zuffa staff who were now employed with the new promotion. Attendance was also a real issue for the IFL since the team concept didn't exactly work, and the shows would travel to cities where none of the teams resided. Regional promotions work off regional fighters, so selling regional teams outside their regions became problematic. In 2008, the made-up regional teams were abandoned for current MMA teams and camps, but by then, it was too late. "They were the nicest guys trying to do the right thing, but they just didn't know what they were doing," said Shamrock. Despite the TV appearance, the IFL didn't make much money and wasn't building up fighters to ever have a chance at pay-per-view. Maurice Smith, Ken Shamrock, and Don Frye were three of several coaches (each paid $5,000 per month) but added very little to the promotion. In May 2008, the company announced a new gimmick with a six-sided cage called "The Hex." "I remember the average amount of money they were spending on a show was $1.3 million," said Meltzer. "Even if they had sold out every arena, they would still lose money. And when you can sell out and lose money, you have a real problem." The IFL closed its doors on July 31, 2008, and the stock plummeted. While HDNet reportedly purchased physical assets for the IFL, including tape libraries for its 23 shows, logos, and rings for $650,000, Zuffa purchased fighter contracts and merely added to their bustling stable of top competition.

HDNet Fights
(October 13, 2007 to December 15, 2007)

Mark Cuban, Dallas billionaire and owner of the NBA's Dallas Mavericks, entered the mixed martial arts market as a promoter in October 2007. After launching HDNet, one of the first high-definition networks, on September 6, 2001, Cuban looked for programming that would entice viewers to add HDNet to their cable bills. When MMA was passed in the state of Texas, Cuban partnered up with Dallas-based Art of War, in addition to Nevada's Steele Cage, and started broadcasting their programs. Viewership shot through the roof, so Cuban decided to get into the mix. After a press conference and marketing campaign through the network, he held two shows in Dallas at Cuban co-owned American Airlines Arena with UFC and Pride vet Guy Mezger serving as president for his new division, HDNet Fights. Neither show was successful as the crowds were a few thousand at best, but that didn't deter Cuban from his love for the sport.

"We didn't want to compete with the promotions we were broadcasting," said Cuban. "Plus, [fight promotion] is harder than it looks. There were a lot of people who over-promised and underdelivered. I just thought it was smarter to partner than compete." After promoting two shows under the HDNet Fights banner, the network left the promotion end to other operators and began partnering with them for live broadcasts. To date, HDNet has produced and broadcast nearly 100 live events from the U.S., Canada, Japan, Korea, and other countries. The HDNet Fights banner is one of the core programs for the network, said Cuban. "The real MMA fans tune in to us because they get a chance to see who is coming up in the sport," remarked Guy Mezger, who personally travels to many of the promotions to ensure they are HDNet quality. "We try to give you a good cross section of MMA—sometimes the biggest, but we can't do that all the time." HDNet Fights also created *Inside MMA*, a weekly news show with newscasters Kenny Rice and Bas Rutten and *Fighting Words with Mike Straka*. The network offers countless fans a wide variety of MMA product, and Cuban even sees 3D programming as the future of the sport.

Yamma Pit Fighting
(April 11, 2008)

In January 2008, former UFC president Bob Meyrowitz announced he was stepping back into the MMA fray with Yamma Pit Fighting through a partnership with Live Nation, the largest live entertainment company in the world. Meyrowitz didn't like how fights would go to the ground and be up against the cage, so he created the "Yamma Pit" whereby the edges of the cage would be raised. "My thought is that it would create more action without demanding that they stand there and punch," said Meyrowitz. "If you pushed a fighter up against the edges of the cage, he could inch himself up and get leverage." Meyrowitz brought back many old-school UFC vets like Don Frye, Maurice Smith, Gary Goodridge, Pat Smith, Mark Kerr, and Oleg Taktarov. Unfortunately, the first three were nixed for various reasons, and the eight-man tournament turned out to be a bust as well.

Since the New Jersey State Athletic Commission only allowed a fighter to compete in five total rounds, the tourney consisted of one five-minute round in the quarterfinals and semifinals, and three five-minute rounds for the finals. "The fact that we tried to do the tournament in one night I think diminished the whole concept because the fighters quickly learned that all they had to do was lay there and hold on to get the one-round win." Only one tournament fight ended in anything but a decision. The only interesting fight was Patrick Smith taking out Toughman competitor Butterbean. The show brought back Bruce Beck and John Perretti as commentators but almost made Yamma completely unwatchable with in-ring announcer Scott Ferrall, whose cackling, robotic voice was all too weird and distracting. Meyrowitz took full responsibility for that, believing he would be unique, but that's not always a good thing. Yamma barely made a blip on PPV, a six-fight deal for Yamma became a one-and-done, and that was all she wrote.

Meyrowitz wouldn't be the only former SEG member to get into MMA. After leaving his post in 1998, David Issacs regrouped with Campbell McLaren and the two created *Iron Ring* in March 2008. The Afro-centric reality series was a cross between the IFL's teams led mostly by rappers and *The Ultimate Fighter*, and it debuted on the BET network but didn't last long. Also in 2008, Art Davie created X-ARM, which was a mixture of MMA and arm wrestling. The show also included several MMA fighters with Gladiator Challenge promoter Tedd Williams as the fight wrangler. "The idea was to bring two athletes into a combat zone, contain them, keep the action going, and create an environment where that would be appropriate," said Davie, who wants to bring the format to smaller forms of media like the iPhone once funding is secure. Even Alyxzander Bear, who was in charge of all the original UFC memorabilia, started his own promotion called Ultimate Pankration back in November 2001, but it went nowhere. Everyone wanted to create his own thing, but nothing was quite like the magic of their joined forces that became the Ultimate Fighting Championship.

Pro Elite
(February 10, 2007 to October 10, 2008)

The story of Pro Elite began in the Amazon jungles of Brazil where UFC fighter Wallid Ismail had become one of the country's best fight promoters for his aptly titled event, Jungle Fight. While in Los Angeles, Ismail told his best friend in the States and "trainer to several pro football players" TJ Goodman that he was shopping a television deal for his promotion, which he began in September 2003. Goodman thought he could help and introduced Ismail to Doug DeLuca, executive producer of *Jimmy Kimmel Live*, in 2006. DeLuca ended up reaching out to an investment group led by David Marshall, who had founded Youbet.com. Ismail thought his dreams were going to be answered, because not only could DeLuca and Marshall bring money to the table, but the Brazilian was also told, according to his lawyer Robert J. Hantman, that he was going to be the richest fighter in history.

According to the *Barron's* article "A Money Manager's Ultimate Fight Game," published June 2, 2008, "The fighter is actually just one of many people affected by Florian Homm and Todd Ficeto, the two gents who financed Pro Elite and dozens of dubious companies in the past 10 years. Those stocks mostly left investors bloodied, but a tally of company filings at the [SEC] shows the two financiers made out with fees and securities worth hundreds of millions." For Ismail's expertise in fight promotion and knowing the MMA game inside and out, he was to get $250,000 a year, plus 24 percent of the company. With a private placement memorandum draft in hand that showed DeLuca as chief executive, the group met with Ken Hershman, sports vice president for Showtime. The *Barron's* article continued: "On September 29, 2006, Ismail and his wife went to a lawyer's office for the scheduled closing of the deal, but no one else showed up. The actual closing, and the reverse merger creating Pro Elite, took place on October 3 without Ismail. In his place as Pro Elite's fight boss was Gary Shaw, a well-known boxing promoter." Ismail would be out of Pro Elite's equation...for now.

Pro Elite was a publicly traded entertainment and media company that used its website as an MMA Internet community to unify the sport, its promoters, and fighters. During its 22 months in operation, the company acquired three MMA promotions: King of the Cage (USA) and Cage Rage (UK) as 100 percent stock purchases and Icon Sport, formerly Superbrawl (Hawaii) as an asset purchase. In addition, the company acquired the asset library for Rumble on the Rock (Hawaii) and invested in Korean-based SpiritMC. Many of these purchases came with strings, some salaries, debt, and not a whole lot of upside. In addition, Pro Elite produced EliteXC and ShoXC for Showtime, with the EliteXC brand even getting exposure on CBS. "I ended up signing a deal, and we were all supposed to be one big happy family taking over the sport of MMA," said Frank Shamrock, "but as soon as the papers were signed, the whole thing fell apart. They didn't know what they were doing at all." Shamrock served as commentator, consultant, and fighter.

At one point, Pro Elite had well over 70 employees, but what business were they in? Was it just a stock play? Was it supposed to turn the website into some kind of MMA Facebook? What role did all of these other MMA promotions that Pro Elite purchased play? And how were these promotions supposed to figure into Pro Elite's own brands? "There were a lot of hands in the pot and a lot of double dipping, and there was a lot of paying themselves first," claimed Shamrock. "And nobody knew what they were doing so they had to actually hire people who knew what they were doing and layers of people who knew what they were doing. It was a big money pit."

The first show, EliteXC: Destiny, took place on February 10, 2007, in Mississippi and featured Frank Shamrock vs. Renzo Gracie. Though Gracie would win by disqualification, the real star of the show was Gina Carano, a beautiful kickboxer whose father Glenn played for the Dallas Cowboys (1977–1983). Her showdown with Julie Kedzie went to a decision with Carano getting the nod, but her personality shined through the cage and a star was born. Forget about the quarter-million-dollar dragonhead entryway where the fighters walked out. EliteXC and its counterpart, ShoXC (for newcomers), had great production value and a stable of nearly 200 fighters, but one stuck out in particular that gave the promotion an extra kick.

Florida-based Kevin Ferguson, also known as Kimbo Slice, was literally born on the Internet when he blew up YouTube with his impromptu streetfights with anyone who wanted a slice. Ferguson was even challenged by part-time MMA fighter, full-time Boston police officer Sean Gannon; the two fought in Rhode Island, and the bout was marketed as an Internet pay-per-view. Gannon's face was literally rearranged, but Slice gassed out and couldn't continue. It didn't matter, with his gold teeth and bling bling, Slice was a walking cartoon character and the perfect type of easy-to-market fighter to promote EliteXC to casual fans. The ploy worked, and Slice, who competed as a heavyweight, was soon popping up all over the place, especially on CBS.

On May 31, 2008, Slice headlined an all-star card that would be the first of three events to air during prime time on CBS. Though Slice had trouble against journeyman Englishman James Thompson, he came out victorious. Gina Carano also strutted her stuff, beating Kaitlin Young. The show averaged 4.85 million viewers and peaked during the main event at 6.51 million viewers; it became the most-watched MMA show in television history.

The live shows and prominence in the marketplace promised good things to come, but things didn't look that way on paper. In January 2007, Showtime paid Pro Elite $5 million for 20 percent ownership into the company. According to *Barron's*, the company was valued at $1.3 billion and was trading at $15 a share at one point, but Pro Elite lost $1.1 million when the quarterly financials were released in March 2008. Scott Coker, whose promotion Strikeforce partnered with Pro Elite, was amazed at what he saw while visiting their offices. "I was like, 'What do all you guys do?' And they just laughed, 'Ha ha.' But I'm thinking, you know, that's overhead right there. That's really unnecessary. And when you saw the operation, it was just such a rich operation in the sense that they were just so deep in Internet. By the time they figured it out and started cutting back, the boat had tipped already too much to ever recover." *The Apprentice* Season 2 winner Kelly Perdew actually headed up Proelite. com, but the site with all the ridiculous overhead wasn't making money.

Robert J. Hantman, a sports and entertainment attorney out of New York, remembered getting a call from Wallid Ismail and couldn't understand what he was talking about. Ismail claimed that he was an owner of Pro Elite, and though he didn't have a contract, he had countless emails—partially because he didn't know how to delete them. After reading various emails from both Doug DeLuca and David Marshall, Hantman thought he had a good case. "I then wrote a letter on behalf of Wallid demanding that Pro Elite pay him some money and/or give him stock as I was trying to resolve it for him," said Hantman. "And next thing I know they filed a lawsuit against him in the state court of California because they wanted jurisdiction in California and 'for him to have to spend money.' They even claimed he stole the idea from them—for MMA fights!" Hantman had the case removed to federal court where it would be mediated between the parties. "We reached a settlement for a large amount of money and stock, but it was subject to approval by CBS, who we were told was considering buying Pro Elite."

All that needed to happen was for the third EliteXC event on CBS to run smoothly. The main event for the card to be held on October 4, 2008, was Kimbo Slice vs. Ken Shamrock, and Gina Carano would be featured on the undercard. Frank Shamrock remembered arriving for dress rehearsal about 4:00 PM that day, as he would be a color commentator, and was told that his adoptive brother Ken might not be able to fight. Ken had sustained a cut above his eye and was not cleared to fight. "It was mayhem," said Frank Shamrock. "They were going to pull the plug; if Kimbo Slice doesn't fight on this show, we got no show." Frank Shamrock raised his hand and offered to take the slot. Even though he weighed far less and hadn't been training, he was up for doing it. Slice turned it down. "We promised Kimbo Slice, marketed Kimbo Slice, and CBS was like, 'Where's our boy?' I couldn't believe I raised my hand; that was insane, but I was worried that our sport was not going to be on CBS tonight, and we needed to be on CBS."

At the last minute an undercard fighter, light heavyweight Seth Petruzelli, agreed to take the fight, and Slice finally gave the okay...for a half million dollars. All of the fights leading up to the main event were exciting, but that's where it ends. Just 14 seconds into their contest, Petruzelli knocked out Slice with Jared Shaw, Gary Shaw's son, jumping up and down in anger. Petruzelli later said he was told to stand, but obviously the promoters didn't know that Petruzelli had been in martial arts all of his life...he loved to stand! CBS backed out of the deal, Showtime wanted their money back (they had lent Pro Elite over a million to keep going), and the whole ship went down almost simultaneously. Though the terms of the deal were confidential, Hantman finished by saying, "Kimbo Slice's loss cost Wallid and me millions, but we are Pro Elite shareholders and hope it gets resurrected under Stratus Media," which took over the company in late February 2010. As of this writing, the stock sat at $.014. King of the Cage, one of the longest-running independent shows, returned to its roots and was the only promotion to salvage itself after the Pro Elite debacle.

Affliction
(July 19, 2008 to January 24, 2009)

While Randy Couture had ongoing litigation with Zuffa, he signed a deal with Affliction to develop a line of Couture-centric T-shirts for the company. Since debuting in 2005, Affliction was pulling in over $125 million in revenue and had major access to retail chains like Nordstrom and Macys around the country. In January 2008, they set up a photo shoot to promote Couture's line with Russian Fedor Emelianenko. Though Affliction had already started sponsoring MMA fighters, several of whom fought in the UFC, this photo shoot served as a catalyst for Dana White banning the clothing company from the promotion. Affliction's response was to get into the fight game itself, so they set up Affliction Entertainment. White did his usual posturing and defense tactics, but Tom Atencio, who had been involved in MMA for many years, wanted to make the promotion a huge, balls-out success.

The first event, titled Affliction: Banned, took place at the Honda Center in Anaheim, California, on July 19, 2008. The show featured Emelianenko vs. former UFC champ Tim Sylvia, along with several top fighters including Andrei Arlovski, Matt Lindland, Josh Barnett, and Vitor Belfort. With the retail presence and some Russian media marketing, the first even garnered around 150,000 buys, along with a paid attendance of 11,242. The disclosed payroll, however, was the highest of any MMA promotion ever in the United States at $3.321 million. "I'm not going to lie, and that's where we made our biggest mistake," said Atencio. "That was the real factor in not continuing. We made a mistake, and it wasn't the fighters, but it was the managers that quite frankly took advantage of us. But that's our fault because we should have found out what they made in their last fights." Arlovski, who was not even the headliner, reportedly walked away with $1.5 million; he made $170,000 for winning his last fight with Zuffa at UFC 82.

On January 24, 2009, Affliction returned and set up the headliner of Emelianenko, who had squashed Sylvia in 36 seconds, against Arlovski. In a battle between Russians, Arlovski got cocky and got knocked out in the blink of an eye. Though the promotion only hit 90,000 buys, it appeared that with Donald Trump on board that Affliction was here to stay. As it turned out, Trump was nothing more than a figurehead, and everything was riding on a third show featuring Emelianenko and American Josh Barnett, who had tested positive for steroids twice before. The California State Athletic Commission conducted a random steroid test on Barnett one month before the show, but Barnett kept it a secret. The results came back positive again just 10 days before showtime. "He knew he got tested and sat there and didn't tell me anything and lied to me," said Atencio. Then he wanted to deny it and went on *Inside MMA*. He was stuttering and stammering because he knew he was dirty, knew he tested dirty, and knew he was at fault for us going down in that third event."

In less than two weeks, Atencio couldn't risk finding a replacement and facing possible lawsuits and pay-per-view refunds. At the time of this interview, Atencio said he was still in litigation with M-1 Global, the company that represents Emelianenko, and could not directly speak on Affliction's fallout. He did say that he met with Zuffa right before the show was cancelled, and today, Affliction is once again a UFC sponsor. "I have no regrets about doing the show, it was entertaining, but we have a great relationship with Zuffa, and we're moving forward."

Bellator Fighting Championships
(April 3, 2009 to Present)

Bjorn Rebney, CEO of Bellator (Latin meaning "warrior") Fighting Championships, started in the fight business in the early 1990s, managing Oscar de la Hoya and promoting boxing events with Sugar Ray Leonard. Even though everything was going well with his boxing promotional career, he became a big MMA fan. In 2008, he formed Bellator, and through a strong connection with ESPN launched the promotion on ESPN Deportes, the network's Spanish-language arm. Instead of a random series of fights, the promotion set up a tournament style over the first season and saw it play out week after week on tape delay. The ratings were solid, but like the IFL, taped fights had a difficult time capturing the general market when viewers were used to live matches.

For the second season launched on April 8, 2010, Rebney and his group relaunched Bellator as a general market product that aired live on Fox Sports Net with taped variations on Telemundo and Canada's The Score, along with a late-night show on NBC. The promotion mainly features newcomers with a few veterans sprinkled in, but the jury is still out as to whether the costly production schedule of shooting a live event every week for 10-plus events will pay off. Despite being off the radar, Zuffa sued Bellator over theft of trade secrets, and Bellator returned fire with tortuous interference of a contract belonging to Bellator fighter Jonathan Brookins, who chose to enter *The Ultimate Fighter* house for Season 12. Lawsuits aside, Bellator has been hard-pressed to fill the seats, namely from the first season when they planned so many shows late in the game. Rebney has talked about getting Bellator on pay-per-view, but with the market so flooded by the UFC, the lack of stars and grassroots marketing would not signal pay-per-view as a wise decision for the relatively new promotion...at least not right away.

Strikeforce
(March 10, 2006 to Present)

With The WEC's merger with the UFC, Strikeforce would have to take the No. 2 slot with a promotion that's now over four years old and seems to be getting stronger and stronger. Promoter Scott Coker started out in kickboxing and ran several shows for ESPN until he became the on-site promoter for Japan's K-1 organization through Maurice Smith. Coker ran several K-1 events in Las Vegas over the years but ultimately knew that MMA would be his calling. In December 2004, he sat down with Frank Shamrock and hatched a plan for him to come out of retirement and fight in front of his hometown crowd in San Jose, California. Problem was, the sport had yet to be passed in the state.

Coker bided his time, until he got a call from then California State Athletic Commissioner Armando Garcia who said the state had passed the sport, and they were giving him the first crack at it since he had held a state license (for kickboxing) since 1985. Partnering up with Silicon Valley Sports & Entertainment, Coker relaunched Strikeforce (which had been a short-lived kickboxing show) as an MMA promotion on March 10, 2006, pitting Frank Shamrock against Cesar Gracie in front of what would become the largest paid attendance in U.S. MMA history: 17,465. "You had to feel it, and it made me shiver with so much energy during that one moment, walking down the ramp," said Shamrock, who crushed Gracie in 21 seconds. With the card loaded with regional superstars from American Kickboxing Academy and the Cesar Gracie Academy, a new promotion was born. According to Coker, the promotion rested on four fighters: Shamrock, Josh Thomson, Gilbert Melendez, and Cung Le.

Over the next two years, Strikeforce solidified itself as a super regional promotion primarily operating in Northern and Central California, with a stop in Washington State and smaller shows at the Playboy Mansion. The promotion really didn't have a television home, doing live Internet-streamed shows and partnering up with HDNet, until March 2008 when they cut a deal to run clip shows on NBC. Hosted by Ken Shamrock, despite being in the twilight hour, the 22-episode show did surprisingly well in the ratings. When word came down that Pro Elite was in trouble financially and looking for a buyer to bail them out of over $3 million in debt, Coker took notice.

Pro Elite and Strikeforce had already partnered on a few shows, so the promoter was well aware of the kind of firepower they had. "It was such a roller-coaster ride," said Coker of the proposed buyout. "I knew we were the right company for the job, but there were a lot of other companies bidding against us. At the end of the day, I said, *If it's meant to be, then it'll be,* and it just worked out." When asked how he thought he could make it work in a sea of others who tried, Coker replied, "I think that when you look at Affliction, IFL, Bodog, Pro Elite, and probably three or four others, the issue was that MMA was not their core business. And with me, it is our core business."

In February 2009, Coker's Strikeforce got a major boost by not only gaining access to Showtime and CBS, but by adding a lot of major stars to their growing stable of fighters. They purchased the video rights and fighter contracts and took over lucrative broadcasting deals where Showtime would pay a premium to broadcast the events, while Coker would get to keep ticket receipts and live sponsorship money. Especially in the middleweight class, Coker had a deeper division to add to Frank Shamrock and his other hometown favorite, Cung Le, a san shou fighter who had successfully crossed over to MMA. The promoter now had Jake Shields, Scott Smith, and Robbie Lawler. He also brought Gina Carano into the fold, knowing her worth as the darling of EliteXC. As for Kimbo Slice, they could not come to terms, and Slice ended up pumping up ratings for Season 10 of *The Ultimate Fighter.* His *TUF* debut fight garnered 5.3 million viewers and became the most-watched original series in Spike's history.

"We definitely have a national promotion now," confessed Coker. "When we started in '06, we did not have a TV deal and had no sponsorships; it was a live gate promotion only. Since we bought Pro Elite's assets and negotiated the deal with CBS and Showtime, we have a national footprint across the country doing fights. Eventually we'll get to Canada and other territories around the world." Coker would be the first one to admit that his business plan was not to rival the UFC. Dana White was actually complimentary of Coker's Strikeforce, until the promoter secured Fedor Emelianenko.

The Russian heavyweight and his management company, M-1 Global, were to be Strikeforce's ticket to pay-per-view, as Emelianenko had developed this mythic-like, unbeatable quality. Nicknamed The Emperor, Emelianenko had never lost a fight, save for an early RINGS bout that was stopped by a cut. On June 26, 2010, he faced off against Brazilian Fabricio Werdum, and after knocking him down early, the Russian overextended himself and the Brazilian capitalized. Just 69 seconds into the match, Emelianenko tapped out from an arm bar and triangle choke. As for Gina Carano, after going on an undefeated tear, she met her match against Brazilian Cristiane "Cyborg" Santos in August the year before. Both women put up an incredible fight for the first-ever middleweight (145 pounds) women's championship, but Santos proved too powerful and won by TKO at 3:40 into Round 3. Carano left the fight game to pursue an acting career, well after being a hit on the revamped *American Gladiators*. Regardless of Carano's return, the promotion has had much success building charismatic female fighters to take her place. Pay-per-view might have to wait, but Coker seems very calculated in terms of what he has done for the promotion thus far.

On a CBS show held April 17, 2010, middleweight champion Jake Shields faced off against the newly UFC-defected Dan Henderson. The gamble was that Henderson was a Strikeforce fighter, and this would be Shields' last fight on his Strikeforce contract. Shields won by decision, and a bidding war almost developed with the UFC, but Strikeforce turned him loose. "There was no reason for them to get into a big money play with the UFC," said Meltzer. "[Strikeforce] is in business to be in business; they are not in business for vanity."

In 2011, Strikeforce launched a monumental eight-man heavyweight tournament to be spread out over several events using the promotion's elite. It appeared that Strikeforce would be the last, stable vestige of being the No. 2 MMA fight promotion. Under Scott Coker, the foolish spending by Pro Elite, the lackadaisical business plan by the IFL, and the pointless vanity of BodogFight was replaced with a true fight promoter who possessed a love for the sport. And maybe that's why Zuffa viewed Strikeforce as a perceived threat that could become a serious rival one day...a day that would never come to be. On March 12, 2011, Zuffa announced that a purchase agreement was finalized to buy Strikeforce, essentially giving Zuffa/UFC a monopoly over professional MMA.

Strikeforce was a safe haven from Zuffa's controlling grip over a fighter's life, no matter the upside. It gave enormous opportunities for female fighters. And it was a promotion that literally kept MMA from being simply known as *the* UFC in the mainstream media. While Dana White contended at the time of the sale that Strikeforce would not change, the same thing was said about Pride Fighting Championships and the WEC before both were folded into the promotional behemoth of the UFC. For now, Coker is still in charge and the fighter contracts remain the same. But from a branding perspective, it makes no sense for Zuffa to keep Strikeforce around when the UFC is the No. 1 MMA brand. The sale begs the question: is the sport simply now known as the UFC? Sure, Bellator and multitudes of regional promotions are still in operation, but to the average person, the UFC is the only name in professional MMA just as the NFL is in football.

Fighting the 800-pound gorilla known as the UFC has been a daunting, if impossible task when you consider the number of people and promotions that have tried and failed over the years. Though class action lawsuits have been bandied about the MMA community against the UFC, it seems, barring any possible antitrust violations, that there is no stopping Zuffa. So many MMA promotions have jockeyed for the "No. 2" slot in the industry, but when it comes right down to it, is it even necessary at this point? Perhaps the sport and the UFC should be one in the same, if public opinion has anything to say about it. Good or bad, the promotion that has been plagued by every type of controversy and rotten luck won't be going anywhere, anytime soon. As for what happens inside the cage, that will change, but fans couldn't be any happier.

23

REAL FIGHTING VERSUS MARTIAL ARTS
BRUCE LEE WAS RIGHT ALL ALONG

Some martial arts are very popular, real crowd pleasers, because they look good, have smooth techniques. But beware. They are like a wine that has been watered. A diluted wine is not a real wine, not a good wine, hardly the genuine article.

Some martial arts don't look so good, but you know that they have a kick, a tang, a genuine taste. They are like olives. The taste may be strong and bittersweet. The flavor lasts. You cultivate a taste for them. No one ever developed a taste for diluted wine.

BRUCE LEE, *TAO OF JEET KUNE DO*

NOTE: This chapter is in no way trying to belittle the men and women who have made martial arts a part of their lives. It is meant to enlighten those who have perhaps taken martial arts under a false pretense. An entire book could be written on this subject alone, but this will only be a general overview of how martial arts has lost its realistic beginnings.

Politics and business aside, the Ultimate Fighting Championship opened the eyes of a world blinded by a centuries-old mystique shadowing martial arts. This was a devastating revelation for those who had bought into that false sense of security taught by their so-called masters. With over 10 million people studying martial arts around the world, it was time for the truth to be told about the synergy between martial arts and reality fighting.

Most martial arts can be traced back to a lawless time when they were crucial to preserving life and limb. They evolved from real-life experiences and became an integral part of cultures that often invested the arts with a spiritual power. Historical warriors were enshrined in folklore, lending their martial arts an almost superhero quality. Traditional techniques were passed down from generation to generation with little regard to practicality.

But something was lost in the translation, making perception greater than reality. Some of the arts ossified over time. They became formal, rigid, and, in truth, ineffective. Many were blatantly commercialized to appeal to the new and wealthy constituency when fighting schools flourished in the United States and Western Europe from the 1960s. They became a money-making enterprise. Westerners were curious, open, and naïve; masters from the Orient were an unknown commodity. Many of their claims were taken at face value; students believed what they were told. Movies were partly to blame. They showed unbelievable feats of physical prowess and fighting techniques foreign to most people on the street. High-flying kicks and the ability to beat several—sometimes dozens—of opponents at once were staples of the martial arts presented on the big screen.

As these arts were being taught in the United States, there was a need to make them accessible to the public. And there was no better way to do this than to turn them into competitive sports, adding credibility and uniformity. The founder of judo, Jigoro Kano, had ended up making his overall self-defense system less effective when he popularized the art as a sport. With countless jujutsu forms being taught in Japan, Kano combined the best elements and formed a very effective *do* system. Judo has now been relegated to throwing movements because the sport dictated that those movements would be the most enjoyable to the crowd. Sport karate was also a product of the twentieth century and became the most popular of all martial arts. Tae kwon do competitions and the flashy stylings of kung fu demonstrations were also well received. The ultimate parlor trick, of course, was breaking a soft balsa wood board that was often baked to ensure it could be torn in half by a karate chop.

Did anything positive develop from the modern-day martial arts movement in America? With schools growing by the thousands and entire federations being built on particular styles, the essence of martial arts got lost in the shuffle. Masters passed along their knowledge to the masses, but how much of this knowledge truly prepared someone for an actual fight? Most Korean systems concentrated on elaborate and often impractical kicking techniques. There's nothing wrong with that, so long as students know what they are getting. "Everyone wants something different from martial arts—not everyone wants to be a no-holds-barred fighter," said kenpo stylist and UFC vet Keith Hackney. "There are still people who only want to do forms and don't want any kind of physical confrontation. They just want to do it as an art form, which is fine as long as they don't pretend that they are doing this for self-defense on the street."

What works on the street is quite different from what works in a dojo because the latter is derived from a precise set of movements carved out by a particular style practiced in a relatively safe environment. In tae kwon do, stances, kicks, and punches dictate a fight. In judo, grappling and throws dictate a fight. But a real-life hand-to-hand confrontation is something that has no form or dictation and follows no particular set of rules. It is an act of aggression built on numerous variables, not formal rules; with the true no-holds-barred contest, a person's morality and judgment as well as his physical prowess will dictate the amount of harm inflicted. While the UFC and other similar competitions are not real fights as they might occur in a bar or in the street, they are as close to real combat as one can acceptably get with two willing and professionally trained athletes in a sporting context.

The myth of the martial arts says that a man with a black belt can defeat almost any opponent with his "empty hand" tools—usually fists and feet. While it's true that there are countless examples of martial artists protecting themselves effectively in real fights, how many of these situations involved opponents who also knew how to fight, possibly from another system? That was the intriguing scenario that drew so much attention to the early UFCs. It quickly provided as many answers as it raised new questions. Most people knew, of course, the hole in martial arts teaching: the fact that years of learning one style could not possibly *guarantee* domination over an opponent from another discipline. "Some guys still believe that their kung fu and karate is so deadly that they can't compete," said former kickboxing champ and MMA star Maurice Smith. "I don't believe that. I think that the smart instructors realize that a lot of stuff that you're taught in traditional martial arts is bullshit."

One man brought the truth about martial arts to the attention of mainstream America, and his name was Bruce Lee. Lee started his martial arts training in Hong Kong at the age of 13, when he learned wing chun kung fu from Master Yip Man. He would have only five years of formal instruction before immigrating to the United States. Lee's greatest strength was his thirst for knowledge in everything he did. Though he adopted wing chun as his base, Lee was left with questions about his style after a real fight against another kung fu exponent. He discovered that much of what he had learned was not truly effective. He knew it would be too time-consuming to try to learn all styles of martial arts, since he found questionable techniques in them as well. Physical conditioning was also a variable he had overlooked up until that point. By applying the philosophy he had been introduced to in college, Lee became a martial arts innovator by creating a concept known as Jeet Kune Do, the "way of the intercepting fist."

Lee made copious notes that were published well after his death as a book, *Tao of Jeet Kune Do*. It is made up of Lee's findings from his own experimentation and from his collection of martial arts books. He came to the conclusion that formlessness keeps one from defining a limited pattern of attack. "It is the artistic process, therefore, that is reality and reality is truth," said Lee. Lee discussed varying stand-up and ground techniques, as well as the importance of being physically fit. The book serves as a basis for enlightenment about an approach to combat, and it's clear the "Little Dragon" was on to something revolutionary. "I thought his principles were the most advanced stuff out there, and I still use a lot of those principles," said karate legend Joe Lewis.

Ironically, Bruce Lee's films were just as responsible for the divergence of martial arts teaching from combat reality as they were for its commercial success. Millions worldwide have seen his films; less than a million bought his book. Many who saw the films swallowed the myth of this tiny, blur-fast dervish, smashing foe after foe with his kicks, punches, and back-fists. It was wildly exciting but hardly realistic. His writings were different, and from them we can assume that, if Lee were alive today, he would revel in the UFC. It broke stereotypes and allowed us to reevaluate the martial arts by defining it as a sum of many parts that otherwise might never have coexisted.

So where does fighting fit into martial arts? "That's really impressive, but would you mind knocking that off," said Campbell McLaren as Bill "Superfoot" Wallace balanced himself on one foot and swept the other over McLaren's head, toying with him. McLaren was working with Wallace to prepare him for the first UFC (which obviously didn't work out).

McLaren asked Wallace, "Do you think we'll see any of this in the Ultimate fights?"

"Are you kidding?" answered Wallace. "If you tried to kick someone like this, they'd rip your balls off!"

"But isn't this what you teach?" said McLaren.

"Yeah, I teach to make money. It has nothing to do with fighting," admitted Wallace, according to McLaren.

"I think that's one of the things that really got the martial arts world involved because so many people were teaching stuff that really had nothing to do with reality," remarked McLaren.

After the second UFC, it was clear that seasoned martial artists could not perform many of their ornate techniques in an actual fighting situation against formidable opponents. There has been a lot of debate on whether the Gracies stacked things in their favor, but the fact is that most people were clueless early on as to the effectiveness of groundfighting. Though the Gracie family tried to treat the UFC as a living infomercial for Gracie Jiu-jitsu, it did prove their contention that the majority of fights would go to the ground. "I had never been on the ground in my life with all the martial arts training that I had," said Kevin Rosier years after his UFC appearance. Some styles of traditional martial arts, such as karate and tae kwon do, include groundfighting, but instructors chose to emphasize the flashier aspects portrayed by the media. Thus, self-defense became hit-or-miss offense based on the high kicks and karate chops people felt they had to learn.

The Gracies proved that an experienced groundfighter can defeat an experienced stand-up fighter simply because it is easier for the stand-up artist to have his tools taken from him. In the *Gracies in Action* videos, there are countless scenes of hapkido, kung fu, and other stand-up styles collapsing against the rudimentary takedowns and eventual submissions of the jiu-jitsu fighters. Once everything goes to the ground, the stand-up martial artist doesn't have the distance or leverage necessary to properly execute kicks or punches. Then, trapped in an unfamiliar environment, he falls victim to the superior ground skills of his opponent. Conversely, wrestlers often proved difficult for jiu-jitsu practitioners, as wrestling is the segue between the stand-up and the ground game. Thus, wrestlers could neutralize jiu-jitsu takedowns, taking the art of submission away from them.

Stand-up martial arts account for most of what is taught in dojos, so they collectively were not supportive of the UFC. In an effort to keep their myths alive, many stand-up arts like karate and tae kwon do claimed that eye-gouging and biting were part of a real fight, thus proving that the UFC—which banned them—was not realistic. But would anyone need martial arts to learn how to do these techniques? How many fights have ended up with someone being eye-gouged? In Japan Vale Tudo '94, Gerard Gordeau eye-gouged opponent Yuki Nakai, but Nakai still pulled out the win. Someone in a street fight could eye-gouge his opponent, step and break his neck, or just kill him. But is every fight life-threatening enough to go to that extreme, and wouldn't the person who took it to that level go to prison? (Incidentally, Gordeau's eye-gouging permanently ended Nakai's MMA career.)

Martial artists also said that going to the ground was not representative of a real fight, despite the men in the Octagon doing what came naturally. When Johnny Rhodes faced David Levicki in UFC II, both men stayed on the ground for the entire duration of the match, even though neither one knew anything about groundfighting. The 1981 Kung Fu and Freefighting Championships held in Hong Kong showcased nothing but stand-up martial artists, but time and again they ended up in a clinch and went to the ground. Clearly, two stand-up fighters can become groundfighters even if they don't know what they are doing down there.

Johnny Rhodes was one of those who questioned the authenticity of the UFC. When he entered the tournament, he had not seen tapes of the first UFC and assumed "THERE ARE NO RULES!" meant just that. "I think that [rules] really hurt it because people don't want to see grappling," said Rhodes. "They want to see blood. People want to see you get beat up. Had the rules been a little bit different, the stand-up fighters would have won back then too because you couldn't bite. If I would have gotten you in a lock, and you would have put your teeth into me, I would have let go. That's how I expected it to be because it said 'no rules.' When I got there, I was not aware that you couldn't bite."

If nothing else, MMA competitions laid to rest the stereotypes surrounding martial arts. Martial artists were finally able to throw punches and kicks at their discretion without any regard for rules germane to their disciplines. The mystique of the black belt, the *dim mak* (death touch), and the lightning-fast kicks that break dozens of boards is a powerful one, often leading followers to believe the performers are deadly. This perception also gives us an unrealistic view of how a real fight unfolds. Would it look as pretty as the movies? Would a martial artist be throwing these beautiful kicks and taking his opponents out with ease? Lee said the martial artist should fight and spar often, just as a swimmer can't practice on dry land. The cold, honest truth lay in the unscripted contests between experienced martial artists who dared to step into the Octagon.

Minutes after Alberto Cerro Leon's defeat at the hands of Remco Pardoel at UFC II, Art Davie came across Leon "crying in the dressing room. He and his manager left the hotel and got on a plane. I had to mail the check to him. The guy was psychologically devastated." He could not believe his art had failed. In a time when Tae Bo exercising and martial arts are said in the same breath, and styles are promoted as "self-defense" by showing one man kick another in the head, it is apparent that the art of war has lost its meaning. How much of martial arts has anything to do with self-defense versus an impractical offense? Many martial arts masters frown upon those who go and learn from other schools. They forget that art is not bound by singularity—especially martial arts. "When he trained me, he said, 'Even though you don't like wrestling, you have to know how to go against a wrestler,'" said Dan Inosanto, who was one of Lee's top students and embodies the legacy of Jeet Kune Do. "Even if you don't like to box, you better know how to go against a boxer. So no matter what formation you have, you have to know their defensive game and you have to know against their offensive game. So everything had to be analyzed, according to Bruce. That's why it was important to study different martial arts, and that's why a lot of people try to make Jeet Kune Do a style, and it isn't a style, it's a way of thinking. It's more of a system rather than it is a style." The true martial artist will arrive at his own conclusion that may start from anywhere but will take him on a road to clarity. The truth of what works and what doesn't work lies beneath a vale of commercialism, greed, and ignorance. Martial arts is a process whereby one must learn "simply to simplify."

Don "The Dragon" Wilson was brought in to serve as color commentator for the UFC based on his name in the martial arts world. Though he had been successful at making the transition from kung fu to full-contact karate, that hardly made Wilson an expert in MMA. "Well if I was in there..." became a Dragonism, so to speak, and many felt he would never have done that well in the Octagon. Play-by-play commentator Bruce Beck finally got tired of Wilson's musings after one UFC event. "He would tell us how he would beat these guys, and I would turn to him later at night at a cocktail party and say, 'Dragon, you would have got your ass kicked and you know it!'

"And Wilson would go, 'Bullshit! You don't know how quick I am. Have you ever seen me with my spinning backfist?'

"I would just say, 'Dragon, you would kick your leg up once, and if you missed, you would be down on the ground, and they would be bashing your head in!'

"'I can beat any of these guys...I can kill any of them!' he would tell me.

"He was always talking about having a big fight for $100,000 or something—'If they give me a million, I'll fight'—and I said, 'Yeah, and you'll get your ass kicked.'" Wilson actually did try to get in the UFC for a million-dollar payday, knowing full well he would price himself out of the market and would never get to perform his spinning backfist. But just because a technique appears improbable, it doesn't mean it's ineffective. Losing his match against Matt Serra at UFC 31, Shonie Carter dropped his opponent with a spinning backfist. He followed that up with a second one to seal one of the most memorable, albeit at the time, victories in the promotion.

Art Davie was swamped with requests by traditionalists who had no fighting experience but wanted to prove themselves in the Octagon. Mitch Cox was a former Army Ranger who taught "realistic combat" martial arts. Davie agreed to see Cox in action, but only on his terms. He took kung fu exponent Tai Bowden to Cox's dojo to set up a makeshift match in Los Angeles, with the winner to fight at UFC IX. Davie drove down in a limousine with Koji Kitao, reporters from Japan's *Baseball* magazine, and Bowden. "Bowden beat the fuck out of him three times and in front of his own students," said Davie. "It wasn't sparring. After the first time, Cox wanted to go again and again, but Bowden would just take him down and pound him out." Bowden got the shot at UFC IX and lost to Steve Nelmark at 7:25. Another fighter desperate to compete was

Thomas Ramirez, who openly complained in magazines that Art Davie wouldn't let him in the show. Don Frye knocked him out in 10 seconds at UFC VIII.

Dan Inosanto began his martial arts training right after World War II. At the age of 74, Guru Inosanto still considers himself a student. "You have to be on the cutting edge," he said. "And that's something, again, I learned from Bruce Lee. That's something he told me—you never leave a stone unturned. Research it. A lot of people might talk trash about a system, but even those classical systems, you need that part of the training." Inosanto's knife and weapons training got him involved with law enforcement on knife defense training; these are the real, life-threatening fights. And yet, he has trained with the Machado family in Brazilian jiu-jitsu and stayed on that cutting edge by doing over 45 around-the-country seminars each year as of 2010. Inosanto is certainly a mixed martial artist and his training and teachings have evolved over the years because that is the thought process behind Jeet Kune Do and the way a martial artist should view his or her journey.

Fred Ettish: Honor Not Lost

Ken Shamrock had to pull out of UFC II due to a broken hand sustained in a training session. Two weeks before the event, Art Davie called Johnny Rhodes and Fredrick Ettish. Rhodes, an alternate, was nursing a broken finger after a bareknuckle fight, but he still moved into Shamrock's slot, while Ettish took over as the alternate. Ettish had expressed interest in the event months earlier but was told the card was full. He accepted the invitation and intensified his training.

Fred Ettish began his martial arts education in 1969 with Chinese kenpo, moving into Okinawan karate 10 years later. He eventually adopted Shorin-ryu Matsumura Kenpo (a Japanese/Okinawan hybrid) as his style and has stuck with it ever since. At age 38, Ettish wanted to enter the UFC because it was a sport that was "a bit more raw, more real, and more honest, that allowed two fighters to be two fighters," he said.

He was not interested in point karate tournaments and believed this would be a good test for his art, though he hadn't seen the first event.

When he arrived in Denver, SEG arranged for Ettish to have some gym time even though he was unlikely to compete. Because there were 16 fighters, an alternate match was unnecessary, so the only way Ettish was going to compete was if someone pulled out before fight time. By 5:30 PM, everyone was healthy and ready to go, so Ettish agreed to help Davie and show producer Michael Pillot with various backstage duties. With all the commotion, the fifth-degree black belt didn't even have time to watch any of the matches.

Later in the evening, Ettish and Rorion Gracie passed each other on a stairway. Gracie asked, "Are you ready to fight?" It would have been an easy question to answer for any fighter in the show, except one whose mind was now elsewhere. Freek Hamaker pulled out of the event after realizing that the UFC wasn't for him. An exhausted Johnny Rhodes was going to pull out too until his cornerman rushed to tell him that a much smaller alternate was taking his opponent's place. Fred Ettish was in; Rhodes took the gamble.

Ten minutes after hearing the news, Ettish donned his traditional gi and made his way to the Octagon, trying to keep calm and ready his mind for the battle at hand. For an introverted man who ran a small dojo back in the remote city of Bemidji, Minnesota, and fought with the blessing of his sensei in Okinawa, this was the moment of truth. As for 39-year-old Rhodes, he was no longer going to use his Shorin Ji-ryu Karate background, which had failed to live up to his expectations against David Levicki, his first-round opponent. Instead, he decided to fall back on his streetwise bravado and bare-knuckle fighting experience.

The match started with a few light kicks from each man until a big right hand from Rhodes sent Ettish reeling, struggling to regain his composure. It was already too late. Rhodes followed that up by grabbing Ettish and forcing him to the canvas after three more hard punches. On the ground, Ettish held one hand up and one hand down trying to keep Rhodes' attack at bay. He absorbed a brutal punch to the face. "I ended up losing the vision in one eye," said Ettish. "It was like trying to look through a glass of milk; everything was very white and totally clouded over." He eventually rolled to his stomach with both hands over his head. Rhodes pounded Ettish unmercifully, landing four knees and scrambling back to his feet.

With Rhodes circling him like a shark, a bloodied Fred Ettish was in serious trouble. "Pride wouldn't let him submit," remembered Rhodes. "I felt bad because I knew if I was in that same situation, it would have been hard for me too." Rhodes eventually took Ettish's back, pulled his hair, and sunk in a basic choke. Ettish, still showing some fight, resisted all he could before finally tapping the mat at 3:07.

It would be two hours before Ettish could see out of both eyes again, but he had learned a powerful lesson. "I was trying to focus on what I was trying to do and not be distracted by the events going on around me. And that's where I was unsuccessful. In my opinion, there are three things that a person needs to be successful in something like that: you need to be physically fit, you need to have a good fighting heart, and you need to have the right psychological mind-set going in. I was two for three."

A month later Ettish sent Art Davie a letter. "It was one of the greatest experiences of his life. He would willingly come back and fight again," said Davie. "That to me says a lot about the competitors who applied to get in the UFC. Some of them didn't actually have a lot of fighting experience, but they came and went all out. And Fred Ettish summed it all up. He had to switch gears so quickly and all of the sudden be a fighter. He wasn't prepared for it; I had him working up to five minutes before that bout. To me, he really typified what the event was all about. I still think about that."

But as the memory of the fight faded, an unconceivable assault beset Ettish and his family, an insult to every man who has the courage to step into the ring. Sometime in 1995, a rogue website was erected to embarrass Ettish, dubbing his style "The Fetal Fighting System" in reference to Ettish's defense from the down position. Many other fighters have fought

REAL FIGHTING VERSUS MARTIAL ARTS

from this position; in fact many jiu-jitsu fighters have simply fallen to their butts to tempt their opponents into a ground game. Yet Ettish was persecuted for the action. "We've had [the site] taken down more than once, but it's like a dandelion...you pluck one out and another pops up somewhere else," said Ettish. "We contacted the hosts of the site and confronted them. After bantering back and forth on the computer, it would go down. Then someone else would pop back up with the exact same website." Ettish fought his heart out, while others have cracked under pressure and gave up. Yet he was mocked and stripped of the basic respect of human dignity he wholeheartedly deserved.

"I've been tried, convicted, and sentenced all on the performance of one night. I think it's a shame to be judged that way," said Ettish. "I've been doing martial arts for decades, and on one night when I step out of the box and do something in a venue foreign to me—and I don't come through—it seems a little harsh. I readily admit that I didn't do well; there is no doubt about that. I bear full responsibility. But I've been misquoted in magazines. There were interviews attributed to me that were in no way, shape, or form things that I said. And that ridiculous website! It goes against everything I believe in and what a martial artist should be. I think I've paid my price and don't need to be subjected to any more of that."

Ettish also felt it was unfair to label him as the sacrificial lamb of traditional martial arts. "I didn't do what I should have done, but does that mean all traditional martial arts are bad? No, it certainly doesn't. I regret that my fight might have tainted traditional martial arts in a lot of people's eyes." Ettish believed that most people do not invest the time and hard work needed to harvest the rewards of traditional martial arts, opting instead for quick satisfaction.

Past the age of 50, Fred Ettish lives with his wife Pam—together they have one son, Nolan—in the forest ranges of Bemidji, Minnesota, where he runs a school with dozens of students inside his own house, part of which has been converted to a dojo. He is now an eighth-degree black belt in Matsumura Kenpo Karate and acts as the United States director and vice president for the Matsumura Kenpo Association. Ettish leads a humble life and admits the experience has made him a better teacher. While still considering himself a traditionalist, he and his students train in a wide variety of submissions. At UFC 45: Revolution, Ettish was flown to Atlantic City and signed autographs alongside many UFC veterans. Not a day goes by that he doesn't think about fighting one more time under better conditions, and he's ventured out on multiple occasions to local Minnesota events and has even served as a judge.

On August 15, 2009, 53-year-old Ettish finally got his chance and fought debut fighter Kyle Fletcher, who was more than half his age, as a welterweight. "I felt incredible pressure and anxiety leading up to the fight until I got in there and the bell rang," said Ettish. "It took 15½ years for everything to fall into place and get back in there. I did not feel as smooth as I had hoped, and my opponent's style was awkward for me. I had a whole lot of things I wanted to do in there, but after a few minutes, I decided to just do what I needed to win the fight." At 3:20, the fight ended with Ettish on top raining down punches, emerging the victor by ref stoppage. Unfortunately there was no fanfare—no website to publicize the win—but Ettish proved something, not only to himself, but to others who have never given up the desire to keep trying. Though he may have been written off as an early MMA casualty, Fred Ettish truly exemplifies a modern mixed martial artist.

Footnote: WOW Promotions presented Helio Gracie with an award in the first UFC for his contribution to the martial arts. On January 29, 2009, he passed away at the age of 95—his legacy will never be forgotten. Ninja Robert Bussey got an award in the second event, and Don "The Dragon" Wilson received one at UFC III. Art Davie was going to honor Frank Dux as well, until the truth came out about his past. From then on, awards were no longer given out. Bruce Lee, who made the biggest contribution to martial arts, never received the recognition he deserved. To this day, almost every fighter attributes their love of fighting and martial arts to the Little Dragon.

24

LIFE AS A
FIGHTER

I'm in the dressing room, pacing back and forth, wondering if all the months of preparation will pay off. The tension builds as I realize that one small mistake can end the fight with hardly a scratch to show for it. Now I'm in the middle of the cage and there's no escape. The crowd is much too loud for me to think. Maybe that's my problem—should I let instinct take over? He doesn't look so tough: the tattoos are window dressing. I stand there with eyes locked on my opponent's. There's a stillness in the air and now everything seems quiet. As the ref motions us to begin, I know I must impose my will over my opponent's to win this real-life chess match.

How and why does one become a mixed martial artist? Obviously, it's not by answering a Wanted advertisement. *Quick thinkers to work in a fast-paced environment with few benefits and the propensity for bodily injury.* Most of the fighters interviewed for this book credit Bruce Lee as their inspiration for getting involved in martial arts. They enjoyed watching Lee onscreen and yearned to attain that athletic body and those powerful yet graceful moves. For John Lober, the *Tao of Jeet Kune Do* outlined a philosophy that combined what worked with one's own physical prowess; he chose to compete under "Jeet Kune Do Concepts" (the name of Lee's philosophy). "Just look at the opening scene from *Enter the Dragon*," said Zane Frazier. "He [Lee] fought with gloves for striking, and there were takedowns and a submission." From kick-boxer Maurice Smith to Brazilian jiu-jitsu stylist Royce Gracie, Bruce Lee is a symbol of excellence that transcended style, culture, and race.

UK fighter Dexter Casey grew up in Hong Kong and saw Bruce Lee as the apex of martial arts. Though he knew most martial arts styles were ineffective in a real situation, "I still wanted to believe in an ultimate war-rior-type person, so I continued." Casey yearned for knowledge of some-thing practical, believing Thai boxing was the answer until he saw the UFC. "Royce Gracie was my new Bruce Lee. The idea that someone the same size as me [at the time] could beat these big monsters was amazing." While Bruce Lee may have been a viable external source for why and how people become fighters, let's examine several different facets of a fighter's life.

Style

The commercialism of traditional martial arts tainted much of its original value by moving away from realistic combative aspects in favor of movie-inspired flashiness. Many sought the true essence of what they had been studying. That truth led them to the belief that one style couldn't beat all, and style was only part of the puzzle. While karate instructors were preaching to their students that they held the answer, Lee professed the opposite. He knew the key was finding that link between one's physical attributes and the gradual process of discovering which fighting concepts worked in reality.

In the first few UFCs, Brazilian jiu-jitsu proved its dominance, because the mainstream martial arts were unfamiliar with groundfighting, nor had anyone expected a tae kwon do black belt to lose in such a manner as a choke or arm bar. To answer that early question of what style reigned supreme, jiu-jitsu won because much of the martial arts community, with their rigid, contained ideals about combat, was asleep. But jiu-jitsu fooled itself in believing its style was superior when it merely supplied a more practical base on which to build on. Once the riddle of jiu-jitsu was solved, people took notice, seeking out new knowledge to sharpen their own fighting skills.

Things have changed since then. "In the beginning, the guy training in jiu-jitsu wouldn't have to train in boxing or wrestling because no one knew about jiu-jitsu," said Wallid Ismail. "I hold the guy and make the guy like a baby. For a no-holds-barred fight, I have to train boxing and wrestling because everyone already knows jiu-jitsu." Rorion Gracie prescribes jiu-jitsu as the basis for effective fighting. "The fight is going to boil down to the ground. So if you know how to get into the clinch, all of that stand-up stuff is going to be gone." Out of jiu-jitsu emerged the submission or hybrid fighter, a term that jiu-jitsu practitioners felt was a ruse to avoid giving credit to the Brazilians. "I think it's ridiculous because they want to start their own little trend," said Rorion. "They don't want to admit that jiu-jitsu is the one that is doing it for them. They want to be originators of their own styles. Joe Son Do? What the heck is Joe Son Do?"

Not so, said submission expert Frank Shamrock. "What I do and what I teach is a bit of wrestling, a bit of sambo, a bit of judo, a bit of jiu-jitsu— a bit of everything because it's a bit of everything that works. Anybody that does jiu-jitsu is very simple. I want a complete fighting system. There has to be more than jiu-jitsu; jiu-jitsu is just a base, like karate. Yeah, they [Gracies] got this thing started, but they're old news now. People just need to understand that. They can call it whatever they want and do whatever they need. Jiu-jitsu is now just another martial art." By 1997, the lines between styles were blurred to such a point that everyone did "a little bit of everything" to be successful in MMA. Stand-up fighters learned the ground, just as groundfighters learned stand-up, and the synergy of those two styles enabled MMA to become a more strategic and complex battle.

Today the sport has two different methodologies. One would have the fighter learn a base style like wrestling or jiu-jitsu and then build around it with free-flowing elements to make complete fighters. The other teaches would-be athletes all forms of mixed martial arts in an integrated forum without a particular base. No two people are alike and there is no specific system that every fighter should follow. Georges St.

Pierre has been called the best wrestler in MMA, yet he came from a traditional martial arts background and had no formalized wrestling accolades. Jon "Bones" Jones had a great amateur wrestling base, and while he liked to perform throws, his style is right out of a fighting video game with wild yet accurate spinning kicks, elbows, and jumping knees. Lyoto Machida was born of Japanese and Brazilian descent, and his style of fighting often favors his karate black belt or his Brazilian jiu-jitsu black belt. His elusiveness and spot-on accuracy with his strikes has made him a difficult opponent to figure out.

Early on, some fighters learned the ground game only for defense. Dutch kickboxer Bob Schrijber could no longer rely on just his fists and feet when he transitioned to MMA. "I wasn't training for getting to the ground to submit somebody," said Schrijber. "I trained [groundfighting] only for defense." Schrijber didn't like training jiu-jitsu because that was not his game, but the thrill of the fight is, and he's defeated experienced ground players before by sprawling, keeping it standing and knocking them out.

"You are a really good martial artist when you can compete under any rules and fight anyone in any style," said Frank Shamrock. Chicago-born Shonie Carter is one such example, a soft-spoken martial arts enthusiast who competed in everything: freestyle and Greco Roman wrestling, judo, jiu-jitsu, boxing, kickboxing, point karate, submission wrestling, and pankration. He competed in different arenas because he saw each one as an individual challenge, acting as a personal release that grounded the nonfighting Carter. He has fought in top MMA promotions from the UFC to Pancrase but often mixed it up in local Chicago nightclubs under not-so-normal rules. One time, Carter and another fighter engaged in a two-on-three match inside a makeshift ring, held for special customers at a bar just after midnight.

There are base styles and variations on styles and that evolution continues even to this day. Eddie Bravo wasn't a fighter, but had trained in Brazilian jiu-jitsu under Jean-Jacques Machado. As a brown belt, he competed against black belt Royler Gracie at the 2003 Abu Dhabi Submission Wrestling Championships and submitted him via triangle choke. Though he now holds a black belt, it's the system he created called the "rubber guard" by which he is mainly known in the fight world. "It didn't happen overnight," remembered Bravo. "It took years, but the idea was born once wrestlers learned how to defend the traditional BJJ guard." A great black belt is not one who masters techniques, but one who creates new ones. His rubber guard, where the bottom fighter uses a leg to keep his opponent down, leaving the arms free for sweeps—defense and offense—has become a fixture in MMA fights today. He has even created different submissions from the position, like the Twister.

New MMA moves are often created on the fly and through trial and error. With barely a minute left in a lightweight title fight in the last WEC, Anthony Pettis leapt up and pushed his right foot against the cage, propelling that foot to drop Ben Henderson after it connected to his head. It was a move he had practiced, like many others, under the tutelage of Wisconsin native Jeff "Duke" Roufus, a retired champion kickboxer. Though he had retired before the MMA boom, he learned to infuse his traditional martial arts base to create new moves to catch opponents off guard in the new fighting sport. During his first fight against Pedro Rizzo, Randy Couture would smash his shoulder into Rizzo's face, something people hadn't seen before. "We just started doing that in training, both from the clinch standing and on the ground," said Couture. "Especially when one guy has your arm, you can come down with the point of your shoulder with quite a bit of force to someone's face." Mixed martial arts is becoming more and more "mixed" as new training philosophies emerge to once again rip the formality away from classic wrestling, jiu-jitsu, and stand-up styles.

Team Sport

Ken Shamrock's Lion's Den emerged as the first American team to prepare fighters for MMA. Single entrants in the UFC just didn't have the same support structure afforded to Royce Gracie with his jiu-jitsu family in tow. Styles for jiu-jitsu, wrestling, and kickboxing formed many teams in the beginning, but eventually the team philosophy rested on the harmonious union of its members striving to become better athletes, adding coaches from different disciplines to sharpen each team. Today's teams are more like brotherhoods, as members rely on one another for training, advice, and sometimes rent money. In pro boxing, a fighter brings his trainer, cut man, manager, and assistants to his bouts. In MMA, a fighter brings as many as a dozen teammates to cheer him on and show their support. And while there are managers, agents, assistants, and the like in MMA, at the end of the day the fighter trusts and respects one of his own...someone who has sweat and bled just like he has on the mats time and time again.

In America alone, there are countless teams in every state, many of which have produced champions at all levels of the game. In New Mexico, Greg Jackson, of Jackson's Submission Fighting, has assembled one of the best teams in the world including Georges St. Pierre, Rashad Evans, and Diego Sanchez. In Iowa, Pat Miletich's Miletich Fighting Systems has spawned Matt Hughes, Jens Pulver, Tim Sylvia, and Robbie Lawler. In San Jose, California, Frank Shamrock student "Crazy" Bob Cook and kickboxer Javier Mendez run American Kickboxing Academy, which has produced several stars including Josh Koscheck, Cain Velasquez, Josh Thomson, and Mike Swick. Florida has the American Top Team, Nevada has Xtreme Couture, North Carolina has Team ROC, and Colorado has the Grudge Training Center. Teams not only prepare their students for MMA, but they also train them for jiu-jitsu and submission matches, kickboxing, and boxing as well. Many fighters even split their time between gyms to never grow stagnant.

Career Choice

Earning a living as a fighter is very difficult. You must train at your own expense and even travel to different countries just to learn a particular choke, new positioning, or way of putting the pieces of the puzzle together. One injury can sideline a fighter for months or even close to a year in some cases. Fights can be planned far in advance, or come out of nowhere for the opportunity of a lifetime to compete in the "big show." It has a tremendous effect on personal relationships where a fighter must juggle so many different variables to keep his or her head in the game. And whether it's for the thrill, the money, or the fame, every fighter must make that commitment to the craft. "I got guys who drive three hours so they can train, and they don't see their families because they stay all weekend," said Frank Shamrock. As others were born to play golf or be pro basketball players, these athletes were born to fight. "I had aspirations of going into boxing or kickboxing, but when I saw the UFC, that is what I wanted to do," said Aaron Riley. Travis Fulton bought into the fantasy of the film *Bloodsport* but made it his goal in life to compete in the UFC when he saw the truth. Today, Fulton has fought in more matches than anyone else—over 250, and he's still going in 2010. "If I had my way, I would fight every day. I'm doing this because this is what I like to do," he said. He sees fighting as a paid vacation that will help him rack up a lot of stories, and today he continues to do what he enjoys most, despite little fanfare.

Unlike boxing, MMA doesn't really have a national amateur league. To gain experience, some first-time fighters put it on the line for as little as $200 in a pro fight. Times have changed from the old days when many shows didn't have insurance, but no doubt, every fighter must start from the bottom and work his way up. When Zuffa took over the UFC, the promotion's normal rate for a first-time entry was $2,000 to show and $2,000 to win. By 2010, the promotion can pay a debuting UFC fighter over $6,000, while dozens earn well over $50,000 a fight. Many UFC fighters make $100,000 or more per year, not including sponsor and endorsement deals. A select few can make several million dollars a year including major sponsor and endorsement deals. The UFC even instituted special bonuses for "Fight of the Night," "Submission of the Night," and "Knockout of the Night." Chris Lytle, a fireman who has fought since 1999, certainly isn't one of the top UFC fighters, but he makes an incredible living putting on a show. He has won these awards on many occasions, earning up to $40,000 in additional money per fight. Matt Hamill's head-kick knockout of Mark Munoz at UFC 96 moved his show/win purse from $40,000 to making an additional $60,000 just for the KO. Today no promotion other than the UFC can pay out these types of purses to fighters.

With gate receipts for some of the UFCs topping $5 million, not including the millions in pay-per-view, critics have often cited that UFC fighters aren't earning enough. But MMA is a sport made up of an ensemble group of fighters in varying weight classes, instead of one heavily promoted fight as in boxing. On a boxing undercard, no one pays attention because the matches don't seem to matter, but in MMA, most every fight is configured into the matrix of sorts as to whether that fighter belongs on the ladder to a title shot. In other words, those fights do matter. "If you are making $80,000 or $90,000 a fight, you lead a very comfortable life, but you really can't afford to take a year off because you may not be able to get that pay again, and your body can only take so much," said Dave Meltzer. "It's not enough to leave the sport. It's comfortable to train and eat well and go on vacation but not too much that they can afford to start skipping fights and lose motivation." By comparison, the top boxers earn in the millions and can dictate where, how, and what about a fight, as in the case of Floyd Mayweather and Manny Pacquiao. When Pacquiao fought Miguel Cotto, the Filipino champion made $22 million while Cotto picked up $12 million. The highest total fight purse for a UFC that includes all the fighters was at UFC 118 for a mere $1.428 million. The main reason for that stemmed from heavyweight boxer James Toney's appearance on the card. The boxer thought he could try his hand at the UFC and knock out Randy Couture on August 28, 2010. Toney picked up half a million dollars for a 199-second match that concluded with Couture submitting Toney with a choke.

MMA is a dream many fighters hope will turn into something more. It started out like bodybuilding where only a handful of people could make any money. Today, many fighters earn a handsome living, and with more sponsors coming onboard and other deals, the fighter must sharpen his business acumen as well as his physical weapons to succeed. Ever since Tito Ortiz started selling t-shirts to fans as a way to earn extra income in 1999, fighters have become tremendous marketers in their own right, maintaining fan websites, developing clothing lines, and offering their services for personal appearances, seminars, and anything to cash in on their names while the getting is good. MMA gave these athletes a way to make real money surrounding the sport, and today there is no limit as to how much they can make.

Motivation

Money wasn't always a motivator behind fighting, as Iowa-born Bobby Hoffman could attest. Hoffman was always a fighter, from as far back as he could remember. At five years old, he was accidentally hit in the head with a garden hoe. The hoe had to be removed by a doctor, and Hoffman spent seven months in a hospital. Hoffman's adulthood didn't fare much better, after a brief stint with the Cleveland Browns football team. "By 1996, I had racked up 14 assault charges in four years. I was actually facing eight years [for assault to commit bodily injury] but served 92 [days] and got out." The gym was the only thing that kept his mind off violence. As fate would have it, Hoffman met a local MMA fighter who was about to turn his life around for the better. Hoffman had no martial arts or boxing background, but as he put it, "My old man was rough on me and boxed me around a lot. I had no type of fight training whatsoever except for bar-room brawls." On two days' notice, the 265-pound, 6'3" Hoffman entered his first MMA fight, Bare Knuckle Brawls. After competing all over the world with great success, his vices got the best of him, and in 2001, he was sentenced to prison for several crimes. He made his comeback more than a year later but wasn't the same fighter as before.

Most career MMA fighters never thought they'd be doing this for a living. Wrestler Mike Van Arsdale saw it as bringing wrestling back to its foundation: "Wrestling was turned into a sport where college kids wouldn't get hurt, so this was just going back to a place in time where wrestling was different." When wrestlers reach that pinnacle and feel they have no more to learn, MMA allows them to apply those skills in a fresh environment. Frank Shamrock needed something in his life to give him perspective. He thought football was too hard and wasn't interested in wrestling, so volleyball and Hacky Sack became his only physical solace. When Shamrock was given the opportunity to be part of the Lion's Den, he seized it as a way to put his life on track. "I never saw myself as a fighter, nor did I want to be a fighter. It was something that was just given to me, so I took it," said Shamrock. It took a couple of years for Shamrock to feel comfortable with the idea, but he learned quickly and became one of the most well-rounded, athletic fighters in MMA. After becoming King of Pancrase, he was able to write his own meal ticket in a sport with little money to go around and a lot of risk to be had.

Mental Edge

The mind-set of a fighter is a hard thing to gauge. Unlike a streetfighter, a professional mixed martial artist must always keep a cool head, since overzealousness might cost him the match. "You have to separate yourself from what you're doing," said Shonie Carter. "A lot of guys get psyched up before a fight, but I'm not like that…you can't have an emotion about fighting because that person has done nothing against you personally. They're just competing to earn money or to test themselves as a fighter." But sometimes a personal element does enter the picture, as in the case of Hawaiian fighter Jay R. Palmer and Brazilian Maurice Corty, who fought at Superbrawl 2 on October 11, 1996. According to Palmer, Corty had the gall to walk up to Palmer's wife and say, "Sorry, I'm going to have to break his arm and send him out on a stretcher." Palmer was beside himself with anger when his wife told him. A camera close-up of Palmer's face revealed a man possessed, marked by heavy breathing and wild eyes. Palmer attacked Corty in the first two and a half minutes with an onslaught of good old-fashioned streetfighting that resulted in the Brazilian being stomped unconscious.

For others, such as Mark Kerr, fighting affects the emotions in a different way. "I brought my brother to the first UFC that I fought in, and these are so emotional for me that I broke down after the fight. I was in tears, and I've probably cried three or four times after a fight. It's just so emotional for me to get it over with, and there is so much tension."

Newcomer Matt Mitrione was a former professional football player whose mind seemed elsewhere during his time on the 10th season of *The Ultimate Fighter*. Since that time, he has bestowed a very carefree attitude, laughing and smiling in the Octagon as he mixes it up with his opponents. He's enjoying what he's doing. Ultimately, each man must find what works best for him, but having the proper mind-set is key.

British fighter Dexter Casey finds he can control the tension—sometimes too much. "I have seen fighters crying before getting in the ring due to the adrenaline running through them," he said. "They think they are scared, but they aren't; it's adrenaline. Being able to control your response to all this adrenaline is the mental aspect. I am a natural performer, and adrenaline does not bother me. This can work against you, as I have recently been going into the ring too relaxed, and because of that, I have been beaten. A bit of tension and edge can keep you alive."

As boxers have long recognized, psychology can be crucial in *mano a mano* contests. Vale, a Neanderthal Russian bouncer, had made quite a name for himself on the east coast of England. Whether it was competing in illegal prizefights or throwing people out on their butts, he was certainly someone to be feared. As MMA events sprouted up around Europe, Casey got the chance to fight him in the ring. "When I got to the arena I was treated like a celeb," he said. "Everybody wanted me to smash his face in, patriotically of course." Meeting for the first time at the weigh-in, Vale claimed Casey was too small to fight him, vexing the Brit in the process. "He was basically assuming, because he outweighed me by 30 pounds, that he was going to run right over me," said Casey, who was a solid 210 pounds.

Two hours before the fight, Casey's mind was off center. Vale's comments enraged him. Devising a strategy, he and his pad man began working Thai kicks just outside of Vale's changing area. "The sound reverberated through his door, and it was really loud. After about 10 minutes of this, I knew he must be wondering what the sound was." Casey knew Vale was a good puncher and solid grappler but wasn't much of a kicker. The sound of Casey's kicks could only plant question marks in Vale's head.

The Brit was the first one to the ring, and he stomped around to let people know he meant business. "When [Vale] came out, I stared at him so hard that he had to break eye contact. I stood in his corner and made him go around me to get in. All these little things made him stiff and nervous." With the sound of the bell, Vale came out just as nervous as his brain and "threw a big right hand that came all the way from Moscow. I slipped the punch and threw a hard low kick. He backed up and I threw another low kick. He looked at me scared, and I threw three more low kicks really fast with complete commitment." Vale crumbled in the corner, and the fight was over within just 18 seconds. Though Casey was disappointed that eight weeks of training led to 18 seconds of ring time, the mental aspect won the fight.

Sometimes that mental aspect has little to do with the fighter but is more about the corner. When UFC lightweight champion Frankie Edgar rematched former titleholder B.J. Penn, many thought Penn would have it in the bag. As the fight progressed, Edgar's corner, Mark Henry, began yelling instruction in Korean. Penn's camp had no idea what he was saying. As it turns out, Penn said after one of his fights that he and his cornermen listened to his opponent's corner yelling instruction and adjusted accordingly. So Henry devised a plan, and during a taping for a UFC special on Edgar's fight with Penn, he taped up some instruction in French on the door. After Edgar defeated Penn for the second time, the Hawaiian sensation told Henry that his cornermen had been studying French in anticipation for the fight. The ruse worked as, in reality, Edgar's instruction for that fight was in Korean. This is one of many instances where people have to think outside the box to create an advantage, and there was nothing illegal about it.

Perhaps there is also a spiritual side to fighting, as many Christians and other religious people also claim MMA professions. "There's certainly nothing wrong with it," said Matt Hume, a devout Christian and head of AMC Pankration in Seattle, Washington. "I'm available to talk with anyone, and even point them to scripture verses if it helps them get their mind right before they step in the ring. There are a couple of scriptures that I use." Texas native Paul Jones, who once worked for a boy's home for troubled teens, came up with the slogan, "Christians Aren't Wimps!" to promote his views. In Hawaii, there was even a pro fighting team called Jesus is Lord. And who could forget the sight of Kimo and Joe Son both carrying crosses and spouting scripture during their debuts in the UFC? UK competitor James Zikic had to wrestle with his Christian beliefs before accepting in his heart that fighting in MMA was something he was born to do. By studying under Frank Shamrock and others, Zikic made a name for himself as one of the best newcomers at the time to come out of Britain.

Physical Edge

On the other side of the coin is the physical aspect: readying a body to perform in an environment full of exhaustive grappling, dangerous striking, and brutal time limits. Successful fighters must train like Olympic athletes to achieve the level of endurance and stamina needed for the profession. Fighters like Tank Abbott, who relied on his one- to two-minute window to knock his opponent out, often tire well before the end of the round due to lack of conditioning. Even Olympic-caliber wrestler Mark Coleman had trouble with Maurice Smith because he didn't have enough gas in the tank to finish with the same level of intensity as he'd started. A fighter can have all the knowledge in the world, but how can he employ this knowledge if his conditioning prohibits him? "Karate people are not athletes," said kenpo exponent Zane Frazier. "Karate, tae kwon do, jiu-jitsu, and kung fu are martial arts disciplines. The reason we didn't win in MMA was simply because our techniques were not trained in the manner that a professional athlete trains." Thus, a world-class athlete with adequate skills can defeat a subpar athlete with above-average skills, in most cases.

Fighters must go through a strenuous program of resistance training, plyometrics [jumping], weight training, and running and be able to separate as well as blend all of the elements in a fight (grappling, submission, striking). This training takes the MMA fighter out of his domain and forces him to look at singular elements, only to understand how to apply, adapt, and add those elements to his existing repertoire. Frequently, he will train with a Muay Thai coach, then spar at a pro boxing gym before rolling with a jiu-jitsu master. These days, all three can be under one roof. Between running and lifting weights, these athletes put in a tremendous amount of training in preparation for one fight. And many training centers not only offer the physical, but also break down a fighter's training on a scientific and psychological level.

Like athletes in other sports, they study their diet and adjust accordingly for weak spots, to maximize their potential in the ring. After losing to Ricco Rodriguez at UFC 36 as a heavyweight, Randy Couture moved down to light heavyweight and worked with a nutritionist to better his conditioning in later rounds. The nutritionist prescribed ample amounts of green, leafy vegetables, which increased the alkalinity of the blood while increasing endurance levels and longevity. Couture's conditioning improved twofold as a result. Some fighters experiment with energy drinks and over-the-counter stimulants like Xenedrine and Ripped Fuel to see how it will affect them in the ring—certainly not the best solution, especially when someone doesn't understand the real problem.

In the past 30 years, sports have been plagued by steroid abuse, and MMA is unfortunately no different. "There are anabolic (stimulates tissue growth and repair) and androgenic (stimulates growth of secondary male sex organs and the synthesis of cellular protein) steroids," said Dr. John Keating, longtime ringside physician and surgeon. "Most sports have moved to outlaw performance-enhancing substances of all kinds, not so much because of the damage it does the athletes, but rather in an effort to keep the playing field level." MMA fighter Travis Fulton was one of the few who commented on his use of steroids. "My wind went downhill big time, and I'm still recovering," said Fulton back in 2000. "I got good steroids; it wasn't like I was doing bad stuff. My body started looking better, and I got a lot stronger and much bigger. It's one of the reasons I got into the UFC, because I was a heavyweight. But to this day, my body aches all the time." Some, like Dan Severn, are adamantly against steroids, even to the point of lobbying for drug-free competitions.

John Keating has this to say about the dangers of steroid use: "The various performance-enhancing agents [in steroids] certainly do enhance performance up to a point. They are extremely effective at developing bulk and strength. Obviously, you can massively overdevelop muscles that create more of an oxygen debt than can be met in sports such as MMA, which require a mix of aerobic and anaerobic capacity. But it's not the short-term oxygen debt problems that concern sports physicians. It is the broad band of side effects that move us to urge athletes to eschew steroid use. They poison your liver, create significant heart changes (both to the muscle itself and to the arteries supplying the heart), promote hypertension, male pattern baldness, and suppress immune function (increasing the likelihood of infection and compromised response to tumor). In fact, longtime steroid users have five thousand times the incidence of liver cancer as the general public."

Benching over 600 pounds, self-proclaimed natural fighter David "Tank" Abbott was also outspoken on the topic. "The first use of steroids was by the Nazis on the front lines so they would be more aggressive. Those guys have to take drugs to think like me. I've taken so many drug and steroid tests, and I have never taken a steroid. Obviously, by looking at my body, you can tell I don't. Steroids ruined real fighting; they ruined the UFC." Though some athletes have used them to become more power-ful, there have been too many cases where all they've done is decreased the endurance and stamina needed to finish a fight.

So if steroid abuse exists, what is to be done about it? "Educate the athlete," said Keating. "Blood testing is expensive and ineffective. I believe the only person harmed by the steroids is the user himself, so the final responsibility lives with the athlete. In the short term, steroids may add some marginal additional risk during the event of a hypertensive episode, but whatever these risks are, they do not substantially add to the danger of what goes on inside the ring."

The first steroid case in MMA occurred on April 22, 2002, when the NSAC filed a complaint against Josh Barnett after winning the heavyweight championship over Randy Couture at UFC 36. The NSAC alleged two positive tests for anabolic steroids from samples taken on November 2, 2001, and March 22, 2002. Barnett was ultimately stripped of the title and given a six-month suspension despite Barnett's camp protesting any usage of anabolic enhancements. Barnett never competed in the UFC again, opting instead to pro wrestle and fight elsewhere. (His testing problems also partially led to the demise of rival promotion Affliction when he was sidelined from the main event in 2009.) Lightning struck again at UFC 44 when Tim Sylvia admitted to steroid use after defending the heavyweight crown. He was also stripped and suspended for four months but stayed with the UFC a short while. A title shot at UFC 47 was postponed when anabolic agents were still found in his bloodstream; he was cleared two days later. Several MMA fighters have tested positive for steroids, including, ironically, Royce Gracie in his rematch against Kazushi Sakuraba. The Gracie name was always built on the smaller guy defeating the bigger guy, but the urge to take steroids has been a powerful one. After delivering a powerful performance against Anderson Silva at UFC 117, middleweight contender Chael Sonnen rose out of obscurity and had a big payday of a rematch on the horizon. He subsequently tested positive for steroids, was sidelined for six months, and would now have to start from scratch.

Similar to what can be found in other professional sports, some fighters also use painkillers to combat the myriad problems these athletes face, especially in the knee and shoulder joints. It's also not uncommon for fighters to partake in recreational drugs, as part of an extremist lifestyle that's hardcore in every respect. Fighters know they can use their occupation to their advantage in social situations. Fighter gyms and teams have their share of groupies much like one would see with rock stars, but as professional athletes, they won't get far if they don't take care of their bodies. Frank Shamrock and Randy Couture are both world-class mixed martial artists; both have taken good care of their bodies, but Shamrock's body was riddled with injuries over the years. "I've broken my face, my cheek, had more stitches than I can ever count, got cauliflower ear, but never had my teeth knocked out," said Shamrock. "My C6 and C7 are all compressed and jammed up. I've torn ligaments in my legs and damaged my right shoulder that had to be arthroscopically repaired. I've broken my right hand three times and my left hand once. I've broken my left elbow and my right leg in the fibula. I broke my left leg and my big toe. I broke my ACL before the Baroni fight. The rest of the stuff was kind of minor. I've torn most of my ribs out and broken my ribs; that's not fun." As for Randy Couture, Dave Meltzer said he was an anomaly in terms of the slight damage his body has taken over the years. "It's doubtful we'll see another one like him."

Performing Artists

MMA is a spectator sport and fighters are performers. They must entertain the audience while trying to win the fight. Upon seeing Tank Abbott's phenomenal success with the crowd, Gary Goodridge became "Big Daddy," giving colorful interview sound bites before walking out to the Octagon. Quinton "Rampage" Jackson, with his trademark chain around his neck, howls into the air before trotting into the cage or ring. His no-bullshit interviews and perceived player lifestyle have made him a huge fan favorite. Heath Herring, known as "The Texas Crazyhorse," used to come out with a different hairdo every time and ham it up in the ring—it made him a star in Pride. Genki Sudo came out as everything from a samurai warrior to a geisha girl for his UFC matches.

No doubt MMA fighters are a different breed. Some have quirks and mannerisms that set them apart from everyone else, and it's the lack of that red tape found in boxing, for example, that allows everyone to see the natural character each fighter possesses. Pride and several Japanese organizations rely more on characters than actual fighting ability, while U.S. promotions took the opposite approach. Either way, every fighter must find and capitalize on what makes him unique, and physical skill isn't always the primary factor.

Case in point is Matt Lindland and Phil Baroni, the two most diametrically opposed fighters in the UFC in the early 2000s. Lindland is an Olympic silver medalist whose all-business demeanor and physical features don't necessarily fit the stereotype of a UFC fighter, compared to the mouthy, brash Phil Baroni, a former bodybuilder and pin-up model who hyped it up every chance he got. Both men represent extremes of perception about what a star is all about, but Baroni carved a niche for himself as being the controversial, unapologetic "New York Badass"— his justified nickname. Baroni's reputation includes a suspension for punching a ref, dropping f-bombs on the mic, and being kicked off fight teams for being too uncooperative. Lindland and Baroni have met twice in the Octagon, and both times, Lindland reigned supreme. Lindland said he can't do anything about "public perception," as people form their opinions in myriad ways. "After much thought, planning, and input from my brilliant staff of 'war room' image makers, I have come up with a spectacular strategy to hold the fan's attention: it's called winning fights," he said laughing.

Building a star in the ring can also have its problems. Dan Severn used "The Beast" and his pro wrestling experience to create a character the audience would remember. After winning a match, Severn will raise his large hands up into the air and let out a roar to get the crowd going. Out of the limelight, Severn is a family man who used to speak frequently of his longtime devotion to his wife (married since 1984) and five children. But not anymore. "I had one of my children almost abducted after my first two years of being involved in this," said Severn in 2001. The Beast promotes himself as a bachelor to the media these days. He ran his own promotion, the Danger Zone, for several years, and his office and training facility sit only 40 yards from his house. In his fifties, he still fights even today.

Part-Time Fighters

Back when then this author originally wrote this book (2000), more than 90 percent of all MMA fighters had full-time jobs; today (2010) it would be closer to 50 percent with more and more opportunities out there to make money. But even some of the top fighters haven't quit their day jobs. Shane Carwin used his mechanical engineering degree to get a job in that profession when he's not fighting for the UFC heavyweight crown. Brett Rogers used to fix tires at a local Wal-Mart but eventually left to pursue his MMA career full time. Gary Goodridge worked a 40-plus-hour week for Honda of Canada Manufacturing in the vehicle quality division. He made fighting a hobby until Japan made him a superstar, affording him the opportunity to fight full-time. Russian immigrant Roman Roytberg is a licensed dentist but competed in kickboxing and MMA. Matt Lindland owned a used car lot in Oregon. Australian standout Elvis Sinosic worked in the telecommunications industry and took time off work to train and fight. Jason Godsey, Phil Johns, and Ron Waterman were all high school teachers. Eugene Jackson ran a trucking business; Genki Sudo and Nicholaus Hill were actors. Since childhood, Oleg Taktarov had always dreamed of being an actor; it just took him being in the Russian Army and a stint as an MMA fighter to get there. After fighting all over the world and mastering English, he's become a successful actor. Randy Couture, who tried acting as an offshoot from his fighting career, has become so popular that he may well hang it up in his forties because the opportunities, and his acting ability, are there to support it.

Here is a partial list of MMA fighters who have appeared in film, television, and commercials:

MMA Fighter	Acting Experience
Randy Couture	*The Expendables* *Scorpion King 2* *Redbelt* *Cradle 2 the Grave*
Quinton Jackson	*The A-Team* *Midnight Meat Train*
Oleg Taktarov	*Predators* *Air Force One* *15 Minutes*
Tito Ortiz	*The Crow: Wicked Prayer* *Cradle 2 The Grave*
Joe Son	*Austin Powers*
Bas Rutten	*The Eliminator* *Shadow Fury* *Martial Law*

MMA Fighter	Acting Experience
Ken Shamrock	*Virtuosity* *The Champions*
Frank Shamrock	*Walker, Texas Ranger* *Burger King* commercial *No Rules*
Lance Gibson	*Rumble in the Bronx* *Romeo Must Die*
Kimo	*Ultimate Fight*
Dan Severn	*Rudy*
Tank Abbott	*Friends*
Maurice Smith	*Bloodfist II* *Fist of Glory*

So what advice can be given to the aspiring mixed martial artist? "Get your head examined!" said Guy Mezger. "And if you get your head examined and find out that you're crazy enough to still do this, it's important that you get well-rounded training and that you get really good-quality training."

"The sport has evolved from a lack of knowledge in the beginning, to a knowledge of submission, to a knowledge of grappling, to a knowledge of striking, and now a knowledge of conditioning," said Maurice Smith. "This is truly a martial art, what these guys are doing now by cross training and becoming hybrid fighters. There will be a guy in the future who is going to have excellent grappling, submission, striking, and strategy skills." Ironically, many of the fighters interviewed for this book spoke of a similar fighter, an almost mythical figure who would emerge to supplant the best of the best today. Georges St. Pierre? Anderson Silva? Fedor Emelianenko? Even in the world of reality fighting, people still believe in mythic heroes and legends. But until they step into the ring or cage, that's all they'll ever be.

25

FIGHTING FOR A MAINSTREAM SPORT

For many casual viewers, mixed martial arts had been a beer-induced fad that came and passed during the mid-1990s. After major pay-per-view companies dropped the UFC, the media had no cause to persecute or milk anymore: it was a "win" for the moral majority. Press coverage died, just as the masses yearned for something else "too taboo." The UFC had breathed new life into a market bored with boxing and pro wrestling, but with MMA out of the spotlight, Vince McMahon of World Wrestling Entertainment came back strong to promote an improved pro wrestling that reclaimed its profitable pay-per-view days. Marketed as sports entertainment, the WWE revamped its programming with raunchy storylines, more scantily clad women, funnier archetypes, and less actual wrestling. The media now had a new villain: sex and violence on television. In the midst of war in the Middle East and risqué reality television, MMA looked rather tame by comparison. MMA now had to survive as a real sport—not just entertainment.

UFC Vice President Joe Silva remembered, while serving as a fight consultant, the time he spoke to programming director Campbell McLaren at Ultimate Ultimate '95: "I told Campbell that we needed to be more like a real sport, and Campbell said, 'The last thing we want to be is a sport.'" Silva became enchanted by MMA after seeing the UFC. "At the end of that first show, I was so happy that I was practically in tears. This is the reality I've been trying to tell people about, what would happen in a real fight. This is not just people running their mouths; this is people putting it on the line." Silva, who had made martial arts a large part of his life, began calling the SEG office, offering up his opinions on how to better the show. His dedication and insight led him to trade ideas for posters and other fan paraphernalia. Silva has been part of the UFC since the third show, from fight consultant to matchmaker to VP and everything in between. From the first show he ever attended, UU '95, Silva told them: "This is a cutting-edge sport, but you guys cover it like it's a fucking golf tournament. It's so boring. I would always just give them my no-holds-barred opinion on things, and I'm sure a lot of times it was very hard to take." But ultimately they listened.

Despite inaccessibility on pay-per-view, MMA created a paradigm shift in the martial arts worldwide. One can't walk into a conventional martial arts school without seeing "submission," "freestyle," "MMA," and "jiu-jitsu" advertised as a way to attract people outside traditional styles. MMA schools often do the opposite by bringing in karate instructors to teach kids classes—the cash cow of the business. Unless students are fighting and the school is making money, it's the kids and the multiple belts that bring in the cash flow to keep schools alive and kicking.

Brazilian jiu-jitsu has been an underlying factor for popularizing MMA. While the sport struggled for sanctioning in the U.S. for years, jiu-jitsu and submission tournaments were left alone and prospered almost from the outset of the first UFC. Arnold Schwarzenegger's "Arnold Classic" bodybuilding and fitness event was one of the first non-martial arts related organizations to add submission wrestling. They created the Arnold World Gracie Submission Championships to add to its growing list of competitive sports. Headed up by Relson Gracie, thousands of people compete each year. People of all ages train jiu-jitsu, much to the delight of Rorion Gracie, who has kept his dream alive in more than one way. His three sons, Ryron, Rener, and Ralek, are "part of the next generation and are teaching and training at the academy now," said Rorion. "It's in their blood; they want to do MMA." While Rener was a state champion wrestler, it would be son Ralek who would forge an MMA career. On May 29, 2010, Ralek stepped into the cage against an older Kazushi Sakuraba, but he defeated him by decision, avenging the name against the man known as the "Gracie Killer."

If there was to be one reason why MMA has stayed around as long as it has without free television, it would be the Internet. "[It] has been amazingly resilient," said Cal Cooper, who has worked on two major MMA websites. "It's a vast, convoluted community, made up of news sites and forums, and it started with the Combat List, an exhaustive email list disseminated to thousands of inboxes per day." Without mainstream sports media, fans, fighters, and promoters relied on the Internet as their biggest source for information. They still do as the community, even with hundreds of websites, blogs, and Myspace and Facebook pages is still a close-knit group. Many Internet journalists write for free, and webmasters keep their sites going by selling merchandise.

Kirik Jenness and David Roy run mma.tv and mixedmartialarts. com, the definitive sounding board for the sport. The site's infamous Underground Forum is the most up-to-date source of information, where insiders and outsiders are free to post anything about the sport and do so regularly. In 2001, the site had over 50,000 members. "The mixed martial arts audience is very well-rounded—people in their seventies to a 12-year-old girl," said Jenness, whose site was started as a vehicle to sell *The Fighter's Notebook*, an instructional book on submission grappling techniques. "I took martial arts for 20 years before watching the UFC, and after that, I came to the realization that I don't know anything." Today, The Forum is a rite of passage for every MMA fan and becomes an obsessive daily, sometimes hourly, fix to see what's happening in the sport. But that's only a small part of the multimedia site that is a superb resource for the sport in general with news, video, and tons of contact information on schools, events, and the like worldwide.

Joel Gold is perhaps the ultimate enterprising fight fanatic. He turned his love for MMA into an empire comprising a newspaper, website, and clothing line. Everything is collectively known as *Full Contact Fighter* (fcfighter.com). In 1993, Gold was training in a local New York boxing gym when he saw the UFC and criticized the stand-up abilities of the first few UFC participants. Intrigued by Brazilian jiu-jitsu, he took up the art and before long the 155-pound Gold was challenging anyone who would put his skills to the test. After taking on guys twice his size, Gold experienced sharp pains in his neck that continued for months. He woke one morning to find the right side of his body paralyzed. Gold went to a sports medicine clinic and discovered that his neck had accumulated three herniated discs. He keeps the X-ray as a reminder. *Full Contact Fighter* grew in page count, added color, and stood as the most reliable news source outside the Internet, but it died out in 2009. Gold said the FCF name would be revived—bigger and better—in 2011.

Full-color magazines, such as *Ultimate Athlete* and *Fightsport*, soon entered the market but couldn't sustain enough revenue to keep going. But that was before 2005. Today there are dozens of MMA magazines on the racks and many more that want to meet that crossover market. MMA Worldwide Inc. even developed two magazines: *TapouT* as the sports-centric product and *MMA Worldwide* as more of a behind-the-scenes, human interest piece. There's *Ultimate MMA*, *Fight!*, *MMA Unlimited*, and even the UFC came out with its own self-titled magazine.

Jeffrey Osborne didn't make his way into MMA as a promoter and journalist because of money. With his long black hair in a ponytail, skinny stature, deep voice, and round-rimmed glasses, it was hard to believe that Osborne was once a hard-core pro wrestler. Unlike the showy WWE, hard-core pro wrestling relies on the use of barbed wire, fire, and other props that could damage the body. In April 1994, Osborne nearly lost his life due to a bad fall. He reconsidered his career and got out of the business: too much attitude, too much drug abuse (Osborne himself never used drugs), and two close friends dying.

Osborne knew about MMA through Japanese promotions like Shooto and Rings. In 1996, he started Hook n' Shoot as a small-time venture in Evansville, Indiana. "The thing I like about MMA is that if you have an ego, it can be crushed at any time," said Osborne. The promotion ran from 1996 to 2009 and was one of the best indie promotions in the country that forged relationships with Shooto and made headlines when it promoted the first all-female event on April 13, 2002. At times, Osborne was a one-man crew, handling commentary, camera work, and postproduction editing. "If I saw someone knocked out or hurt, I would leave the production booth and get up to the ring because I'm genuinely concerned," said Osborne, who has even fought in MMA himself.

Along with one-time partner Miguel Itturate, they ran one of the first Internet websites, Fight World, that sold merchandise and also produced a series of documentaries long before any major media took notice. The duo also headed up one of the first submission-only organizations in the world called Abu Dhabi Combat Club during the late 1990s. Before the horrible terrorist attacks on September 11, 2001, the Abu Dhabi World Submission Wrestling Championship was held in the United Arab Emirates for the sole purpose of entertaining Sheik Tahnoon and other wealthy oil tycoons who enjoy the competition. The show became a who's who in the submission world and paid large purses, since the Sheik had enough money to get any fighter he chose. In 2001, Osborne briefly took over from Jeff Blatnick as color commentator for the UFC. He cut his ponytail, replaced his glasses with contacts, and wore a suit, but comedian Joe Rogan replaced him a year later. Osborne later worked with Calvin Ayre on Bodog and has continued to work behind the scenes, namely in the women's MMA movement in Indiana.

◆ ◆ ◆

IN ALMOST EVERY CONCEIVABLE PLACE around the U.S.A., and even the world, MMA promotions are flourishing, including Mainland China and Dubai. Most of these shows give up-and-coming fighters, who perform in front of crowds from 300 to 6,000, a chance to ply their trade. Though attempts have been made to form amateur MMA organizations to create a network as vast as Golden Gloves, there are few solid amateur entities. Many promoters have swarmed the market in their respective states, all but three with state sanctioning (another three have no athletic commissions), and some hold shows on American Indian land, under a veil of secrecy in small, off-the-map venues. Since October 1999, Terry

Trebilcock's King of the Cage has become one of the most profitable MMA promotions of all time, using a tribal land casino model with local fighters to sell tickets. Having promoted shows around the U.S. and in several countries, the production is kept lean and mean for on-site fees and sponsorship money.

It's been a mixed blessing for a sport trying to find its way, with solidarity being the key issue. No neutral body oversees MMA, as there are too many promotions with too many individual ideas on how it should be governed. Some matches are held in a ring, some in a cage. The unified rules have become the norm, though some promoters will make changes, like the absence of elbow strikes to the face that can force significant cuts. In the beginning, fight promotions deemed bouts as Pancrase style with open-palm strikes or NHB (no-holds-barred) with closed fist. Today, the sport is regulated enough to where the vast majority are MMA under these unified rules. While there is no official ranking system, there are few variations in reference to gloves (typically four ounce, but up to six depending on opponent's weight) and weight classes, listed below:

Flyweight	125 pounds
Bantamweight	135 pounds
Featherweight	145 pounds
Lightweight	155 pounds
Welterweight	170 pounds
Middleweight	185 pounds
Light Heavyweight	205 pounds
Heavyweight	265 pounds
Super Heavyweight	Over 265 pounds

Websites offer a primitive semblance of ranking by having journalists decide who is the best of the best on that day. Since the UFC controls most of the professional talent, they have their own rankings. Promoters used to manage fighters in their own shows, and they still do, but with more state sanctioning, this typically only happens in regional, independent events. Before 2005, some fighters took their lives in their hands by competing in as many as 10 matches a year, even after knockouts, but today, they are far more picky because each fight is no longer just a paycheck—it could be a launching pad for a bigger opportunity. Fighters used to self-manage themselves or have their coaches, friends, or fathers do it. That's still true, but now many have agents, managers, management firms, and the like; the sport of mixed martial arts is a business.

When the UFC first roared onto the scene, weigh-ins were relegated to tiny rooms meant for managers and fighters only. After Zuffa took over, weigh-ins attracted thousands of fans, matching and eclipsing the attendance for UFCs during the so-called "Dark Ages." The old UFC also had very little merchandising strength, offering only standard shirts and caps, many of which just stated the date. Just before Ultimate Ultimate '95, SEG debuted *Secrets of the Octagon*, a five-videotape instructional set featuring Ken Shamrock, Dan Severn, Oleg Taktarov, and Keith Hackney. "The set didn't have Brazilian jiu-jitsu, which was the only secret of the Octagon at that point," said Art Davie, who claimed it was Bob Meyrowitz's idea to add products for the franchise. "Anybody who was a serious devotee, a fan of the UFC at that point, quickly got the buzz out on them through the bulletin board and word of mouth that there were really no secrets of the Octagon in *Secrets of the Octagon*. I mean, Oleg Taktarov showing you how to do a punch!" The set never made it into stores, and only a thousand, if that, were made. The tapes have become true, if laughable, collector's items.

It wasn't the UFC or any promotion in particular that opened up the true fandom of mixed martial arts; it was the grassroots movement of believing in a cause and being willing to wear the war paint to fight for it. That war paint can arguably be traced to a couple of budding entrepreneurs from San Bernardino, California, named Charles Lewis and Dan Caldwell, better known as "Mask" and "Punkass." When the MMA scene in California was relegated to tribal land, fans would sometimes drive through crazy terrain to pack the bleachers, mostly outside, for

History of the Unified Rules

Today mixed martial arts has a template aptly named the "unified rules" that most states have adopted ever since they were originally codified by the New Jersey State Athletic Commission in 2001. Most promotions have adopted these rules with few variations (namely the omission of elbows to the head) for safety or liability reasons. During the days of SEG and the first few UFCs, the organization ran through the International Fighting Council, the Ultimate Fighting Alliance, and the Mixed Martial Arts Council (MMAC). All three of these organizations were self-serving for the UFC only, though to Art Davie's credit, 85 percent of what can be found in the five different updates of the UFA still hold up today in the unified rules through trial and error of what occurred in the Octagon.

The genesis of the unified rules can be traced back to the Mecca of MMA, California, where due to the enormous amount of Indian casinos, fight promotions were as plentiful as blondes in bikinis. Paul Smith of the IFC, Ryan Chenoweth of amateur league Neutral Grounds, and others desperately tried to get the sport legalized in California since the late 1990s, and many others have claimed that "they" were the ones who showed the California State Athletic Commission (CSAC) how to do it. Commissioner Rob Lynch said he was inundated with different rules from different promotions, so a meeting was called amongst anyone who wanted to attend to discuss those rules in Sacramento on June 5, 1998. The commission met on June 12, 1998, and motioned to reestablish the Martial Arts Advisory Committee (MAAC), which on March 26, 1999, voted in the following members: Paul Smith, Ryan Chenoweth, Nelson Hamilton, Herb Cody, Mark Krieger, Dan Stell, and Tony Thompson. The first meeting of MAAC was held on June 12, 1999, and after streamlining the rules, the first draft of the unified rules was sent to the CSAC on December 14, 1999. The commission would review and discuss these rules over the next few months. Jeff Blatnick, working for SEG, entered the process on April 13, 2000. On April 28, 2000, the CSAC passed the "unified rules" to legally sanction mixed martial arts. Unfortunately, the state didn't have the budget to move forward, and for one reason or another, the rules sat in limbo. No budget; no MMA.

Enter Howard Petschler, Smith's business partner from the IFC, who had kept in touch with his contacts from the kickboxing side on the East Coast. After being allowed to hold an exhibition in mid-2000 on a kickboxing card, New Jersey State Athletic Commissioner Larry Hazzard decided to give the IFC a test case for those same

California-passed unified rules on September 30, 2000, at the Tropicana. The show wasn't anything special and barely made a blip on the radar in terms of the MMA press, but Hazzard was impressed nonetheless. The unified rules were amended to omit knees to the head of a downed opponent after Gan McGee's TKO of Brad Gabriel, which cut open his cheek, proved to be too brutal. The door was now open for SEG to stage UFC 28, held November 15 of that year at the spectacular Taj Mahal casino.

On April 3, 2001, a commission meeting was called by Larry Hazzard that can be called one of the most important steps toward legitimacy. This epochal meeting set standards on several issues with the unified rules, while Marc Ratner, representing the Nevada State Athletic Commission, listened via conference call to report back the findings. After all, Nevada is the king of combat sports and all eyes were on legislation passing in the state. When the NJSAC sanctioned the UFC, the MMAC was disbanded, but the MAAC that worked to pass the rules in California remained. The "unified rules" created by this meeting was one of the few instances of solidarity among the top promoters in the country. Fighters now have to compete without shoes for uniformity and safety, and after Nevada (covered in Chapter 21), everyone else followed suit…in their own way.

New York withstanding, California was the next to be on the hit list to finally get sanctioning. After all, this is where the unified rules came from, and there were promoters aplenty already holding shows on tribal land—only the state wasn't getting any money from it. The tortuous deregulation of water in California (which bankrupted businesses and upset the economy) buried any new legislation in 2002, but many hoped that when Arnold Schwarzenegger became governor, that a pro-MMA bill could pass. But MMA was taking place, legally, off tribal land through a loophole that Greg "Kazja" Patschull had been using to run his Kage Kombat events since 1997. As long as promoters provided a list of winners of "predetermined" bouts for real fights to the CSAC, the commission was fine.

This author, living in California at the time and yearning to promote an MMA event, decided to give this loophole a shot with business partner Clint Santiago Dahl. With commission approval and even telephone conversations with Lynch, a promotion called Venom was set for January 11, 2003, at the Grand Olympic Auditorium. Unlike Kazja's event locations, the Grand Olympic was a historic site in Los Angeles. And that was a big mistake since it caught the attention of both the UFC and King of the Cage, whose attorneys promptly met with the commission on December 12, 2002, to shut the show down. Despite the wink and the nod from the commission, Venom cancelled two weeks before the show ala something out of Donald Zuckerman's handbook. Figuring out another loophole to promote the event on private property at a sound stage, Venom did come off in Long Beach, California, on September 18, 2004…without a hitch. "We bused all the fighters in, with only a select few knowing where the location was, and we shot the show with 20 fights," said Dahl. "Terry Trebilcock had people trying to find the location, but nobody found us."

Whether it was the tribal land shows or the commission playing games allowing the sport to go on unsanctioned, it was only a matter of time before it was legalized. On December 28, 2005, California finally sanctioned MMA and gave Strikeforce promoter Scott Coker, who had an existing CSAC license since 1985 for kickboxing events, the first shot at it. With New Jersey, Nevada, and California, the unified rules spread like wildfire. In Texas, Steve Nelson had been running MMA events since 1996 under a pro wrestling license, but that was discontinued. With the help of longtime kickboxing promoter Steve Armstrong and Guy Mezger—and the unified rules—the Texas Department of Licensing & Regulation legalized MMA in 2007. Denver, Colorado, promoter Sven Bean didn't need New Jersey's blessing, and after learning from promoter Steve Nelson in Texas and pitching the Colorado Athletic Commission, he held the first sanctioned show on March 18, 2000. Iowa promoter Monte Cox, who had ties with the Iowa commission, approached them right away and had no problem promoting shows; the UFC even used his rules when they held a show there in June 2000. He's been promoting sanctioned events since November 23, 1996. On March 26, 2004, a bill banned MMA events in Washington State after Matt Hume had been legally running shows during the mid-nineties; today the sport is legalized.

On May 15, 2006, Marc Ratner, former executive director of the Nevada State Athletic Commission, became vice president of regulatory affairs for the UFC after being one of the sport's biggest opponents during the nineties. Working alongside Randy Couture, he has traveled across America and met with state athletic commissions to get the sport passed. Thanks to his efforts, Alabama and Tennessee can now be added to that list. In fact, longtime UFC judge Jeff Mullen runs the new Tennessee State Athletic Commission.

King of the Cage, World Extreme Cagefighting, and the like throughout Central and Southern California. The fighters weren't paid much, most of the fans were friends, girlfriends, or other fighters, but during those renegade days, it was a family of people who lived MMA. And Lewis and Caldwell decided to do something about it and created the name brand TapouT in 1997.

The designs were "in ya face" as the motto came to be known, and like the skateboard and surfer craze of colorful apparel, so did MMA have its own style. To say that these two, who would be joined by a third individual named Tim "SkySkrape" Katz, were entrepreneurs would be an understatement. They would pack their van with clothes and drive for hours, pile into one room or sleep in fighters' rooms, and try to get their gear into as many hands as possible. Sure, there were a few other apparel names out there like Bad Boy, which came over from Brazil, but the TapouT crew as they would be called were always a welcome addition to any show. Mask always had his face painted, Punkass looked rather unremarkable with his short stature, and SkySkrape was towering with big, funky wigs and dark glasses. A fourth member and eventual UFC fighter, Mike "The Joker" Guymon, was also part of the crew for a short while.

TapouT grossed $30,000 in 1999, and through a decade of hard work, a television show, and multiple other revenue streams, the brand grossed $200 million in 2009. On September 7, 2010, Authentic Brands Group acquired both TapouT and Silver Star, which started in 1993, to take both brands to newer heights. TapouT already has both an athletic supplement line and a training facility to get behind the science of athletes. Sadly, Charles Lewis, who created the designs for TapouT, would not get to see how his empire would prosper; on March 11, 2009, his life was tragically cut short in a high-speed automobile accident. The 46-year-old who lived life to the fullest posthumously became the first and only nonfighter to ever be inducted into the UFC Hall of Fame in July 2009, and his name is etched into the top, inside ring of the famous UFC Octagon.

TapouT's success ushered in a whole new way of looking at MMA. And after the success of *The Ultimate Fighter*, there would be no shortage

Female Fighters

By 2010, MMA was overflowing with female fighters, building up four weight classes: 115, 125, 135, and 145 pounds. Strikeforce built up the latter two weight classes, Bellator ran a 115-pound women's tournament, and several events from around the country are staging events with ladies. Back in August 1996, Japan was the first country to step up and produce a women's event, U-Top Tournament, which assembled fighters from all over the world. Despite its ties to pro wrestling, it set a precedent for the fairer sex to have their day in the ring. On December 5, 2000, Japan hosted the ReMix World Cup 2000, a 16-woman tournament with fighters from Japan, Russia, the U.S., and Holland. The open-weight-class event showed just how far women had come in the sport, drawing over 6,500 attendees. The real showstopper saw Dutch import Marloes Coenen, weighing 145 pounds, employ a flying arm bar to dispatch undefeated 200-plus-pound Becky Levi at 1:24.

According to Levi, she pushed to have the first female fight in the UFC. "The night of Ultimate Ultimate '95, Art Davie pulled me aside and said they would like to find me an opponent to fight," said Levi. "The next thing I knew it was squashed because Meyrowitz didn't want to involve women because of the controversy already surrounding the sport." Levi would become the first female fighter to compete in MMA on American soil, where she defeated Betty Fagan at IFC 4 on March 28, 1997.

Jeff Osborne of Indiana-based Hook n' Shoot has been a cheerleader for the women's MMA movement since 2000. He promoted the first all-female event in the U.S., Hook n' Shoot: Revolution, on April 13, 2002, and later made the cause his sole focus. Along with judo and MMA practitioner Patricia VanderMeer, he created the G-Fight Summit, a yearly, week-long agenda of seminars, grappling matches, and fights— all dedicated to women. "I think it's just a matter of time before Dana eventually puts 16 women in a house together," he said laughing.

The biggest trendsetter for getting people to take notice of women's MMA is Gina Carano, who started out as a champion Muay Thai fighter and was featured on *Fight Girls*, a reality show akin to *The Ultimate Fighter* on the Oxygen network featuring female kickboxers. Carano and several of the ladies from that show crossed over to MMA to join the hundreds who were already in the game. Dallas-born Carano made her debut in EliteXC, but with her signature style and well-spoken personality, she was far from just another fighter. She ranked fifth on Yahoo's "Top 10 Influential Women of 2008" and took the 16th spot in

Maxim magazine's Top 100. After losing her 145-pound Strikeforce belt to heavy-hitting Cristiane Cyborg, she moved on to taking a lead role in director Steven Soderbergh's *Haywire*. Carano may hang up the gloves for good, but her presence really gave prominence to the female MMA scene.

The UFC has yet to take the plunge, though Dana White was interested in the Cyborg/Carano match before it took place in Strikeforce. The biggest reason stems from a lack of depth in the different female divisions. There just aren't enough top female fighters today to create a real, long-lasting division. That will change in the years to come as more female fighters arrive on the scene. Pioneers in the movement, like Erin Toughill, Debi Purcell, Tara La Rosa, and Roxanne Modafferi, have sent a message to the sports world that women belong in MMA and have just as much to offer. It will be interesting to see how the women's side takes shape, but in just 10 years, it has grown tremendously.

of collectibles, keepsakes, and the like. From Topps trading cards to an Octagon play set with figurines to Round 5 sculpted figures, the MMA market beyond fighting seems to hold no bounds. Brett Kawczynski even started the MMA Museum and has over 10,000 different items, including many rare items and one-of-a-kind gloves and memorabilia, to showcase for fans. Video stores have full shelves of MMA DVDs, and the UFC video game has been a smashing success. The sport has become so big that the UFC has started hosting Ultimate Fan Expos that draw hundreds of thousands of people each year. For many years, bootlegging was the only way to get many of these fights on DVD or video, but now they are coming out so fast commercially and through different forms of multimedia through downloads, iPhone, and other new forms of technology that put most every current fight at the fan's fingertips.

Ten years ago, this author said, "The jury is still out on whether MMA will take off." It's safe to say that jury unanimously voted to allow MMA to flourish and evolve, not just with the athletes, but with the sport itself, in different countries and hopefully one day as part of school curriculums. There has been talk of bringing submission wrestling into high schools already, but collegiate wrestling is already in decline. "Wrestling is dying on the vine," said collegiate wrestler and former MMA fighter Scott Adams. "We've already lost UC Davis where Urijah Faber wrestled. Fresno State is gone, and University of Oregon, once home to Chael Sonnen, is already gone. I'm trying to save my old alma mater, Cal Poly, along with Bakersfield." Adams runs a program called Fight for Wrestling that is devoted to raising awareness for amateur wrestling. He promotes MMA fights as charities to raise money. Even bigger, the status of UFC and its tremendous power has allowed the promotion to stage charity events for severely wounded U.S. military personnel and their families through the Intrepid Fallen Heroes Fund.

◆ ◆ ◆

So is mixed martial arts a mainstream sport? "I wouldn't consider it mainstream in the sense that it's not like the NBA or NFL," said Dave Meltzer. "I don't know where it would sit on the list. To me, mainstream means when you go and talk to your parents and list off some names... see if they know who you are talking about. If they do, that means mainstream." He went on to say that in another 10 years, if the sport keeps growing like it is, and the fans of today have kids who will ask them that question, the sport is mainstream. "It's on the verge of getting there." This author originally called this chapter "Fighting for a Renegade Sport." While renegade certainly no longer fits, it would be a true assumption that all of the people who have worked so hard to make this a viable sport are fighting to make it mainstream. And they can do that every day by wearing TapouT shirts, showing someone a magazine article, or inviting them over for a Saturday night to watch a UFC pay-per-view.

While MMA has been dubbed "the fastest growing sport in the world," mmapayout.com proved that factoid in an article called "The UFC Fan Base," on November 29, 2010. According to the site, it mined data from Simmons Research Database, comparing the UFC to the NFL, MLB, NBA, NHL, NASCAR, and MLS. According to the research, the size of the UFC fan base is 31 million people. Simmons also recorded that the UFC and NHL were the only two "sports" that could grow their avid fan bases over the three years. While the data suggested a male/female split of 75/25, it also pointed to the fact that the numbers for the 18–34 demographic weren't so different from that of the NFL or MLB. While mmapayout.com says that the NFL is "the" model to follow, according to Simmons data, there has been a 30 percent increase in growth by the UFC. "The UFC owns an interest level commensurate with lower-tier sports leagues like the NHL and MLS; no one would dismiss the fan bases of those two leagues as insignificant," the site said.

From November 12, 1993, a sport-in-the-making evolved from the concept of testing martial arts in a reality-based setting. It needed a little extra sauce on the steak to make it work, but the taste grew more inviting. The fight outside the cage continued long after the politicians and the media gave up on it. The sport only got stronger, and while it had to prove itself time and time again, finally people took notice thanks to the countless efforts of a grassroots movement born out of the Internet age. Bombarded with top-flight programming on television and through commercials and film, new fans don't have to face those old enigmas of a bloodsport that made people feel guilty to watch. Fans are educated, and they are drawn to this new age of warrior who could just as well be the kid from college as he could be the businessman that works in the office down the way. To quote Dan Severn, MMA is the ultimate test of mental and physical fortitude, and the athletes and the sport itself are only getting stronger. The only history left is seeing how the fighter of today will stack up against the fighter of tomorrow. Let this tome stand the test of time for all those who have sacrificed so much to make mixed martial arts what it is today and what it will be for the future.

26

JAPANESE MMA: HISTORY AND BEYOND

Japan's MMA genesis can arguably be traced to pro wrestling when Antonio Inoki and Akira Maeda put themselves over by beating top fighters from other martial arts in mostly worked bouts. Though Brazilian jiu-jitsu paved the way for the UFC and similar events in the U.S., pro wrestling served as the springboard for MMA in the Land of the Rising Sun.

In the 1960s and 1970s, American pro wrestler Karl Gotch, known for his legit submission wrestling abilities as a "shooter," was invited by Antonio Inoki to teach wrestlers for his New Japan Pro Wrestling (NJPW) organization. Gotch and Inoki even faced off in the inaugural NJPW show on March 6, 1972. The Japanese pro wrestlers really liked the shoot style of pro wrestling as compared to the theatrics embraced by the American scene. Gotch taught Inoki, Akira Maeda, Satoru Sayama, and Yoshiaki Fujiwara, four men whose legacy kick-started the Japanese MMA scene.

While Inoki continued to wrestle shooters with NJPW, Akira Maeda had other plans. Maeda started pro wrestling at age 18 in 1977. At 6'4"and well over 200 pounds, a giant by Japanese standards, he quickly became one of the group's most popular wrestlers. Maeda eventually left New Japan and started Universal Wrestling Federation (UWF), where the new shoot style could have its own forum. When he was joined by rising star Satoru Sayama—better known as the original "Tiger Mask"—as well as Yoshiaki Fujiwara and Nobuhiko Takada, the organization flourished, developing a harder style of stiff-worked matches using solid ground techniques with open-hand strikes. Dissention in the ranks, however, built to a head when a pro wrestling match between Maeda and Sayama turned into a real fight. The company folded soon after, and Maeda, Fujiwara, and Takada eventually returned to NJPW in 1986. In November 1987, Maeda was involved in another ruckus with pro wrestler Riki Choshu and was kicked out of the organization.

Sayama moved out on his own and began prepping fighters for a new organization called Shooto. Though Sayama had been one of the most flamboyant Japanese pro wrestlers, the organization that debuted in 1987 promoted shoots only—the first of its kind in Japan. Sayama would often come out to the uniquely staged mat that originally hosted the fights and perform an impromptu exhibition of what the audience might see, plus a little showboating.

Maeda and Takada restarted the UWF in 1988, and Maeda, following in Inoki's footsteps, put himself over by fighting legit outsiders. His first big match was against Holland's Gerard Gordeau in August 1988. After defeating another Dutchman, Chris Dolman, in May 1989, he beat judo silver medalist Willie Wilhelm in November 1989 in what became the first Tokyo Dome sellout of any combat sport. Even Mike Tyson vs. Buster Douglas couldn't sell out the venue. But despite its initial success, the promotion folded on December 1, 1990.

Nobuhiko Takada formed Union of Wrestling Forces International (UWFI) using leftover UWF talent soon after. According to Steve Nelson, who wrestled for the organization, no one really knew any submission holds and everyone was basically learning together. "We would train five days before the night of the show and frequently had the best Americans spar with the Japanese wrestlers," said Nelson.

Using his contacts from Europe, Maeda created Rings, which debuted on May 11, 1991. It looked similar to UWF, but Maeda made enough slight changes to sell the show as being completely legit. In reality, most of the matches were stiff worked, save for the occasional shoot involving non-Japanese. Maeda spun off the Rings name to form the Rings Fighting

Network that would encompass Ring incarnations in other countries. Most European Rings matches were shoot, save for those involving occasional marquee Japanese fighters.

On March 4, 1991, Yoshiaki Fujiwara stepped into the spotlight by starting Pro Wrestling Fujiwaragumi (PWFG). The organization enjoyed great success, partly due to the addition of Masakatsu Funaki and Minoru Suzuki, who had both wrestled for NJPW and the UWF. While American Bart Vale had close ties with Fujiwara in the new organization, Ken Shamrock's impressive debut in 1992 made him one of Japan's few non-Japanese breakout stars. (Ken initially went by the name Wayne Shamrock because he had worked on tour for All Japan Pro Wrestling using his real name, and the UWF didn't want Japanese fans thinking he was a pro wrestler.)

Eventually, Funaki grew tired of putting over older wrestlers like Fujiwara, and he too wanted to branch out on his own. On September 21, 1993, Funaki launched Pancrase with Suzuki and Shamrock. Pancrase looked like Rings and employed similar rules, but it promoted mostly shoot fights.

After the success of the UFC, Satoru Sayama and investors promoted Japan Vale Tudo '94, a gala MMA event copromoted by Frederico Lapenda with Rickson Gracie competing in an eight-man tournament. Gracie tore through the competition to take the top prize, establishing himself in Japan just as Royce had done in the States. Yoji Anjo, Takada's UWFI stablemate, thought he could become a star by fighting the Brazilian so he flew to Los Angeles with press in tow for an impromptu challenge. On December 7, 1994, Rickson beat Anjo down for three minutes inside his local gym. The press wasn't allowed to view the fight, only the aftermath—Anjo waking up from being choked out.

Back in Japan, "everyone expected Takada to seek revenge as the head of the stable in Japanese martial arts tradition," said pro wrestling expert Dave Meltzer. "Takada's fans thought he was the real deal since UWFI was sold as being legit and Takada was the star of the group. When he didn't work to make the Rickson match happen, and didn't challenge him, UWFI fans lost [respect for] Takada." The UWFI suffered as a result. Steve Nelson remembered the scene quite vividly. "Takada embarrassed the company. Between the Japanese reporters taking pictures of the fight, running the story, and hiring Van Vader (a pro wrestler from American promotion World Championship Wrestling) and allowing him to wear his mask, they ruined one of the top companies in Japan." The UWFI ended up needing NJPW to bail the company out of debt in exchange for Takada losing the world championship to NJPW's Keiji Mutoh on May 3, 1995. After problems with New Japan and failing to align successfully with other groups, the UWFI held its final show on December 27, 1996. Some former UWFI members then joined Takada's upstart stiff-worked pro wrestling show, Kingdom, which had ties with the group copromoting the UFC Japan show the following year. UWFI members Yoji Anjo and Kazushi Sakuraba competed on that card.

◆ ◆ ◆

AFTER REBUILDING HIMSELF, Takada fought Rickson Gracie for a new organization called Pride on October 11, 1997, in front of 47,000 fans. The show featured several UFC alumni with Gracie vs. Takada headlining. It took Gracie less than five minutes to submit the pro wrestler with an arm bar. Kakutougi Revolution Spirits (KRS), the company that produced Pride, wanted to take up where Japan Vale Tudo left off by creating an ongoing promotion to topple the fledgling pro wrestling scene. Realizing both Renzo and Rickson Gracie would win their matches, they cut deals with John Dixson and Nathan Jones (who played the giant that Brad Pitt killed at the beginning of *Troy*) to work their bouts against Japanese opponents, according to Dixson.

Frequently, Japanese promotions will bring in outsiders to serve as tomato cans for Japanese fighters, throwing money at them on late notice to make the journey. Often the outsider hasn't had time to prepare and succumbs to the readied Japanese fighter. KRS needed to build Takada back up with another bout and wasn't about to take any chances. "The key for Pride's early success was Takada," said Meltzer. "It was okay that he lost, but he needed to win some of the time." American Kyle Sturgeon was secured to throw the match against Takada at Pride 3. "We had all the details worked out for Kyle to lose the match against Takada around the 10-minute mark," said Sturgeon's former manager, Clint Dahl. "I remember getting a call from him in Japan the night before the fight. He told me the Brazilians were egging him on to beat Takada anyway and deviate from the plan. I informed him that KRS had make it very clear that if Sturgeon doesn't do the job, he won't be coming back home." During the fight, Sturgeon threw a high kick a little too hard and dropped Takada to the canvas. Nervous that he would not get up, Sturgeon danced around, wasting enough time for Takada to regain his composure. Takada submitted Sturgeon with a heel hook less than a minute later.

The win set up the rematch between Takada and Rickson Gracie; it took nearly 10 minutes for the Brazilian to submit him this time. Despite over 30,000 people in attendance, Pride 4 would be the final event for KRS. The company sold Pride to Dreamstage Entertainment, which drove the franchise to record attendance numbers, American pay-per-view, and steady merchandise sales. Dreamstage knew it had to make an impact by leveraging the pro wrestling fan base with real fighting. Takada was obviously someone they had to protect. After dropping three bouts in a row, former UFC champion Mark Coleman was given an offer he couldn't refuse to drop a bout to Takada at Pride 5. "I had no other choice," said Coleman. "I had a child and another one on the way. If I didn't have any kids, maybe I wouldn't have done that. I was absolutely backed into a corner. Bills were coming in, and the UFC wasn't going to pay me squat, so I did it and I'm not ashamed of it at all." A year later, Coleman would sweep the Pride Grand Prix 2000 16-man tournament for real and get his comeuppance.

With Takada's days as a viable star numbered, Kazushi Sakuraba became the unexpected answer. His first Pride wins over Vernon White and Carlos Newton proved the victory over Conan Silveira at UFC Japan was no fluke. Sakuraba wasn't a big draw in Kingdom, but his skills as a shooter made him Pride's poster boy. After frustrating and decisioning Vitor Belfort, Sakuraba faced off against Royler Gracie at Pride 8 on November 21, 1999. "Takada couldn't keep competing forever, so when Sakuraba defeated Royler Gracie, that was the true birth of Pride as a company," said Meltzer. Sakuraba would become known as "The Gracie Hunter" and ended up defeating Royce, Renzo, and Ryan Gracie. Eventually, Sakuraba burned himself out by not maintaining his health (bad smoking and drinking habits) and fighting in too many matches against tough opposition.

Dreamstage followed a traditional pro wrestling strategy by building up fighters against tomato cans until they were ready to fight for a belt. Most cards featured one-sided fights mixed with a couple of well-matched bouts. But the colorful characters, production design, and raw energy were hard to dismiss. When Dreamstage first took over the organization, it relied on using Japanese pro wrestlers to drive ticket sales, but outside of Sakuraba, most couldn't cut it against top opponents. Dreamstage even tried promoting a pro wrestling bout between Takada and Alexander Otsuka at Pride 8, but it didn't seem to work. Now Pride had stars from Brazil, Russia, and the U.S., along with a few Japanese thrown in for good measure.

On August 28, 2002, Dreamstage pulled off its biggest show to date by cross-promoting with K-1, Japan's premier kickboxing organization. Shockwave 2002 or K-1 Dynamite (the promotion went by both names) drew 71,000 fans, the largest audience ever assembled for an MMA promotion. Since Dreamstage came onto the scene, it attracted several UFC stars but failed to break into the U.S. market. (Pride became Pride Fighting Championships to play off the UFC name.) Delayed pay-per-views and two American shows couldn't do much to build the brand. Pride even started hosting tournaments that became a big hit for new fans, who missed the drama of the early UFC format. But K-1 had a plan of its own, and Pride found competition right in its own backyard.

◆ ◆ ◆

MASTER KAZUYOSHI ISHII ESTABLISHED seidokan karate schools around Osaka in the 1970s and staged countless karate tournaments during the late 1980s. In 1991, he worked for one year in the front office for Maeda's Rings organization, learning about pro wrestling angles and marketing stars—the missing ingredients to take his own promotional aspirations to the next level. In 1993, Ishii invented K-1, a splashy kickboxing show with colorful athletes and world-class production. "K" stood for many martial arts styles (karate, kung fu, kickboxing) while "1" represented only one weight class: heavyweight. The K-1 Grand Prix became the hot ticket in Japan, where year after year the elite eight fighters from around the world met in a one-night, winner-take-all tournament, much like the original UFC. Dutchmen Ernesto Hoost and Peter Aerts became superstars, and with Fuji Television onboard, the promotion sold out shows all over Japan and in European countries. K-1 twice failed to break into the American market before establishing a smaller-scale, success-ful promotion in Las Vegas in 1999 under the watchful eye of eventual Strikeforce promoter Scott Coker.

Moving into 2000, the organization faced trouble as K-1's stars were get-ting old, Master Ishii was looking at jail time for tax evasion, and Pride was gaining momentum. Enter Bob Sapp, a 377-pound, 6'4" former pro football player whose injuries sidelined a promising career. Sapp was spotted in a toughman contest against ex-Chicago Bear William "The Refrigerator" Perry. His sloppy skills beat the out-of-shape Perry, and K-1 liked his look. Taking a gamble, they decided to transform him into a fighter. Sapp was flown to Seattle, Washington, and began training for kickboxing under the tutelage of K-1/UFC kickboxer Maurice Smith and for submission wrestling under Matt Hume. K-1 allowed Sapp to fight for Pride first, and after destroying his opponent, Norihisa Yamamoto, he competed in several kickboxing matches with great success. The audience couldn't get enough of Sapp and loved his over-the-top personality and superhuman girth.

Nicknamed "The Beast," he bounced between Pride and K-1 until the latter made him their signature star. Sapp resurrected the K-1 franchise with dozens of sponsorship tie-ins and TV appearances, becoming a national icon in Japan. He even released a record entitled *Sapp Time*; the album cover ripping off Michael Jackson's *Thriller*. Sapp's unbelievable success transformed K-1 into something of a circus act by bringing in over-the-hill boxers like Francois Botha (who lost his first four K-1 bouts) and old sumo wrestlers like Yokozuna Akebono in the hopes of creating another Sapp. Unfortunately, K-1 lost a lot of credibility as a kickboxing promotion in the process. (K-1 Max, featuring lightweight fighters, did earn the respect of honest kickboxing fans throughout the world.)

In 2003, K-1 signed a promotional contract with Mike Tyson, putting the company in the spotlight with a debut set for 2004. Even K-1 wasn't safe from scrutiny and misinformation, as evidenced by this April 2004 quote from World Boxing Council President Jose Sulaiman. "The World Boxing Council deeply regrets the fact that the great world ex-heavyweight champion Mike Tyson is thinking of the possibility of contending in a sport known as K-1, which represents a huge and regrettable return to the most savage times in which respect to human life did not exist at all—as this 'sport' is one of the most violent and less humane practices anyone can ever witness." One week later, K-1 announced that Tyson would stick with boxing, under their new banner—Fighting Entertainment Group, but nothing ever really came up; Tyson was washed up, and a subsequent matchup with Bob Sapp was put on ice.

K-1 became a profitable powerhouse relying on pro wrestling gimmickry over conventional sports wisdom. On December 10, 1994, K-1 promoted its first MMA bout between UFC alumni Kimo and Pat Smith, held in an Octagon. K-1's top stars commented on the fight, saying it wasn't a real sport. Nearly a decade later, K-1 started promoting MMA-only cards, luring fighters from other promotions with top-dollar purses. Ishii eventually stepped down from K-1 but never served a day in jail. Today K-1 is still running strong, and though some of the older fighters still compete, a clear superstar has yet to emerge. Like so many pro wrestling promotions, real or scripted, popularity comes and goes.

◆ ◆ ◆

ON FEBRUARY 15, 2002, Maeda officially promoted the last Rings Japan show. Rings couldn't compete with Pride and made the erroneous decision of moving to shoots with closed-fist strikes. Most people thought this added credibility to the organization by enriching the promotion to compete against Pride, but Rings fans were pro wrestling fans. When stars like Kiyoshi Tamura could no longer be protected, the fan base dried up. Rings Japan went through many ups and downs, but it ended on a high note by producing two of the most interesting 32-man tournaments in the sport's history. Rings wasn't completely dead and continued to produce regular shows in Holland and Lithuania. Pride was more than happy to take Rings' talent, cleaning them out with Brazilians Rodrigo "Minotauro" Nogueira and Ricardo Arona, Russian Fedor Emelianenko, and Dutchman Gilbert Yvel. Pride destroyed Tamura by having the 185-pounder face Wanderlei Silva and the monstrous Bob Sapp back to back, instead of rebuilding him as their new star.

Since its inception, Pancrase turned out many great champions under founder Masakatsu Funaki, including Ken and Frank Shamrock, Bas Rutten, Guy Mezger, Semmy Schilt, Yuki Kondo, and Nate Marquardt. In the late 1990s, the promotion lost steam and money and even changed its rules to incorporate closed-fist strikes as well. By that time, the stars were gone and the fans were tuning in to Pride. Founder Masakatsu Funaki competed in a retirement match against Rickson Gracie in Coliseum, a joint effort between Pancrase and Rings. Though Funaki lost by choke, he stayed on with the organization he created and became a film actor to boot, appearing in a modern sequel in the Godzilla franchise. Today, Pancrase no longer sells out the major venues and is almost completely devoid of foreign talent. That said, they are still actively promoting shows and staying in the game.

The country's longest-running and most consistent series, Shooto, stayed active by focusing on the lighter weight classes. Fighters like Rumina Sato, Hayato Sakurai, Takanori Gomi, and Caol Uno became legends, but the promotion's appeal is strictly for hard-core fans. Sayato Sayama eventually left Shooto and turned back to his roots in pro wrestling, but Shooto has never promoted a worked match in its history.

◆ ◆ ◆

DESPITE DECENT RATINGS, Pride had its share of problems, and on January 8, 2003, a bombshell dropped on the MMA community. Pride President Naoto Morishita called a press conference to announce both a middleweight and heavyweight grand prix to be spread out over the coming months and then returned to his hotel room. At 12:20 AM, Morishita was found dead from an apparent suicide by hanging. Rumors surfaced that his death could be attributed to everything from a romantic affair gone awry to continuing pressure from Dream Stage brass to improve revenue figures. No one knew for sure, and many thought Pride was officially dead.

Nobuhiko Takada took over for the interim before Dream Stage hired Nobuyuki Sakakibara, who was Morishita's right-hand man, to be the new president. Takada would now serve as general director for the organization, but his role was rumored to be largely that of a public figurehead. With the change, Pride put plans to enter the U.S. market (Dream Stage obtained a NSAC license in 2003) on the backburner and started a sister organization called Pride Bushido showcasing lighter-weight fighters.

December 31, 2003, will be a day that all Japanese fight fans remember. Pride Shockwave 2003 headlined Royce Gracie vs. former Olympic judo medalist Hidehiko Yoshida; K-1 promoted its first MMA-heavy show with Sapp vs. Akebono; and Antonio Inoki assembled a lackluster card borrowing stars from Pride and K-1. In the end, K-1 won the ratings war and made a statement that Pride wasn't the only show in town. As for Inoki, to this day, no one really knows just how much power he wields in Japan. Despite nearly destroying pro wrestling with the Ali debacle, his name has reached iconic proportions. After promoting MMA bouts in three separate promotions, Inoki took a formal position with K-1.

• • •

DESPITE ZUFFA TAKING CONTROL of the UFC, Pride Fighting Championships had managed to build the greatest heavyweight stable of fighters in the world. After mining the befallen Rings, nearly every show highlighted major bouts among the sport's top heavyweights. Croatian Mirko "Cro Cop" Filipovic became one of the promotion's biggest stars, as did Brazilian Rodrigo "Minotauro" Nogueira and Russian Fedor Emelianenko. Even Pride's lower weight classes were strong with American Quinton "Rampage" Jackson, Brazilians Wanderlei Silva and Mauricio "Shogun" Rua, and of course Kazushi Sakuraba was still a main draw. But even before the apparent "suicide" of Pride President Naoto Morishita, rumors had circulated that Pride was a front for the Japanese yakuza. Pride may have had some of the best fighters in the world, but they couldn't stop Japan-based Fuji Network from terminating all of Dream Stage's contracts for Pride, Pride Bushido, etc. on June 5, 2006. "When Pride lost TV over that scandal, I knew Pride was done," said Dave Melzter. "Had they trimmed their business and tried to survive, maybe they could have lasted, but when they couldn't get TV, you pretty much knew that was it."

Just a few months earlier on April 7, 2006, Dream Stage signed a deal with gaming industry pioneer Ed Fishman to pay him $200,000 a year plus 10 percent of ticket sales to become the chairman and co-promoter of Dream Stage Entertainment USA to promote American events. On October 21, 2006, Pride made its American debut with its 32nd show dubbed "Real Deal." Although gate figures toppled $2 million, far below what the promotion would get in Japan, pay-per-view buy rates were 40,000. By comparison, just 28 days later UFC 65 pulled in around the same gate figures, but buy rates were estimated to be 500,000. Dream Stage would promote a second show in America ironically called "Second Coming" on February 24, 2007.

One month later on March 27, Zuffa made a landmark announce-ment to purchase Pride—the price tag rumored to be anything from $12 million to over $70 million. At a press conference held on that day, it was agreed that Pride President Nubuyuki Sakaibara would step down after one final show, Pride 34: Kamikaze, on April 8. Zuffa co-owner Loreno Fertitta was quoted as saying, "This is really going to change the face of MMA. Literally creating a sport that could be as big around the world as soccer. I liken it somewhat to when the NFC and AFC came together to create the NFL." Months later, Dana White told Dave Meltzer that the purchase was "the worst deal done in the history of business." Zuffa would be unable to secure a new television deal for Pride; White professed the difficulties of working in Japan and that he wasn't welcome. On October 4, the Pride Japan office was closed down. All 20 employees were terminated over the phone. Pride Fighting Championships was officially dead. It's questionable as to what Zuffa actually got out of the deal, aside from video rights to broadcast old shows on U.S. cable television. Zuffa had to renegotiate fighter contracts, Mirko Cro Cop had already defected before the sale, and they didn't get Fedor Emelianenko, who was Pride's No. 1 heavyweight.

The Japanese scene today is unfortunately a shell of its former self. "It's been going down for a long time," said Meltzer. "The big problem is that they needed a world beater, someone like Sakuraba. Yoshida was big for a bit and won a lot of matches; they thought he was a world beater and a big deal." On February 13, 2008, former Dream Stage executives banded together with another Japanese promotion, Hero's, and formed Dream. The promotion can certainly be called the second coming of Pride, but it's nowhere near the heyday of the latter, with few notable stars. On September 25, 2010, Dream 16 was held as a supposed last-ditch effort to raise ratings and bring an influx of capital into the cash-strapped company. But ratings dropped, and now Dream may have died or has little chance for survival. The Japanese MMA scene could have an entire book written about its vast history and contribution to the sport overall. And like all product cycles, it may have run its course...for now. But the future of this great sport is never-ending, and Japan has the talent and the fan base—it just needs a new hero.

27

MMA AROUND THE WORLD

Brazil

Brazilian vale tudo had dried up during the early 1990s until the UFC came along. The controversial decision in the Marco Ruas–Oleg Taktarov fight at Ultimate Ultimate '95 prompted Ruas' manager Frederico Lapenda to rebuild the fighter by staging the World Vale Tudo Championship (WVC). Debuting August 4, 1996, the first show was held in Japan, implementing the standard eight-man heavyweight tournament with few rules and bare fists. The headliner pitted Ruas against UFC III champ Steve Jennum. The ex-cop didn't stand a chance, while Taktarov, who faced Joe Charles, also won his match with ease.

Lapenda set up the rematch between Ruas and Taktarov for WVC 2 in Brazil, just 11 months after their first meeting. This time Ruas pummeled Taktarov for 30 minutes. The two battled toe-to-toe with no groundwork, but this was by design. "[Lapenda] wanted to make this fight look so good that he paid me extra money at the time," said Taktarov. "We reached an agreement where I would not fight Marco on the ground." According to Ruas, Lapenda told him he was not allowed to kick the Russian. "He said that if I kick, I have to pay Oleg $1,000. Then he said that I would have to fight with open hand. I refused, but said I wouldn't kick. Then during the fight, Oleg kicked me first, so I kicked [back]. After the fight, Oleg's manager tried to sue and there were a lot of problems. Oleg agreed not to take me down." For 29 minutes, Taktarov stood and took a beating. As the final minute ticked away, Taktarov's corner said the word, and the Russian took Ruas down immediately and established half mount just to show he could.

The match was ruled a draw under their agreement, since Ruas couldn't knock him out and the fight went the distance. "That fight was a draw because both of our hands were up when I was there," said Taktarov. "When everyone left, [Lapenda] raised Ruas' hand while he stood by himself." Only the shot of Ruas as the winner appeared on the video. Taktarov wanted to set up a third fight, but no one was interested. According to Lapenda, his referee Sergio Batarelli had theorized that Ruas was being underpaid versus what Lapenda was getting from the broadcaster. "Ruas came to me and doubted me," said Lapenda. "He said I was pocketing extra money, and I was really hurt by that because I was a very loyal manager. I created the show for Marco because I thought the Ultimate was unfair." Lapenda and Ruas parted ways. On March 7, 2002, the WVC promoted its final show in Jamaica. Lapenda had made a lasting impact on the Brazilian scene, not only with the WVC, but by creating the World Vale Tudo Council that presided over the WVC and other events like the Brazilian Vale Tudo series. Teaming up with Dutch promoter Bas Boon, he also produced the Absolute Fighting Championship in Russia and was responsible for producing the immensely popular *The Smashing Machine*, starring former WVC and UFC star Mark Kerr. He currently lives in Los Angeles, where he works as a successful low-budget film producer.

Lapenda's original referee, former kickboxer Sergio Batarelli, started the International Vale Tudo Championship (IVC) when personal problems forced him to leave after WVC 4. Batarelli employed similar rules and built the show around Brazilian talent but brought in several Westerners for the first event, held July 7, 1997. In the eight-man tournament, Gary Goodridge made it to the finals to face Pedro Otavio, who wore down his larger opponent on the ground. During the 16-minute match, Goodridge held Otavio in his guard, using his feet to keep him out of striking range. Goodridge's tactic worked until his toes started wiggling inside Otavio's trunks. "My foot slipped out the back of his pants, so I'm trying to pull them back, and I felt his jock, so I thought, *why don't I just kick his jock out, and I'll freakin' knee him in the nuts?"* remembered Goodridge. After a brief restart, the two fell into the same position, where Otavio complained to ref Batarelli about Goodridge's actions. Batarelli let them continue, and Goodridge finally gained the upper hand, tapping out Otavio with strikes. Rumors circulated that Goodridge was playing footsie with Otavio's balls. "Sergio owed me $22,000 and told me that I ruined his show," said Goodridge. "I told him to keep the money, and let's get a doctor to inspect his testicles. If there's anything wrong with them, you keep the money. They didn't want to go that route." On October 16, 1998, Batarelli copromoted UFC Brazil, giving Americans their first glimpse at Brazilians Pedro Rizzo and IVC star Wanderlei Silva. The IVC made a superstar out of Wanderlei Silva and out of Silva's fellow team member at the time, Jose "Pele" Landi-Jons. One of the latter's toughest fights was against a green Chuck Liddell, who he dropped with a head kick. "Yeah, that was fun. The look on his face when I stood up was worth it to me," said Liddell. "I made his face drop; it was great." Liddell won by unanimous decision and said it was a great experience. It took the UFC 12 years to return to Brazil with an event aptly named UFC Rio on August 27, 2011, but Batarelli soldiered on, producing IVCs in Venezuela, Yugoslavia, and Portugal. After producing the last IVC in 2003, he continued his involvement in the vale tudo scene.

Two months after the inaugural IVC, Pentagon Combat took place in Rio de Janeiro, setting up a grudge match between luta livre's Eugenio Tadeu and jiu-jitsu's Renzo Gracie. Ill will between these two fighting factions put this event in the history books for a different reason. According to event promoter Nelson Monteiro, 10 minutes into their battle, "members of the luta livre group invaded the outer ring area and also started climbing the ring's lighting structure. Because of the weight of the people, the light structure started collapsing." As tension built, the angry luta livre mob got out of hand, and someone stabbed Renzo in the back with a sharp object. "A riot broke out, complete anarchy, chairs were flying, fists were flying, even gunshots were being fired, and all coming from the luta livre side," said Monteiro. Talk of banning vale tudo in Brazil worried fans but eventually subsided after safer security measures became prevalent in future shows.

The rivalry between jiu-jitsu and luta livre eventually petered out, but a milder rift surfaced between the Brazilian Top Team (BTT) and the Chute Boxe Academy. Both Brazilian schools turned out top talent, and Pride Fighting Championships had their hooks in both, keeping the conflict in the ring. BTT emerged from a fallout between Carlson Gracie and his students. Under the leadership of Ze Mario Sperry, the team consisted of Murilo Bustamante, Ricardo Arona, and identical twins Rodrigo and Rogerio Nogueira. Rodrigo could arguably be called the best heavyweight submission fighter in the world, using his long arms and legs to trap his opponents when they made a mistake. Hailing from Bahia, Brazil, he hungered for sports growing up, until a life-threatening accident at age 11. A bus plowed into the youngster, first leaving him in a coma and then without hope of walking for nearly two years. With badly scarred lungs that required 13 operations, Rodrigo defied the odds, taking up boxing as part of his recuperation. Eventually he began training in jiu-jitsu with Carlson Gracie disciples. In his twenties, he moved to Florida to join his mother and brother Rogerio. When Rodrigo started competing in Japan, first in Rings and then in Pride, he moved back to his native land and joined Brazilian Top Team. After becoming the 2000 Rings King of Kings champion, he moved over to Pride, defeating several marquee names to ultimately become the Pride heavyweight champion. His favorite move was the triangle choke, but Rodrigo continually surprised his opponents by pulling submissions from any position. After the fall of Pride, Rodrigo and Rogerio defected to the UFC and enjoyed long careers.

In 1980, Rudimar Fedrigo opened the Chute Boxe Academy (*Chute Boxe* means *Muay Thai* in Brazil) in Curitiba and assembled one of the toughest groups of fighters to ever come out of the country. Unlike most Brazilian teams, the Chute Boxe Academy relied more on striking as its base, though jiu-jitsu was part of the program as well. A war with capoeira fighters prompted Fedrigo to stage his first vale tudo event in 1991; Chute Boxe won all their matches. On November 1, 1996, Campeonato Brasileiro de Vale Tudo saw Chute Boxe student Jose "Pele" Landi-Jons win a four-man tournament, ending with a defeat over BJJ black belt Jorge "Macaco" Patino. The back-and-forth action lasted nearly 15 minutes, and it became one of the most talked about fights in modern Brazilian vale tudo history. Both men developed a hatred for one another, and Pele won the rematch at WVC 4 after Patino's overzealous efforts forced him out of the ring, stopping the fight on a cut. Though he was one of Fedrigo's first students, Pele left Chute Boxe in 2002, while strangely enough, Patino joined a year later. The team fielded great fighters, including Mauricio "Shogun" Rua, brother Murilo "Ninja" Rua, and Anderson Silva, but when people think of the team, only one name comes to mind: Wanderlei Silva. After the fallout from Pride, they all went their separate ways, with Anderson Silva becoming one of the pound-for-pound best UFC middleweight champions. Though Anderson Silva enjoyed success outside the UFC, he became virtually unstoppable after jumping on the Zuffa train. With his long, wiry body type, he can strike from odd angles and knock out an opponent before they ever see it coming. As a BJJ black belt, he is just as dangerous on the ground, equally submitting the same level of fighter he can best standing up. Former Pride middleweight champion Mauricio "Shogun" Rua also enjoyed similar success in the UFC at light heavyweight, while Wanderlei Silva has reinvented himself as a more cerebral fighter at 185 pounds.

Without a doubt, Wanderlei Silva had the most spot-on, ferocious staredowns in the sport, with his menacing scowl, shaven and tattooed head, and vicious fighting style. Growing up in Curitiba, Brazil, Silva joined the Chute Boxe Academy at age 13, learning discipline, and competing first in kickboxing before a brief stint in the Brazilian army. After several bloody vale tudo battles in Brazil, he enjoyed huge success in Pride, but his overzealousness cost him several matches. At UFC Brazil, he wanted to show off his skills against fellow Brazilian Vitor Belfort, but didn't get the chance, as "The Phenom" crushed him in 53 seconds. Silva recommitted his work ethic, improved with every fight, and eventually became the long-term Pride middleweight champion. One of his biggest tests came at Pride 13 when he faced Kazushi Sakuraba, who had dispatched many top Brazilians, including Belfort. At 1:38 into the first round, Silva stomped Sakuraba's face into mush. He went on to defeat Sakuraba (twice), Guy Mezger, and Quinton "Rampage" Jackson. Silva's popularity carried over to signing endorsement deals and doing Japanese commercials. After winning the Pride Grand Prix middleweight tournament, he seemed content to punish whoever was brave enough to step in the ring with him. Defecting to the UFC, he was no longer as dominant, trading wins and losses, but fans and opponents alike still remember the fearlessness he once bestowed in his prime years.

Although Brazil has produced many top stars that have moved abroad, the local scene has pretty much evaporated. Brazilian shows eventually started adopting Pride rules to better prepare their athletes for the big time, but Pride's death cut off many opportunities for the country's up-and-coming talent. Rudimar Fedrigo started Meca Vale Tudo in Curitiba in 2000, which became one of the country's top shows; it lasted five years. His Chute Boxe student, Rafael Cordeiro, copromoted Storm Samurai, a Muay Thai event; it lasted four years from 2003 to 2007. Rodrigo Nogueira got into the promotion game by starting Conquista Fight in Bahia that lasted four shows. In July 2003, Heat Fighting Championship debuted in Natal, stepping up the Brazilian scene with better production value; it promoted two other shows and folded in 2005. In mid-2007, American Jason Atkins of Florida-based Tough Sports Live launched Rio Heroes, which actually turned out to be a misnomer since partner and BJJ black belt Jorge Pereira meant to say "real heroes." The name stuck, and the plan was to stage good old-fashioned, bare-knuckle, "anything goes" vale tudo fights in parking lots and gyms. That lasted a year and a half before the Brazilian government shut them down; it became popularized on the *Howard Stern Show*, which crashed Rio Heroes' servers trying to broadcast an Internet pay-per-view.

Today, it's a toss-up as to who will survive and keep the Brazilian vale tudo legacy going. Amaury Bitetti, who fought at UFC IX, started Bitetti

Combat Nordeste in 2002, and it still continues today. Wallid Ismail, who spent time working with Antonio Inoki, started Jungle Fights in the Amazon on September 13, 2003. Seven years later and with a judgment from Pro Elite, he has produced 22 events, the last being in Sao Paulo, Brazil. Ismail may end up being the promoter who keeps the spirit of vale tudo alive in the country that started it all.

Europe

In January 1990, Akira Maeda traveled to Holland and met up with Chris Dolman, a multitime sambo and judo champion who popularized his name by competing in stiff-worked pro wrestling matches in Japan. The two hatched an idea to take Maeda's Rings to the next level, and by March 1991, the Rings Fighting Network was born. Starting with Rings Holland run by Dolman, the promotion branched out to Russia, Georgia, Bulgaria, Australia, and the U.S. Dolman is considered the godfather of European MMA, as he paved the way for homegrown talent to cross over into the Rings organization. European Rings shows rarely promoted works, but the rules were the same, allowing for open-hand strikes, rope escapes, and submissions.

Even with Rings taking off, the more brutal style of MMA reared its head in Europe. Headbutts, elbows, and bare fists were commonplace. Men like "Dirty" Bob Schrijber, who had well over 100 kickboxing matches, didn't care; it was just another fight. In June 1993, Schrijber competed in his first Rings match upon winning the European Kickboxing Championship. He also competed in one of the first closed-fist MMA bouts in Europe, called the Cage Fight Tournament, held in Belgium in January 1995. Due to the lack of alternates and lack of submission experience, Schrijber fought twice and lost twice in the same night. He began training with Dolman, Remco Pardoel, and others to understand the submission game. Schrijber's ring prowess was outmatched only by his looks, which included polka dot dye in his hair before he shaved it bald. As one of Holland's biggest stars, he hung up his gloves in October 2003 upon losing five of his last six matches. He returned once in 2005 and once in 2008, losing both times. His wife, Irma Verhoeff, was also a well-known MMA fighter; she retired in 2004. Together they run Team Schrijber preparing the next crop of Dutch fighters, like UFC's Stefan Struve.

Fellow kickboxer Gilbert "The Hurricane" Yvel also emerged as a household name among Dutch MMA purists. Though he never seriously studied traditional martial arts, he took up Thai boxing at age 16, and after winning the European Full Contact Karate Championship, he signed on with Rings Holland. There he enjoyed much success, knocking out opponents left and right, mostly using his long legs and knees. Schrijber handed Yvel his first major loss to win the finals of a European promotion called KO Power Tournament. Yvel had met his real mother for the first time two days before their fight, and his mind was elsewhere. Schrijber had just lost to Yvel two months prior, and five years would pass before they met a third time. In 2002, Yvel knocked his fellow countryman out after a gutsy war.

Yvel, along with brothers Valentijn and Alistair Overeem, Remco Pardoel, and Semmy Schilt, formed Golden Glory. As Holland's premiere fighting team, they have competed in the U.S., Russia, Japan, Brazil, and Aruba in the West Indies. "We train hard, and we have the best trainers in Holland, who have produced many world champions," said Yvel. "Dutch people in general are pretty tall compared to fighters in other countries; it's a big advantage."

The man behind Golden Glory, Bas Boon, has also been the braintrust behind the Cage Fight Tournament events that broke new ground in Europe. "After the Belgium and Holland shows in 1996, the sport was still in a very negative light," said Boon. "But the controversy drew a lot of media attention that I pushed myself. The second Cage Fight Tournament in Emmen (Netherlands) in 1996 had a total viewership in Europe of over 38 million viewers, and the tone was set. It would still take a long fight to get the sport more regulated and accepted, though." He created Golden Glory after World Vale Tudo Championship 9 sparked interest in Dutch fighter Gilbert Yvel. He also took on American Heath Herring, whose B-level fighter status became a thing of the past after spending time with the rest of the crew. Boon has put Golden Glory fighters in the UFC, Pride, and K-1. Though many MMA stars have tried their hand at kickboxing, Golden Glory fighters Semmy Schilt and Alistair Overeem have won K-1 Grand Prix championships. Overeem became the first combat sports fighter to simultaneously hold titles in both MMA (Strikeforce) and K-1 when he won the K-1 2010 Grand Prix. Of course, Boon casts his fighters in several Holland promotions. 2 Hot 2 Handle was the flagship promotion in Holland, complete with laser light shows, a magic act, and even a miniature blimp that flew over the crowd. Boon has copromoted shows in several European countries, including Germany and Russia. Georgy Kobylyansky, who copromoted the inaugural IFC, started up the first Russian organization, Absolute Fighting Championship, but M-1 Mix-Fight has been the country's top show since 1997. The promotion builds fighters for the Red Devil Team, taking its name from a popular energy drink that also sponsors M-1, allowing Boon to cross-promote using his fighters. M-1, thanks to Russian heavyweight Fedor Emelianenko, became popularized in the States when the promotion cut a deal for its international tournament with HDNet Fights.

• • •

CHRIS DOLMAN AND RINGS also heavily influenced the UK scene. Bob Schrijber turned Lee Hasdell on to Rings after his pro kickboxing career grew stagnant. "Maeda saw me and invited me to study with him in Japan, so two months later I went to Rings Japan," said Hasdell. The soft-spoken Brit eventually formed Night of the Samurai, one of the UK's first promotions using rules similar to Rings, but it didn't last long. As British fighters began learning submission, other promotions came along. On December 5, 1999, Andy Jardine's Millennium Brawl gave rising British talent an opportunity to compete at home, but it folded in 2002. Cage Warriors Fighting Championships debuted in 2002 and promised to step things up to an international level. The promotion is still running strong today.

Mark Weir is something of an anomaly. He took up martial arts for the most basic need: survival. Growing up in a racially biased neighborhood, he needed protection and took up boxing, judo, and later tae kwon do. Martial arts was something that made his life complete, not just a hobby or an extension of childhood rage. After winning two tournament championships, Weir lost his motivation, and tae kwon do lost its luster. Everything changed after he saw the UFC. "Anybody who's looking to actually improve in martial arts as a whole will eventually end up in MMA, no matter what foundations or background you have."

Before *The Ultimate Fighter*, Britain was not that influential in the MMA world, as few competitors had fought abroad in bigger shows. The country was far behind Russia and Holland, which had both produced top names. Weir noted that part of the problem lied in the fact that martial arts never really took off as a whole in Britain: unlike judo's wide acceptance in France and Thai boxing's popularity in Holland, Britain never really claimed an art or a system of its own. Boxing is still the king of combat sports in Britain, where the Queensberry Rules originated. "[MMA] is new to this country; [Britain] is only beginning to accept it, and they're airing more about the sport on national TV," said Weir in 2002.

Britain's most active fighter for many years was Ian Freeman, who had competed in Japan, Holland, Russia, and the U.S. He never really had a martial arts background *per se* but learned boxing at age 20. "I was more of a brawler than a boxer," said Freeman, who migrated to jiu-jitsu after his fists failed to subdue an opponent when he was 32 years old. He never really understood groundfighting until real life showed him what he was missing. Freeman was puzzled by the early UFCs, wondering why they weren't standing up and fighting. After taking jiu-jitsu and finding success in his club, Freeman ventured out to test himself: part martial arts, part machismo practice. He found there was still much to learn.

On March 10, 2000, Freeman became the first Brit to compete in the UFC, fighting submission specialist Scott Adams on four days' notice. Freeman even paid for his own airfare. The match stayed competitive until both men went for leg locks. "Scott snapped the ligaments in my ankle three times in that fight, and afterwards I had to have a cast put on my leg," said Freeman. "I never knew how far the U.K. was behind the U.S.A. in terms of fighting until I entered the UFC. I was beating the best in the U.K. in less than five minutes, but it's a big step when you fight in America."

After losing to Adams, he had varied success worldwide. Freeman later chronicled his exploits in an autobiography, *The Machine*, in 2001, which described his moving from a 9-to-5 job as a salesman to an ultimate fighter. It was one of the first autobiographies from an MMA fighter. "Along the way I was beaten up by a gang of skinheads and spent a long time in the hospital, going into deep depression. I gained acceptance as a streetfighter in my hometown and began to lead an army of doormen. It is funny, [contains] horrific fight scenes, and most of all, it's enjoyable to read." Freeman loved fighting all over the world and ultimately retired in 2008.

• • •

BRITAIN AND THE REST OF EUROPE are growing more supportive of MMA. In 2001, the British Association of Mixed Martial Arts was established to bring attention to the sport. The rising number of European competitors means the sport's popularity will no longer be anchored by the U.S., Brazil, and Japan alone. The grassroots movement, along with promoters and pioneers like Bas Boon, Lee Hasdell, Bas Rutten, and U.K. fight promoter Chris Zorba, has sustained the growth of a sport whose flame has no chance of dying out...not now, not ever.

In 2002, Zuffa introduced a regular television program on the UFC to the U.K. market (on Sky). It failed to find an audience, but Zuffa was able to secure a pay-per-view deal for their shows. On July 13, 2002, UFC 38 was held at the famous Royal Albert Hall in London. The show was a huge success, with Mark Weir defeating Eugene Jackson with one of the fastest knockouts in UFC history: 10 seconds. Ian Freeman shocked everyone by beating down Frank Mir, forcing a ref stoppage and dedicating the fight to his father, who was in a nearby hospital. Freeman's father had actually passed away the night before the match, but his family didn't want to upset him with the news, knowing Freeman's father would have wanted him to do his best.

The event ended with an afterfight party that once again supplied extra fireworks. At a nearby bar, a friendly bit of roughhousing escalated into a street fight involving then UFC light heavyweight champ Tito Ortiz and Britain's Lee Murray. "Tito came right at me and hit me in the ear," said Murray, who gave his account to Dutch journalist Wiggert Meerman. "We clinched, and I punched him two straight ones, two uppercuts, and then he went down, and I kicked him in the face." Murray, who had a reputation for his powerful hands, made a name for himself in the States, but it didn't get him any offers. He knocked out Jose Landi-Jons in a local event exactly one year after UFC 38, earning his shot in the UFC six months later and a long-term contract. Unbelievably Murray's career was cut short when he was arrested on June 25, 2006, for his involvement with the Securitas depot robbery, the largest cash robbery in British history, estimated at $92.5 million. Murray would serve a 10-year jail sentence for his troubles.

In 2003, Granada, the U.K. company responsible for the infamous Michael Jackson exposé *Living with Michecl Jackson*, produced *Ultimate Warriors*, a 13-hour look at MMA and other combative sports. Camera crews were dispatched to the U.S., Japan, Thailand, and throughout Europe, interviewing hundreds of people. To date, it is the most comprehensive documentary series ever produced on the subject. For American fans, Englishman Michael Bisping is the most widely known European mixed martial artist, thanks to his participation in the third season of *The Ultimate Fighter*. The charismatic Bisping has the look of a marquee fighter and gives it his all every single time. After winning that season, he has been the UFC's primary vehicle for opening up Britain and gaining access to other European markets like Germany. Bisping would return to *TUF* to coach the ninth season called United States vs. United Kingdom where the Brits would win both weight classes. Since 2005, the European scene has been on an explosion with an influx of new fighters and new promotions.

Canada

Two years after Extreme Fighting 2's debacle, Mike Thomas worked with Quebec's gaming commission to bridge the relationship with the Mohawks. Thomas, a Mohawk native, befriended the commission and gained clearance for the IFC to hold the first sanctioned Canadian event on May 30, 1998. Dubbed Montreal Cage Combat, the show was a success, ending with Vladimir Matyushenko defeating Anthony Macias in 15 seconds. The rules disallowed punching with a closed fist to the head on the ground, but the commission reinstated the tactic for future events.

Quebec-born Stephane Patry was soon approached to serve as director of operations for the company, since Thomas needed someone who could speak French and understood the game. Patry had successfully lobbied the Canadian Radio-Television and Telecommunications Commission to bring the UFC back to pay-per-view. He had also worked with SEG to translate press releases into French for the Quebec press and serve as the French color commentator for UFC pay-per-views. Patry managed several French fighters, who participated in the Montreal IFC events. After working on two shows, he left the organization over "creative differences" and in February 2000, cofounded the Universal Combat Challenge. (The IFC wouldn't promote another Canadian event until 2009.) Patry teamed up with New York–born Pete Rodley, whose passion for the sport was just as strong. After moving to Ontario, Rodley took up karate at the same school that produced the UFC's first Canadian entry, Harold Howard. Later Rodley managed fighters who competed against Patry's in the IFC, for which he also worked as an Ontario liaison. "We wanted to build the sport so we could pay them what they should be paid," said Rodley. "We wanted to give the fans what we felt they deserved, and there were no bigger fans than me and Stephane at the time."

With Patry as president and Rodley as VP, the UCC held its first show on June 2, 2000. Their headliner fell apart when Kimo no-showed due to injury and Canadian Kristophe Midoux pulled out after a car accident. The main event of Australian Elvis Sinosic vs. Canada's own Dave Beneteau ended up being a snoozer, but the first UCC was a learning experience. The organization had its work cut out in rebuilding the relationship with fans miffed over Kimo's absence.

UCC 6: Redemption, held October 19, 2001, was the turning point for the promotion when Patry signed former ranked pro boxer Stephane Ouellet. Quebec rallied behind the boxer, and Patry felt the big name could double his audience. Ouellet destroyed Jeff Davis in six seconds, and the UCC sold out a venue of 6,000 compared to 3,000 from previous shows. The ploy worked to familiarize fans with UCC stars like David "The Crow" Loiseau, Shawn "Pain" Peters, and Justin Bruckmann. Ouellet was no match for Peters in the following event, however, and disqualified himself with illegal headbutts. The crowd embraced Peters, who everyone thought would be another Ouellet casualty. With his frazzled beard, crazied eyes, and off-the-wall antics (riding a motorcycle down to the ring while wearing a *Halloween* Michael Myers mask), Peters surfaced as one of the country's early, likable stars. Loiseau, with his lightning-fast hands, also become a breakout hit with the audience. Born in Montreal, the bilingual Loiseau would rev up the crowd by saying, "What time is it? It's Crow Time!" Despite the promotion's lack of heavyweights, it compiled a stable of lighter-weight fighters, each with his own style and appeal that worked for the culturally diverse audience.

Before Zuffa's reign, Gary Goodridge and Carlos Newton were Canada's best-known fighters. While Goodridge made waves all over the world with his colorful persona, Newton's path was guided by something more spiritual. At age 16, Newton, who emigrated from the British Virgin Islands to Vancouver, Canada, was introduced to *The Book of Five Rings*, written by a samurai warrior named Miyamoto Musashi in 1645. "I was drawn to seeking the path of the warrior and being a fighter by living my life through contest," said Newton. A breakup with his girlfriend and lack of concentration in the ring sent him on a worldwide quest to find himself. At age 20, he assumed the role of ronin, or masterless samurai, and lived in Japan, Australia, Thailand, Greece, and Egypt over a two-year period. In May 2001, Newton was a changed man and stepped up to face Pat Miletich for the UFC welterweight title. He caught

Miletich with a side choke in the third round and joyously performed his trademark move by firing an imaginary energy ball—a reference to the Japanese animae *Dragonball Z*. While Newton lost his first title defense, his graceful demeanor and skills made him a hot property in both Pride and the UFC for years. Newton, whose nickname is Ronin, is the epitome of dedication, heart, and showmanship.

With pay-per-view, a sister show building new fighters, frequent coverage on free TV, a bevy of high-profile sponsors (Coors Light, Pepsi), and a fighter-centric website, the UCC was hailed as arguably the second-best promotion in North America behind the UFC. But outside of Canada, no one was really paying attention. The UCC brought in a few fighters from the U.S. and Brazil, and even held a cross-promotion in Hawaii, but couldn't turn heads outside of Quebec. That changed on January 25, 2003, when the UCC took a chance by headlining its 12th show with two big American names: Duane Ludwig vs. Jens Pulver. The rest of the event was packed solid with top Canadian talent like Georges St. Pierre and Steve Vigneault, along with four other Americans. For the 3,500 in attendance, it was the best UCC ever produced, lighting up message boards and MMA Internet news sites, talking up Ludwig's demolition of Pulver at 1:13 into the first round.

Ironically, the show everyone touted as a major achievement also sent shockwaves through the MMA community over allegations of unpaid fighters and unreturned phone calls. MMA forums were used as a virtual battlefield for President Stephane Patry to defend his position against countless people wanting answers. Joe Ferraro was cofounder of Showdown Fight Wear, one of UCC's first sponsors. He eventually served under Patry in several capacities, from commentator to VP of talent relations. As time went on, he felt the heat of what he called "shady" business practices. "I was the cleanup man for years, for various 'messes' [Stephane] would create," alleged Ferraro. "From manager Monte Cox to a DVD replication house to everyone in between, I would be the soundboard of how everyone and their brother was owed money." Patry didn't want to comment on specific allegations but said, "The UCC was losing money, a lot of money especially after the UCC 8 and UCC 12 fiascos. I was the only one in this company putting money in show after show right after UCC 3." (After all the momentum built from UCC 7, the eighth show was held in Rimouski, Quebec, 10 hours north of Montreal; attendance was less than 1,000.)

Pete Rodley, who didn't even attend UCC 12, was fed up and wanted out. "[Stephane] was surprised I didn't attend the show, but I told him it would be a good idea if I did not see him in person at this time," said Rodley. He said Patry frequently contradicted him behind his back, and he could no longer take it. "For over three years I would defend his actions and make good for his lies. After realizing this trend was not going to end, I had to preserve my reputation and bowed out of the project." Rodley left the organization and sold his shares of the company to Patry. He continued working in the scene, even copromoting a show with this author and Clint Dahl on July 9, 2005. Freedom Fight 2005: Canada vs. USA became one of the first prime-time events to be shown in North America on Canadian sports network TSN. Ferraro unwillingly took over as VP of the UCC, despite being owed money himself.

On September 6, 2003, the UCC became TKO Major League MMA and started promoting events as usual. But the problems didn't go away, and some of Patry's most trusted employees were finding it difficult to stay onboard. By November 2003, color commentator JT McCarthy and Joe Ferraro had resigned. Canadian MMA forums were swamped with threads concerning Ferraro's departure and subsequent defection to a new but short-lived Canadian promotion, Shut Up and Fight (SUAF). "Rumors floated around about money, dirty politics, and shady relationships," said Ferraro, "but the big one concerned a merger between two bitter enemies, Patry and Mark Pavelich." Pavelich had set up shop in Alberta and promoted Maximum Fighting Championships since March 2001. Despite 2,300 miles separating them, Pavelich and Patry allegedly tried to put each other out of business through fighter exclusivity contracts, forum trolling, and personal bickering. Strangely enough, both men set aside their differences, forming a relationship to own Canada's MMA scene. Pavelich took over for Ferraro as VP of TKO, and Patry became VP of MFC.

Their first order of business, according to Ferraro, was to shut down Shut Up. Ferraro said Pavelich, on advice from Patry, began informing authorities, sponsors, local papers, and local radio stations that an illegal, unsanctioned event was taking place in British Columbia. "Everything the MMA community was used to fighting against, all the education we bestowed on the ignorant, was used against us...by one of our own," said Ferraro. Patry vehemently denied any involvement with the SUAF situation, saying he was working 20-hour days on TKO 14 at the time. True, the event was nonsanctioned, but seven events had already taken place in the same city, and the local government was fully aware and approved SUAF to take place. On December 5, 2003, just one day before showtime, the Canadian government shut down the event. "December 6 became known as 'Black Friday' for Canadian MMA fans," said Ferraro, since British Columbia would no longer sanction MMA events...but that wouldn't last forever.

After the SUAF incident, there was never any mention of Patry and Pavelich working together. On November 15, 2008, Stephane Patry stepped down from his post as president of TKO, following what would become TKO's last show on October 3, 2008. Patry kept managing top fighters like Georges St. Pierre and Patrick Cote for a time, but the sport would lose one of its biggest promotions. Despite all the posturing, Maximum Fighting Championships became the country's No. 1 promotion, namely because of a deal with HDNet to air live fights to millions of homes. "MFC is the frontrunner in Canada," said Ferraro. "Trailing behind them are the likes of W-1, Ringside, MFL, Aggression, and The Fight Club." Every promotion is only as good as its last show, and for so many upstarts—no matter the location—it can all come to an end overnight.

Nothing behind the scenes has kept fighters from the Great White North from making a name for themselves. Although Joe Doerksen, David Loiseau, Patrick Cote, and John Alessio paved the way for many Canadian fighters to cross over to the big leagues, there is one name that has truly made a difference: Georges St. Pierre. The French Canadian, with his boyish good looks, charm, and chiseled physique, has become one of the sport's most celebrated fighters and has been called pound-for-pound the best MMA fighter in the world. "GSP has been an integral part of the sport's growth in Canada," said Ferraro. "His elite status and positive image has taken MMA mainstream. Every time he fights, every time he speaks, every time he does anything, it's automatic news on the mainstream Canadian networks." In 2008 and 2009, he was named Canadian Athlete of the Year by Rogers Sportsnet. The country also produces more and more fighters every year, ready for the big leagues, with no doubt a future season and series of *The Ultimate Fighter* in its midst. "Canadians have always done well at sports you can train indoors [for] because of our harsh winters," said Donald Boswell, who heads up the Calgary Combat Sports Commission. "Fighting and competing hard has always been part of being a Canadian. For a country with such a small population, I believe our pugilistic record speaks for itself."

Showdown, the company founded by Ferraro along with partners Danny Yen, Paul Mitchell, and Mike McNeil, keeps the scene alive in Ontario, running the country's top MMA store and magazine of the same name. Ontario is the Mecca for the sport in Canada, just as California is in the U.S., and it's had its share of problems getting sanctioned. The UFC, thanks to St. Pierre and the incredible fan base, has done extremely well in Canada, bringing in millions of dollars of revenue. After the sport got sanctioned in Vancouver, British Columbia, UFC 115, held June 12, 2010, completely sold out in 30 minutes. Ontario finally relented in mid-August 2010 to officially start sanctioning events in 2011. "Ontario has the greatest concentration of MMA athletes and fans," said Yen, who said they used to have to drive up to six hours to compete and enjoy the shows in Quebec. Now they can do it at home. Canada boasts one of the highest per-capita audiences for the sport. On April 18, 2009, the UFC broke all attendance records with UFC 97: Redemption, which drew 21,451 people in Montreal, Quebec—Georges St. Pierre wasn't even on the card. With Ontario now ready, the UFC and MMA will most likely copy what they did in the U.S. to make Canada another UFC stronghold.

APPENDIX I

THE BEST OF
TANK ABBOTT

Love him or hate him, David "Tank" Abbott was never at a loss for words. During three interviews with Abbott (all of which took place via telephone from an undisclosed bar), he had plenty to say and talked for hours. From his UFC appearances and the three interviews conducted for this book, here are some of his more revealing quotes.

Growing up

I was brought up during Reaganomics, and there were a lot of people who shouldn't have had money, but did. At that time, I had a lot of resentment towards that because my parents didn't think the same way I did. So I was like, "Who the fuck are these guys?" I hung around with their group because they saw me as an asset. I was like their trained pet who would beat the hell out of anyone who got too close. But they didn't realize that they were my trained pet because I was enjoying all of their stuff—climbing on their boats, going out partying, and doing their women because I'm their trained chimp.

How much of Tank is David Abbott?
Both of them are me. If you cross my path, you're fucked brother.

Tank says that he is the first one to have a real fight in the Octagon. Well, tell that to Andy Anderson, who lost sight out of one eye (see Chapter 8).

391

That was a joke and a half! Those guys couldn't even hold a candle to my jock strap, brother! That is ridiculous! They couldn't even trim my toenails, and you're telling me that "Oh, they had a real—FUCK!" I've seen two drunks have a real fight in a bar! And you're telling me that was a real fight! It's because they didn't have an interest in fighting the Gracies, but they were absolute garbage! Those guys are trash! Do you understand what I'm saying to you or not? For the first five shows of the Ultimate Fighting, it was the biggest joke, professional work—all to put the Gracies over and to sell their stupid fucking martial arts that any stupid, average guy could learn. So you are telling me that two jokers that might as well be throwing water balloons at each other are being tough guys? They were the absolute jokers of the century! For you to say that these guys...

No, I'm not saying it was any kind of great match with great technique, but it was a no-holds-barred match.
Yeah, so is my mother and grandmother when they go at it! It doesn't make any difference; it's still girls fighting. But please don't tell me about two doughboys, pieces of shit that were set up for the Gracies to beat. That was a joke! Those are not fighters! They are absolute jokers, but if you want to use them as fighters, go ahead, but you are terribly, terribly wrong!

Have you ever got your ass kicked on the street?
Yeah. There have been three or four times where I've gotten the living fucking piss kicked out of me. I got beat up by four Samoans one time. I couldn't sleep for three days because I couldn't put my head down. The cops called me and said, "Hey, let's put these guys down," and I said, "Hey man, it's my turn for my ticket to get punched."

Fighting and Fame
I have 13 arrests for fighting in public to attempted murder. I have four convictions...I have served seven months in prison because bottom line is this: I'm not a bully; there are two willing participants that want to fight and

then someone ends up on the short end of the stick. But when someone ends up on the short end of the stick so many times, they have to finally say that someone has a problem because you have so many pencil-pushing jack-offs who want to cause a problem. Modern society has adopted this philosophy that explains it, and this is it: we are the weak, and we are going to band together against people who can impose their will against us. That's why all the fuckers in Ultimate Fighting—they are not fighters, they are ultimate jokers. They are ultimate posers, every single one of them, and the biggest one is Ken Shamrock. He's not a fighter; he's a joke. Let me explain something to you. I'm in the professional wrestling business. You want to know what the No. 1 fucking claim by professional wrestling is? I want to be famous for something that's easy! Ken Shamrock wants to be famous, and that's his whole motivation in life. He was a professional wrestler before he ever got into professional fighting. He's an absolute jokeaholic. He's a steroided, 180-pound joke. He ain't nothing but a joke. He had two times to fight me and he ran! And you want to know what? A fighter does not care about losing. This is supposed to be about real fucking fighting, and this is supposed to be about doing jail time for your passion. I am Nelson Mandela of fucking no-holds-barred, but no one seems to get that because they all want to fucking live vicariously through a joker that says if you own my book of tools, you can be tough too. It's a joke!

Prefight interview for UFC VI
My name is Tank Abbott. I'm going to be the most athletic person that has ever stepped into the Octagon. That, coupled with my experience, will definitely make me the UFC VI champ.

Watching tape of his win over Paul Varelans at UFC VI
I'm starting to get sexually aroused so you better take that off.

Talking about his suspension at UFC X
When I count days, I'm counting days to get out of a cage. Now I'm counting days, 70 and running, to get back into a cage. You've seen the

Discovery Channel. You've seen some animals rip apart a gazelle. That's what's going to happen.

Jeff Blatnick asks Tank about respecting the traditional martial arts

Well that's for Don "The Dragonfly" Wilson, and let him go do...where's he at? He's probably making a Godzilla voiceover that you'll see at three in the morning.

On Shamrock vs. Severn II

You saw Glamrock and you saw Freddie Mercury look-alike or whatever. They fought for 27 minutes, and they all hid behind a second clock of a hand. They didn't go out there to fight. When I go in there, I'm not going in there to win. I'm going out there to fight!

After defeating Cal Worsham at Ultimate Ultimate '96

My fire is basically all about fighting. I'm a warrior...if I wouldn't be in the Octagon, I'd be in a bar, I'd be in an intersection—fighting.

After knocking out Steve Nelmark at Ultimate Ultimate '96

I'm healthy...I'm like fire through bushes, baby. I do all my talking in the ring. It ended up the way it should. He was staggering, but he wasn't hurt. That's all part of the fight game. If you get on Queer Street, you make a right turn and get back to Main. I was just on him and not letting him turn.

Tony Blauer asks Tank if this is retribution for getting into the finals again at Ultimate Ultimate '96

I just come here to fight and it don't matter. Win or lose, I still put a... there's an ass-kicking either way. One goes on me or the other person. I'm not part of the quick-tap club...I go out there to bang.

Bruce Beck asks Tank about Shamrock

He's appropriately named Sham-rock. He's a fake. He's a fraud. He's a sham.

APPENDIX II
BAS RUTTEN:
THE FLYING DUTCHMAN

With his devilish smile and mesmerizing eyes, the bald, charismatic Bas Rutten can not only claim to be the most famous European mixed martial artist, but also a Renaissance man with a carefree way of juggling everything life has to offer. He kicks ass too.

Rutten's trademark jumping splits and aggressive fighting style started with a 12-year-old boy wandering into a French cinema to catch a glimpse of Bruce Lee in *Enter the Dragon*. Born in Tilburg, Netherlands, he grew up with very conservative parents and was not allowed to partake in any type of martial arts. As a young teen, he faced constant taunting from other children because he suffered badly from the skin condition eczema. "My hands were so bad that I couldn't even grip a pen at times," said Rutten, who often wore gloves to protect them. He had bad asthma to boot.

Rutten's parents finally allowed him to take up tae kwon do at age 14. As the skin disease cleared up, he set out for revenge on those who had persecuted him. "After two weeks, I broke somebody's nose in a street fight and that was it...no more martial arts." Four years later, with his eczema cleared up, Rutten used his looks to land modeling gigs around Holland. Moving out of the house at age 20, Rutten took up kyokushinkai karate and tae kwon do, subsequently earning black belts in both. He enjoyed performing katas because the breathing exercises helped to control his asthma.

Balancing his college work, Rutten became a cook specializing in French cuisine before working as a bouncer, which paid more money in less time and allowed him to take better classes at a neighboring college.

It also afforded him more time to train, and he eventually took up Thai boxing as a more effective form of street defense than his traditional training. One of his training partners was 15-year-old Peter Aerts, who went on to become one of K-1's greatest stars. "Once I started to come to the set for a [modeling] photo shoot with black eyes from training, I didn't get asked [to model] anymore," said Rutten, who began competing in matches just three weeks after he started training.

Rutten won 14 straight matches but also found the rough and tumble streets of Amsterdam an irresistible attraction. He often spent nights in jail after rousing, drink-soaked parties and had effectively given up the sport until an unlikely New Year's celebration at age 26. Drunk and out of hand, Rutten unknowingly agreed to take on well-known stand-up fighter Frank Lobman two months later. The promoters reminded him four weeks before the fight; Rutten had completely forgotten. "I realized that I had said yes, so I started training. At that time, I had not trained in four years, so I couldn't even finish my warm-up with rope skipping." Rutten lost by TKO.

In an effort to set things straight, he stepped up his training to fight top Dutch kickboxer Rene Rooze. Rutten dominated the first round, but Rooze developed a case of Tysonitis and bit a hole in his ear during the second round. "I told him to let go, he didn't, so I kneed him in the groin as hard as I could, and the whole audience started to fight," said Rutten, who had brought 30 bouncer friends to watch. The ensuing brawl ended the fight.

His final match came on the heels of a four-day sentence in jail. "One day before the fight [against France's Alexes Burger], they turned me loose, but I had caught an infection in one of my balls. I decided to fight anyway. I knocked the guy down three times during the first round, but I couldn't come out to the second round because I was cramped."

Rutten decided to retire after that second loss, realizing his fans were no longer with him. He found work doing martial arts shows around Holland, where he used his athleticism and uncanny comedic timing to entertain live audiences. The shows turned out to be so popular that Rutten soon found himself on Dutch TV and then European TV. "There were a lot of acrobatic jumps and kicks and stuff like that. We made it very funny."

Pro wrestler and former sambo/judo champ Chris Dolman approached Rutten at one show and asked if he would consider trying out for Rings Holland, a European flavor of Akira Maeda's Rings. Rutten resisted at first, not wanting to make the nearly two-hour drive to Amsterdam from his home in Idolan to train. He worked out with Dolman a handful of times, and, as luck would have it, he was at the right place at the right time on one particular night. Pro wrestlers Masakatsu Funaki and Minoru Suzuki were scouting for their new shoot promotion, Pancrase, and wanted to see if Dolman had any notables in his midst. "One of the Rings Holland guys tried to put the pressure on me to show off in front of them, and I ended up kicking him in the head and sending him to the hospital for stitches," said Rutten. "Five weeks later and I was fighting in Pancrase."

On September 21, 1993, Rutten made his MMA debut in the inaugural Pancrase event against Ryushi Yanagisawa, but first he had to take care of a little problem. Though his asthma had been attributed to stress while competing in Holland, Rutten felt relaxed in Japan but needed an extra reminder. "I was always really relaxed until somebody hit me, and then I totally lost it. That's not good because sometimes you have to fight more than one round. That's dangerous because you can lose all your power." So before stepping into the ring, Rutten painted large Rs on his wrists. Since Pancrase was open-hand fighting, he would be able to see the Rs to reference "rustick," which means "relax" in Dutch. "The next time that somebody hit me, I look at my hands and say to myself, 'Relax Bas, relax...relax.'" Rutten knocked out Yanagisawa in 43 seconds and completed his new career start in a unique fashion. Taking a tip from his days as a martial arts performer, Rutten leapt up and did the splits, repeating it to each corner. The crowd went wild. "I had so much adrenaline in my body that I just jumped up [and it] became my trademark after that. Sometimes I did it for fun, but never in the ring."

If Rutten wanted to become the next big thing, he needed to learn submission fighting, something he was unfamiliar with until Pancrase founder

Funaki submitted him in his third match. "They called me for a meeting, and I thought, *that's it*. That's when I thought they were going to ask me to start doing fixed fights," said Rutten, who had heard the rumors about Japanese promotions. "Instead, they invited me to dinner and gave me a book and told me to study it." Yoshiaki Fujiwara penned the book, which described in great detail the submission holds he had learned from Karl Gotch.

Rutten was well on his way to becoming a superstar, but after losing once to Frank Shamrock and twice to Ken Shamrock, he swore he would never lose again and started grappling twice a day. From April 1995 to September 1998, he won 18 matches and had one draw. On September 1, 1995, Rutten won his first King of Pancrase title, and after besting such luminaries as Maurice Smith, Frank Shamrock, and Guy Mezger, he defeated Pancrase founder Funaki on September 7, 1996, to win his second KOP title. "He was incredible, and it took a lot of conditioning to beat him," said Rutten.

Of course, the wild side of Bas Rutten came out every once in a while. Visiting Sweden in 1997, he found himself inebriated in a local pub where everyone knew who he was. "The bouncers there were called mafia bouncers, and they pushed me between two doors into the marble stairway, the fire escape. They told me to leave and I said okay, but [I needed] to tell my friend that I was leaving and that I'll be gone. One guy started pushing my chest with his finger, and I told him not to touch me." One more push created the swell of anger within him. Then one of the bouncers poked Rutten in the eye. "While I was holding my eye, he poked my other eye too. That's when I knocked him out, and then all hell broke loose. I ended up fighting five bouncers, and that was pretty rough. Three of them ended up in the hospital; they were pretty hurt. I had an instructional series at the time, so in the newspaper they put the picture [of me] demonstrating my street defense."

After winning the King of Pancrase for the third time, Rutten had accomplished all of his goals in Japan. A meeting with UFC matchmaker John Perretti gave him the opportunity to test his skills in the U.S. "I fought guys who had won in the UFC and became champions, so I thought that it isn't much of a difference," said Rutten. The Dutchman was originally to face Randy Couture on October 16, 1998, but Couture left the UFC over a contract dispute. To make matters worse, Rutten suffered a neck injury leading up to his eventual match against Tsuyoshi Kosaka at UFC 18 on January 8, 1999. After an exhausting war that lasted 14:15, Rutten knocked him out. He then earned a shot at the heavyweight title against Kevin Randleman at UFC 20. Rutten had his hands full for the first four minutes of the match when Randleman took him down and grounded and pounded him. Unable to see out of one eye, the match was momentarily stopped for a doctor to check his nose, which appeared broken. "What many don't know is that I have a silicon nose," said Rutten, who kept going and won by a split decision.

Riddled with injuries, Rutten retired from fighting and with the UFC losing the pay-per-view battle at the time, he wasn't missing anything. He stayed in America and found he liked it much more than Holland. Today, he lives in the Los Angeles area with his second wife Karin and their two daughters, Sabine and Bianca. He also has a third daughter, Rachele, who lives in The Netherlands. He turned to acting, taking parts

A Night Out with Bas

A bar in Louisiana the night before UFC XXII was virtually taken over by MMA fighters needing a place to relax. The locals didn't know what to make of it. Bas Rutten was in pure form that night, hamming it up with fellow fighters and cracking jokes. As the night wore on and the alcohol started to flow, the Dutchman really came out of his shell. At one point, two particularly big cowboys were shooting a game of pool. During the game, Rutten literally walked over and pushed all their balls into the pockets. Normally, this type of behavior would lead to a bar fight, but there's something about Rutten that says, "Don't mess with him." Rutten then proceeded to hop onto the pool table and crash out, while the rest of the bar went about its business. Rutten made it home okay, while John Lober tried a parlor trick outside the bar of cutting the top off a beer bottle with a karate chop. Lober nearly sliced his hand in half, bleeding all over the bar entrance; Andy Anderson took him to the hospital for over a half-dozen stitches. It was all in good fun.

in Sammo Hung's short-lived martial arts series *Martial Law* and in 2002 played opposite Pancrase founder Funaki, fighting him to a duel in the Japanese copromotion, *Shadow Fury.*

Though he may have been out of the fight game in the ring, Rutten showed no signs of not being the life of the party. He attended a fight in Hawaii in May 2002, and after a drunken but relatively tranquil evening, he returned to his hotel room. With so much liquor in his system, Rutten took a shower before bedtime. "When I got out, for some reason, I knocked out the toilet with my head," laughed Rutten. "The whole fucking thing exploded into a hundred pieces. It looked like a ritual killing with blood everywhere." Tired and out of his mind, Rutten simply threw some blankets down and passed out. The next morning, he woke up to find a new toilet had been fitted. Apparently his fight with the porcelain god had flooded the entire 35th floor of the hotel. Security entered his room, and the hotel cleaned everything up, replaced the toilet, and on top of that, gave everyone on the floor a complimentary breakfast for their troubles. Rutten kept a piece of the broken toilet as a souvenir.

Rutten went on to serve as color commentator for Pride Fighting Championships and released the two-volume *Bas Rutten's Big Book of Combat*, an illustrated look at the techniques that made him famous. Over the years, Rutten has become one of the foremost authorities on MMA fighting techniques, and favors strikes to the liver. On July 22, 2006, he would step back into the cage one more time for the short-lived World Fighting Alliance where he knocked out Ruben Villareal by leg kicks. Though he is often referred to by the moniker El Guapo (meaning "The Handsome One" in Spanish), the fighter Bas Rutten finished his career with a 28-4-1 record with a 22-fight unbeaten streak (21 wins, 1 draw). In 2010, he released BAS (Body Action System), a mixed martial arts workout system. He also became an integral part of the now defunct International Fight League. Since 2007, he has served as cohost for a weekly MMA news program on HDNet called *Inside MMA*. Rest assured, no matter where he is, Bas Rutten is flying high.

APPENDIX III

MIXED MARTIAL ARTS

AN ILLUSTRATED LOOK AT BASIC
POSITIONS AND SUBMISSIONS

There is no universally recognized set of terms for the fundamental techniques used in mixed martial arts. Some use a single word to describe what others see as a variety of different moves, each with a different name.

Groundfighting recognizes positions of control, striking, and submissions by joint lock or choke. Listed here is a brief description of fundamental techniques, with photos alongside each description to further demonstrate. English, Japanese, and Brazilian Portuguese pronunciations are listed with each term.

This section is by no means comprehensive, but is meant to provide the reader with a better understanding of the most basic positions and submissions used in the sport. While there are many MMA-centric technique books, fans can see some of the sport's top stars performing many different techniques—striking, wrestling, and submission—with *MMA Lessons* from MMA Worldwide and published by Triumph Books. MMA Worldwide provided the photos in the accompanying pages.

MOUNT

With the knees straddling either side of the opponent, the top player can control the other's torso and end the fight with strikes or a submission hold, all while remaining protected from his strikes. When these three criteria (torso control, protection from strikes, and finishing opportunities) are present, the controlling player is said to have "position."

English: *Mount*

Japanese: *Tate-shiho-gatame*

Brazilian Portuguese: *Montada*

BACK MOUNT

When the player is controlling the other's torso, but both are facing the same direction. It can be used with both players facing up or down. The controlled player is more vulnerable to chokes and has fewer opportunities to strike back, putting him at a greater disadvantage.

English: *Back Mount*

Japanese: *Ushiro-tate-shiho-gatame*

Brazilian Portuguese: *Montada Pelas Costas*

SIDE MOUNT

A large number of positions exist where the top, controlling player is on the side of the other.

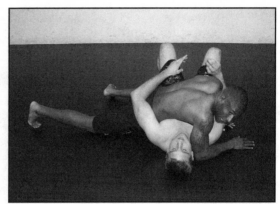

English: *Side Mount*

Japanese:
Mune-gatame,
Yoko-shiho-gatame

Brazilian Portuguese:
Cem Quilos Ou Atravessada

CLOSED GUARD/ OPEN GUARD

While the top is preferable, the bottom player can control his opponent's torso, be protected significantly from strikes, and have opportunities to finish the fight. Two broad variations are recog-

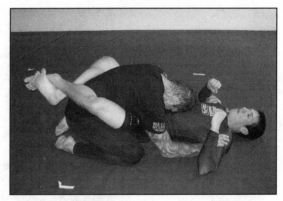

nized: (1) closed guard, where the legs are locked around the other player and (2) open guard, where the feet are unlocked.

English: *Closed Guard* (shown here)

Japanese: *Do-jime*

Brazilian Portuguese: *Guarda Fechada*

English: *Open Guard*

Japanese: *Do-basami*

Brazilian Portuguese: *Guarda Aberta, many named variations*

ARM BAR

One of the most frequently used submissions. The arms control the wrist, the legs control the torso, and the hips are brought forward, hyperextending the elbow joint until the opponent submits by tapping out.

English: *Arm Bar*

Japanese: *Ude-hishigi-juji-gatame, usually abbreviated to Juji-gatame*

Brazilian Portuguese: *Chave de Braço*

ARM LOCK

This lock attacks the shoulder joint by rotating it forward or backward. Variations of the hold can also be done against the elbow or even the wrist.

English: *Key Lock, Entangled Arm Lock, Arm Lock*

Japanese: *Ude-garami*

Brazilian Portuguese: *Americana (forearm points up), Kimura (forearm points down)*

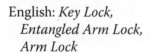

REAR NAKED CHOKE

A choke can be applied across the windpipe, closing off the air, or against the carotid artery on either side of the neck, causing rapid, though brief, unconsciousness. The rear naked (the word *naked* makes reference to the fact that no clothing is employed) is generally executed from  back mount; the bicep and forearm close off the carotid.

English: *Rear Naked*

Japanese: *Hadaka-jime*

Brazilian Portuguese: *Mata Leão*

ARM TRIANGLE CHOKE

This choke is caused by the bicep and the opponent's own shoulder together closing off the carotid artery on both sides. It can be executed from mount, from side control, or from guard.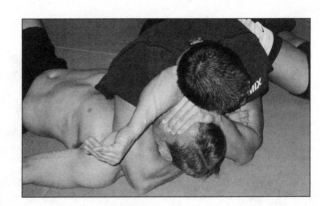

English: *Arm Triangle, Arm Choke*

Japanese: *Kata-gatame*

Brazilian Portuguese: *Katagatami*

GUILLOTINE CHOKE

The guillotine is by far the most successfully employed standing submission and is also effective from the guard. Here the forearm applies the upward pressure into the throat and neck.

The guillotine is perhaps even more effective in the guard; as in addition to a choke, it can also be applied against the spine, called a "crank."

English: *Guillotine (from Guard)*

Japanese: *Mae-hadaka-jime*

Brazilian Portuguese: *Guilhotina, Gravata Técnica*

TRIANGLE CHOKE

The legs can also be used to choke the opponent. The triangle is similar to the arm choke, except that instead of the choke being caused by the opponent's own shoulder and your bicep, it is caused by the shoulder and your thigh.

English: *Triangle Choke*

Japanese: *Sankaku-jime*

Brazilian Portuguese: *Triângulo*

D'ARCE CHOKE

A variation of the arm triangle choke from the headlock position, whereby the choking arm is threaded under the near armpit and across the opponent's neck, grabbing your bicep so that arm can clutch the opponent's back.

The choke gets its name from Renzo Gracie black belt Joe D'Arce, who had much success with the maneuver even before it had a proper name (shown here).

If used with a gi, the move is often called a "brabo choke."

The reverse of this choke

is called the "anaconda choke," whereby the choking arm is threaded across the neck and through your opponent's armpit, grabbing your bicep so that arm can clutch the opponent's back.

English: *D'Arce*

Japanese: *Kuzure Kata-gatame*

Brazilian Portuguese: *Brabo (there is no technical "Brazilian" name for the choke, but this term is readily used by Brazilian speakers)*

NECK CRANK

This technique causes a relatively minor choke effect, but its primary effectiveness comes from applying pressure to the vertebrae in the neck. Here are two different variations of a neck crank.

English: *Neck Crank (Crucifix)*

Japanese: *Jigoku-jim*

Brazilian Portuguese: *Crucufixo, Cervical (general term)*

HEEL HOOK

Perhaps the most feared leg lock is the heel hook, which applies rotational pressure to the knee and ankle joint. As there are few nerve endings

in the affected parts of the knee, injury can result unexpectedly.

English: *Heel Hook*

Japanese: *Ashi-garami*

Brazilian Portuguese: *Chave de Calcanhar*

KNEE BAR

Just as the arm bar hyperextends the elbow, the knee bar hyperextends the knee. The foot is trapped securely by the arms (which can readily transition to

a toe hold), the leg is trapped by the legs, and the force is applied by the forward movement of the hips.

English: *Knee Bar*

Japanese: *Hiza-juji-gatame*

Brazilian Portuguese: *Chave de Joelho*

ANKLE LOCK

Similar to the toe hold, but here the foot is trapped under the arm of the attacking player. Again, the result properly applied is the hyper-extension of the ankle joint.

English: *Ankle Lock (where foot is trapped under the arm)*

Japanese: *Ashi-gatame*

Brazilian Portuguese: *Chave de Tornozelo*

TOE HOLD

The joints of the legs as well as those of the arm can have holds applied to them. As it is necessary to lose position to

effectively apply most leg locks, the limb must be trapped as securely as possible.

English: *Toe Hold, Foot Lock (where foot is held by the hand)*

Japanese: *Ashi-gatame*

Brazilian Portuguese: *Chave De Pe*

All photos courtesy of MMA Worldwide (www.mmaworldwide.com)

REFERENCES AND INTERVIEWS

References

Alonso, Marcelo. "João Alberto Barreto." *Full Contact Fighter*. January 2002.

Alpert, Bill. "A Money Manager's Ultimate Fight Game." *Barron's*. June 2, 2008.

Barry, Dan. "Outcast Gladiators Find a Home: New York." *New York Times*. January 15, 1997.

Barry, Dan. "Giuliani to Try to Prevent 'Extreme Fighting' Match." *New York Times*. January 16, 1997.

Barry, Dan. "Commission Approves Rules for Sport of Ultimate Fighting." *Metropolitan Desk*. January 31, 1997.

Barry, Dan. "Seasoned Lobbyist Gave No Quarter in Quest to Legitimize Bloody Sport." *New York Times*. February 7, 1997.

Barry, Dan. "Rules Upheld, So a Bout Leaves New York." *New York Times*. February 7, 1997.

Bash, Alan. "Brawls Punch up Pay-Per-View Numbers." *USA TODAY Life*. April 7, 1995.

Bunk, Tom. "The Extremely Ultimate Fights." *MAD Magazine*. August 1996.

Brunt, Stephen. "Sign of the Apocalypse: Call it Ultimate Fighting." *Toronto Globe*. December 4, 1995.

Cavalcanti, Keo. "The History of Kudokan Judo." judoinfo.com/jhist.htm

Chen, Jim (M.D.). "Masahiko Kimura: The Man Who Defeated Helio Gracie." www.judoinfo.com. 1996.

Corcoran, John & Farkas, Emil. *The Original Martial Arts Encyclopedia*. California: Pro-Action, 1993.

Crompton, Paul. *The Complete Martial Arts*. New York: McGraw-Hill, 1989.

Edison Media Research. "Ultimate Fighting Championship Market Research." July 16, 1996.

Finnegan, Michael. "Big Brawl Has Pataki on Ropes." *DKA News*. September 16, 1995.

Friend, Tad. "Getting Medieval." *New York*. February 19, 1996.

Gorsuch, Mark. "Mitsuyo Maeda Biography"—based on review of *A Lion's Dream: The Story of Mitsuyo Maeda* by Kohyama, Norio. April 1998.

Gross, Josh. "Rodrigo Nogueira." *Ultimate Athlete.* November 2001.

Gross, Josh. "Wanderlei Silva—The Axe Murderer." *Ultimate Athlete.* December 2001.

Hamilton, Kendall. "Brawling over Brawling." *Newsweek.* November 27, 1995.

Hanania, Joseph. "No Mercy: The 'Ultimate Fighting Championship V' Returns Tonight on Pay-Per-View TV." *Los Angeles Times.* April 7, 1995.

Henican, Ellis. "Selling Blood Sport." *Newsday.* February 9, 1997.

HR&A Advisors. "New York State MMA: Economic & Fiscal Benefits." January 2011.

Jordan, Pat. "BAD." *Playboy.* September 1989.

Kagan, Paul. "It's Bloody, It's Violent, It's PPV's Newest Hit." *The Pay TV Newsletter.* January 31, 1995.

Kano, Jigaro & Lindsay, T. "Jujitsu." *Transactions of the Asiatic Society of Japan, Volume 15.* 1887.

Kano, Jigaro. *Kodokan Judo.* Japan: Kodansha International, 1957.

Kessler, Sandra E. "Shotokan, Taekwondo and Kung Fu Challenge Jujutsu." *Black Belt.* April 1994.

Kriegel, Mark. "Gentlemen, Start Your Bleeding." *Esquire.* March 1996.

Lane, Randall. "It's Live, It's Brutal." *Forbes.* May 22, 1995.

Lee, Bruce. *Tao of Jeet Kune Do.* California: Ohara Publications, 1975.

Linderman, Larry. "Fast Forward Section." *Penthouse.* October 1994.

Logan, Greg. "SPECIAL REPORT: Concussions in Sports/Damaging Blows for Boxing." *Newsday.* July 10, 1996.

Marks, John. "Whatever It Takes to Win." *U.S. News & World Report.* February 24, 1997.

McBride, Clay. "The Ultimate Fighting Championship II: Fighter Biographies." *WOW Promotions.* 1994.

McBride, Clay. "The Ultimate Fighting Championship: Various Articles." *Martial Arts Legends Magazine.* 1994.

McBride, Clay. "The UFC Special Section." *Martial Arts Ultimate Warriors.* February 1995.

Meerman, Wiggert. "Lee Murray: British Bad Boy." *Ultimate Athlete.* January 2003

Meyrowitz, Robert. "A Survival Guide for Producers." *Multichannel News.* April 3, 1995.

Miller, Matthew. "Ultimate Cash Machine." *Forbes.* May 5, 2008.

Minzesheimer, Bob. "N.Y. Deals Blow to Extreme Fighting." *USA TODAY.* February 6, 1997.

Mitchell, Paul. *The Overlook Martial Arts Handbook.* New York: The Overlook Press, 1988.

Newfield, Jack. "Should We Let Boxing Die?" *Parade.* May 2, 2004.

Paul Newport, John. "Blood Sport." *Details*. March 1995.

Plummer, William. "Blood Sport." *People*. March 11, 1996.

Poliakoff, Michael. *Combat Sports in the Ancient World: Competition, Violence, and Culture*. Connecticut: Yale University Press, 1995.

Postell, Robin & Coleman, Jim. "Ultimate Fighting Championship Fails to Live Up To Its Billing." *Black Belt*. April 1996.

Rist, Curtis. "Hit-Com Pay-Per-View Mega-Brawl Has Socko Ratings." *Newsday*. August 31, 1994.

Rosato, Bill. "BOX: Sweden to Review 30 Year Old Boxing Ban." *AAP Sports News (Australia)*. December 16, 1999.

Rosenberg, Howard. "'Ultimate' Lives Up to Name.'" *Los Angeles Times*. November 15, 1993.

Ruibal, Sal. "Fatalities Infrequent but Devastating." *USA TODAY Sports*. December 13, 2000.

Sokolove, Michael. "Bloodbath." *Philadelphia Inquirer*. February 25, 1996.

Stone, Andrea. "Fans See Fun in Brawls Where Anything Goes." *USA TODAY*. December 19, 1995.

Svinth, Joseph R. "Death under the Spotlight: The Manuel Velazquez Boxing Fatality Collection." *Journal of Combative Sport*. November 2007.

Umstead, Thomas. "Three Events Boost Early April PPV Revenues." *Multichannel News*. April 17, 1995.

Umstead, Thomas. "Operators Struggle Again with UFC Time Overrun." *Multichannel News*. September 18, 1995.

Umstead, Thomas. "InterMedia Nixes 'Ultimate Fighting'-Type Events." *Multichannel News*. January 1, 1996.

Umstead, Thomas. "SEG Gets Clearance in N.Y. for Ultimate Events." *Multichannel News*. November 18, 1996.

Umstead, Thomas. "UFC Prospers Despite Dwindling Support." *Multichannel News*. February 26, 1996.

Van Gelder, Lawrence. "Promoter Postpones 'Ultimate Fight' in Manhattan." *Metropolitan Desk*. February 6, 1997.

Warner, Gene. "Crowd-Pleasing Attraction Triggers Heated Debate." *Buffalo News*. January 27, 1997.

Weiner, Stewart. "Fast Forward Section." *Penthouse*. December 1993.

Weiss, Al & Weiss, David. *The Official History of Karate in America*. California: Pro-Action, 1997.

White, Nadia. "Arizona Senator: Stop 'Bloody' Fight in Casper." *Casper Star Tribune*. June 12, 1996.

Will, George. "'Extreme' Fighting: Just Today's Ultimate." *Newsday*. November 26, 1995.

Yan, Ellen. "Gov.: No Sport About Ultimate Fighting." *Newsday*. January 18, 1997.

Interviews

All interviews were conducted between mid-1999 and October 2010.

Abbott, David, telephone interview by author.

Adams, Scott, telephone interview by author.

Anderson, Andy, telephone interview by author.

Atencio, Tom, telephone interview by author.

Ayre, Calvin, email interview by author.

Beck, Bruce, telephone interview by author.

Beneteau, David, telephone interview by author.

Blatnick, Jeff, telephone interview by author.

Bohlander, Jerry by Joe Silva.

Bonnar, Stephan, email interview by author.

Boon, Bas, telephone/email interview by author.

Boswell, Donald, email interview by author.

Bravo, Eddie, email interview by author.

Buffer, Bruce by author.

Burnett, Mikey by Joe Silva.

Carter, Shonie by author.

Casey, Dexter, email interview by author.

Chenoweth, Ryan, phone interview by author.

Coker, Scott, phone interview by author.

Coleman, Mark by author.

Cooper, Cal, telephone interview by author.

Couture, Randy, telephone interview by author.

Cox, Monte, telephone interview by author.

Cuban, Mark, email interview by author.

Dahl, Clint Santiago by author.

Davie, Arthur, telephone/email interview by author.

DeLucia, Jason, telephone interview by author.

DePersia, Robert, telephone interview by author.

Dixson, John, telephone interview by author.

Ettish, Fred, telephone/email interview by author.

Ferraro, Joe, email interview by author.

Ferrozzo, Scott, telephone interview by author.

Fertitta, Lorenzo, telephone interview by author.

Frazier, Zane, telephone interview by author.

Freeman, Ian, email interview by author.

Frye, Don, telephone interview by author.

Fulton, Travis, telephone interview by author.

Goes, Allan, by author.

Gold, Joel, telephone interview by author.

Goldman, Eddie, telephone interview by author.

Goodridge, Gary, telephone interview by author.

Gordeau, Gerard, telephone interview by author.

Gracie, Relson, telephone interview by author.

Gracie, Rorion, telephone interview by author.

Gracie, Royce, telephone interview by author.

Hackney, Keith, telephone interview by author.

Hall, Mark, telephone interview by author.

Hantman, Robert, telephone/email interview by author.

Hasdell, Lee, telephone interview by Carl Fisher.

Herrera, Paul, telephone interview by author.

Hoffman, Bobby, by author.

Hume, Matt, telephone interview by author.

Inosanto, Dan, telephone interview by author.

Inoue, Enson, telephone interview by author.

Isaacs, David, telephone interview by author.

Ismail, Wallid, telephone interview by author.

Jardine, Andy, email interview by author.

Jenness, Kirik, telephone interview by author.

Jimmerson, Art, telephone interview by author.

Johnston, Brian, telephone interview by author.

Keating, John, telephone interview by author.

Kerr, Mark, telephone interview by author.

Kidd, Kathy, telephone interview by author.

Lapenda, Frederico, telephone interview by author.

Leininger, Christophe, telephone interview by author.

Levi, Becky, telephone interview by author.

Lewis, Joe, phone interview by author.

Lewis, John, by author.

Liddell, Chuck, phone interview by author.

Lindland, Matt, email interview by author.

Lober, John, telephone interview by author.

Lucadamo, Gino, telephone interview by author.

McBride, Clay, phone interview by author.

McCarthy, Elaine, telephone interview by author.

McCarthy, John, telephone interview by author.

McLaren, Campbell, telephone interview by author.

Meltzer, Dave, telephone interview by author.

Meyrowitz, Robert, telephone interview by author.

Mezger, Guy, telephone interview by author.

Miletich, Pat, telephone interview by author.

Nelson, Steve, email interview by author.

Ortiz, Tito, telephone interview by author.

Osborne, Jeffrey, telephone interview by author.

Owen, Steve, telephone interview by author.

Palmer, Jay R, telephone interview by author.

Pardoel, Remco, email interview by author.

Patry, Stephane, email interview by author.

Patschull, Greg, phone/email interview by author.

Paulson, Erik, phone interview by author.

Perretti, John, telephone interview by author.

Peters, Christopher, telephone interview by author.

Petschler, Howard, telephone interview by author.

Postell, Robin, telephone interview by author.

Rhodes, Johnny, telephone interview by author.

Riley, Aaron, by author.

Rodley, Pete, email interview by author.

Rosier, Kevin, telephone interview by author.

Ruas, Marco, phone interview by author.

Rutten, Bas, phone interview by author.

Schrijber, Bob, telephone interview by Wiggert Meerman.

Severn, Dan, telephone interview by author.

Shamrock, Bob, by author.

Shamrock, Frank, telephone interview by Joe Silva and author.

Shamrock, Ken, by author.

Silva, Joe, telephone interview by author.

Silveira, Marcus, telephone interview by author.

Smith, Maurice, by author.

Smith, Patrick, telephone interview by Jake Rossen.

Smith, Paul, telephone interview by author.

Sperry, Ze Mario, email interview by author.

Tabbs, Leon, by author.

Taktarov, Oleg, telephone interview by author.

Telligman, Tre, by author.

Tew, Rick, email interview by author.

Thatch, Clarence, telephone interview by author.

Thomas, Mike, telephone interview by author.

Thompson, TJ, telephone interview by author.

Tuli, Teila, telephone interview by Jake Rossen.

Vale, Bart, telephone interview by author.

Van Arsdale, Mike, by Joe Silva.

Van Clief, Ron, telephone interview by author.

Weir, Mark, email interview by author.

Woodard, Julian, email interview by author.

Yen, Danny, email interview by author.

Yvel, Gilbert, telephone interview by Wiggert Meerman.

Zinoviev, Igor, telephone interview by author.

Zuckerman, David, telephone interview by author.

INDEX

A

Abbott, David "Tank", 113–14, 116–17, 119–21, 123–28, 131–32, 170, 187–91, 193, 195–200, 202–3, 205, 212, 214–15, 234, 242, 244–45, 247, 252, 254–55, 259–60, 262, 268, 279, 337, 339, 341, 344, 391–94
ABC's Wide World of Sports, 110
Abramson, Michael, 38
Absolute Fighting Championship, 177, 374, 381
Abu Dhabi Combat Championships, 215
Abu Dhabi Combat Club, 349
Abu Dhabi Submission Wrestling Championships, 328
Abu Dhabi World Submission Wrestling Championship, 349
Adams, Scott, 164–65, 290–91, 358, 382–83
Adkins, Sam, 130, 189
Aerts, Peter, 139, 367, 396
Affliction Entertainment, 304
aikido, 69, 78
Akebono, Yokozuna, 368, 370
Alabama State Fair Arena, 182, 193
Alaska Fighting Championship, 166
Albin, Buddy, 97, 112–13, 118, 120, 169–72, 174, 176–79
Albritton, Wes, 234
Alegria, Ralph, 31
Alessio, John, 389
Alexio, Dennis, 103
Alger, Royce, 233–34
Ali, Muhammad, 7–8, 11, 39, 45, 92, 172, 370
All Japan Pro Wrestling, 8, 363
American Airlines Arena, 297
American Gladiators, 309
American Kickboxing Academy, 286, 290, 307, 330
American Medical Association, 133-34
American Sumo Association, 46

Amtrak, Ken Wayne, 133
Anderson, Andy, 104–5, 117–18, 121, 169–73, 175–76, 178–80, 251, 256, 268, 273, 391, 399
Anderson, Mike, 11, 162
Andrade, Alex, 268
Anjo, Yoji, 252, 363–64
Arlovski, Andrei, 305
Armstrong, Steve, 354
Arnold World Gracie Submission Championships, 346
Arona, Ricardo, 369, 376
Atencio, Tom, 304
Atkins, Jason, 378
Atlanta Underground, 129
Augusta-Richmond Civic Center, 188, 231
Authentic Brands Group, 355
Ayre, Calvin, 294–96, 349

B

Bare Knuckle Brawls, 333
Barnett, Josh, 305, 339
Baroni, Phil, 341–42
Barreto, João Alberto, 16, 18, 20–21, 53
Barretto, Carlos, 220, 242
Barrie, Canada, 127
Barry, Dan, 156, 160, 166
Batarelli, Sergio, 260, 374
Battle Management, 293
Battlecade Inc., 142–43, 156, 227
Bean, Sven, 166, 229, 354
Bear, Alyxzander, 299
Beck, Bruce, 93, 105–6, 118, 199, 251, 299, 319, 346
Belfort, Vitor, 105, 194, 210–12, 214–15, 241, 243–44, 247–49, 254–55, 261, 263, 277–78, 305, 366, 377–78
Bell Canada, 149
Bellagio, 278
Bellator Fighting Championships, 306, 310, 356

Beneteau, David "Dave", 105, 117, 123, 134, 203, 242–43, 385
Berger, Steve, 278
Bertelsmann Music Group (BMG), 35, 39, 41, 58
Bessac, Scott, 48
Bhering, Marcelo, 24
Bigelow, Bam Bam, 196
Bingo Palace, 272
Bisping, Michael, 384
Bitetti Combat Nordeste, 378
Bitetti, Amaury, 135, 269, 378
Bitonio, Mike, 140, 208
Bjornethun, Todd, 164
Black Belt, 67–69, 86, 139–40
Black Friday, 389
Blanks, Billy, 50
Blatnick, Jeff, 93, 99, 104, 117–18, 131, 203, 211–12, 254–56, 271, 349, 352, 394
Blauer, Tony, 197, 203, 394
Blind, Tim, 73
Bobish, Dan, 236–38
Boddidharma, 13
BodogFIGHT, 294–96, 310
BodogMUSIC, 295
BodogTV, 295
Body Action System (BAS), 400
Bohlander, Jerry, 127–30, 188–89, 193, 210, 249–50, 263
Bonnar, Stephan, 282
Boon, Bas, 374, 380–81, 383
Borga, Ludwig, *see also* Tony Halme, 232
Bossett, Marcus, 99
Boswell, Donald, 390
Botha, Francois, 368
Bougara, Redone, 162
Boutwell Arena, 235
Bowden, Tai, 319
Bowen, Melton, 97–98
Boztepe, Emin, 84, 102
Bravo, Eddie, 328
Brazilian Amazon, 16, 210, 300, 379
Brazilian jiu-jitsu (BJJ), 17, 21, 43, 53, 68–69, 75–76, 79–80, 87, 145, 164, 209, 215, 219, 242, 259, 262, 273, 292, 320, 326, 328–29, 346, 348, 351, 361, 377–78
Brazilian Top Team (BTT), 376
Bren Center, 34
Bristow, Lonnie, 133–34
British Association of Mixed Martial Arts, 383
Brookins, Jonathan, 306
Broughton, Jack, 6
Brown, Jim, 53, 58, 65, 73, 118
Bruckmann, Justin, 386

Bruno, Joseph, 155, 157, 160
Buckner, Amanda, 295
Budokan Arena, 8
Buffer, Bruce, 215, 253
Buffer, Michael, 71, 115
Buffer Partnership, 115
Bulman, Bob, 155
Burger, Alexes, 396
Bussey, Robert, 77, 324
Bustamante, Murilo, 219, 277, 376
Butler, Todd, 236
Butterbean, 299

C

Cablevision, 127, 231
Cage Fight Tournament, 379–80
Cage of Rage, 34, 116
Cage Rage, 301
Cage Warriors Fighting Championships, 381
Caldwell, Dan, 268, 351, 355
Calgary Combat Sports Commission, 390
California Amateur Mixed Martial Arts Organization (CAMO), 294
California State Athletic Commission (CSAC), 294, 305, 352–54
Campbell, Ben Nighthorse, 126
Campetella, John, 184
Canals, Jason, 150
Cantu, Robert, 163
Carano, Gina, 301-303, 308–9, 356–57
Carano, Glenn, 301
Carter, Shonie, 319, 328, 334
Carwin, Shane, 342
Casey, Dexter, 326, 335–36
Casino Magic Dome, 241
Cason, Dwane, 243
CBS, 10, 301–4, 308–9
Century Plaza Hotel, 50–51
Cesar Gracie Academy, 18, 20, 43, 71, 102, 111, 290, 307
Chapirelli, Ricco, 233
Charles, Joe, 103, 249, 254, 373
Chenoweth, Ryan, 294, 352
Chinese Goju, 6
Chivichyan, Gokor, 104, 120, 147
Choon Chu era, 13
Choshu, Riki, 362
Christopher Peters Entertainment, 141
Chute Boxe Academy, 376–78
Citrus Bowl, 128
Civilian Martial Arts Review Board, 71
Cleveland Browns, 333
Clube Remo, 16
CNBC, 276

CNN Sports, 136–37
Cobo Arena, 134
Cody, Herb, 352
Coenen, Marloes, 356
Coker, Scott, 302, 307–10, 354, 367
Coleman, Jim, 69, 139-141
Coleman, Mark, v, 158, 181–82, 184–93,
    196, 204, 223, 236, 238–41, 253, 255,
    259–60, 265, 268, 337, 365
Conquista Fight in Bahia, 378
Continental Airlines Arena, 276
Cook, Bob, 330
Cooper, Cal, 178, 347
Cordeiro, Rafael, 378
Corty, Maurice, 334
Cote, Patrick, 389
Cotto, Miguel, 332
Couture, Randy, 121, 164, 232–33, 235,
    241, 243–45, 247–49, 253, 255–56,
    262–63, 269–70, 275, 281, 283, 286, 304,
    329, 332, 338–41, 343, 354, 399
Cox, Mitch, 319
Cox, Monte, 166, 221–23, 229, 267–68,
    354, 387
Crunkilton, Richard, 290
Cuban, Mark, 297–98
Curitiba, 376–78
Cusson, Jason, 38

D

Dahl, Clint Santiago, ix, 197, 200, 353–54,
    365, 388
Dallas Mavericks, 297
Danger Zone, 342
Daugherty, Sean, 68
Davie, Arthur (Art), ix, 32–40, 43–44,
    48–50, 53–55, 57, 60–61, 67–76, 81–86,
    88, 90–91, 94–95, 101–3, 106–8, 111–
    14, 116, 118, 120–21, 123–24, 126–28,
    132, 139, 141–42, 146, 159, 166, 182,
    187–91, 198, 200, 202, 213, 236, 242,
    249, 251–52, 258–59, 275, 299, 318–22,
    324, 351–52, 356
Davis, Jeff, 386
de Bola, Pé, 16
de la Hoya, Oscar, 306
Dedge, Douglas, 161–62, 258
DeLuca, Doug, 300, 303
DeLucia, Jason, 65, 68, 74, 78–79
Denver Coliseum, 39
Denver Post, 85
DePasquale, Michael Jr., 237
DePersia, Robert, 129, 182, 194, 199–201,
    247–48
DeSouza, Tony, 277

Diaz, Megaton, 87
Dixson, John, 173, 177, 219, 364
Doerksen, Joe, 389
Dolan, Jim, 127
Dolman, Chris, 362, 379, 381, 397
Douglas, Buster, 362
Draka, 162
Dream Stage Entertainment, 365–66,
    370–72
Duarte, Hugo, 36, 259
Dux, Frank, 50–51, 324

E

Edgar, Frankie, 336
Edison Media Research, 187
Electra, Carmen, 275
EliteXC, 294, 301–3, 308, 356
Emelianenko, Fedor, vii, 295, 304–5, 309,
    344, 369, 371–72, 381
Erikson, Tom, 181, 219, 227
Escovedo, Cole, 290–91
ESPN, 142, 221, 228, 306–7
Estwanik, Dr. Joseph, 90, 163
Ettish, Frederick "Fred", 74, 79, 85, 320–24
Ettish, Nolan, 324
Ettish, Pam, 323
European Full Contact Karate
    Championship, 380
European Kickboxing Championship, 379
European Rings, 363, 379
Evans, Rashad, 287, 330
Executive Tower Inn, 54
Expo Square Pavilion, 97
Extreme Challenge, 221–22, 267
Extreme Fighting, 4, 143–48, 155, 157, 164,
    170, 179, 160, 205, 222, 227–28, 257,
    384,

F

Faber, Urijah, 291, 293, 358
Fabrikant, Gennadiy, 170
Fagan, Betty, 179, 356
Fairn, Jason, 99
Fantasy Island, 25
Fata, Matsui, 45
Faulkner, Steve, 150
Featherstonhaugh, James D., 154
Fedrigo, Rudimar, 376, 378
Ferguson, Kevin, *see also* Kimbo Slice, 302
Ferrall, Scott, 299
Ferraro, Joe, 387–90
Ferrozzo, Scott, 128–29, 189–90, 193, 203,
    212, 214
Fertitta, Frank III, 272–74, 286
Fertitta, Frank Jr., 272–74, 292

Fertitta, Lorenzo, 272, 274–77, 281, 284, 286, 292, 372
Ficeto, Todd, 300
Fiedler, Scotty, 184
Fight Girls, 356
Fighting Entertainment Group, 368
Fighting Words with Mike Straka, 298
Fightsport, 21, 348
Filipovic, Mirko, 371
Fishman, Ed, 371
Fitch, Jon, 285
Flash Entertainment, 286
Fletcher, Kyle, 324
Florida, 27, 46, 198, 207, 330, 376
Flynt, Mike, 221
Forbes, 281, 286, 294
Ford, Willa, 283
Foreman, George, 45, 92
Forum, The, 293, 347
Fox International, 142
Fox Sports Net, 278, 296, 306
France, 5–6, 382, 396
Franklin, Rich, 293
Franks, Carl, 150
Frazier, Zane, 50–51, 54–55, 57, 59–60, 63, 165, 326, 337
Freedom Fight 2005, 388
Freeman, Ian, 164–65, 382–83
Friends, 344
Frye, Don, 128–30, 135, 181–87, 190–91, 193–95, 199–204, 203, 217, 233, 297–98, 320
Frye, Molly, 186, 202
Fryklund, Anthony, 236–37
Fuji Network, 371
Fuji Television, 367
Fujiwara, Yoshiaki, 46–47, 207, 361–63, 398
Full Contact Fighter (FCF), 16, 258–59, 277, 284, 347–48
Fulton, Travis, 248, 331, 338
Funaki, Masakatsu, 46–48, 62, 363, 369, 397–98, 400
Furey, Matt, 194

G

Gable, Dan, 228
Gabriel, Brad, 353
Gannon, Sean, 302
Garcia, Armando, 286, 307
Garcia, Sal, 262, 264, 271–72
General Media Inc, 142
Georgia, 188, 217
Geringer, Jim, 116
German, Harold, 146

G-Fight Summit, 356
Gibson, Lance, 344
Gladiator Challenge, 299
Global Domination, 180
Gnap, John, 195
Godsey, Jason, 343
Godzilla, 369, 394
Goes, Allan, 131, 164, 208
Goins, Rich, 58
Gold, Joel, 258–59, 277, 284
Goldberg, Mike, 251, 271
Golden Glory, 380–81
Golden Gloves, 349
Gomes, Helio Vigio, 53–54
Gomes, Ivan, 21–22
Gomi, Takanori, 369
Goodman, Ross, 293
Goodman, Roy, 143, 154–56
Goodman, TJ, 300
Goodridge, Gary, 127, 129–30, 134–35, 183–85, 195, 200, 298, 341, 343, 374–75, 386
Gordeau, Gerard, 48–49, 55, 58–60, 63, 65–66, 73, 75, 124, 316, 362
Gordon Biersch Brewing Company, 272, 283
Gotch, Karl, 46, 48, 64, 207, 361, 398
Gracie Diet, 17
Gracie Jiu-Jitsu, 25–27, 30, 209, 316
Gracie, Carley, 26
Gracie, Carlos, 16–18, 26, 53
Gracie, Carlson, 21–22, 24, 131, 145, 147–48, 208–11, 219–20, 225, 242–43, 262, 376
Gracie, Cesar, 307
Gracie, Charley, 23
Gracie, Gastão, 16
Gracie, Helio, 17–21, 27, 32–33, 53, 60, 65, 81, 101, 324
Gracie, Ralek, 346–347
Gracie, Ralph, 145–46, 150, 152, 205, 207, 210
Gracie, Relson, 17, 23–24, 60, 89–90, 232, 346
Gracie, Rener, 346
Gracie, Renzo, 139–41, 210, 219–20, 222, 301, 364, 366, 375
Gracie, Reylson, 17, 53, 127
Gracie, Rickson, 22, 43–44, 60, 81, 112, 139, 242, 247, 363–65, 369
Gracie, Robson, 24
Gracie, Rockson, 70
Gracie, Rolls, 23
Gracie, Rorion, 20–21, 24–27, 29–34, 37–39, 43–44, 48–50, 52–53, 55, 57, 66,

69–71, 79, 81, 84–85, 91, 101–2, 106–8, 111–12, 123, 137, 139–40, 142, 321, 327, 346
Gracie, Royce, 32, 43, 50, 55, 60–61, 63–66, 68, 76, 78–81, 83–84, 88–90, 95, 97–108, 123, 131, 133, 210, 238, 280–81, 326, 329, 340, 366, 370
Gracie, Royler, 22, 33, 60, 328, 366
Gracie, Ryan, 366
Gracie, Ryron, 346
Grady Cole Center, 84
Graham, Steven, 232, 235
Grand Olympic Auditorium, 353
Great American Mat Endeavors (GAME), 94
Greco, Sam, 139
Griffin, Forrest, 283
Grudge Training Center, 330
Guccione, Bob, 142, 151
Guerus, Igor, 174
Guiliani, Rudy, 156
Gunn, Billy, 198
Gurgel, Fabio, 189, 236
Guymon, Mike, 355

H

Hackleman, John, 259
Hackney, Keith, 85–86, 89, 97–99, 123–24, 127, 129, 313, 351
Hall, Mark, 124, 183–84, 186, 194, 199–202
Halme, Tony, *see also* Ludwig Borga, 232, 235
Hamaker, Freek, 75, 321
Hamill, Matt, 331
Hamilton, Joe, 212
Hamilton, Nelson, 352
Hamilton, Richard, 129, 181–82, 184–85, 187, 191
Hantman, Robert J., 300, 303–4
Harris, Gerry, 171, 173
Harris, Reed, 290
Hasdell, Lee, 381, 383
Hawaii, 83, 144, 211, 224, 232, 250–51, 260, 301, 337, 387, 400
Haywire, 357
Hazzard, Larry, 269, 274, 352–53
HDNet Fights, 297–98, 381, 389, 400
Hearns, Thomas, 52, 61
Heat Fighting Championship, 378
Hebestreit, Eric, 173
Henderson, Ben, 329
Henderson, Dan, 227–28, 250, 309
Henry, Mark, 336
Hernandez, Noe, 259

Herrera, Paul, 120–21, 127, 129–31, 215, 234, 252, 256, 268
Herring, Heath, 341, 380
Hershman, Ken, 300
Hess, John, 104–5, 211
Hex, The, 297
Hill, Nicholaus, 343
Hindery, Leo J. Jr, 213
Hisamori, Tenenuchi, 14
Hoffman, Bobby, 333
Holland, 65, 149, 175, 356, 362, 369, 382, 395–97, 399
Homm, Florian, 300
Honda Center, 304
Hong Kong, 6, 96, 314, 317, 326
Hoost, Ernesto, 367
Horenstein, Moti, 183–84, 236–37
Horn, Jeremy, 217, 261, 273
Howard, Harold Clarence, 84, 87–92, 183, 385
Howard Stern Show, 378
Huggins, Tom, 218
Hughes, Matt, 225, 280, 330
Hume, Matt, 131, 166, 223–24, 227–28, 336, 354, 367
Hunt, Loretta, 285
Hunter, Alex, 252
Huntington, John, 292
Hustler, 142

I

Ichihara, Minoki, 76
Icon Sport, 301
Inoki, Antonio, 7–8, 22, 203, 361–62, 370, 379
Inosanto, Dan, 2, 26, 318, 320
Inosanto, Guru, 320
Inoue, Egan, 251
Inoue, Enson, 232–34, 249–51, 257
International Fight League (IFL), 257, 296–97, 306, 308, 310, 400
International Fighting Championships (IFC), 7, 169, 172, IFC, 178–79, 290
International Fighting Council, 39, 166, 352
International Professional Kickboxing League (IPKL), 170–71
International Shoot Fighting Association, 207
International Taekwondo Council, 117
International Vale Tudo Championship (IVC), 374–75
ION television, 295
Iron Gladiator Championships, 7
Iron Ring, 299

Isaacs, David, 36–37, 68, 73, 88, 93, 113, 122, 135, 149, 158, 160, 182, 188, 191, 202, 243, 248–49, 251, 256
Ishii, Master Kazuyoshi, 367
Ismail, Wallid, 210, 215, 300, 303, 327, 378–79
Istrico, Dr. Richard, 165, 234, 264
Itturate, Miguel, 349

J

J & P Marketing, 32
Jacare, 75
Jack, Yukon, 127
Jackson, Eugene, 343, 383
Jackson, Greg, 330
Jackson, Howard, 11, 143
Jackson, Kevin, 223, 225, 232, 235–37, 240, 249–50, 253
Jackson, Quinton, 287, 293, 343, 371, 378
Jackson's Submission Fighting, 330
Jacques, John, 46
Japan Vale Tudo, 81, 249, 251, 316, 363, 364
Japanese MMA, 242, 361, 372
Japanese Pro Sumo Association, 46
Japanese Sumo Federation, 45
Jardine, Andy, 381
Jeet Kune Do, 2, 26, 40, 140, 311, 314, 318, 320, 325
Jenkins, Trent, 65, 78, 183
Jenness, Kirik, 347
Jennum, Steve, 85, 91–92, 95, 98–99, 123–24, 373
Jenson, Kirk, 208
Jimmerson, Arthur "Art", 52, 55, 58, 60–62, 97
Jiu-Jitsu Federation, 53
Johns, Phil, 343
Johnson, Marvin, 165
Johnston, Brian, 118, 183–85, 188–89, 194, 203–4, 236–37
Johnston, Teiana, 204
Joint, The, 293
Jones, Jon, 328
Jones, Nathan, 364
Jones, Paul, 150, 337
Jordan, Pat, 31
judoka, 7, 15, 19, 87
jujutsu, 13–18, 67, 312
Jungle Fight, 300

K

K-1, 12, 139, 195, 259, 307, 366–68, 370, 381, 396
Kage Kombat, 116, 353

Kahnawake, 148, 178
Kakutougi Revolution Spirits (KRS), 364–65
Kamay, Randy, 176
Kano, Jigoro, 312
Karate Kung Fu Illustrated, 31
Karelin, Alexander, 112
Kata, 9
Kato, 5, 19
Katz, Tim, 355
Kawczynski, Brett, 357
Kazunari, Murakami, 206–9, 226–27
Keating, Dr. John, 217–27, 338–39
Kedzie, Julie, 301
Kelly, Jim, 40
Kenpo, 50–51, 54, 59, 65, 85, 97, 116, 124, 205, 313, 320, 323–24, 337
Kerr, Mark, 121, 181, 236–38, 241–43, 247–48, 253, 296, 298, 334, 374
Khmelev, Peter, 174
Kidd, Kathy, 91, 139–41
Kimura, Masahiko, 19–21, 53
King of Pancrase (KOP), 249, 250, 264, 334, 398
King of the Cage, 180, 301, 304, 349, 353, 355
Kirkham, Michael, 162
Kitao, Koji, 183, 319
Knobbs, Brian, 47
KO Power Tournament, 380
Kobylyansky, Georgy, 177, 381
Kodokan judo, 14
Kohler, Brad, 164, 248–49
Kondo, Yuki, 271, 369
Kosaka, Tsuyoshi, 263, 399
Koscheck, Josh, 330
Krieger, Mark, 352
Kriviy, Ruslan, 174
Kumite, 50–51
kung fu, 2, 6, 13, 24, 65, 67, 75, 78, 96, 102, 143, 174, 313–14, 316–19, 337, 367
Kyokushinkai karate, 12, 45, 395

L

La Rosa, Tara, 357
Landi-Jons, Jose, 375, 377, 384
Lane, Mills, 72
LaPaglia, Lenny, 52
Lapenda, Frederico, 122, 125, 135, 145, 177–78, 363, 373–74
Lappen, Jeremy, 293–94
LaRosa, Tara, 295
Larry King Live, 153
LaVerne, Marie, 150
Lawler, Robbie, 278, 308, 330

Le, Cung, 307–8
LeBell, Gene, 7, 71, 143, 145, 228
Lee, Brandon, 100
Lee, Bruce, 1–2, 32, 39, 45, 66, 205, 223, 311, 314–15, 318, 320, 324–26, 395
Lee, Felix, 89
Lee, Phyllis, 94, 115
Leininger, Christophe, 87, 231–34
Leito, Roberto Sr., 24
Leninger, 234
Leon, Alberto Cerro, 76, 318
Leonard, Sugar Ray, 306
Leopoldo, Kimo, 83, 127, 196, 279, 293
Lesnar, Brock, 287
Lethal Weapon 3, 31
Levi, Becky, 129, 179, 186–87, 194, 212, 356
Levicki, David, 74, 317, 321
Lewis, Bobby, 45
Lewis, Charles, 351, 355
Lewis, Joe, 9, 70, 315
Lewis, John, 144–45, 147–48, 150, 205, 207, 223, 225, 269, 273, 292–93
Liddell, Chuck, vi-vii, 259, 271–72, 277–78, 281, 283–85, 287, 290, 375
Lindland, Matt, 293, 305, 341, 343
Lion's Den, 62, 112, 127–29, 132, 189, 206, 210–11, 232–33, 239, 249–50, 256, 260, 263–64, 268, 278, 329, 334
Live Nation, 298
Lober, John, 171–73, 223, 225, 249, 261–62, 266, 325, 399
Lobman, Frank, 396
Loeb, Steven, 121
Loiseau, David, 386, 389
Long, Kathy, 53, 58
Los Angeles Police Department, 71
Los Angeles Times, 142, 213
Lucarelli, Robert, 77, 85
Ludwig, Duane, 387
Lumax Cup, 207
Luster, Thaddeus, 75
Luta Livre Americana, 21
Luthor, Lex, 284
Lyle, Ron, 45
Lynch, Rob, 352–53
Lytle, Chris, 331

M

M-1 Global, 305, 309
M-1 Mix-Fight, 381
Machado family, 26, 43, 143, 145, 320
Machado, Carlos, 26
Machado, Jean-Jacques, 328
Machado, Rod, 65

Machida, Lyoto, 293, 328
Macias, Anthony, 98, 118, 120, 169, 178, 208, 219, 385
Madison Square Garden, 52, 93, 167
Maeda, Akira, 46, 48–49, 361–62, 367, 369, 379, 381, 397
Maeda, Mitsuyo, 15–19
Mak, Tai, 96
Makoto Murako, 146
Makushita Class, 46
Malenko, Dean, 47
Mammoth Arena, 73
Mammoth Gardens, 124
Man, Master Yip, 314
Manaus, 16
Mandalay Bay Events Center, 287, 292
Maracana Stadium, 20
Marquardt, Nate, 369
Marshall, David, 300, 303
Martial Arts Advisory Committee (MAAC), 352–53
Martial Arts Reality Superfighting (MARS), 170, 217–21
Martial Law, 343, 400
Martin, John, 10
Matua, John, 116–17, 120
Matyushenko, Vladimir, 277, 385
Maxim, 275, 357
Maximum Fighting Championships (MFC), 388–89
Mayweather, Floyd, 332
McBride, Clay, 57, 66, 69, 107–8, 141
McCain, Senator, John, 116, 126, 153–55, 166, 258
McCarthy, Elaine, 127, 131, 159, 187
McCarthy, John, 71–72, 74, 77, 85, 104, 106–7, 116–17, 119, 124–25, 130, 132–35, 184, 186, 188, 190, 196, 201, 212–13, 233–35, 237–38, 240–41, 244–45, 253, 256, 261, 264
McCarthy, JT, 388
McCormick, Jan, 100
McCully, Sean, 141
McGee, Gan, 353
McLaren, Campbell, *see also* Marky D. Sodd, 36–40, 59, 68, 70, 72–73, 83–84, 94, 96–97, 113, 120, 127, 133–34, 149, 161, 299, 315, 345
McMahon, Vince, 35, 284, 345
McNeil, Mike, 390
McNichols Sports Arena, 39, 57, 73
Meadowlands, 276
Meca Vale Tudo, 378
Medina, Todd, 173
Meerman, Wiggert, 384

Melendez, Gilbert, 290, 307
Meltzer, Dave, ix, 8, 67, 92, 166, 199, 277,
  280, 282, 287, 289, 292, 294, 297, 309,
  332, 341, 358, 363, 366, 372
Memorial Auditorium, 122
Mendez, Javier, 330
Meyrowitz, Bob, 35–36, 39–40, 57–58, 68,
  72, 96, 100–103, 107–8, 113, 123, 127,
  132–33, 135, 149, 153–60, 169, 172, 191,
  194, 213, 251–52, 258–59, 264–65, 269,
  273, 276, 284, 298–99, 351
Meyrowitz, David, 273–74
Mezger, Guy, 99, 118, 211, 232–35, 249–50,
  263–64, 297–98, 344, 354, 369, 378, 398
MGM Grand, 277–78
Midoux, Kristophe, 385
Mihoubi, Ali, 207
Miletich Fighting Systems, 225, 330
Miletich, Pat, 215, 221–22, 224–25, 236,
  257, 330, 386
Milius, John, 33-34, 37–38, 40, 101
Millennium Brawl, 381
Miller, Matthew, 281
Mir, Frank, 165, 287, 383
Mitchell, Felix, 89
Mitchell, Paul, 390
Mitrione, Matt, 335
Mixed Martial Arts Council (MMAC), 352
MMA Unlimited, 348
MMA Worldwide, ix, 348
MMA Worldwide Inc., ix, 348
MMApayout.com, 296, 358–59
Mo, Da, 13
Modafferi, Roxanne, 357
Mohawk Council, 148
Mohawk Peacekeepers, 151
Mohawk Territory, 178
Mohawks, 148–49, 151, 385
Mohegan Sun Casino, 291
Moldavian, 177
Molina, Flavio, 23
Moncayo, Rudyard, 117, 146–47
Monday, Kenny, 223, 225, 228
Monteiro, Nelson, 375
Montreal Cage Combat, 385
Montreal IFC, 385
Moreira, Joe, 127, 129, 132, 236
Morishita, Naoto, 370–71
Morris, Scott, 77, 85
Morris, William, 101
Moses, Brett, 221
Mr. T, 146
MTV, 84, 207
Muay Thai, 9–10, 77–78, 88, 98, 122, 209,
  222–24, 338, 356, 378

Muay Thai Kickboxing Championships, 78
Muhle, Doug, 166
Mullen, Jeff, 354
Mullen, Jim, 210, 212
Munich, Germany, 83
Munoz, Mark, 331
Murray, Lee, 384
Musashi, Miyamoto, 386
Mutoh, Keiji, 364
Myers, Gary, 146

N

Nakai, Yuki, 316–17
Nakao, Jutaro, 277–78
Nassau Coliseum, 160
Nasty Boys, 47, 198
Natal, 378
National Sports Palace, 172
National Wrestling Alliance, 105
Nationals, 111, 233
Nazri, Reza, 188
NBC, 10, 306–7
Nelmark, Steve, 199, 319, 394
Nelson, Gordon, 150
Nelson, Steve, 149–51, 166, 354, 362, 364
Nevada State Athletic Commission
  (NSAC), 258, 264, 272–73, 276, 286,
  339, 353–54, 370
New Full Contact, The, 178
New Japan Pro Wrestling (NJPW), 7, 203,
  361-364
New York Daily News, 155
New York Division of the Military and
  Naval Affairs, 156
New York State Athletic Commission, 155,
  157–58, 160, 165
New York State Senate, 143, 154
New York Times, 156–57, 159–60
Newsday, 85, 127
Newton, Carlos, 151, 227, 365, 386–87
Night of the Samurai, 381
Nikulin, Valery, 174
Ninjutsu, 68, 77, 91
No Rules, 344
Nogueira, Rodrigo "Minotauro", 369, 371,
  378
Nogueira, Rogerio, 376
Norris, Chuck, 26, 53
Norris, Orlin, 61
North Phoenix Baptist Church, 182
NSAC, 264, 276, 286, 339, 370

O

O'Reilly, Kelli, 157
O Globo, 18

Oliveira, Johil De, 207
Ortiz, Jacob Christopher "Tito", v, 214, 234–35, 262–64, 266–68, 271–72, 274–75, 277–81, 285, 287, 332, 343, 384
Osaka, Tsuyoshi, 49, 367
Osborne, Jeffrey "Jeff", 295, 348–49, 356
Otavio, Pedro, 374–75
Otsuka, Alexander, 366
Otto, Kurt, 296
Ouellet, Stephane, 386
Overeem, Alistair, 380–81
Overeem, Valentijn, 164
Owen, Steve, 186, 191, 194, 201

P

Pacquiao, Manny, 332
Paige, Woody, 85
Pain Inc., 204
Palace, The, 290
Palazzo, Louis, 292
Palmer, Jay R. 334
Pancrase Hybrid Wrestling, 48
Pardoel, Remco, 75–79, 318, 379–80
Park Slope Armory, 143, 155–56
Parker, Ed, 50–51
Pataki, George, 153, 155
Patino, Jorge, 377
Patry, Stephane, 385–89
Patschull, Greg, 34, 116, 284, 353
Patterson, Floyd, 154
Paulson, Erik, 26, 140, 224
Pavelich, Mark, 388
Payne, Roland, 87
Pederneiras, Andre, 147, 273
Pencak silat, 68, 76
Penn, B.J., 287, 336
Pentagon Combat, 375
Penthouse, 75, 142, 151–52, 227
Penthouse Pets, 146
Perdew, Kelly, 302
Pereira, Jorge, 378
Perretti, John, 143, 145–50, 152, 205, 207, 218, 224–25, 227–28, 256, 261, 263, 275, 299, 398
Perry, Ben, 40
Perry, William, 367
Peters, Christopher, 139–41
Peters, Shawn, 228, 386
Peters, Jon, 139
Petruzelli, Seth, 303–4
Petschler, Howard, 10–11, 170–72, 175–80, 218, 352
Pettis, Anthony, 329
Pillot, Michael, 57, 72, 91, 93, 170, 321
Pinduka, Fernando, 24

Pinto, Samuel, 16
Playboy, 31–32, 36, 43, 142, 275
Playboy Mansion, 307
Point karate, 9–11, 41, 96, 206, 232, 321, 328
Polygram, 142
Pontchartrain Center, v
Porto Alegre, Brazil, 16
Portugal, Antonio, 18
Predators, 343
Pride 3, 364
Pride 4, 364
Pride 5, 365
Pride 8, 365–66
Pride 13, 108
Pride 34, 372
Pride Bushido, 370–71
Pride Fighting Championships, 310, 366, 371–72, 376, 400
Pride Grand Prix 2000, 365, 378
Pride Japan, 281, 304, 372
Pride Shockwave 2003, 195, 370
Pro Elite, 300–304, 308, 310, 379
Professional Karate Association (PKA), 11–12, 170, 205
Pulver, Jens, 225, 269, 330, 387
Purcell, Debi, 357
Putin, President Vladimir, 295
Professional Wrestling Fujiwara Gumi (PWFG), 46–47, 363

Q

Quad City Ultimate, 222
Queensbury Rules, 6
Quine, Judy, 11

R

Radnov, Mike, 136
Ramirez, Thomas, 86, 129, 320
Randleman, Kevin, 191, 265–70, 399
Ranger International Performance (R.I.P.), 242
Ratner, Marc, 154, 286, 353–54
Real American Wrestling (RAW), 84, 233, 255, 320, 366
Rebney, Bjorn, 306
Red Belt, 343
ReMix World Cup 2000, 356
Request TV, 227
Rhee, Jhoon, 10–11
Rheingans, Brad, 203
Rhodes, Johnny, 68, 74–75, 79, 317, 320–22
Rice, Kenny, 298
Riley, Aaron, 331

Ring of Fire, 229
Rings Fighting Network, 362–63, 379
Rio Heroes, 378
Riviere, Jean, 151
Rizzo, Pedro, 260, 267, 275, 329, 375
Robert Bussey's Warriors International, 77
Robinson, Sugar Ray, 32
Robotae, 45
Rodley, Pete, 385, 388
Rodriguez, Ricco, 338
Rogan, Joe, 349
Rogers Sportsnet, 390
Rogers, Brett, 342
Rooze, Rene, 396
Rosier, Kevin, 49, 55, 57, 59–60, 63, 69, 73, 316
Roufus, Jeff, 329
Roy, David, 347
Royal Albert Hall, 383
Roytberg, Roman, 343
Rua, Mauricio, 371
Ruas, Marco, 23–24, 122–25, 135, 170, 177, 219, 260, 373–74
Ruas Vale Tudo, 122
Ruiz, Eddie, 120–21, 215, 252, 256
Rumble on Rock, 301
Ruska, Willem, 8
Rutten, Bas, v, 172, 175, 249, 262–63, 265, 293, 298, 343, 369, 374, 380, 383, 395–400
Rutten, Bianca, 399
Rutten, Karin, 399
Rutten, Sabine, 399

S

S.L.O. Kickboxing, 290
Sabaki Challenge, 45
Sakakibara, Nobuyuki, 370, 372
Sakuraba, Kazushi, 252–54, 340, 347, 364–66, 371–72, 378
Sakurai, Hayato, 369
Sambo, 68, 75, 109–11, 117, 126, 145, 150, 201, 223, 327, 379, 397
San Jose Razorclaws, 296
Sanchez, Diego, 330
Sanchez, Julian, 188
Santana, Waldemar, 20
Santos, Christiane "Cyborg", 309, 357
Sanzo, Nick, 210
Sapp, Bob, 367–70
Sato, Rumina, 369
Sauer, Pedro, 111, 242
Savage, Milo, 7
Savate, 49, 58, 60
Sayama, Satoru, 361–63

Sayama, Sayato, 370
Scantelbury, Nigel, 150
Schilt, Semmy, 369, 380–81
Schrijber, Bob, 328, 379–81
Schultz, Dave, 94
Schultz, Mark, 94, 112, 134–35, 183
Schwarzenegger, Arnold, 34, 346, 353
Scientific Aggressive Fighting Technology of America, 104
Score, The, 306
Seagal, Steven, 69, 78
Semaphore Entertainment Group (SEG), 35–40, 53, 57–58, 61, 67–68, 72, 82–83, 86, 93, 95–97, 99–100, 107–8, 113–16, 118–19, 121, 126–27, 132, 136–37, 139, 142, 149, 153–55, 157–61, 163, 182, 187–89, 193–95, 197, 202, 210, 213, 220–21, 231, 233, 242–43, 247–48, 250–51, 253–57, 259–65, 267, 269, 271, 273–75, 281, 286, 291, 299, 321, 346, 351–53, 385
Serra, Matt, 319
SET, 35–36
Severn, Daniel "The Beast", 94, 105, 126, 129, 187, 342, 367
Shamrock, Amy, 267
Shamrock, Angelina Brown, 250
Shamrock, Bob, 47, 62, 103, 106, 112, 135-137, 206
Shamrock, Frank Juarez "King of Pancrase", 194, 208, 227–28, 240, 249–51, 253–55, 257, 261–62, 264, 266–68, 373, 296, 301, 307–8, 327–28, 330–31, 333–34, 337, 340, 344, 369, 398
Shamrock, Ken, *see also* Vince Torelli, v, 47–48, 54–55, 57, 62–64, 66, 79, 83, 87, 89, 91, 94, 102–3, 105–6, 112, 115, 118–19, 121–23, 126–29, 131, 133–34, 137, 154, 170, 182, 189, 193–94, 197–99, 202, 204, 206–7, 232, 235, 237–38, 247–48, 250, 264, 278–81, 297, 303, 307, 320, 329, 344, 351, 363, 393, 398
Shamrock, Nicolette, 267
Shamrock, Tina, 279
Shamrock, Tonya, 279
Shamus, Gareb, 296
Shaw, Gary, 300, 304
Shaw, Jared, 304
Sheinberg, Jeff, 101
Shelby, Sean, 291
Sher, John, 142
Sherdog.com, vi, 284, 289
Sherk, Sean, 280
Shields, Jake, 308–9
Shootfighting, 207–8

Shooting Stars, 218–19
Shooto, 140, 164, 232, 348, 362, 369–70
Shootwrestling, 93
Shorin Ji-ryu Karate, 321
Shorin-ryu Matumura Kenpo, 320
Showdown Fight Wear, 387
Showtime, 170, 300–302, 304, 308
ShoXC, 301
Shut Up and Fight (SUAF), 388–89
Sieglen, William, 217
Silicon Valley Sports & Entertainment, 307
Silva, Anderson, vii, 287, 340, 344, 377
Silva, Joe, v, ix, 195, 199, 249, 251, 261–62,
    275, 279–80, 291, 345–46
Silva, Wanderlei, 260–61, 266–67, 271,
    369, 371, 375, 377
Silveira, Marcus "Conan", 145–47, 150,
    205–6, 209, 240, 252–55, 365
Silver Star, 355
Simpson, Mike, 101
Sinosic, Elvis, 343, 385
Slice, Kimbo, *see also* Kevin Ferguson,
    302–4, 308
Smith, James, 51, 165
Smith, Maurice, 121, 205–9, 223, 226, 235,
    238–41, 244–45, 247, 249, 252–53, 255,
    259–60, 263, 265, 297–98, 307, 314, 326,
    337, 344, 367, 398
Smith, Patrick "Pat", 45, 62, 77, 79–80, 102,
    117–18, 120–21, 124, 147, 196, 298–99,
    368
Smith, Paul, ix, 7, 166, 180, 273, 290, 294,
    352
Smith, Scott, 308
Snow, Al, 94–95, 98
Sodd Marky D., *see also* Campbell
    McLaren, 133
Soldier of Fortune, 51
Son, Joe, 83–84, 88, 90, 95, 97–98, 327,
    337, 343
Sonnen, Chael, 291, 295, 340, 358
Soranaka, Masami "Sammy", 46–47, 207
South Atlantic Professional Wrestling
    Association, 47
Sperry, Ze Mario, 145–48, 220, 376
Spijkers, Ben, 140–41
Spike TV, 282–83, 285
Spinks, Leon, 51, 172, 243
SpiritMC, 301
Sports Illustrated, 136–37, 283
St. Pierre, Georges, vii, 287, 327–28, 330,
    344, 387, 389–90
Stankie, Al, 215
Stann, Brian, 291
State Supreme Court (New York), 156

Station Casinos, 272–73, 286
Steele Cage, 297
Steele, JT, 294
Stell, Dan, 352
Stepanov, Dmitri, 232
Stone, Mike, 10
Stott, Greg, 242
Storm Samurai, 378
Stratus Media, 304
Strikeforce, 302, 307–10, 354, 356–57, 367,
    381
Struve, Stefan, 380
Sturgeon, Kyle, 365
submission fighting, 3, 127, 173, 221, 223,
    250, 397
Sudo, Genki, 341, 343
Sulaiman, Jose, 368
Sumo, 45–46, 59, 73, 84–86, 183, 368
Sunkist Kids, 182
Superbrawl, 211, 249–51, 301
Superbrawl 2, 334
Suzuki, Minoru, 47, 206, 363, 397
Svinth, Joseph R., 162
Swick, Mike, 330
Sylvia, Tim, 165, 225, 304–5, 330, 340

T

Tabbs, Leon, 122, 125–26, 165, 234
Tachi Palace, 290
Tadeu, Eugenio, 375
Tae Bo, 2, 318
Tae kwon do, 6, 11, 23, 36, 45, 67–68, 75,
    83, 104, 115–17, 143, 162, 173–74, 196,
    205, 313, 316, 326, 337, 382, 395
Tahnoon, Sheik, 349
Takada, Nobuhiko, 242, 247, 252, 361–62,
    370
Takahashi, Kazuo, 136
Takahashi, Yoshiki, 210
Takase, Daiju, 273
Taktarov, Oleg, 103–4, 109–12, 117–20,
    122, 126, 131, 145, 169–70, 218–21, 298,
    343, 351, 373–74
Tamura, Kiyoshi, 266, 369
Tanner, Evan, 274
TapouT, 348
TapouT, 355, 358
Tatarkin, Victor, 146
TCI Cable, 213
TCI Canada, 231
Teachout, Jim, 150
Team ROC, 330
Telligman, Tra, 210–11, 249
Tennessee State Athletic Commission, 354
Texas Department of Licensing, 354

The Best Damn Sports Show...Period!, 278
The Cobra Challenge, 202
The Contenders, 227–28, 250, 253
The Crow: Wicked Prayer, 343, 386
The Last Dragon, 96
The Love Boat, 25
The Ultimate Fighter, 2, 282–83, 293–94,
    299, 306, 308, 335, 355–56, 382, 384, 390
The World Championship of Jiu-jitsu, 20
The World's Best Fighter, 37–38
The Wrestling Observer, 67, 294
Theodosius, 5
Theriault, Jean Yves, 170
Theriault, Roger, 86
Theriault, Victor, 170
Thomas, Dave, 113, 131
Thomas, Mike, 148–49, 151–52, 170, 176,
    178–80, 384
Thompson, James, 302
Thompson, T.J., 249–50
Thompson, Tolly, 188
Thompson, Tony, 352
Thomson, Josh, 307, 330
Thunderdome, 251–52
Time Warner, 213, 227, 231
TKO Major League MMA, 388
Tokyo Dome, 203, 362
Tomita, Tsunejiro, 15
Toney, James, 164, 332
Torelli, Vince, *see also* Ken Shamrock, 47
Tough Man, 163
Tough Sports Live, 378
Toughill, Erin, 357
Traven, Roberto, 191
Trebilcock, Terry, 349–350, 354
Trejo, Frank, 50
tribal land, 149, 350–51, 353–54
Tropicana, 353
Troy, 364
Trump Taj Mahal, 269, 274, 276, 353
Trump, Donald, 305
TSN, 388
TUF, 283, 308, 384
Tuli, Teila, *see also* Taylor Wiley, 45–46,
    54–55, 58–60, 66, 73
Turner Broadcasting, 115
Turner, Karyn, 45
Turner, Ted, 115
TV Guide, 32, 73
TVKO, 35–36, 217, 221
Tyson, Mike, 35, 92, 161, 362, 368

U

U Japan, 194, 199
U.S. Junior Open, 105

U.S. Open Taekwondo Championship, 162
UCC, 385–88
UCC 3, 388
UCC 6: Redemption, 386
UCC 7, 387
UCC 8, 387
UCC 12, 387
UFA, 352
UFC I, 67
UFC II, 57, 67, 70, 72, 77–78, 81, 84–85,
    102, 124, 149, 164, 317–18, 320
UFC III, 81, 83–84, 92, 94, 103, 123, 127,
    129, 137, 163, 170, 182, 232, 324, 373
UFC IV, 93, 95, 97, 232
UFC V, 103, 107, 112–13, 123, 166, 169,
    238, 268
UFC VI, 109, 113, 115, 123, 137, 147, 199,
    206, 393
UFC VII, 68, 122–24, 139, 153, 155, 183,
    217
UFC VIII, 131, 169–70, 189, 233, 320
UFC IX, 132, 165, 182, 276, 319, 378
UFC X, 181–83, 185, 187, 191, 393
UFC XI, 132, 187–88, 191, 210, 234
UFC XII, 158–59, 191, 210, 213, 231
UFC XIII, 87, 215, 231–34, 277
UFC XIV, 235
UFC XV, 241–43, 252
UFC XVII, 259
UFC XVIII, v, 262
UFC XIX, 263, 265, 278
UFC XX, 265
UFC XXI, 273
UFC XXII, 266, 399
UFC XXIII, 265
UFC XXIV, 267
UFC XXV, 165
UFC XXVI, 268
UFC XXVII, 269
UFC 28, 269, 353
UFC 29, 271–72
UFC 30, 274
UFC 31, 275, 319
UFC 32, 372
UFC 33, 276–78
UFC 34, 275, 277, 293
UFC 36, 338–39
UFC 38, 383–84
UFC 40, 278–80, 283
UFC 41, 280
UFC 42, 280
UFC 43, 281
UFC 44, 281, 340
UFC 45, 281, 324
UFC 47, 281, 340

UFC 48, 165
UFC 52, 283
UFC 60, 280
UFC 61, 294
UFC 65, 371
UFC 82, 305
UFC 96, 331
UFC 97, 390
UFC 100, 287
UFC 111, 277
UFC 115, 390
UFC 118, 164, 332
UFC 121, 287
UFC 122, 287
UFC Brazil, 262, 375, 377
UFC Hall of Fame, 281, 355
UFC Japan, 245, 247, 256, 364–65
UFC Octagon, 355
UFC Rio, 375
UFC Unleashed, 283, 291
Ultimate Brazil, 260
Ultimate Fan Expos, 357
Ultimate Fight, 344
Ultimate Fight Night Live, 283
Ultimate Fighting Alliance, 166, 352
Ultimate Fighting Challenge, 58
Ultimate Fighting Champion, 65, 92, 101
Ultimate MMA Fight!, 348
Ultimate Pankration, 299
Ultimate Ultimate (UU), 123, 135, 193, 201
Ultimate Ultimate '95, 123, 129, 153, 170, 183, 345–46, 351, 356, 373
Ultimate Ultimate '96, 193–94, 201–2, 237, 394
Ultimate Warriors, 170–71
Ultimate Warriors, 384
Underground Forum, 347
Union of Wrestling Forces International (UWFI), 362–64
United Full Contact Fighting, 145, 224
United Shoot Wrestling Federation, 152
Universal Combat Challenge, 385
Universal Television, 11
Universal Vale Tudo Fighting Championship, 6, 242
Universal Wrestling Federation (UWF), 46–48, 64, 93, 206–7, 247, 361–63
Uno, Caol, 369
Urquidez, Benny, 29–30, 71, 142
USA TODAY, 123, 162
USA Wrestling, 227–28
U-Top Tournament, 356

V

Vale Tudo, 2, 16, 18, 20–21, 23, 25, 33, 43, 53, 81, 122, 142, 219, 236, 242, 249, 251, 260, 316, 363–64, 373–80
Vale Tudo No Maracanãzinho, 23
Vale Tudo on TV, 21
Vale, Bart, 102, 140, 206–9, 226, 335–36, 363
Valente, Pedro Sr., 53
Van Arsdale, Mike, 333
Van Clief, Ron "Black Dragon", 6, 95–97, 120, 170–72
Van Vader, 364
VanderMeer, Patricia, 356
Varelans, Paul, 117–18, 122–24, 127, 129–30, 173–75, 194, 196–97, 200–201, 236, 393
Vasquez, Sam, 162
Vaulin, Yuri, 236
Velasquez, Cain, 287–88, 295, 330
Velazquez, Manual, 162
Venom, 353–54
Verhoeff, Irma, 380
Vigneault, Steve, 387
Villareal, Ruben, 400
Virtuosity, 102, 343
Vocsh, Johan, 48
Vovchanchyn, Igor, 174–77, 194
Vunak, Paul, 40

W

Wall, Bob, 139
Wallace, Bill, 11, 53, 58, 61, 69, 315
Warring, James, 140–41
Waterman, Ron, 343
WBF Intercontinental Boxing Champion, 97
WEC 4, 291
WEC 19, 291
Weir, Mark, 381, 383
Weit, Orlando, 77, 85, 149–50
Weller, Jeff, 179
Werdum, Fabricio, 309
White, Dana, 271–74, 276–77, 279–80, 283–86, 291–92, 294, 304, 309–310, 357, 372
White, Vernon, 365
Wide World of Entertainment, 11
Wide World of Sports, 10
Wiley, Taylor, *see also* Teila Tuli 46
Wilhelm, Willie, 362
Williams, Pete, 260, 265
Williams, Tedd, 299
Wilson, Don, 52, 205, 318–19, 324, 394
World Boxing Council, 52, 368

World Championship Karate, 49

World Championship Wrestling (WCW), 115, 198, 203, 364

World Combat Championship (WCC), 139–41, 150, 208

World Extreme Cagefighting, 180, 290–91, 294, 307, 329, 355

World Fighting Alliance (WFA), 292–93, 400

World Freefighting Championships, 6, 96

World Kickboxing Association (WKA), 205–6

World Kickboxing Commission, 45

World Vale Championships 2, 219

World Vale Tudo Championship (WVC), 373–74, 377, 380

World Vale Tudo Council, 374

World War II, 6, 58, 320

World Wrestling Entertainment (WWE), 274, 279–80, 345, 348

World Wrestling Federation (WWF), 35, 198, 203, 206, 232, 247, 278–79

Worley, Pat, 10

Worsham, Cal, 117, 165, 195, 394

WOW Promotions, 34–35, 44, 53, 55, 57, 81, 91, 100, 107–8, 111–12, 134, 324

X

Xtreme Couture, 330

Y

Yamaguchi, 19

Yamamoto, Norihisa, 367

Yamasaki, Fernando, 75

Yamashita, Yoshiaki, 15

Yamma Pit Fighting, 298

Yanagisawa, Ryushi, 397

Yarbrough, Emmanuel, 84–86, 88, 127

Yen, Danny, 390

YMCA, 20, 29, 259

Yoshida, Hidehiko, 370

Young, Kaitlin, 302

Young, Robert, 141

YouTube, 302

Yvel, Gilbert, 369, 380

Z

Zikic, James, 337

Zinoviev, Igor, 145–51, 149, 151, 225, 227, 257

Zorba, Chris, 383

Zuckerman, Donald, 141–44, 148–49, 151–54, 156, 222–23, 227, 354

Zuffa Entertainment, 166–67, 271, 274–92, 294, 296–97, 304–6, 310, 331, 351, 371–72, 377, 383, 386